GLOBAL
DATA
LOCATOR

GLOBAL DATA LOCATOR

GEORGE THOMAS KURIAN

BERNAN PRESS
LANHAM, MARYLAND

Published 1997 by Bernan Press, an imprint of Bernan Associates
Printed in the United States of America

99 98 97   4 3 2 1

∞ ™

Bernan Press
4611-F Assembly Drive
Lanham, MD 20706-4391
(800) 274-4447
e-mail: info@bernan.com

ISBN: 0-89059-039-7

TABLE OF CONTENTS

INTRODUCTION

Global Data Locator is a user's guide and road map to global statistical information sources. It provides annotated and descriptive reviews as well as tables of contents for 240 statistical publications published by both official and commercial organizations.

Global statistics is a relatively young phenomenon. Only a handful of publications listed in this book predate 1945 and the establishment of the United Nations (UN) Statistical Office. Before that date some of the more advanced countries produced statistical compendia mainly for the use of their diplomatic corps or military personnel, and the information contained in them was limited to certain broad areas such as population and commerce. The 50 years since the end of World War II have witnessed two related developments. First, organizations publishing international data have proliferated, and the range and variety of data also have expanded so that there is virtually no field in which data are not collected in however rudimentary a form. Second, there has been an even more appreciable growth in the number of consumers of global statistical data representing a variety of needs and constituencies. These users have become more demanding in their search for value-added quality data, even though many of them are not trained professionals. Both of these developments have contributed to what may be best described as the Age of Popular Statistics. Data are no longer esoteric. They have become basic ingredients of social and economic analysis, and they are being constantly evaluated for their reliability, vintage, and provenance. To rephrase an old aphorism, statistics have become too important to be left to the statisticians. Global Data Locator tries to bring the producers and consumers of global statistics together. It is addressed particularly to the latter group.

The quality of global statistics has improved over the years but continues to suffer from many deficiencies, some of them inherent in the mechanisms of collection and dissemination. The availability of data varies from topic to topic and from country to country. In some there is such an abundance of data that it constitutes an embarrassment of riches; in others there is such a paucity of data that one has to scrape the bottom of the barrel to find some crumbs. Some are what could be described as hard data—figures that have been verified and well documented, while others seem to be, at least figuratively speaking, pulled out of a hat. And there is always the perennial, and often daunting, problem of comparability and recency. Some statistical publications are extremely regular, include data of fairly recent vintage, and are frequently updated and revised. There are other publications that are hopelessly outdated with time lags of up to eight years. In some cases there is no assurance that these volumes will be published again.

Fortunately, the number of books in the first group has increased during the past decade while those of dubious quality in the second group have actually decreased. This is perhaps the most hopeful sign of the continuing health of global statistical efforts.

A word of explanation is in order because popular misconceptions of the credibility of statistics have persisted despite these positive trends. Unlike mathematics, its sister science, statistics are not required to be infallible or absolute. Given that statistical collections are dependent on exogenous factors, such as the efficiency of the collectors, the extent and scope of the collection basin, and the reliability of the pipelines, they are always subject to a margin of error. They are, to use the old Latin legal term, cy pres, or approximations of truth within certain orders of magnitude. For example, when it is said that the global population in 1997 is 5.8 billion, it could be off the mark by several hundred millions or by a few thousands. No one knows and no one will ever know. (In any case it changed while you were reading this sentence). However, even approximate data are useful in establishing trends, devising projections, and determining rates of growth. The problem of recency is less troublesome because there are no out-of-date data. Data can always be pickled and preserved as time series for the use of historians and cliometricians. In fact, historians have become inveterate users of statistics, and there is no aspect of modern world history that does not require a reference to the data contained in one or the other of the publications cited in this book.

There was a time when statistical publications were considered forbidding and unattractive because of their format—large masses of closely printed figures that would leave even an accountant dazed. This has changed in recent years. Many, especially those published by commercial organizations, are printed on glossy paper and have the appearance and feel of corporate annual reports. The increasing use of graphics and color also has helped to make statistics more presentable.

The Information Superhighway will obviously have a direct impact on global statistics, not merely in its extraordinary number-crunching ability, but also by presenting more data more quickly to more users. To devise a rough principle, only about 30 percent of the data that can be collected are being collected now and presented in print form. Of that, only about 25 percent are being used in any form. These figures are likely to double within the next decade. The Internet itself is likely to emerge as a vast data sink, expanding data resources both vertically, as time series, and horizontally, as networks of datasets on related subjects. New computer modeling techniques using global statistics as raw materials are making quantitative projections and creating multiple scenarios of the future.

Statistics has remained a very structured discipline, mostly isolated from branches of knowledge other than mathematics. The next step in the data revolution will be to create new linkages between statistics on the one hand and the humanities, social sciences, and natural sciences on the other, so that statistics provides the nexus on which every type of analysis can be based. Religious statistics is a good example. Virtually unknown about two decades ago, religious statistics has thrived providing grist for both evangelists and religious sociologists. Similar linkages can be established in history, sociology, psychology, and other disciplines.

Work on this project was made smoother by the dedication and support of Marc Beauboeuf, editor at Bernan Press. He has made significant contributions to the scope and structure of the book. Above all, my unabashed gratitude goes to the one person who earns it every day, my wife Annie Kurian.

—George Thomas Kurian

SECTION ONE:

STATISTICS IN PRINT

The Statistics in Print Section of the *Global Data Locator* is the largest portion of this book. It was the sole section in its predecessor, *Sourcebook of Global Statistics*, published 10 years ago. Most of the publications reviewed in the earlier edition have survived, thus revealing the stability of the field of global statistics.

The print section covers primarily books, annuals, monthlies, and irregular serials. It excludes certain types of publications, such as almanacs, yearbooks, and encyclopedias that include statistical data exclusively borrowed from primary or secondary sources. For this reason, the reader will not find publications, such as the *Europa Yearbook*—an extraordinarily useful annual—or Euromonitor publications which simply recycle available data in excruciatingly expensive formats. The reader also will not find *The World Almanac* and similar publications.

Entries in the *Global Data Locator* are arranged according to a standard format providing five segments of information: (1) Facts at a Glance—which features bibliographic information, including author, number of volumes, number of pages, periodicity, and publisher; (2) Purpose and Scope; (3) Data Organization; (4) Methodology; and (5) Contents. Any information that was accessible or available to the author at the time that the book was compiled is included. However, some of the entries are incomplete due to the many different publishing styles and requirements used by the various

publishers in producing their books. In every case the review is based on an actual physical examination of the publication and not on secondary reports.

Whenever possible, the author has taken introductory text directly from the source, thereby giving the reader a clear and objective representation of the elements of each book.

Unlike in the first edition, entries are not arranged alphabetically, but according to a subject thesaurus specifically devised for this edition. The headings are designed to make it easier for users to locate publications so long as they know what topics they are looking for. An alphabetical index at the end will help those users who are looking for specific titles rather than topics. As in the first edition, only English language publications are covered. Most UN publications, however, are issued simultaneously in French, Spanish, and other languages.

There is some confusion regarding the vintage of data. This book is not intended to include or represent the most recent editions of works published, rather, it should be used as a sourcebook which lists the most authoritative books containing international statistics. Generally, if there is a year in the title, then that refers to the year of publication and not the time frame of the data in the book. Data collection methodologies vary from organization to organization and are spelled out in monographs or manuals published by the same organization.

Five Most Important General Global Statistical Sourcebooks

HUMAN DEVELOPMENT REPORT

FACTS AT A GLANCE

Number of Pages: 226

Periodicity: Annual

Publisher: United Nations

PURPOSE AND SCOPE

The sixth edition of the *Human Development Report* is a report card on the pace and extent of development and the state of the developing world versus the developed world. Its purpose is to explore the gaps, inequalities, and disparities between the two worlds and the drag that maldevelopment exerts on global economic and social progress.

DATA ORGANIZATION

The key to the report is the Human Development Index (HDI), a composite index based on the Life Expectancy Index (life expectancy at birth), the Literacy Index (mean years of schooling and adult literacy rate), the Educational Attainment Index (combined first, second, and third gross enrollment ratios), and the GDP Index (real gross domestic product per capita adjusted). The first 19 countries on the list are industrial countries and the remaining 154 countries are developing ones. The first 26 tables (2-27) following the HDI are limited to developing countries; and the remaining 23 tables (28-50) are limited to industrial countries. Table 51 presents regional aggregates of human development indicators and Table 52, the final table, presents the HDI and income aggregates of human development indicators. Countries are ranked in the descending order of the HDI.

METHODOLOGY

The *Human Development Report* and Index are based on official government data collected by the United Nations Statistical Division and related agencies. Almost all of the sources are published materials, except in a few cases, where for the sake of completeness, UNDP has used its own estimates. Because of the varying provenance and vintage of these data, they bear the usual cautionary notes regarding interpretation and analysis.

CONTENTS

Key to Indicators

Key to Countries and Areas

Selected Definitions

Classification of Countries

Table 1: Human Development Index - All Countries

Table 2: Profile of Human Development - Developing Countries

Life Expectancy at birth. Population with access to health services. Population with access to safe water. Population with access to sanitation. Daily calorie supply as percent of requirements. Adult literacy rate. Enrollment ratio for all levels. Daily newspapers. Televisions. Real gross domestic product (GDP) per capita. Gross national product (GNP) per capita.

Table 3: Profile of Human Deprivation - Developing Countries

People in absolute poverty: total and rural. Refugees. Population without access to health services. Population without access to safe water. Population without access to sanitation. Illiterate adults. Illiterate females. Children not in primary school. Malnourished children under five. Children dying before age five.

Table 4: Trends in Human Development - Developing Countries

Life expectancy at birth. Infant mortality rate. Population with access to safe water. Malnourished children, percent underweight. Adult literacy rate. Enrollment ratio for all levels. Real GDP per capita.

Table 5: Human Capital Formation - Developing Countries

Adult literacy rate. Literacy rate, age 15-19. Mean years of schooling. Scientists and technicians. R&D scientists and technicians. Tertiary graduates. Science graduates.

Table 6: Narrowing South-North Gaps - Developing Countries

Life expectancy. Adult literacy. Daily caloric supply. Access to safe water. Under-five mortality.

Table 7: Widening South-North Gaps - Developing Countries

Real GDP per capita. Mean years of schooling. Overall enrollment.

Table 8: Status of Women - Developing Countries

Life expectancy at birth. Average age at first marriage. Literacy rate, age 15-24. Enrollment ratios by level. Tertiary science enrollment. Administrators and managers. Parliament.

Table 9: Female-Male Gaps - Developing Countries

Life expectancy. Population. Literacy. Years of schooling. Primary enrollment. Secondary enrollment. Tertiary enrollment. Labor force.

Table 10: Rural-Urban Gaps - Developing Countries

Rural population as percent of total. Population with access to health services. Population with access to water. Population with access to sanitation.

Rural-urban disparity in health services. Rural-urban disparity in water. Rural-urban disparity in sanitation. Rural-urban disparity in child nutrition.

Table 11: Child Survival and Development - Developing Countries

Pregnant women receiving prenatal care. Pregnant women with anemia. Births attended by health personnel. Low birth-weight babies. Maternal mortality rate. Infant mortality rate. Median duration of breast-feeding. One-year-olds immunized. ORS access rate. Malnourished children, percent underweight. Under-five mortality rate.

Table 12: Health Profile - Developing Countries

Years of life lost to premature death. Tuberculosis cases. Malaria cases. AIDS cases. Population per doctor. Population per nurse. Nurses per doctor. External aid flows to health. Public expenditure on health. Total expenditure on health.

Table 13: Food Security - Developing Countries

Food production per capita index. Agricultural production as percent of GDP. Daily calorie supply per capita. Daily calorie supply as percent of requirements. Food import dependency ratio. Cereal imports. Food aid.

Table 14: Education Flows - Developing Countries

First-grade intake rate. Primary enrollment ratio. Primary repeaters. Completing primary level. Transition to secondary level. Primary entrants proceeding to secondary schooling. Secondary enrollment ratio. Secondary repeaters. Tertiary enrollment ratio.

Table 15: Education Imbalances - Developing Countries

Pupil-teacher ratios, primary and secondary. Secondary technical enrollment. Tertiary science enrollment. Tertiary students abroad. Public expenditure on education. Public expenditure on primary and secondary education. Public expenditure on higher education. Public expenditure per tertiary student.

Table 16: Communication Profile - Developing Countries

Radios. Televisions. Cinema attendances. Daily newspapers. Book titles published. Printing and writing paper. Post offices. Letters posted. Telephones. Motor vehicles.

Table 17: Employment - Developing Countries

Labor force as percent of total population. Women in labor force as percent of total. Percentage of labor force in agriculture. Percentage of labor force in industry. Percent of labor force in services. Earnings per employee annual growth rate.

Table 18: Wealth, Poverty, and Social Investment - Developing Countries

Real GDP per capita. GNP per capita. Income share of lowest 40 percent of households. Ratio of income of highest 20 percent of households to income of lowest 20 percent. People in absolute poverty, total, rural, and urban. Social security benefits expenditure. Public expenditure on education. Public expenditure on health. Total expenditure on health.

Table 19: Aid Flows - Developing Countries

Official development assistance (ODA) received. ODA as percent of GNP. ODA per capita. ODA per poor person. Bilateral aid social allocation ratio. Bilateral aid social priority ratio. Bilateral aid human expenditure ratio. Human priority aid as percent of total.

Table 20: Resource Flow Imbalances - Developing Countries

Total external debt. Total external debt as percent of GNP. Debt service ratio. Export-import ratio. Trade dependency. Terms of trade. Workers' remittances from abroad. Gross international reserves. Current account balance.

Table 21: Military Expenditure and Resource Use Imbalances - Developing Countries

Military expenditure as percent of GDP. Military expenditure as percent of combined education and health expenditure. Arms imports. Arms imports as percent of national imports. Armed forces per 1,000 people. Armed forces per teacher. Armed forces per doctor.

Table 22: Growing Urbanization - Developing Countries

Urban population as percent of total. Urban population annual growth rate. Population in cities of more than one million as percent of urban population. Population in largest city. Population in cities of more than one million as percent of total population. Major city with highest population density.

Table 23: Demographic Profile - Developing Countries

Estimated population. Annual population growth rate. Population growth rates over time. Population doubling date. Crude birth rate. Crude death rate. Fertility rate. Fertility rates over time. Contraceptive prevalence rate.

Table 24: Natural Resources Balance Sheet - Developing Countries

Land area. Population density. Arable land. Pesticide consumption. Forest area. Production of fuel wood. Deforestation. Internal renewable water resources. Fresh water withdrawals as percent of water resources. Fresh water withdrawals per capita. Irrigated land. Global emissions share.

Table 25: Energy Consumption - Developing Countries

Total commercial energy consumption. Commercial energy consumption per capita. Energy imports. Rate of change in commercial energy consumption. Commercial energy efficiency.

Table 26: National Income Accounts - Developing Countries

Total GDP. Agricultural production. Industrial production. Services. Private consumption.

Government consumption. Gross domestic investment. Gross domestic savings. Tax revenue. Central government expenditure. Exports. Imports.

Table 27: Trends in Economic Performance - Developing Countries

Total GNP. GNP annual growth rate. GNP per capita annual growth rate. Rate of inflation. Exports as percent of GDP, annual growth rate. Tax revenue as percent of GDP, annual growth rate. Direct taxes. Overall budget surplus/deficit.

Table 28: Profile of Human Development - Industrial Countries

Life expectancy at birth. Maternal mortality rate. Population per doctor. Scientists and technicians. Enrollment ratio for all levels. Tertiary enrollment ratio. Daily newspapers. Televisions. Real GDP per capita. GNP per capita.

Table 29: Profile of Human Distress - Industrial Countries

Total unemployment rate. Youth unemployment rate. Adults with less than upper-secondary education. Ratio of income of highest 20 percent of households to income of lowest 20 percent. Female wages as percent of male wages. Rate of inflation. Years of life lost to premature death. Injuries from road accidents. Intentional homicides. Reported rapes. Sulfur and nitrogen emissions.

Table 30: Weakening Social Fabric - Industrial Countries

Total prisoners. Juvenile prisoners. Intentional homicides by men. Reported rapes. Drug crimes. Asylum applications. Divorces. Births outside marriage. Single-female-parent homes. Suicides by men.

Table 31: Trends in Human Development - Industrial Countries

Life expectancy at birth. Tertiary enrollment ratio. Real GDP per capita. GNP per capita. Education expenditure. Health expenditure.

Table 32: Human Capital Formation - Industrial Countries

Mean years of schooling. Scientists and technicians. R&D scientists and technicians. Expenditure on research and development. Upper-secondary graduates. Tertiary graduates. Science graduates.

Table 33: Status of Women - Industrial Countries

Life expectancy at birth. Average age at first marriage. Maternal mortality rate. Secondary enrollment ratio. Upper-secondary graduates. Tertiary enrollment ratio. Tertiary science enrollment. Labor force. Administrators and managers. Parliament.

Table 34: Female-Male Gaps - Industrial Countries

Life expectancy. Population. Years of schooling. Secondary enrollment. Upper-secondary graduates. University enrollment. Tertiary science enrollment. Labor force. Unemployment. Wages.

Table 35: Health Profile - Industrial Countries

Years of life lost to premature death. Deaths from circulatory system diseases. Deaths from malignant cancers. AIDS cases. Alcohol consumption. Tobacco consumption. Population per doctor. Health bills paid by public insurance. Public expenditure on health. Total health expenditure. Private expenditure on health.

Table 36: Education Profile - Industrial Countries

Enrollment ratio for all levels. Upper-secondary enrollment ratio. Upper-secondary technical enrollment. Nineteen-year-olds in full-time education. Tertiary enrollment ratio. Tertiary science enrollment. Expenditure on tertiary education. Public expenditure per tertiary student. Total education expenditure. Public expenditure on education.

Table 37: Communication Profile - Industrial Countries

Radios. Televisions. Cinema attendances. Museum attendances. Registered library users. Daily newspapers. Book titles published. Printing and writing paper. Letters posted. Telephones. International telephone calls. Motor vehicles.

Table 38: Employment - Industrial Countries

Labor force as percent of total population. Percentage of labor force in agriculture. Percentage of labor force in industry. Percentage of labor force in services. Future labor force replacement ratio. Earnings per employee annual growth rate. Earnings disparity. Percentage of labor force unionized. Weekly hours of work. Expenditure on labor market programs.

Table 39: Unemployment - Industrial Countries

Unemployed persons. Total unemployment rate. Total rate including discouraged workers. Female unemployment rate. Youth unemployment rate. Male youth unemployment rate. Unemployment benefits expenditure. Incidence of long-term unemployment. Regional unemployment disparity. Unemployment by educational level.

Table 40: Wealth, Poverty, and Social Investment - Industrial Countries

Real GDP per capita. GNP per capita. Share of industrial GNP. Income share of lowest 40 percent of households. Ratio of income of highest 20 percent of households to lowest 20 percent. Social security benefits expenditure. Education expenditure. Health expenditure.

Table 41: Aid Flows - Industrial Countries.

Official development assistance (ODA) disbursed. ODA as percent of GNP. ODA as percent of central government budget. ODA per capita. Bilateral aid social allocation ratio. Bilateral aid social priority ratio. Bilateral aid human expenditure ratio. Bilateral aid for human priorities. Aid to least developed countries. Multilateral aid.

Table 42: Resource Flow Imbalances - Industrial Countries

Export-import ratio. Export growth rate as percentage of import growth rate. Trade dependency. Terms of trade. Workers' remittances from abroad. Public debt. Government debt interest payments. Gross international reserves. Current account balance.

Table 43: Military Expenditure and Resource Use Imbalances - Industrial Countries

Military expenditure as percentage of GDP. Military expenditure as percentage of combined education and health expenditure. ODA as percentage of military expenditure. Arms exports to developing countries. Share of arms exports to developing countries. Armed forces per 1,000 people. Armed forces per teacher. Armed forces per doctor.

Table 44: Urbanization - Industrial Countries

Urban population as percentage of total. Urban population annual growth rate. Population in largest city. Population in cities of more than one million as percentage of urban population. Population in cities of more than one million as percentage of total population. Major city with highest population density. Population exposed to road traffic noise.

Table 45: Demographic Profile - Industrial Countries

Estimated population. Annual population growth rate. Fertility rate. Fertility rates over time. Contraceptive prevalence rate. Dependency ratio. Population aged 60 or over. Life expectancy at age 60.

Table 46: Natural Resources Balance Sheet - Industrial Countries

Land area. Population density. Arable land and permanent crop land. Permanent grasslands. Forest and wooded land. Irrigated land. Internal renewable water resources. Fresh water withdrawals as percentage of water resources. Fresh water withdrawals per capita.

Table 47: Energy Consumption - Industrial Countries

Total commercial energy consumption. Commercial energy consumption per capita. Share of world commercial energy consumption. Rate of change in commercial energy consumption. Commercial energy efficiency.

Table 48: Environment and Pollution - Industrial Countries

Major city with highest sulfur dioxide concentration. Sulfur and nitrogen emissions. Global emissions percentage share. Pesticide consumption. Nuclear waste. Hazardous and special waste production. Municipal waste. Waste recycling.

Table 49: National Income Accounts - Industrial Countries

Total GDP. Agricultural production. Industrial production. Services. Private consumption. Government consumption. Gross domestic investment. Gross domestic savings. Tax revenue. Central government expenditure. Exports. Imports.

Table 50: Trends in Economic Performance - Industrial Countries

Total GNP. GNP annual growth rate. GNP per capita annual growth rate. Rate of inflation. Exports as percentage of GDP, annual growth rate. Tax revenue as percentage of GNP, annual growth rate. Direct taxes. Overall budget surplus/deficit.

Table 51: Regional Aggregates of Human Development Indicators - All Countries

Table 52: HDI and Income Aggregates of Human Development Indicators - All Countries

Boxes

A world social charter. A proposed action agenda for the Social Summit. Poverty reduction. Employment creation. Social integration. Human security—as people see it. Starvation amid plenty—the Bengal famine of 1943. HIV and AIDS—a global epidemic. The rising tide of disasters. The international narcotics trade. Selected indicators of human security. Job-sharing. Credit for all. Armed conflicts within states increasing. The continuing nuclear threat. A Central American accord for human development. A new horizon for Subic Bay. The human development cost of arms imports. How industrial countries rank on human development indicators. HDI values. Gender-disparity-adjusted HDI. Income-distribution-adjusted HDI.

Figures

Similar incomes—different human development. Falling incomes threaten human security. High unemployment in industrial countries. Children's health. More than a billion people in developing countries still lack safe drinking water. Profile of human distress in industrial countries. The widening gap between the rich and the poor. Refugees of the past three years could populate a major city or a country. World military spending equals the income of nearly half the world's people. The human cost of military spending in developing countries. The permanent members of the UN Security Council supply the most weapons to developing countries. Suppliers of weapons to three trouble spots. Military spending and the peace dividend. Private flows to developing countries exceed ODA. More from workers' remittances than from ODA. Global economic disparities. Net flows to developing countries turning positive again. Net transfers to developing countries from Bretton Woods institutions. Burden of debt shifts to poorest regions. ODA distribution not linked to human development objectives. The majority of the world's people have shifted from low to medium and high human development. Global improvement, but growing intercountry disparity. Top ten performers in human development. South Africa: disparity between blacks and whites four times larger than in the United States. Regional disparities in Brazil and Mexico. Regional disparities needing urgent attention in Nigeria. Human development lagging in rural Upper Egypt. China: good overall performance, extreme regional differences. Malaysia: all improve, but some faster. The legacy of land-mines. The United Nations Register of Conventional Armaments. The UN's mandate for conflicts within nations. A $50 billion bill for trade barriers on textiles and clothing. The cost of agricultural protection. Payment for services rendered—forest conservation in Costa Rica. Tradable permits for global pollution. Global human security compacts. Successes of foreign assistance. Public opinions on aid. A 20:20 compact on human development. Why failed economists visit. Does the United Nations work in the development field? A primer on the human development index.

Tables

Similar income, different HDI, 1991/92. Indicators of food security in selected countries. Ethnic and religious conflicts. Ratios of military to social spending, 1990/91. Global military expenditures and the peace dividend. High military spending among poor countries. Estimates of worldwide military assistance. Sales of major conventional weapons. Deliveries by ten suppliers to countries at war, 1980-89. Arms trade, 1988-92. Potential benefits from the Uruguay Round in 2002.

ODA to the poorest. The World Bank and the poorest people, 1989/92. Human priorities in bilateral aid allocations. Human priorities in multilateral aid, 1989/91. Human priorities in bilateral aid expenditures. U.S. ODA to selected strategic allies and to poor nations. World Bank lending to countries experiencing a major rise or fall in military spending. World Bank loans and democracy. Fixed maximums and minimums for HDI values. HDI ranking for industrial countries. HDI ranking for developing countries. Distribution of counties by human development group, 1960-92. HDI values by region, 1960-92. Top performers in human development, 1960-92. How developing countries rank on human development indicators.

THE ILLUSTRATED BOOK OF WORLD RANKINGS

FACTS AT A GLANCE

Author: George Thomas Kurian

Number of Pages: 400

Periodicity: Quadrennial

Publisher: M.E. Sharpe

PURPOSE AND SCOPE

The *Illustrated Book of World Rankings* (IBWR) is the fourth edition of a standard reference work first published in 1979 as the *Book of World Rankings*. Its second (1984) and third (1991) editions were known as the *New Book of World Rankings*. IBWR is one of the most comprehensive datasets in the field of international statistics. It ranks the performance of over 191

nations of the world in over 300 subject areas ranging from population and land area to culture and cities.

DATA ORGANIZATION

The *Illustrated Book of World Rankings* presents data organized under 25 headings. The tables themselves are derived from published sources, principally the United Nations and its affiliated organizations—the World Bank, the International Monetary Fund, and the Organization for Economic Cooperation and Development. Whereas the population and land area tables are complete, many of the other tables reflect the scarcity of data on the less developed countries. Each table is preceded by an introduction highlighting the salient features of the table, noting the share of the leading nations or their dominance. The tables themselves are divided into Top 10, Upper Middle, Lower Middle, and Bottom 10.

METHODOLOGY

The *Illustrated Book of World Rankings* presents the best available data for the latest available year. Generally, the IBWR data provides information on a large number of countries though this data may not be the most recent.

CONTENTS

Preface

Notes on Format and Entry Order

Prologue

The Use of Statistics

Profile of the Planet

130. Energy Production Growth Rate
131. GDP Output Per kg of Energy
132. Nuclear Power Production

Section XIII. Labor

133. Labor Force
134. Organized Labor as Percentage of Labor Force
135. Civil Servants as Percentage of Labor Force
136. Youth Unemployment Rate Male/Female
137. Percentage of Labor in Services
138. Percentage of Labor in Manufacturing
139. Percentage of Labor in Agriculture
140. Self Employed and Employers
141. Activity Rate
142. Women in the Labor Force
143. Workers' Remittances from Abroad

Section XIV. Transportation & Communications

144. Airfields
145. Cycling
146. Inland Waterways
147. Civil Aviation: Passengers
148. Cargo Handled by Ports: Loaded
149. Cargo Handled by Ports: Off-loaded
150. Merchant Marine
151. Rail; Freight Traffic
152. Railway Trackage
153. Rail Passenger Traffic
154. Commercial Vehicles
155. Passenger Cars
156. Length of Roads
157. Pipelines
158. Tourist Receipts
159. Tourist Expenditures by Nationals Abroad
160. Persons Per Motor Vehicle
161. Cargo by Road
162. Air Freight
163. Tourist Arrivals
164. Telephones Per Capita
165. Domestic Mail Per Capita
166. Volume of Mail
167. Post Office
168. Telephones
169. Fax Machines
170. Cellular Phones
171. International Telephone Traffic

Section XV. Environment

172. Deforestation
173. Protected Areas
174. Greenhouse Emissions Per Capita
175. Forest Land
176. Population Served by Wastewater Treatment Plants
177. Waste Recycling of Paper and Paperboard
178. Hazardous Waste Production
179. Population Served by Municipal Waste Services
180. Nuclear Wastes from Spent Fuel
181. Annual Freshwater Withdrawals
182. Internal Renewable Water Resources
183. Sulfur and Nitrogen Emissions
184. Carbon Monoxide Emissions
185. Space Objects in Orbit

186. Carbon Emissions
187. Domestic Water Shortage
188. Endangered Species

Section XVI. Consumption

189. Gold
190. Alcoholic Liquors
191. Meat
192. Chocolate
193. Butter
194. Cigarettes
195. Newsprint
196. Sugar
197. Coffee
198. Per Capita Consumption
199. Paper
200. Gasoline
201. Fish

Section XVII. Housing

202. Size of Dwellings
203. Dwellings with Toilets
204. Dwellings with Electric Lights
205. Dwellings with Piped Water
206. Home Ownership

Section XVIII. Health & Food

207. Public Health Expenditures as Percentage of GDP
208. Health Expenditures per Capita
209. Underweight Children and Low Birth Weight Infants
210. Breast Cancer Rate
211. Suicides
212. Death Rate from Cancer
213. Causes of Death—Accidents
214. Causes of Death—Respiratory Diseases
215. Causes of Death—Circulatory Diseases
216. Food Supply—Proteins
217. Food Supply—Calories
218. Deaths from Motor Vehicle Accidents
219. Maternal Mortality Rate
220. Hospital Admissions
221. Hospital Beds
222. Pharmacists
223. Nurses
224. Dentists
225. Physicians
226. Population per Physician
227. Hospitals
228. Hospital Bed Occupancy Rate
229. Population with Access to Safe Water
230. Food Supply as Percentage of FAO Requirements
231. AIDS

Section XIX. Education

232. Male Literacy Rate
233. Female Literacy Rate
234. Tertiary Institutions
235. Secondary Schools
236. Academic Attainment
237. Students at the Tertiary Level Per 100,000

UNESCO STATISTICAL YEARBOOK

FACTS AT A GLANCE

Number of Pages: 900

Periodicity: Annual

Publisher: United Nations Educational, Scientific, and Cultural Organization (UNESCO)

PURPOSE AND SCOPE

The *UNESCO Statistical Yearbook* is the premier statistical collection on educational and cultural activities and institutions throughout the world. It is prepared by the Division of Statistics of UNESCO in cooperation with national UNESCO commissions and statistical services. Its publication is mandated by Article VIII of the UNESCO Constitution.

DATA ORGANIZATION

The first part of the *Yearbook* consists of four tables—two on population, one on illiteracy, and one on educational attainment. The remaining tables deal with first, second, and third level educational systems, cohorts, enrollments, teachers, and other data, science, culture, and mass media and communications.

METHODOLOGY

Data are gathered mainly from official replies to UNESCO questionnaires and special surveys, supplemented by official reports and publications. Some 200 countries and territories respond to the questionnaires every year. Data are generally presented for the latest year, but by using the current edition in combination with earlier ones, a meaningful time series can be developed. Introductions to each table are presented in English, Spanish, and French. Translations of these texts appear in Russian and Arabic in Appendix F and G respectively.

CONTENTS

Introduction

Explanatory Note

List of Countries and Territories

1. Reference Tables

Population, area, and density, 1970, 1980, 1986, 1990, and 1991. Estimated total population and population 0-24 years old, by continents, major areas, and groups of countries, 1970-2010. Illiterate population 15 years of age and over and percentage illiteracy by age group and by sex. Percentage distribution of population 25 years of age and over, by educational attainment and by sex.

Education

2. Summary Tables for All Levels of Education, by Continents, Major Areas, and Groups of Countries

Teaching staff and enrollment by sex for education preceding the first level. Total and female enrollment by level of education. Total enrollment percentage distribution by level and percentage female at each level. Total and female teaching staff by level of education. Teaching staff distribution by level of education and percentage female at first and second level. Index numbers of total and female enrollment by level of education (1975=100). Education at the second level: percentage distribution of enrollment and teaching staff by type of education. Estimated gross enrollment rations by level of education. Estimated enrollment ratios by age group and sex. Public expenditure on education, in United States dollars.

3. Education By Level and By Country

A. Educational Structures and Enrollment Ratios
National education systems. Enrollment ratios by level of education.

B. Education at the Pre-Primary, First, and Second Levels
Education preceding the first level: institutions, teachers, and pupils. Education at the first level: institutions, teachers, and pupils. Education at the first level: percentage distribution of enrollment by grade. Education at the first level: percentage of repeaters by grade. Education at the second level (general teacher-training and vocational): teachers and pupils. Education at the second level (general): percentage distribution of enrollment by grade. Education at the second level (general): percentage of repeaters by grade.

C. Education at the Third Level
Education at the third level: number of students per 100,000 inhabitants. Education at the third level: teachers and students by type of institution.

Education at the third level: enrollment by sex, and by ISCED level and field of study. Education at the third level: number of foreign students enrolled. Education at the third level: foreign students by country of origin, in 50 selected countries.

4. Educational Expenditure

Public expenditure on education: total and as percentage of the GNP and of all public expenditure. Public current expenditure on education: distribution according to purpose. Public current expenditure on education: distribution by level of education. Public current expenditure on education: distribution by level of education and purpose.

5. Science and Technology

A. Summary Data for R&D Scientists and Engineers and for Expenditure
Figure: Distribution of R&D scientists and engineers and expenditure by groups of countries: estimated percentage for 1980, 1985, and 1990.
Tables: Scientific and technical manpower: estimates for 1980 and 1985. Scientists and engineers engaged in R&D and expenditure for R&D: estimates for 1980, 1985, and 1990.

B. Scientific and Technical Manpower
Scientific and technical manpower. Number of scientists, engineers, and technicians engaged in research and experimental development. Total personnel engaged in research and experimental development by sector of performance and by category of personnel.

C. Expenditure on Research and Experimental Development
Total expenditure for research and experimental development by type of expenditure. Total expenditure for the performance of research and experimental development by source of funds. Current expenditure for research and experimental development by type of R&D activity. Total and current expenditure for research and experimental development by sector of performance. Expenditure for national research and experimental development activities by major socio-economic aim.
Culture and Communication

6. Summary Tables for Culture and Communication Subjects by Continents, Major Areas, and Groups of Countries

Number of book titles published. Number and circulation of daily newspapers. Newsprint production and consumption. Production and consumption of other printing and writing paper. Production of long films. Number and seating capacity of fixed cinemas. Annual cinema attendance. Number of radio broadcasting receivers and receivers per 1,000 inhabitants. Number of television receivers and receivers per 1,000 inhabitants.

7. Printed Matter

A. Libraries
Libraries by category: number, collections, additions, registered users. Libraries of institutions of higher education: collections, registered users, works loaned out, current expenditure, employees. School libraries: collections, registered users, works loaned out, current expenditure, employees.

B. Book Production
Book production: number of titles by UDC classes. Book production: number of titles by subject group. Book production: number of titles by language of publication. Book production: number of copies by UDC classes. Book production: number of copies by subject group. Production of school textbooks: number of titles and copies. Production of children's books: number of titles and copies. Translations by country of publication and by UDC classes. Translations by original languages and by UDC classes. Translations by country of publication and by selected languages from which translated. Translations by original language and by selected languages into which translated. Authors most frequently translated.

C. Newspapers and Other Periodicals
Daily newspapers: number and circulation (total and per 1,000 inhabitants). Non-daily newspapers and periodicals: number and circulation (total and per 1,000 inhabitants).

D. Cultural Paper
Newsprint and other printing and writing paper: production, imports, exports, and consumption (total and per 1,000 inhabitants).

8. Film and Cinema
Long films: number of films produced. Long films: number of long films imported, by country of origin. Cinemas: number, seating capacity, annual attendance, and box office receipts.

9. Broadcasting
Radio broadcasting: number of receivers and receivers per 1,000 inhabitants. Television broadcasting: number of receivers and receivers per 1,000 inhabitants. Radio broadcasting: programs by function and by type of institution. Television broadcasting: programs by function and by type of institution. Radio and television broadcasting: personnel employed by type of personnel and type of institution. Radio and television broadcasting: annual revenue by source and by type of institution. Radio and television broadcasting: annual current expenditure by purpose and by type of institution.

10. International Trade in Printed Matter
Importation and exportation of books and pamphlets: 1980, 1985, and 1991. Importation and exportation of newspapers and periodicals: 1980, 1985, and 1991.

11. Cultural Heritage
Number of museums by subject of collection or type of institution: annual attendance, receipts, personnel, and current expenditures.

Appendixes
Member States and Associate Members of UNESCO. School and Financial Years. Exchange Rates. Selected List of UNESCO Statistical Publications. Tables Omitted. Introductory Texts in Russian, Introductory Texts in Arabic.

UNITED NATIONS STATISTICAL YEARBOOK

FACTS AT A GLANCE

Number of Pages: 1,109

Periodicity: Annual

Publisher: United Nations

PURPOSE AND SCOPE

The major purpose of the *Statistical Yearbook* is to provide, in a single volume, a comprehensive compilation of international statistics on social and economic conditions and activities, at the world, regional, and national levels covering roughly a 10-year period.

DATA ORGANIZATION

The reorganized *Yearbook* consists of four parts: Part One—World and Regional Summary, is essentially unchanged from previous issues. Parts Two, Three, and Four deal with Population and Social Topics, National Economic Activity, and International Economic Relations. Part Two integrates population and social statistics. Part Three is based on the International Standard Industrial Classification of all Economic Activities. Part Four covers merchandise trade, international tourism, and financial transactions, including development assistance. Each chapter includes technical notes on statistical sources and methods. Complete references to sources and methodology are provided at the end. Important additions include two detailed tables of statistics and indicators on the environment and pollution, and the deletion of certain commodities from the commodity production tables in Part Three. The list of tables added to or omitted from the last two issues are given in Annex III.

The current issue continues to make extensive use of the microcomputer database, spreadsheet, and typesetting technologies. It employs the open-table design which is easier to photocompose than the enclosed designs using horizontal and vertical rules and boxes common to the pre-computer era.

The statistics presented in the *Yearbook* are extracted from other publications and compilations. While these specialized publications focus on particular fields, the *Statistical Yearbook* provides data for comprehensive overall structures, conditions, trends, changes, and activities. The goal has been to systematize essential components of comparable statistical information on a broad range of subjects at world, regional, and national levels. The emphasis is on those issues which are of immediate concern to the United Nations and its agencies, such as population, economic growth, urbanization, employment, inflation, wages, energy, trade, food, finances, external balance of payments, education, environment, and development assistance. More information on statistical concepts, definitions, and classifications are provided in the Technical Notes that accompany each chapter. Information on the methodology used for the computation of data can be found in the *1977 Supplement to the Statistical Yearbook.*

Part One illustrates the *Yearbook's* principal concern with the global situation and contains 10 tables. Part Two contains 18 tables, Part Three, 87 tables, and Part Four, 16 tables. Annex I provides information on countries and areas covered in the Yearbook tables and their grouping into geographical regions. The geographical regions are generally continents. The terms "developing" and "developed countries" are used in the conventional sense, more for statistical convenience than as a judgment on the economic stature of the country.

Although the *Yearbook* attempts to present internationally comparable data by coordinating base years, time periods, and dollar exchange values, much work remains to be done. Many tables serve only as a rough source of data and, when derived through vastly different methodologies, may actually be misleading. Because of the frequent and wide fluctuations in the market rates of the numeraire, or the United States dollar, in international transactions and the resulting distortions in the purchasing power parities, the computations of national prices, cost of living, and wages may be off the mark by several degrees of magnitude.

METHODOLOGY

The *Yearbook* is based on data compiled by the Statistics Division in the fields of demography, national accounts, industry, energy, and international trade. Data provided by the 20 offices of the United Nations System, and transport data provided directly by countries.

CONTENTS

Part One: World and Regional Summary

1. World and Regional Summary
Tables 1-10. Technical notes.

Part Two: Population and Social Statistics

2. Population and Human Settlements
Tables 11 and 12. Technical notes.

3. Education and Literacy
Tables 13-18. Technical notes.

4. Health and Child Bearing; Nutrition
Tables 19-22. Technical notes.

5. Culture
Tables 23-28. Technical notes.
Part Three: Economic Activity

6. National Accounts
Tables 29 and 30. Technical notes.

7. Government Finance
Tables 31-35. Technical notes.

8. Labor Force
Tables 36 and 37. Technical notes.

9. Wages and Prices
Tables 38-40. Technical notes.

10. Agriculture, Hunting, Forestry, and Fishing
Tables 41-60. Technical notes.

11. Mining and Quarrying
Tables 61-67. Technical notes.

12. Manufacturing
Food, beverages, and tobacco, Tables 68-76. Textile, wearing apparel, and leather industries, Tables 77 and 78. Wood and wood products; paper and paper products, Tables 79-81. Chemicals and related products, tables 89-96. Non-metallic mineral products and fabricated metal products, machinery, and equipment, Tables 97-99. Technical notes.

13. Transport and Communications
Tables 100-105. Technical notes.

14. Energy
Tables 106 and 107. Technical notes.

15. Environment and Land Use
Table 108-110. Technical notes.

16. Science and Technology; Intellectual Property
Tables 111-115. Technical notes.
Part Four: International Economic Relations

17. International Trade
Tables 116-121. Technical notes.

18. International Tourism
Tables 122-124. Technical notes.

19. Balance of Payments
Table 125. Technical notes.

20. International Finance
Tables 126-129. Technical notes.

21. Development Assistance
Tables 130 and 131. Technical notes.

Annexes
Country and area nomenclature, regional, and other groupings. Conversion coefficients and factors. Tables added and omitted. Statistical sources and references.

Index (English Only)

List of Tables

Part One: World and Regional Summary

1. World and Regional Summary

Selected series of world statistics. Population, rate of increase, birth and death rates, surface area and density. Index numbers of total agricultural and food production. Index numbers of per capita total agricultural and food production. Index numbers of industrial production; world and regions. Index numbers of industrial employment: world and regions. Index numbers of labor productivity in industry: world and region. Production, trade, and consumption of commercial energy. Total exports and imports (SNA countries). Export price index numbers of primary commodities and non-ferrous base metals.

Part Two: Population and Social Statistics

2. Population and Human Settlements

Population by sex, rate of population increase, surface area, and density. Population in urban and rural areas, rates of growth, and largest city population.

3. Education and Literacy

Education preceding the first level. Education at the first level. Education at the second level. Education at the third level. Public expenditure on education at current market prices. Illiterate population by sex.

4. Health and Child-Bearing; Nutrition

Vital statistics summary and expectation of life at birth. Selected indicators of life expectancy, child-bearing, and mortality. Estimates/projections of total AIDS cases and cumulative HIV infections and number of reported AIDS cases. Estimated cumulative HIV infection to the end of 1991, and projections for year 2000. Reported, estimated, and projected AIDS cases to December 1990. Reported AIDS cases, 1991. Food supply.

5. Culture

Newsprint consumption. Book production: number of titles by UDC classes. Book production: number of titles by language of publication. Daily newspapers. Non-daily newspapers and periodicals. Television and radio receivers.

Part Three: Economic Activity

6. National Accounts

Gross domestic product and net material product. Million national currency units. Million US dollars. Index numbers of industrial production.

7. Government Finance

Money supply. Rates of discount of central banks. Government bonds. Market prices of industrial shares. Money market rates.

8. Labor Force

Employment by industry. Unemployment.

9. Wages and Prices

Earnings in manufacturing. Producers prices and wholesale prices. Consumer price index numbers.

10. Agriculture, Hunting, Forestry, and Fishing

Agricultural production (index numbers). Cereals. Wheat. Rice (rough or paddy). Maize (corn). Soybeans. Coffee. Coffee consumption. Tea. Tobacco. Cotton (lint). Livestock. Wool. Roundwood. Natural rubber. Fish catches. Tractors in use. Nitrogenous fertilizers (consumption). Phosphate fertilizers (consumption). Potash fertilizers (consumption).

11. Mining and Quarrying

Diamonds. Uranium. Iron-bearing ores. Bauxite. Phosphate rock. Silver. Gold.

12. Manufacturing

A. Food, Beverages, and Tobacco
Sugar. Sugar consumption. Meat. Butter. Cheese. Wheat flour and flour of other cereals. Wine. Beer. Cigarettes.

B. Textile, Wearing Apparel, and Leather Industries
Cotton (industrial consumption). Wool (industrial consumption).

C. Wood and Wood Products; Paper and Paper Products
Sawnwood. Paper and paperboard. Wood-based panels.

D. Chemicals and Related Products
Rubber: synthetic and reclaimed. Rubber (industrial consumption). Tires. Nitrogenous fertilizers. Phosphate fertilizers. Potash fertilizers. Cement.

E. Basic Metal Industries
Pig-iron and crude steel. Aluminum. Copper. Lead. Magnesium. Tin. Tin (industrial consumption). Zinc.

F. Non-metallic Mineral Products and Fabricated Metal Products, Machinery, and Equipment Radio and television receivers. Merchant vessels. Passenger cars.

13. Transport and Communications

Railways: traffic. Motor vehicles in use. Merchant shipping: fleets. International maritime transport. Civil aviation. Telephones.

14. Energy

Production, trade, and consumption of commercial energy. Production of selected energy commodities.

15. Environment and Land Use

Selected indicators of environmental pollution and management. CO_2 CFCs halons;

drinking water and sanitation; paper consumption and recovery; and protected area. Sulphur dioxide at selected sites. Global water quality in selected rivers—pollution indicators, 1984-1988 (mean values). Surface and land area and land use.

16. Science and Technology; Intellectual Property
Number of scientists, engineers, and technicians in research and experimental development. Expenditure for research and experimental development. Patents. Industrial designs. Trademarks and service marks.

Part Four: International Economic Relations

17. International Trade
External trade conversion factors. Total imports and exports. World exports by commodity classes and by regions. Total imports and exports: index numbers. Manufactured goods exports. Structure of world exports by commodity classes and regions.

18. International Tourism
Tourist arrivals by region of origin. Tourist arrivals and international tourism receipts. International tourism expenditures.

19. Balance of Payments
Summary of balance of payments.

20. International Finance
Exchange rates. International reserves excluding gold. Gold reserves. External debt of developing countries. Total external debt. Public and publicly guaranteed long-term debt.

21. Development Assistance
Disbursement to developing countries or areas of bilateral and multilateral official development assistance through the United Nations system. Development grant expenditures. Development loan and relief expenditures.

WORLD DEVELOPMENT REPORT

FACTS AT A GLANCE
Number of Pages: 254

Periodicity: Annual

Publisher: World Bank/Oxford University Press

PURPOSE AND SCOPE
The 17th edition of the *World Development Report* (including the *World Development Indicators*) provides economic, social, and natural resource indicators for selected periods or years for 207 countries or territories and various analytical and geographic groups of countries. Data in the *World Development Indicators* are supplemented by other World Bank publications, such as the *World Bank Atlas, World Tables, World Debt Tables,* and *Social Indicators of Development.*

DATA ORGANIZATION
Data are presented for all industrialized and developing countries with a population of one million or more. Only basic data are given for countries with sparse data, such as Afghanistan, Angola, Bosnia and Herzegovina, Cambodia, Croatia, Cuba, Eritrea, Haiti, Iraq, North Korea, Kuwait, Lebanon, Liberia, Libya, Macedonia, Viet Nam, Yugoslavia, and Zaire. Changes in this edition relative to the previous ones include a new table on Infrastructure and deletion of the table on Consumption. Aggregates for severely indebted middle-income economies are also presented. The indicators in Tables 1 and 1a give summary profiles of economies. Data in the other tables fall into seven categories: production, domestic absorption, fiscal and monetary accounts, core international transactions, external finance, human resources development, and environment. All economies are listed in ascending order of GNP per capita, except those for which no such figure can be calculated. Those are italicized and listed in alpha order at the end of the appropriate group.

METHODOLOGY
Differences in the data between this year's and previous editions reflect not only updates but also revisions to historical series and changes in methodology. The summary measures in the colored bands in each table are totals (t), weighted averages (w), or median values (m), calculated for groups of economies. Group aggregates include countries for which country-specific data do not appear in the tables. Where missing information accounts for a third or more of the overall estimate, the group measure is not reported. The key shows the years of the most recent census, demographic survey, or vital registration-based estimates. This information is included because demographics affect the overall quality of per capita rates and ratios.

Technical notes outline the methods, concepts, and definitions and data sources used in compiling the tables. Country notes to the world tables provide additional explanations of sources used, breaks in comparability, and other exceptions to standard statistical practices.

CONTENTS
1. **Tables**
   Basic indicators.

2. **Production**
   Growth of production. Structures of production. Agriculture and food. Commercial energy. Structure of manufacturing. Manufacturing earnings and output.

3. **Domestic Absorption**
   Growth of consumption and investment. Structure of demand.

4. **Fiscal and Monetary Accounts**

   Central government expenditure. Central government current revenue. Money and interest rates.

5. **Core International Transactions**

   Growth of merchandise trade. Structure of merchandise imports. Structure of merchandise exports. OECD imports of manufactured goods. Balance of payments and reserves.

6. **External Finance**

   Official development assistance from OECD and OPEC members. Official development assistance receipts. Total external debt. Flow of public and private external capital. Aggregate net resource flows and net transfers. Total external debt ratios. Terms of external public borrowing.

7. **Human Resources Development**

   Population and labor force. Demography and fertility. Health and nutrition. Education. Gender comparisons. Income distribution and PPP estimates of GNP.

8. **Environmentally Sustainable Development**

   Urbanization. Infrastructure. Natural resources.

9. **Table 1a**

   Basic indicators for other economies.

10. **Technical Notes**

11. **Data Sources**

12. **Classification of Economies**

13. **Text Figures**

    As a country's income grows, the amount of infrastructure increases. The composition of infrastructure changes with country income level. Infrastructure has expanded tremendously in recent decades. Urban populations have better access to safe drinking water than rural populations. Annual gains from eliminating mispricing and inefficiency are large relative to investment. Public infrastructure investment is a large fraction of both total and public investment in developing countries. Per capita availability of major infrastructure is closely related to income levels. Infrastructure services differ substantially in their economic characteristics across sectors, within sectors, and between technologies. The rural-urban gap in access to power and water in developing countries narrowed over the past decade. Efficient and effective delivery of infrastructure services does not always accompany increased availability. There is very high unmet demand for telephone connection. Walking is a transport mode used frequently by the poor. The adoption of commercial principles in 1984 allowed Togo's water utility to increase coverage and production, but a performance agreement in 1989 was needed to improve financial outcomes. Costs are seldom fully recovered in infrastructure. Unbundling activities increase the options for competition and private sector involvement. Leases and concessions in infrastructure sectors are common, even in low-income countries. Privatizations in telecommunications can lead to large gains. Countries with decentralized road maintenance have better roads. Participation increases water project effectiveness by improving maintenance. In water and sewerage, the better-off often get more subsidies than the poor. Even in some formerly centrally planned economies, infrastructure subsidies went mainly to the better-off. Large shares of official development finance for infrastructure go to energy and transport. Official lending for infrastructure has increased, but publicly guaranteed private loans have fallen. Infrastructure is a large share of privatization proceeds; foreign financing of infrastructure privatization is important in Latin America. Infrastructure equities are contributing to the growth of Argentina's capital market. Infrastructure equities have outperformed other stocks by a huge margin. Options for financing increase with administrative capacity and maturity of domestic capital markets.

14. **Text Tables**

    Value-added of infrastructure services by country groups. Average economic rates of return on World Bank-supported projects. Expansion of infrastructure coverage in low-, middle- and high-income economies, recent decades. Percentage of the poorest and richest population quintiles with access to infrastructure, various countries. Common management problems in public sector infrastructure entities, 1980-92. Contractual arrangements for private water supply. Value of infrastructure privatizations in developing countries. Portfolio and foreign direct investment in developing countries. Infrastructure project financing for projects funded and in the pipeline, October 1993. Project financing of funded infrastructure projects, by sector, October 1993. The main institutional options for provision of infrastructure. Country infrastructure coverage and performance. Feasibility of private sector delivery varies by infrastructure components. Options in telecommunications and energy. Options in water and waste. Options in transport. Fiscal burden of underpriced infrastructure. Savings from increased efficiency.

15. **Appendix Table**

    Physical measures of infrastructure provision. Access to drinking water and sanitation. IBRD and IDA commitments. Official development finance commitments.

Other General Global Statistical Sourcebooks

GALE COUNTRY AND WORLD RANKINGS REPORTER

FACTS AT A GLANCE

Number of Pages: 1,091

Periodicity: Annual

Publisher: Gale Research

PURPOSE AND SCOPE

The purpose of the *Gale Country and World Rankings Reporter* is to present comparative rankings data on 235 countries culled from published sources and organized into 3,246 tables.

DATA ORGANIZATION

The *Country and World Rankings Reporter* comprises five thematic profiles organized first by broad subject categories, broken down into alphabetically arranged chapters and then subdivided by specific topics. Topics and tables are presented in alphabetical order. The five topical profiles are:

1. Social - covering demographics, education, health and welfare, home and family, religion, labor, leisure, and entertainment.
2. Physical - covering agriculture, environment, natural resources, and geography.
3. Transportation and Public Utilities - covering communications, energy and utilities, infrastructure, transportation, travel, and tourism.
4. Political - covering defense, government, politics, international relations, law, and criminal justice.
5. Economic - covering industry, economy, marketing, and trade.

The tables are followed by a keyword index with cross-references, a list of statistical sources and a list of acronyms and abbreviations.

METHODOLOGY

A typical ranking presents data for countries or territories (in some cases corporations, brands, or people) ranked either according to values or alphabetically. Whenever possible, tables show data by world regions; thus all of the regional tables must be read together to obtain the global data. Data with equal values within a table receive the same ranking. There are tables with as few as two countries . In the case of absolute numbers, value-added data (such as per capita) were derived from them and then ranked. There is no analysis of the data nor any attempt to highlight the more important features.

CONTENTS

Part I: Social Profile

Chapter 1: Demographics

Crops: Cash Grains

Water

Part III - Transportation and Public Utilities Profile

Chapter 10: Communications

News Media

Radio

Heat Content

Land
Table 1848: Car Rental in Asia
Table 1849: Car Rental Taxes in Europe
Table 1850: Cars in Europe
Table 1851: Motor Vehicles in Taiwan and China, 1990
Table 1852: Passenger Car Registrations in Caribbean Countries, 1990
Table 1853: Passenger Car Registrations in East Asia, 1990
Table 1854: Passenger Car Registrations in Europe, 1990
Table 1855: Passenger Car Registrations in Middle America, 1990
Table 1856: Passenger Car Registrations in North America, 1990
Table 1857: Passenger Car Registrations in Oceania, 1990
Table 1858: Passenger Car Registrations in South America, 1990
Table 1859: Passenger Car Registrations in South Asia, 1990
Table 1861: Registered Vehicles in Caribbean Countries, 1990
Table 1862: Registered Vehicles in East Asia, 1990
Table 1863: Registered Vehicles in Europe, 1990
Table 1864: Registered Vehicles in Middle America, 1990
Table 1865: Registered Vehicles in North America, 1990
Table 1866: Registered Vehicles in Oceania, 1990
Table 1867: Registered Vehicles in South America, 1990
Table 1868: Registered Vehicles in South Asia, 1990
Table 1869: Road Accident Death Costs
Table 1870: Road Accident Deaths, 1990
Table 1871: Traffic Accident Death Rates in Selected Caribbean Countries
Table 1872: Traffic Accident Death Rates in Selected East Asian Countries
Table 1873: Traffic Accident Death Rates in Selected European Countries
Table 1874: Traffic Accident Death Rates in Selected Middle American Countries
Table 1875: Traffic Accident Death Rates in Selected North American Countries
Table 1876: Traffic Accident Death Rates in Selected Oceania Countries
Table 1877: Traffic Accident Death Rates in Selected South American Countries
Table 1878: Traffic Accident Death Rates in Selected South Asian Countries
Table 1879: Traffic Accident Death Rates Worldwide
Table 1880: Traffic Accident Deaths in Selected Caribbean Countries
Table 1881: Traffic Accident Deaths in Selected East Asian Countries
Table 1882: Traffic Accident Deaths in Selected European Countries
Table 1883: Traffic Accident Deaths in Selected Middle American Countries

Table 1884: Traffic Accident Deaths in Selected North American Countries
Table 1885: Traffic Accident Deaths in Selected Oceania Countries
Table 1886: Traffic Accident Deaths in Selected South American Countries
Table 1887: Traffic Accident Deaths in Selected South Asian Countries

Land: Rail
Table 1988: Rail Freight Traffic Growth, 1985-1992
Table 1889: Rail Passenger Traffic Growth, 1985-1992

Logistics
Table 1890: Distribution Costs of Administration as Percent of Sales
Table 1891: Distribution Costs of Inventory as Percent of Sales
Table 1892: Distribution Costs of Order Entry and Customer Service as Percent of Sales
Table 1893: Distribution Costs of Transportation as Percent of Sales
Table 1894: Distribution Costs of Warehousing as Percent of Sales
Table 1895: Logistics Administration Costs in Europe and the United States
Table 1896: Logistics Customer Service Costs in Europe and the United States
Table 1897: Logistics Inventory Costs in Europe and the United States
Table 1898: Logistics Transportation Costs in Europe and the United States
Table 1899: Logistics Warehousing Costs in Europe and the United States
Table 1900: Storage Expenditures for Hire
Table 1901: Storage Expenditures for Insurance
Table 1902: Storage Expenditures for Labor
Table 1903: Storage Expenditures for Maintenance
Table 1904: Storage Expenditures for Pallets
Table 1905: Storage Expenditures for Power
Table 1906: Storage Expenditures for Rent
Table 1907: Storage Expenditures for Security
Table 1908: Storage Expenditures for Staffing
Table 1909: Transport Expenditures for Fuel
Table 1910: Transport Expenditures for Garages
Table 1911: Transport Expenditures for Hire
Table 1912: Transport Expenditures for Insurance and Licensing
Table 1913: Transport Expenditures for Labor
Table 1914: Transport Expenditures for Maintenance
Table 1915: Transport Expenditures for Staffing

Space
Table 1916: Decayed Space Objects
Table 1917: Ground Crews for Space Vehicles
Table 1918: Launch Cost of Space Vehicles
Table 1919: Payload of Space Vehicles
Table 1920: Reliability of Space Vehicles
Table 1921: Space Objects in Orbit

Table 2182: Polling in Latin America
Table 2183: Polling in Western Europe
Table 2184: Voter Turnout in Europe, 1994
Table 2185: Women's Right to Vote

Chapter 17: International Relations

Foreign Aid
Table 2186: Environmental Assistance to Central and Eastern Europe, 1990-1992
Table 2187: Environmental Financial Assistance From G-24 Nations, 1990-1992
Table 2188: Food Aid from the United States, 1992
Table 2189: Foreign Aid from the United States, 1982-1991
Table 2190: Foreign Aid from the United States - Leading Recipients, 1993
Table 2191: Foreign Aid to Eastern Europe through the PHARE Program, 1992
Table 2192: Foreign Aid to Ex-Soviet Countries through the TACIS Program, 1992
Table 2193: Foreign Aid to the West Bank and Gaza Strip
Table 2194: Humanitarian Aid for Yugoslavian Refugees, 1991-1991
Table 2195: Inter-American Foundation Grants to Latin America, 1990
Table 2196: Private Aid to Developing Countries, 1990
Table 2197: Public Aid to Developing Countries, 1990

International Organizations
Table 2198: European Community Directives
Table 2199: NATO Countries' Shares of Military Budget Support
Table 2200: NATO Forces on Duty in Europe, June 1992
Table 2201: United Nations Army Forces on Duty
Table 2202: United Nations Contributions, 1994
Table 2203: United Nations Debt
Table 2204: United Nations Peacekeepers - Highest Numbers, 1994
Table 2205: United Nations Peacekeepers - Lowest Numbers, 1994
Table 2206: United Nations Peacekeeping Forces, by Country
Table 2207: United Nations Peacekeeping Forces Costs, 1994
Table 2208: United Nations Peacekeeping Forces Deaths
Table 2209: United Nations Peacekeeping Forces Locations, 1994
Table 2210: United Nations Peacekeeping Services Debt
Table 2211: United Nations Unpaid Contributions

Military Aid
Table 2212: Military Assistance Requests, 1993
Table 2213: Military Construction Sales Deliveries of the United States, 1991
Table 2214: Operation Desert Shield/Desert Storm - Cash Contributions from Foreign Governments

Table 2215: Operation Desert Shield/Desert Storm - Receipts-in-Kind from Foreign Governments
Table 2216: Operation Desert Shield/Desert Storm - Total Contributions of Financial Assistance from Foreign Governments
Table 2217: U.S. Military Assistance Program Deliveries and Expenditures in American Republics, 1991
Table 2218: U.S. Military Assistance Program Deliveries and Expenditures in Europe and Canada, 1991
Table 2219: U.S. Military Assistance Program Deliveries and Expenditures in Near East and South Asia, 1991

Trade Partners
Table 2220: Export Partners of Antigua and Barbuda
Table 2221: Export Partners of Australia
Table 2222: Export Partners of Austria
Table 2223: Export Partners of Bahrain
Table 2224: Export Partners of Bangladesh
Table 2225: Export Partners of Barbados
Table 2226: Export Partners of Belgium
Table 2227: Export Partners of Benin
Table 2228: Export Partners of Bermuda
Table 2229: Export Partners of Brazil
Table 2230: Export Partners of Brunei
Table 2231: Export Partners of Bulgaria
Table 2232: Export Partners of Burkina
Table 2233: Export Partners of Burundi
Table 2234: Export Partners of Cape Verde
Table 2235: Export Partners of Chile
Table 2236: Export Partners of Colombia
Table 2237: Export Partners of Comoros
Table 2238: Export Partners of Cuba
Table 2239: Export Partners of Cyprus
Table 2240: Export Partners of Denmark
Table 2241: Export Partners of Djibouti
Table 2242: Export Partners of Dominican Republic
Table 2243: Export Partners of Equatorial Guinea
Table 2244: Export Partners of Farce Islands
Table 2245: Export Partners of Fiji
Table 2246: Export Partners of Finland
Table 2247: Export Partners of France
Table 2248: Export Partners of French Guiana
Table 2249: Export Partners of French Polynesia
Table 2250: Export Partners of Gabon
Table 2251: Export Partners of Germany
Table 2252: Export Partners of Ghana
Table 2253: Export Partners of Greece
Table 2254: Export Partners of Greenland
Table 2255: Export Partners of Guadeloupe
Table 2256: Export Partners of Guam
Table 2257: Export Partners of Guinea
Table 2258: Export Partners of Guyana
Table 2259: Export Partners of Haiti
Table 2260: Export Partners of Honduras
Table 2261: Export Partners of Hong Kong
Table 2262: Export Partners of Hungary
Table 2263: Export Partners of Iceland
Table 2264: Export Partners of India

Chapter 18: Law and Criminal Justice

Espionage and Piracy

Homicide

Illegal Substances

Legal Fees

Penalties and Punishments

Part V - Economic Profile

Chapter 19: General Indicators

Banking and Financial Services

Exchange Rates

Exports, by Commodity

Table 2933: Air Conditioner Exports of the United States

Table 2934: Aluminum-Vanadium Master Alloy Exports of the United States, 1992

Table 2935: Aluminum-Vanadium Master Alloy - Value of Exports of the United States, 1992

Table 2936: Ammonia Compressor Exports by the United States

Table 2937: Barley Exports of Europe, 1992

Table 2938: Barley Exports of North America, 1992

Table 2940: Bicycle Exports

Table 2941: Butter Exports of Europe, 1992

Table 2942: Butter Exports of North America, 1992

Table 2943: Butter Exports of Oceania, 1992

Table 2944: Cattle Exports of Europe, 1992

Table 2945: Cattle Exports of Latin America and the Caribbean, 1992

Table 2946: Cattle Exports of North America, 1992

Table 2947: Cattle Exports of Oceania, 1992

Table 2948: Cheese Exports of Europe, 1992

Table 2949: Cheese Exports of North America, 1992

Table 2950: Cheese Exports of Oceania, 1992

Table 2951: Chemical Exports of the United States, 1990

Table 2952: Chemical Product Exports of European Markets, 1992

Table 2953: Cigarette Exports from the United States, 1993

Table 2954: Coffee Exports of Africa, 1992

Table 2955: Coffee Exports of Asia, 1992

Table 2956: Coffee Exports of Latin America and the Caribbean, 1992

Table 2957: Compressor Parts Exports of the United States

Table 2958: Copper (Refined) Exports of the United States, 1990

Table 2959: Copper (Unalloyed) Scrap Exports of the United States, 1990

Table 2960: Copper-base Scrap Exports of the United States, 1990

Table 2961: Corn Exports of Africa, 1992

Table 2962: Corn Exports of Asia, 1992

Table 2963: Corn Exports of Europe, 1992

Table 2964: Corn Exports of Latin America and the Caribbean, 1992

Table 2965: Corn Exports of North America, 1992

Table 2966: Corn Exports of Oceania, 1992

Table 2967: Cotton Exports of Africa, 1992

Table 2968: Cotton Exports of Asia, 1992

Table 2969: Cotton Exports of Europe, 1992

Table 2970: Cotton Exports of Former Soviet Union, 1992

Table 2971: Cotton Exports of Latin America and the Caribbean, 1992

Table 2972: Cotton Exports of Near East, 1992

Table 2973: Diammonium Phosphates Exports of the United States, 1992

Table 2974: Drinking Water Cooler Exports of the United States

Table 2975: Egg Exports of Asia, 1992

Table 2976: Egg Exports of Europe, 1992

Table 2977: Egg Exports of Latin America and the Caribbean, 1992

Table 2978: Egg Exports of Near East, 1992

Table 2979: Egg Exports of North America, 1992

Table 2980: Elemental Phosphorus Exports of the United States, 1992

Table 2981: Elemental Phosphorus - Value of Exports of the United States, 1992

Table 2982: Ferromanganese Exports of the United States, 1992

Table 2983: Ferrosilicon Exports of the United States, 1992

Table 2984: Ferrosilicon - Value of Exports of the United States, 1992

Table 2985: Ferrovanadium - Exports of the United States, 1992

Table 2986: Ferrovanadium - Value of Exports of the United States, 1992

Table 2987: Fiber Exports from the United States to Latin American Destinations

Table 2988: Fiber Exports from the United States to Middle Eastern and African Destinations

Table 2989: Fiber Exports from the United States to Western Europe

Table 2990: Fluid Milk Exports of Europe, 1992

Table 2991: Fluid Milk Exports of Oceania, 1992

Table 2992: Freezer Display Cases Exports of the United States

Table 2993: French Fry Exports of the United States, 1991

Table 2994: Gold Exports of the United States, 1992

Table 2995: Ice Cream Exported from the United States, 1991

Table 2996: Ice-Making Machine Exports of the United States

Table 2997: Machine Tool Export Shipment Values, 1990

Table 2998: Machine Tool Exports as Percent of Production

Table 2999: Machine Tool Exports in Selected Countries, 1991

Table 3000: Machinery Exports to the United States

Table 3001: Manganese Metal Exports of the United States, 1992

Table 3002: Manganese Ore Exports of the United States, 1992

Table 3003: Medical Equipment Exports to Germany, 1992

Table 3004: Monoammonium Phosphate Exports of the United States

Table 3005: Nonrubber Footwear Exports of the United States

Table 3006: Oat Exports of Europe, 1992

Table 3007: Oat Exports of Latin America and the Caribbean, 1992

Table 3008: Oat Exports of North America, 1992

Table 3009: Oxides and Hydroxides - Value of Exports of the United States

Table 3010: Paper and Paperboard Exports of the United States

Imports

INSTAT: INTERNATIONAL STATISTICS SOURCES

FACTS AT A GLANCE

Number of Pages:
Volume One: 426; Volume Two: 449

Periodicity: Irregular

Publisher: Routledge

PURPOSE AND SCOPE

INSTAT provides a comprehensive subject guide to sources of international statistical data. Its purpose is to lead users quickly and easily to sources of international data on particular subjects. Among the more than 400 sources included are statistical data published by both public and private bodies. Purely national sources restricted to one country are not included.

DATA ORGANIZATION

Because user needs were the major consideration in the design of the book, it is organized by subject rather than by source. Subjects are analyzed at two levels: a cross classification of 46 broad subject areas in the overview; and detailed topical breakdowns of these 46 subject areas.

The purpose of the overview is to provide users with a quick source of reference from which a user can gain access to the range of sources covering a subject area and the range of subjects covered in any one source. The detailed subject subclassifications bring all the materials from the diverse range of sources together under a strict subject arrangement, organized into 46 chapters. These chapters constitute the core of *INSTAT.*

METHODOLOGY

All publications and their sources are referred to by code in the body of the book. Full bibliographical details of these publications arranged by these codes

are given in Appendix A. Appendixes B and C list these publications by title and the name of the publisher respectively. No restriction is imposed on the range of the subject matter. Among the sources excluded from *INSTAT* are those issued by international organizations that may contain extensive statistical data but whose purpose is not statistical as such.

CONTENTS

Volume 1

Volume 2

19. Finance

19.1	Financial System - Structure
19.2	Financial Markets
19.2.1	Assets and Liabilities
19.2.2	Banking Industry
19.2.3	Capital Market
19.2.4	Corporate Finance
19.2.5	Credit
19.2.6	Deposits and Savings
19.2.7	Exchange Rates
19.2.8	Insurance
19.2.9	Interest Rates
19.2.10	International Finance
19.2.11	Money Supply
19.2.12	Personal Finance
19.2.13	Stock Exchange
19.3	Investment
19.3.1	Domestic Investment
19.3.2	Foreign Investment
19.4	Public Finance
19.4.1	Central Government
19.4.2	Local Government

20. Fishing

20.1	Consumption
20.2	Fish
20.2.1	Catches
20.2.2	Processed
20.2.3	Products
20.3	Fish Farming
20.4	Industry
20.5	International Trade
20.6	Labour
20.7	Vessels

21. Forestry

21.1	Consumption
21.2	Damage
21.3	Employment
21.4	Financial Accounts
21.5	Holdings/Wooded Areas
21.6	International Trade
21.6.1	Direction of Trade
21.6.2	Exports and Imports
21.7	Industry
21.8	Investment
21.9	Prices
21.10	Production

22. Health

22.1	Alcoholic Beverages Consumption
22.2	Child Health
22.3	Disability
22.4	Expenditure
22.5	General Statistics
22.6	Hospitals, Services
22.6.1	Beds
22.6.2	General
22.7	Immunization
22.8	Nutrition
22.9	Personnel
22.10	Resources
22.11	Smoking
22.12	Vital Statistics
22.13	Water, Sanitation
22.14	Women's Health and Health Services

23. Housing

23.1	Construction
23.1.1	Authorized, Permits Issued
23.1.2	Completions
23.1.3	Expenditure and Output
23.1.4	Starts
23.2	Energy Consumption
23.3	Finance
23.4	Households and Housing Occupancy
23.5	Housing Stock
23.5.1	Characteristics
23.5.2	Size of Stock
23.6	Prices
23.7	Rents

24. Income and Wealth

24.1	Earnings
24.1.1	All Workers
24.1.2	Industrial Analysis
24.1.3	Distribution
24.1.4	Manual Workers
24.1.5	Non-Manual Workers
24.2	Income Distribution
24.3	Labour Costs
24.4	Purchasing Power
24.5	Wealth
24.6	Wage Rates
24.6.1	Chemical Industry
24.6.2	Food, Beverages, and Tobacco Industry
24.6.3	Metal Industry
24.6.4	Textile Industry

25. Industries

Note: Some industries are covered in separate subject sections. A list of these is given at the end of the introduction to this chapter below.
Introduction to Section 25 - Content and Coverage

26. Intellectual Property

27. International Trade and Finance

INTERNATIONAL HISTORICAL STATISTICS: EUROPE

FACTS AT A GLANCE

Author: B.R. Mitchell

Number of Pages: 942

Periodicity: Irregular

Publisher: Stockton Press

PURPOSE AND SCOPE

Statistics are used not just as illustrations or to give a rough sense of proportions or magnitudes involved, but as a major raw material of much economic history, especially of economic growth. Since the subject is by its very nature concerned with quantities, this is an inevitable and welcome development, though no sensible historian would ever claim that statistics can tell the whole story. Aggregative national statistics conceal local and regional detail which may be important in explaining the national picture, and no one doubts that an average may hide as much as it reveals.

In response to the demand for historical statistics, there has appeared since the late 1950s a number of collections for individual countries. The U.S. was the pioneer in this respect, followed by a majority of European countries. Not all are as complete as one would wish. Czechoslovakia (since World War II), Denmark, Italy, the Netherlands, Norway, Sweden, the USSR (since 1917), and Yugoslavia have all been covered more or less comprehensively by publications sponsored by their governments. The French have long designated occasional volumes of their Annuaire Statistique as Volumes Retrospectifs, though sadly none since 1966. In addition, the Bank of Finland has produced several Studies of Finland's Economic Growth which include many historical series, notably one by Riitta Hjerppe, which has been translated into English. Other countries have been covered unofficially—Austria-Hungary, Belgium, Germany, Spain, and the United Kingdom.

When the first edition of this book was conceived over 20 years ago, many of these publications had not appeared. The time then seemed ripe for gathering the major statistical series for a number of different countries, especially in light of burgeoning interest in comparative development. That interest has not abated and there still remains the need for a collection covering many countries. The objective of this volume is to fulfill this need—to provide economists and historians with a wide range of mainly economic statistical data without the difficulty of identifying sources and the considerable labor of extracting data from many different places, and of transforming variously defined annual figures into long comparable time-series.

There is a variety of statistical data going back into the Middle Ages for some countries but it is usu-

ally of a rather haphazard and incomplete nature—
the output of precious metals, the trade of a particular port or in a particular commodity. In view of this and of the fact that modern economic growth is generally held to have begun with the British industrial revolution, which is dated at the earliest from the middle of the eighteenth century, it was decided to fix the starting date of this volume at 1750. This is not to imply that there are no useful statistics for earlier periods. It will be obvious even to the casual user of this work that there was no sudden beginning to the collection of large numbers of statistical series in the second half of the eighteenth century.

However, there is this to be said for 1750. With the single exception of price data for Spain and northwestern Europe, a few series of overall economic significance began before that date. The finishing date for most series in this edition is 1988, the latest date for which data were generally available at the time of compilation. Even so, it must be realized that many of the statistics for the later 1980s are provisional and will be subject to revision in the future.

That there are pitfalls for the unwary user of statistics needs no saying and this is not the place to attempt to summarize those traps of which any introductory textbook will warn. However, there are certain problems of particular prominence in historical statistics to which attention may properly be drawn. The biggest single and most obvious problem is lack of availability of the data we would like to have, at any rate until the last four or five decades. There is a comparable though less apparent problem in the existence of data which seem to relate to the same things in different countries or at different times, but which do not do so. Some sort of data are available in these cases but not the precise sort which we require. Basically, these are problems of definition. For example, in some times and places exports include bullion, in others they do not. Pig iron can include or exclude ferro-alloys; bank deposits may include those of other banks or they may not; corn output can be measured by volume or by weight; and so on. Often there is nothing one can do about this lack of uniformity except indicate its existence and warn against glib comparisons. One can find little comfort, however, in the fact that failure to observe such warning is one of the main reasons why statistics have sometimes been held to be worse than "damned lies!" Kindred definitional difficulties are provided by the numerous changes in the boundaries of European countries during the 240 years covered here.

Two problems are peculiar to historical statistics. The first is a mechanical one created by the variable and unknown efficiency of past collectors and compilers of statistics (including the present one), and their printers, and the impossibility of ever being able to check on these qualities. This is a situation with which one has to live, keeping a vigilant eye on one's credulity and endeavoring to estimate margins of error. Too often users of historical statistics—and we are nearly all guilty of this—take best-estimate figures for their calculations without working out the effects on their analysis of compounding margins of error.

The second peculiar problem concerns the purposes for which statistics were collected up to the end of the nineteenth century and indeed the purposes for which they are still compiled. William Robson has rightly said that the most important methodological development of the present century is the "introduction of measurement in varying degrees in virtually every one of the social sciences." It is only with this development that there has come much collection and publication of statistical material for its own sake. In some countries it began to happen a little before the end of the nineteenth century. But it is generally true to say that most statistics prior to 1900 were by-products of taxation or military preparedness, although some of these, notably population censuses, had outgrown their origins some time before then. Many early series, therefore, have to be viewed with a measure of skepticism because there was clearly a premium on evading inclusion in the data. Registration of one's true age if one was a young man liable to miliary service, and the smuggling of dutiable imports, are only two of the most obvious examples. Understatement is not the only error to which early statistics were liable. Some countries found it convenient to inflate their population or wealth in order to impress potential enemies. There is no ready solution to all these difficulties. All one can do is to be careful and to keep a firm rein on credulity without resorting to stultifying total skepticism.

However, two problems do arise. The first is the omission from statistical annuals of some statistics for some years—either through accidents of publication or because a series had ceased to be or had not yet become of clear general interest and significance. The second problem is the universal habit of government statistical services of changing the detail of coverage and of concepts from one yearbook to the next. Such changes often do occur in the collection of the statistics and there is nothing that can be done about it other than by indicating the break in continuity. Frequently, the changes relate only to presentation in the yearbook and access to more detailed sources can enable one to reconstruct the original format. With few exceptions, it has not been possible for me to do this in the tables that follow and as a result they undoubtedly contain more breaks in continuity than are strictly unavoidable. However, both this latter problem and the one caused by non-publication in statistical annuals have been mitigated to some extent by the co-operation which I have had from colleagues in various European universities and from officials of several national statistical offices and central banks. This assistance is acknowledged below and, where appropriate, in the notes to the tables. It must be stated that this is not to any great extent a work of original research, in the sense that comparable time-series have been compiled where only the raw materials for such a compilation existed in the sources. It is, rather, almost entirely a collection of already published statistics, with many of their inconsistencies not eliminated.

These few general remarks are not intended as a critique of the usefulness of statistics in historical studies but as a warning against their careless and casual use in comparisons over time and between different countries. It has been rightly said that "numbers are useful when they attain a level of subtlety and precision beyond that of words." Let the user of this volume be in no doubt of the need to seek for subtlety and of the difficulties in the way of precision.

DATA ORGANIZATION

While the general plan of previous editions in this series has been followed in this one, a number of changes have been made. The most obvious is the deletion of the section on climate. The main reason for this has been the desire to save space coupled with the opinion which has often been expressed by users that these were among the least useful tables. An additional reason is that some of the data for the past two decades have not been fully available. No other table has been omitted, though some have been compressed. The amount of rounding has been increased, again in the interest of space saving. Requests for additional material have been met in three cases. One completely new table has been added showing money supply statistics for the last four decades. Data on telephone calls have been put into a separate table, to which have been added statistics of the number of instruments in use. In addition, a large amount of new material for earlier years has been added, mainly thanks to some of the work on national historical statistics referred to above.

METHODOLOGY

Some of the problems peculiar to each topic are mentioned briefly in the introduction to each of the separate sections, but it must be pointed out that these are not intended to be comprehensive critiques of the statistics presented. To do this properly would require at least another volume. The intention here is only to draw the user's attention to the main types of difficulty in interpreting the statistics. The problems for each individual country are not generally dealt with unless they are outstandingly important. However, most of them are readily apparent from a careful use of the notes and footnotes to the tables.

CONTENTS

Introduction

Official Sources

Acknowledgements

Weights and Measures: Conversion Ratios

Symbols

A. Population and Vital Statistics

1. Population of Countries at Censuses (in thousands)
2. Population of Countries by Sex and Age Groups
3. Population of Major Districts (in thousands)
4. Population of Major Cities (in thousands)
5. Mid-year Population Estimates (in millions)
6. Vital Statistics: Rates per 1000 Population
7. Deaths of Infants under One Year Old (per 1000 live births)
8. Emigration from Europe by Decades
9. Annual Migration Statistics (in thousands)

B. Labor Force

1. Economically Active Population by Major Industrial Groups (in thousands)
2. Unemployment
3. Industrial Disputes
4. Money Wages in Industry
5. Money Wages in Agriculture

C. Agriculture

1. Area of Main Cereal, Potato, and Sugar Beet Crops
2. Output of Main Cereal, Potato, and Sugar Beet Crops
3. Area of Vineyards and Output of Wine
4. Area and Output of Mediterranean Crops
5. Numbers of Livestock
6. Output of Cows Milk
7. Butter Output
8. Meat Output
9. Landings of Fish
10. External Trade in Corn
11. Exports of Agricultural, Fishing, and Forestry Products

D. Industry

1. Indices of Industrial Production
2. Output of Coal (in millions of metric tons)
3. Output of Crude Petroleum
4. Output of Natural Gas
5. Output of Main Non-Ferrous Metal Ores
6. Output of Main Non-Metallic Minerals
7. Output of Iron Ore
8. Output of Pig Iron
9. Output of Crude Steel
10. Output of Aluminum
11. Imports and Exports of Coal by Main Surplus and Deficient Countries
12. Imports and Exports of Petroleum by Main Surplus and Deficient Countries
13. Imports and Exports of Iron Ore by Main Trading Countries
14. Raw Cotton Consumption Indicators
15. Cotton Spindles
16. Output of Cotton Yarn
17. Output of Cotton Tissues
18. Raw Wool Consumption Indicators

19. Output of Wool Yarn
20. Output of Wool Tissues
21. Output of Artificial and Synthetic Fibres
22. Linen Industry Indicators
23. Output of Sulfuric Acid
24. Timber Industry Indicators
25. Output of Motor Vehicles
26. Output of Beer
27. Output of Electric Energy

E. External Trade

1. External Trade Aggregate Current Value
2. External Trade (by value) with Main Trading Partners

F. Transport and Communications

1. Length of Railway Line Open
2. Freight Traffic on Railways
3. Passenger Traffic on Railways
4. Merchant Ships Registered
5. Inland Navigation Traffic
6. Motor Vehicles in Use
7. Commercial Aviation
8. Postal and Telegraph Services
9. Telephone Services
10. Radio and Television Receiving Licenses

G. Finance

1. Banknote Circulation
2. Deposits in Commercial Banks
3. Deposits in Savings Banks
4. Money Supply
5. Total Central Government Expenditure
6. Government Revenue and Main Tax Yields

H. Prices

1. Wholesale Price Indices
2. Cost-of-Living/Consumer Price Indices

I. Education

1. Children and Teachers in Schools
2. Number of Students in Universities

J. National Accounts

1. National Accounts Totals
2. Proportions of National Product by Sector of Origin (percent)
3. Balance of Payments

INTERNATIONAL HISTORICAL STATISTICS: THE AMERICAS

FACTS AT A GLANCE

Author: B.R. Mitchell

Number of Pages: 817

Periodicity: Irregular

Publisher: Stockton Press

PURPOSE AND SCOPE

Compilers of historical statistics are suppliers of raw materials for historians, social scientists, and economists. They differ from other types of statisticians because their focus is on time-series, that is data over a period of time. Their work is also more difficult because they are essentially attempting to bring together disparate materials and then weave together a reasonably coherent set of comparable statistics. Their success is often dependent not on their skills or their knowledge, but on the quality, vintage, and provenance of the sources.

National compendia of statistics often date back to the early part of the century in many European countries, and to the middle of the century in many developing countries. There is a variety of statistical data going back to the Middle Ages for some countries, but it is fragmentary, and it is well known that fragmentary data are as good as no data at all. At some point collections of these statistics appeared providing some continuity to the statistical efforts. Since a large part of Africa and Latin America as well as some countries in Asia were Western possessions, the colonial powers took the initiative in collecting rudimentary statistical data on these countries to improve their administrative systems. Some of these statistical efforts continued after the countries became independent in the late 1940s, 1950s, and 1960s. The data themselves were crude without any claim to scientific accuracy; nevertheless they are the only data available on these countries.

The problems with constructing global historical statistics on the basis of such haphazard and fragmentary statistics are obvious. There are breaks in continuity, as governments change or wars intervene. New sources being uncovered may require large scale revisions in coverage; changes in format may make some data obsolete and others irrelevant. Even more irritating are the gaps in series as a result of official negligence or ignorance on the part of compilers. Biases of the compilers toward some subjects and against others may lead to lop-sided presentations. Boundary changes may make certain data aggregates totally incomparable over a period of time. Aggregate international statistics conceal, as well as reveal, just as averages may distort and make data meaningless.

However, the most serious problems relating to historical statistics are two classic ones: One relates to the differences in the definitions of terms. Simple terms, such as "bullion" or "pig iron" may mean different things in different countries, and the national statisticians are under no obligation to follow any convention in this regard other than their own. The second, and the more intractable one, is the variable and unknown efficiency and respect for accuracy of past collectors and compilers of statistics, and of their printers. After all, national statistics can be self-serving exercises. No one wants data that make them look less powerful or important than their neighbors, and a little doctoring may go a long way toward improving the political value of the data. All too often historical statisticians simply take the best-estimate figures (or figures at the high end of a range) without any concern how such an estimate might skew extrapolations or compound margins of error.

As an example, it only needs to be recalled that most statistical collections in earlier decades served a purpose. Prior to 1900, population counts were thinly disguised attempts to estimate the number of young men eligible for the military draft or to check on potential taxpayers. In both cases, the enumerees had every reason to understate their age or their income or both, which left the compilers with totals far less than actual. But understatement was not the only error to which statistics were liable. Population and wealth were inflated by pulling numbers out of a hat to impress the friends and enemies of a country or ruling group.

B.R. Mitchell's second edition of the *Historical Statistics* is an ambitious attempt to conflate the existing national statistical compendia. He has done that with remarkable fidelity. However, the cautionary notes stated above need to be carefully weighed before using the data in these books for any analytical or sociological purposes. This is by no means a work of original research. It is, rather, almost entirely a collection of already published statistics with some of their inconsistencies removed.

The modern world may be said to have begun with the Industrial Revolution in Britain in the middle of the eighteenth century. The starting point of the this volume is thus fixed at 1750. The cut off date is 1988. The series thus covers 240 years.

DATA ORGANIZATION

Each volume follows a rather standard format and sequence. Chapters are numbered alphabetically from A to J. The series begins with the core tables on population and vital statistics, which, as in many other books, are the most complete. The section includes the population of the most important cities and districts as well as breakdowns by age and sex. The sections following deal, in order, with Labor, Agriculture, Industry, External Trade, Transport and Communications, Finance, Prices, Education, and National Accounts.

METHODOLOGY

Some of the problems peculiar to each topic are mentioned briefly in the sectional introductions. The problems peculiar to each country are not dealt with unless they are important. While the general plan of the previous editions in this series has been followed, a number of changes have been made. The most obvious is the deletion of the section on climate. No other table has been omitted although some have been compressed. Figures are rounded in the interests of saving space. Two new data elements have been added including the number of telephones in use and money supply for the past four decades.

CONTENTS

Table

Number

Introduction

Official Sources

Acknowledgements

Weights and Measures

Symbols

A. Population and Vital Statistics

1. Population of Countries
2. Population of Major Countries by Sex and Age Groups
3. Population of Major Administrative Divisions
4. Population of Major Cities
5. Mid-year Population Estimates
6. Vital Statistics: Rates per 1000 Population
6a. Coliver's Estimates of Average Vital Rates for Quinquennia 1850-1959
7. Infant Mortality Rates
8. International Migrations

B. Labor Force

1. Economically Active Population by Major Industrial Groups
2. Unemployment (numbers and percentages)
3. Industrial Disputes
4. Money Wages in Industry
5. Wages in Agriculture

C. Agriculture

1. Area of Main Arable Crops
2. Output of Main Arable Food Crops
3. Output of Sugar
4. Area of Flax, Groundnuts, and Soya Beans
5. Output of Main Oil Crops
6. Area and Output of Cotton and Tobacco
7. Output of Cocoa, Coffee, and Tea
8. Output of Fruit
9. Area of Vineyards and Output of Wine
10. Numbers of Livestock
11. Output of Cows Milk
12. Output of Butter
13. Output of Meat
14. Landings of Fish
15. Exports of Wheat by Main Trading Countries
16. Exports of Sugar by Main Trading Countries
17. Exports of Principal Livestock Products by Main Trading Countries
18. Exports of Various Agricultural Commodities by Main Trading Countries
19. Exports of Timber Products by Main Trading Countries

D. Industry

1. Indices of Industrial Production
2. Output of Coal

3. Output of Crude Petroleum
4. Output of Natural Gas
5. Output of Iron Ore
6. Output of Main Non-ferrous Metal Ores
7. Output of Main Non-metallic Minerals
8. Output of Pig Iron
9. Output of Crude Steel
10. Output of Aluminum
11. Output of Refined Copper, Lead, Tin, and Zinc
12. Raw Cotton Consumption
13. Cotton Spindles
14. Output of Cotton Yarn
15. Output of Cotton Tissues
16. Wool Industry Indicators
17. Output of Artificial and Synthetic Fibres
18. Output of Sulfuric Acid, Hydrochloric Acid, Nitric Acid, and Caustic Soda
19. Timber Industry Indicator
20. Output and Assembly of Motor Vehicles
21. Output of Beer
22. Output of Electric Energy
23. Imports and Exports of Coal by Main Trading Countries
24. Imports and Exports of Petroleum by Main Trading Countries
25. Imports and Exports of Iron Ore by Main Trading Countries

E. External Trade

1. External Trade Aggregates in Current Values
2. External Trade (in current values) with Main Trading Partners
3. Major Commodity Exports by Main Exporting Countries

F. Transport and Communications

1. Length of Railway Line Open
2. Freight Traffic on Railways
3. Passenger Traffic on Railways
4. Merchant Ships Registered
5. Inland Waterway Traffic
6. Motor Vehicles in Use
7. Civil Aviation Traffic
8. Postal and Telegraph Traffic
9. Number of Telephones in Use
10. Radio and Television Sets in Use

G. Finance

1. Currency in Circulation
2. Deposits in Commercial Banks
3. Savings Bank Deposits
4. Money Supply
5. Total Central Government Expenditure
6. Central Government Revenue, with some Main Tax Yields
6a. Total Revenue of Canadian Colonies before Confederation

H. Prices

1. Wholesale Price Indices
2. Consumer Price Indices

I. Education

1. Pupils and Teachers in Schools
2. Students in Universities

J. National Accounts

1. National Accounts Totals
2. Proportions of GDP by Sector of Origin
3. Balance of Payments

STATISTICAL ABSTRACT OF THE WORLD

FACTS AT A GLANCE

Number of Pages: 1,111

Periodicity: Annual

Publisher: Gale Research

PURPOSE AND SCOPE

The *Statistical Abstract of the World* is a comprehensive presentation of data on 185 countries of the world in a uniform format. Large and small countries are given the same treatment in terms of data format.

DATA ORGANIZATION

For each country, the data are shown in five or six pages beginning with a country and regional map followed by 42 panels. The panels are grouped by topics. All panels are numbered and titled and may hold tables or text. If no information is available for a panel, it is shaded gray. Where detailed information is lacking for small countries for certain topics such as energy or manufacturing, variant formats are used. Thus for small countries, the fourth page has an energy resource summary rather than the regular panels. An Industrial Summary replaces detailed data and appears in a combined fifth and sixth page. Thus smaller countries are covered in five pages and larger ones in six, but the panel numbers and locations remain the same. Information in each panel is generally drawn from the same source except where alternative sources had to be used.

METHODOLOGY

Data for the panels are drawn from standard sources, such as the United Nations and the World Bank and there is very little analysis or highlighting. Data gaps are common, especially in the case of small island states, the former Soviet Union, and Yugoslavia.

CONTENTS

WORLD BANK ATLAS

FACTS AT A GLANCE

Number of Pages: 36

Periodicity: Annual

Publisher: World Bank

PURPOSE AND SCOPE

The *World Bank Atlas* presents key economic and social information organized under three headings: People, Economy, and the Environment.

DATA ORGANIZATION

The *Atlas* covers 207 countries, seven more than the previous edition. New data in this edition include infant mortality rates, child malnutrition, net primary school enrollment, and inflation.

METHODOLOGY

Estimates for the former Soviet Union countries are preliminary.

CONTENTS

WORLD STATISTICS IN BRIEF: UNITED NATIONS STATISTICAL POCKETBOOK

FACTS AT A GLANCE

Number of Pages: 112

Periodicity: Annual

Publisher: United Nations

PURPOSE AND SCOPE

The *World Statistics in Brief* is a condensed version of the *United Nations Statistical Yearbook* and presents basic statistics for all countries of the world.

DATA ORGANIZATION

The data are presented under 41 time series tables. Six tables deal with population and the remaining deal with economy, labor, agriculture, manufacturing, trade, tourism, communications, transportation, education, and health. The white pages show important and frequently consulted statistical indicators for 168 countries or areas. The colored pages contain economic and social statistics for the world as a whole and for selected major regions.

METHODOLOGY

The data are reproduced from major statistical publications of the United Nations system.

CONTENTS

Surface Area and Density
Currency
Largest City or Agglomeration

Total Population
Population Sex Ratio
Age Group 0-14 Years
Age Group 60 Years and Over
Urban Population and Growth Rate
Annual Growth Rate of Population
Gross Domestic Product (GDP)
Long-Term Rate of Change in GDP
Per Capita GDP
Economically Active Population
Rate of Change of Economically Active Population
Gross Fixed Capital Formation
Agricultural Production
Labor Force in Agriculture
Agricultural Production Index
Per Capita Food Production Index
Total Industrial Production
Labor Force in Industry
Manufacturing
Industrial Production Index
Commercial Energy Production
Merchandise Exports

Merchandise Imports
Exchange Rate
Balance of Payments, Current Account
Tourist Arrivals
Consumer Price Index
Motor Vehicles in Use
Telephones in Use
Television Receivers in Use
Illiterates Aged 15 Years and Over
Primary-Secondary Gross Enrollment Ratio
Third-Level Students
Government Education Expenditures
Life Expectancy Birth
Infant Mortality Rate
Health Services Personnel
Average Food Supply: Calories

WORLD TABLES

FACTS AT A GLANCE

Number of Pages: 749

Periodicity: Annual

Publisher: World Bank and The Johns Hopkins University Press

PURPOSE AND SCOPE

World Tables presents core socio-economic indicators for 160 countries including many countries of the former Soviet bloc. Basic indicators for an additional 47 economies with sparse data are presented in Table A-1.

DATA ORGANIZATION

The core of the *World Tables* are the topical pages, two double-page spreads. Two new topical pages are included in the current edition covering gross domestic product in constant and current prices. Topical pages recast some of the indicators from the country pages. The current edition also includes six new poverty-related social indicators covering gender-disaggregated data on education and child malnutrition.

The country pages include time series concerned with national accounts and international transactions, manufacturing, monetary, fiscal and social indicators, and external debt.

METHODOLOGY

World Tables uses data from the International Monetary Fund and the Organization for Economic Cooperation and Development as well as from national publications.

CONTENTS

Topical Pages
Table 1. Gross National Product Per Capita
Table 2. Gross National Income Per Capita
Table 3. Private Consumption Per Capita

Country Pages

Topical Statistical Sourcebooks

ACCIDENTS

STATISTICS OF ROAD TRAFFIC ACCIDENTS IN EUROPE

FACTS AT A GLANCE

Number of Pages: 113

Periodicity: Annual

Publisher: United Nations (UN)

PURPOSE AND SCOPE

The purpose of *Statistics of Road Traffic Accidents in Europe* is to provide basic data on road traffic accidents and casualties in European countries, Canada, and the United States.

DATA ORGANIZATION

The scope of the statistics comprises road traffic accidents involving personal injuries only, excluding accidents with material damage. Data relates to accidents by type, accidents due to the influence of alcohol, and the number of persons killed or injured by category of road user and age group. Background statistics including data on the number of road vehicles in use, registration of new vehicles, and estimates of population and distribution by age groups are given in Tables 6, 7, and 8.

METHODOLOGY

The publication is compiled by the UN Economic Commission for Europe on the basis of data supplied by countries directly.

CONTENTS

Tables

Accidents and Casualties
1. Road Traffic Accidents Involving Personal Injury
2. Persons Killed or Injured in Road Traffic Accidents
3A. Road Traffic Accidents by Time of Occurrence and Surroundings, 1991 and 1992
3B. Road Traffic Accidents by Nature of Accident, 1991 and 1992
4. Persons Killed or Injured in Road Traffic Accidents by Category of User and Age Group, 1980, 1991, and 1992

   Austria
   Belarus
   Belgium
   Bulgaria

Canada
Croatia
Cyprus
Czech Republic
Denmark
Estonia

Finland
France
Germany
Greece
Hungary
Iceland
Ireland
Italy
Latvia
Lithuania

Luxembourg
Malta
Netherlands
Norway
Poland
Portugal
Republic of Moldova
Romania
Russian Federation
Slovak Republic
Spain
Sweden
Switzerland
Turkey
Ukraine
United Kingdom
United States

5. Road Traffic Accidents Involving One or More Persons Under the Influence of Alcohol, 1992

Background Statistics
6. Road Vehicles
7. Estimated Vehicle Kilometers Run
8. Estimates of Population and Distribution by Age Group

ACP (AFRICAN-CARIBBEAN-PACIFIC) COUNTRIES

ACP BASIC STATISTICS

FACTS AT A GLANCE

Number of Pages: 253

Periodicity: Annual

Publisher: European Communities

PURPOSE AND SCOPE

ACP Basic Statistics brings together the principal economic indicators of the ACP (African-Caribbean-Pacific) states associated with the European Union (EU).

DATA ORGANIZATION

The tables cover the 66 countries which signed the third Lomé Convention as well as some Mediterranean states linked to the European Union by special agreements. There are three kinds of tables: (1) summary tables presenting the situation in ACP countries; (2) tables on the situation in each member country; and (3) tables relating to the application of the agreements between EU and ACP countries. The current edition also contains results of the Phase V (Africa) International Comparison Project carried out in 23 African countries.

METHODOLOGY

Most of the statistics are derived from the Developing Countries Data Bank set up by the European Union Statistical Office.

CONTENTS

Introduction

Methodologist Notes and Sources

Part I. The ACP Countries in the World

Graphs

Tables

Production

External Trade

Assistance

Part II. Principal Economic and Social Indicators by ACP State

Somalia
Sudan
Suriname
Swaziland
Tanzania
Chad
Togo
Tonga
Trinidad and Tobago
Uganda
Vanuatu
Western Samoa
Zaire
Zambia
Zimbabwe

Part III. EDF and EIB Interventions Under the Lome Conventions

Tables

1. Financing Situation in 1986 by Method of Financing and by Administrative Body - Lomé I
2. Financing Situation in 1986 by Method of Financing and by Administrative Body - Lomé II
3. Fourth EDF: Aid by Economic Sector and Beneficiary Country (31.12.1986)
4. Fifth EDF: Aid by Economic Sector and Beneficiary Country (31.12.1986)
5. Fifth EDF: Aid by Type and Beneficiary Country
6. The Six EDFs: A Breakdown of the Cumulative Payments by Beneficiary Country (1960-1986)
7. Stabex: Aggregate Balance Sheet by ACP State
8. Stabex: Aggregate Balance Sheet by Product
9. EIB Loans (Lomé II)
10. EIB Loans (Lomé III)

Part IV. Mediterranean Countries

Tables

Algeria
Cyprus
Egypt
Israel
Jordan
Lebanon
Libya
Malta
Morocco
Syria
Tunisia
Turkey
Yugoslavia

Part V. ICP International Comparison Project

Purchasing Power Parity
Table 1: Gross Domestic Product for 1985
Table 2: Foodstuffs by Product Group per Head of Population for 1985

Food Prices and Nutritive Value in 1985
Table 3: Unit Price per Kilo-calorie; Miscellaneous Products
Table 4: Unit Price per 1000g of Protein; Miscellaneous Products

AFRICAN STATISTICAL YEARBOOK

FACTS AT A GLANCE

Year of Publication: 1993

Periodicity: Annual

Publisher: United Nations

PURPOSE AND SCOPE

The *African Statistical Yearbook* (ASY) is the regional counterpart of the *United Nations Statistical Yearbook* and is designed to provide comprehensive and inclusive data on the principal sectors of the economy, society, and trade of the continent.

DATA ORGANIZATION

The data are arranged by country, and for each of the 51 Economic Commission for Africa (ECA) member states, ASY provides 42 tables grouped in nine chapters: Tables 1 to 5 deal with population; Tables 6 to 9 with national accounts; Tables 10 to 15 with agriculture, forestry, and fishing; Tables 16 to 21 with industry; Tables 22 to 27 with transport and communications; Tables 28 to 34 with foreign trade; Table 35 with prices; and Tables 36 to 42 with finance, education, and health.

METHODOLOGY

Section A contains subregional summary tables. The data follow the pattern of the *United Nations Statistical Yearbook*.

CONTENTS

Volume I:
Part 1: North Africa
Part 2: West Africa

Volume II:
Part 3: East and Southern Africa
Part 4: Central Africa

Section A
Sub-regional summary tables which generally cover the years 1970, 1975, 1980 and the period 1985-1991.

Section B

Population
Table 1: Total and Urban Population
Table 2: Total Population by Age Group and Sex
Table 3: Economically Active Population by Sector and Sex

COMPENDIUM OF STATISTICS

FACTS AT A GLANCE

Number of Pages: 80

Periodicity: Annual

Publisher: African Development Bank

PURPOSE AND SCOPE

The *Compendium of Statistics* is designed to provide access to the databases of the African Development Bank, the African Development Fund, and the Nigeria Trust Fund.

DATA ORGANIZATION

The tables are divided into five sections. The first four provide, in a symmetrical fashion, data on loan approvals, commitments, cancellations, effective loans, disbursements and repayments, and disbursed debt outstanding.

METHODOLOGY

The current issue provides data on the value of goods and services procured. Also included is additional information on the lending operations of the banks.

CONTENTS

5.01 Composition of African Development Bank Membership as at 31 December 1993

5.02 Composition of African Development Fund Participants as at 31 December 1993

Notes on Tables

SELECTED STATISTICS OF REGIONAL MEMBER COUNTRIES

FACTS AT A GLANCE

Number of Pages: 87

Periodicity: Annual

Publisher: African Development Bank (ADB)

PURPOSE AND SCOPE

Selected Statistics of Regional Member Countries is an annual publication of the African Development Bank

DATA ORGANIZATION

The current issue consists of 56 tables on selected social and economic indicators of the 51 regional member countries. The areas covered are: population and social statistics, national accounts, agriculture, external trade, balance of payments, external debt, finance, and prices.

METHODOLOGY

The compilation makes liberal use of statistics published by international organizations. They are supplemented by data from national sources and estimates made by ADB.

CONTENTS

1. Area and Mid-year Population Estimates
2-3. Selected Social Indicators
4. Labor Force
5. Gross Domestic Product at Current Market Prices
6. Gross Domestic Product at Constant 1985 Market Prices
7. Per Capita GDP at Current Market Prices
8. Per Capita GDP at Constant 1985 Market Prices
9. GDP by Kind of Economic Activity at Current Factor Cost
10. GDP by Kind of Economic Activity at Current Factor Cost - Percentage Distribution
11. Expenditure on GDP at Current Market Prices - Percent Age Distribution
12. Gross Domestic Investment as Percentage of GDP
13. Gross Domestic Savings as Percentage of GDP
14. Agricultural Food Production
15. Per Capita Agricultural Food Production
16. Agricultural Food Consumption
17. Per Capita Agricultural Food Consumption
18. Agricultural Food Self-Sufficiency Ratio
19. Value of Exports
20. Percent Share of Major Commodities in Total Value of Exports
21. Per Capita Exports
22. Intra-African Exports as Percent of Total Value of Exports
23. Exports as Percentage of Imports
24. Exports as Percentage of GDP
25. Purchasing Power Indices of Exports
26. Quantum Indices of Exports
27. Unit Value Indices of Exports
28. Value of Imports
29. Petroleum Imports as Percent of Total Value of Imports
30. Petroleum Imports as Percent of Total Value of Exports
31. Food Imports as Percent of Total Value of Imports
32. Food Imports as Percent of Total Value of Exports
33. Per Capita Imports
34. Intra-African Imports as Percent of Total Value of Imports
35. Imports as Percentage of GDP
36. Quantum Indices of Imports
37. Unit Value Indices of Imports
38. Balance of Trade
39. Terms of Trade Estimates
40. Free Market Prices of Selected Primary Commodities
41. Balance of Payments
42. External Public Debt Outstanding (Including Undisbursed)
43. External Public Debt Outstanding (Disbursed Only)
44. External Public Debt Outstanding (Disbursed Only) by Category of Lenders
45. External Public Debt Outstanding (Disbursed Only) as Percent of GNP at Current Market Prices
46. External Debt Service
47. External Debt Service as Percent of Exports of Goods and Services
48. External Debt Service as Percent of GNP at Current Market Prices
49. Net Total Financial Flows
50. Net Direct Investments from DAC Countries
51. Money
52. International Reserves
53. Exchange Rates
54. Index of Real Exchange Rates
55. Consumer Price Index - All Items
56. Consumer Price Index - Food

AGRICULTURE

AGRICULTURE: STATISTICAL YEARBOOK

FACTS AT A GLANCE

Number of Pages: 238

Periodicity: Annual

Publisher: European Communities

PURPOSE AND SCOPE

The *Agriculture: Statistical Yearbook* is the annual statistical survey of agriculture in European Union (EU) countries. It covers agriculture, forestry, and fisheries and for each sector includes data on production, trade, area, and yields.

DATA ORGANIZATION

The data are organized in eight sections: (1) General, with four figures and 11 tables giving general statistics on world agriculture, area, trade, production, employment, and livestock; (2) Area and Crop Production, with six figures and 13 tables which focus on supply balances, arable land, and production; (3) Animal Production, with 17 tables which focus on livestock, pig, sheep, goats, and milk; (4) Structure of Agricultural Holdings, with 13 tables which focus on modes of tenure, types of holdings, margin of profit, and labor force; (5) Prices and Price Indices, with 12 tables which focus on producer and consumer prices; (6) Agricultural Accounts, with seven figures which focus on final output and net value; (7) Forestry, with one figure and five tables which focus on holdings and roundwood; and (8) Fisheries, with four tables.

METHODOLOGY

The data are produced by the national EU statistical offices or ministries and then compiled by Eurostat.

CONTENTS

1. General

Figures
1.1 Distribution of Total Area by Main Category 1992
1.2 Selected Crop Production in the World 1992
1.3 Livestock Numbers in the World 1992
1.4 Meat Production in the World 1992

Tables
1.1 Total and Agricultural Area 1982 and 1992
1.2 Civilian Employment by Sector of Activity 1981 and 1991
1.3 Gross Value Added at Factor Cost by Group of Economic Branches 1981 and 1991

1.4 EU Trade in Agricultural Commodities 1991 and 1992
1.5 Intra Trade in the European Union, Food and Live Animals 1992
1.6 External Trade of the Member States, Food and Live Animals 1992
1.7 External Trade of the European Union, Food and Live Animals 1992
1.8 External Trade of the Member States, Food and Live Animals 1983-1992
1.9 Selected Crop Production in EU and in the World, 1986 and 1992
1.10 Livestock Numbers in EU and in the World, 1986 and 1992
1.11 Meat Production in EU and in the World, 1986 and 1992

2. Area and Crop Production

Figures
2.1 Distribution of the Utilized Agricultural Area by Member States 1992
2.2 Distribution of Total Area by Member States 1992
2.3 Distribution of Harvested Production by Member States 1992
2.4 Development of Yields of Important Crops 1983-1992
2.5 Distribution of Fruit Trees Areas by Member States 1990
2.6 Distribution of Fruit Trees Production by Member States 1990

Tables
2.1 Total and Agricultural Area by Main Category 1983-1992
2.2 Arable Land by Category 1992
2.3 Land Under Permanent Crops by Category 1992
2.4 Important Crops, Harvested Area and Production 1983-1992
2.5 Important Cereal Crops, Harvested Area and Production 1992
2.6 Important Fresh Vegetables, Harvested Area and Production 1983-1992
2.7 Harvested Production of Selected Fresh Vegetables 1992
2.8 Important Fruits, Main Area and Harvested Production 1983-1992
2.9 Supply Balance Sheet, Cereals 1982/83 - 1991/92
2.10 Supply Balance Sheet, Oilseeds 1982/83 - 1991/92
2.11 Supply Balance Sheet, Dried Pulses 1982/83 - 1991/92
2.12 Supply Balance Sheet, Sugar 1982/83 - 1991/92
2.13 Supply Balance Sheet, Wine 1982/83 - 1991/92

Text
Methodological Notes: Area and Supply Balance Sheets

Text

Methodological Notes: Wooded Area and Supply Balance Sheets

8. Fisheries

Tables

Text

Methodological Notes: Catches and Fishing Fleet

EARNINGS IN AGRICULTURE

FACTS AT A GLANCE

Number of Pages: 95

Periodicity: Triennial

Publisher: European Communities

PURPOSE AND SCOPE

Earnings in Agriculture presents the results of a 1991 survey on the earnings of permanent agricultural workers in European Union member states.

DATA ORGANIZATION

The survey covers actual earnings of full-time permanent workers and/or seasonal workers of both sexes employed in clearly agricultural pursuits and excludes gardeners and such. In addition to information on wages, the survey also includes data on size and geographical location of the agricultural employer, benefits, type of work done, and the level of qualification required for the work. Data on seasonal workers are provided for only three countries—Greece, Italy, and Spain. In Greece only one percent of all agricultural workers are permanent. Therefore, the Greek chapter covers seasonal workers only.

METHODOLOGY

The survey was carried out during different months in the EC member countries depending on the agricultural seasons. Wages are expressed in terms of hourly earnings so that they are comparable with average gross earnings of workers in industry.

CONTENTS

General Results

Number of permanent manual workers employed full-time, hourly earnings, and number of hours paid. Number of manual workers and indices of average gross hourly earnings by size of farm and by sex.

Number of manual workers and indices of average gross hourly earnings by type of work carried out and by sex. Number of manual workers and indices of average gross hourly earnings by provision of benefits in kind and by sex. Number of manual workers and indices of average gross hourly earnings by sex and age group.

Results for Each Country

Belgium: Number of manual workers. Average number of hours paid per month. Average gross hourly earnings (BFR). Professional qualification. Number of manual workers and average gross hourly earnings by provision of benefits in kind, by sex and age group.

Denmark: Number of manual workers. Average number of hours paid per month. Average gross hourly earnings (DKR). Professional qualification. Number of manual workers and average gross hourly earnings by provision of benefits in kind, by sex and age group.

Germany: Number of manual workers. Average number of hours paid per month. Average gross hourly earnings (DM). Professional qualification. Number of manual workers and average gross hourly earnings by provision of benefit in kind, by sex and age group.

Spain: Number of manual workers. Average number of hours paid per month. Average gross hourly earnings (PTA). Professional qualification. Number of manual workers and average gross hourly earnings by provision of benefits in kind, by sex and age group.

France: Number of manual workers. Average number of hours paid per month. Average gross hourly earnings (FF). Professional qualification. Number of manual workers and average gross hourly earnings by provision of benefits in kind, by sex and age group.

Ireland: Number of manual workers. Average number of hours paid per month. Average gross hourly earnings (IRL). Professional qualification. Number of manual workers and average gross hourly earnings by provision of benefits in kind, by sex and age group.

Italy: Number of manual workers. Average number of hours paid per month. Average gross hourly earnings (LIT). Professional qualification. Number of manual workers and average gross hourly earnings by provision of benefits in kind, by sex and age group.

Luxembourg: Number of manual workers. Average number of hours paid per month. Average gross hourly earnings (LFR). Professional qualification. Number of manual workers and average gross hourly earnings by provision of benefits in kind, by sex and age group.

Netherlands: Number of manual workers. Average number of hours paid per month. Average gross hourly earnings (HFL). Professional qualification. Number of manual workers and average gross hourly earnings by provision of benefits in kind, by sex and age group.

Portugal: Number of manual workers. Average number of hours paid per month. Average gross hourly earnings (ESC). Professional qualification. Number of manual workers and average gross hourly earnings by provision of benefits in kind, by sex and age group.

United Kingdom: Number of manual workers. Average number of hours paid per month. Average gross hourly earnings (UKL). Professional qualification. Number of manual workers and average gross hourly earnings by provision of benefits in kind, by sex and age group.

Results by Region

Belgium: Number of manual workers, average number of hours paid per month, and average gross hourly earnings (BFR).

Germany: Number of manual workers, average number of hours paid per month, and average gross hourly earnings (DM).

Spain: Number of manual workers, average number of hours paid per month, and average gross hourly earnings (PTA).

Italy: Number of manual workers, average number of hours paid per month, and average gross hourly earnings (LIT).

Portugal: Number of manual workers, average number of hours paid per month, and average gross hourly earnings (ESC).

United Kingdom: Number of manual workers, average number of hours paid per month, and average gross hourly earnings (UKL).

Seasonal Workers

Average gross daily earnings and average number of hours worked per day.

FAO PRODUCTION YEARBOOK

FACTS AT A GLANCE

Number of Pages: 281

Periodicity: Annual

Publisher: Food and Agriculture Organization (FAO)

PURPOSE AND SCOPE

The *FAO Production Yearbook* is a compendium of data on production of agricultural commodities worldwide.

DATA ORGANIZATION

The data are organized in nine sections. Section I, deals with land and land use; Section II, with population; Section III, with indices; Section IV, with world and regional agricultural production in summary form; Section V, with crops; Section VI, with livestock; Section VII, with food supply; Section VIII, with means of production; and Section IX, with prices.

METHODOLOGY

The data are based on official sources and publications supplemented by FAO estimates. Both types of data are provisional.

CONTENTS

I. Land
 1. Land Use (Total Area, Land Area, Arable Land, and Land under Permanent Crops, Permanent Meadows and Pastures, Forest and Woodland, and Other Land, by Countries)
 2. Irrigation

II. Population
 3. Total Population, Agricultural Population, and Economically Active Population

III. FAO Index Numbers of Agricultural Production
 4. Total Food Production
 5. Total Agricultural Production
 6. Total Crop Production
 7. Total Production of Livestock Products
 8. Total Cereal Production
 9. Per Caput Food Production
 10. Per Caput Agricultural Production
 11. Per Caput Crop Production
 12. Per Caput Production of Livestock Productions
 13. Per Caput Cereal Production

IV. Statistical Summary
 14. Statistical Summary of World and Regional Agricultural Production

V. Crops
 15. Cereals, Total
 16. Wheat
 17. Rice, Paddy
 18. Coarse Grains
 19. Barley
 20. Maize
 21. Rye
 22. Oats
 23. Millet
 24. Sorghum
 25. Roots and Tubers, Total
 26. Potatoes
 27. Sweet Potatoes
 28. Cassava
 29. Yams
 30. Taro
 31. Pulses, Total
 32. Dry Beans
 33. Dry Broad Beans
 34. Dry Peas
 35. Chick-peas
 36. Lentils
 37. Soybeans
 38. Groundnuts in Shell
 39. Castor Beans
 40. Sunflower Seed
 41. Rapeseed
 42. Sesame Seed

43. Linseed
44. Safflower Seed
45. Seed Cotton
46. Cottonseed, Olives, Olive Oil
47. Coconuts, Copra, Tung Oil
48. Palm Kernels, Palm Oil, Hempseed
49. Total Production of Vegetables, Fruits and Berries, Nuts
50. Cabbages
51. Artichokes
52. Tomatoes
53. Cauliflowers
54. Pumpkins, Squash, and Gourds
55. Cucumbers and Gherkins
56. Eggplants
57. Green Chillies and Peppers
58. Dry Onions
59. Garlic
60. Green Beans
61. Green Peas
62. Carrots
63. Watermelons
64. Cantaloupes and Other Melons
65. Grapes
66. Wine, Raisins, Dates
67. Sugar Cane
68. Sugar Beets
69. Centrifugal Sugar (Raw Value), Non-centrifugal Sugar, Apples
70. Pears, Peaches and Nectarines, Plums
71. Oranges, Tangerines, Mandarins, Clementines and Satsumas, Lemons and Limes
72. Grapefruit and Pomelos, Citrus Fruit NES, Apricots
73. Avocados, Mangoes, Pineapples
74. Bananas, Plantains, Papayas
75. Strawberries, Raspberries, Currants
76. Almonds, Pistachios, Hazelnuts (Filberts)
77. Cashew Nuts, Chestnuts, Walnuts
78. Coffee, Green
79. Cocoa Beans
80. Tea
81. Hops
82. Tobacco Leaves
83. Flax Fibre and Tow
84. Hemp Fibre and Tow
85. Jute and Jute-like Fibres
86. Sisal
87. Cotton (Lint), Fibre Crops NES, Natural Rubber

VI. Livestock Numbers and Products

Livestock Numbers
88. Horses, Mules, Asses
89. Cattle, Buffaloes, Camels
90. Pigs, Sheep, Goats
91. Chickens, Ducks, Turkey

Slaughterings, Average Dressed Carcass Weight, and Production of Meat from Slaughtered Animals
92. Beef and Veal
93. Buffalo Meat
94. Mutton and Lamb
95. Goat Meat
96. Pig Meat
97. Horse Meat, Poultry Meat, Total Meat

Production of Meat from Indigenous Animals
98. Beef and Buffalo Meat, Mutton and Goat Meat, Pig Meat

Milk, Cheese, and Other Livestock Products
99. Cow Milk, Whole, Fresh (Milking Cows, Milk Yield, and Milk Production)
100. Buffalo Milk, Sheep Milk, Goat Milk
101. Cheese, Butter and Ghee, Evaporated and Condensed Milk
102. Dry Whole Cow Milk, Dry Skim Milk and Buttermilk, Dry Whey
103. Hen Eggs, Eggs, excluding Hen Eggs, Honey
104. Silk, Raw and Waste, Wool, Greasy, Wool, Scoured
105. Cattle and Buffalo Hides, Fresh Sheepskins, Fresh Goatskins, Fresh

VII. Food Supply
106. Calories
107. Protein
108. Fat

VIII. Means of Production

Farm Machinery
109. Agricultural Tractors, Total, Harvester-threshers, Milking Machines

IX. Prices
110. Price Series of International Significance
111. Index Numbers of Prices Received by Farmers and Prices Paid by Farmers

FAO TRADE YEARBOOK

FACTS AT A GLANCE

Number of Pages: 361

Periodicity: Annual

Publisher: Food and Agriculture Organization (FAO)

PURPOSE AND SCOPE

The *FAO Trade Yearbook* presents data on worldwide trade in agricultural commodities.

DATA ORGANIZATION

The *Yearbook* is divided into four parts: Part I gives FAO indices of agricultural trade by region. Part II gives total merchandise; trade; trade in agricultural, fishery, and forestry products; total agricultural products; and total food excluding fish and fishery products. It also presents 120 tables of detailed data on types and categories of agricultural products. Part III shows trade in means of agricultural production, such as fertilizers, tractors, and pesticides. Part IV gives value of agricultural trade by countries.

METHODOLOGY

Data are derived from official reports and publications, and trade information from national and international agencies and organizations. Where information is available in terms of units only, corresponding values are estimated by FAO based on data from trading partners.

CONTENTS

PATTERNS AND TRENDS IN WORLD AGRICULTURAL LAND USE

FACTS AT A GLANCE

Number of Pages: 21

Periodicity: Irregular

Publisher: U.S. Department of Agriculture (USDA)

PURPOSE AND SCOPE

The U.S. Department of Agriculture's International Division keeps a close watch on foreign agricultural practices, prices, and markets. *Patterns and Trends in World Agricultural Land Use* is one of the USDA publications designed to inform agricultural specialists about data relating to land.

DATA ORGANIZATION

Among the topics explored in the book are land trends and the composition patterns of cropland. Based on the data, the book concludes that the world population is increasing at a much faster pace than the increase in agricultural land. More land is being lost to urban, commercial, and recreational uses. Many countries have little or no room for cropland expansion.

METHODOLOGY

The data are collected and analyzed by the economists and statisticians at the U.S. Department of Agriculture.

CONTENTS

Land Use Data

Trends in Agricultural Land Use
Global Land-use Patterns
Trends in Composition of Land Use
Trends in Cropland Use
Per Capita Cropland Availability and Trends
Factors Causing Changes in Agricultural Land Use Trends

Conclusion

References

Appendix Tables

THE STATE OF FOOD AND AGRICULTURE

FACTS AT A GLANCE

Number of Pages: 306

Periodicity: Annual

Publisher: Food and Agriculture Organization (FAO)

PURPOSE AND SCOPE

The State of Food and Agriculture includes data on the global agricultural situation and agricultural economics, regional trends and policy developments, profiles of country performances, and examines the sector's future prospects.

DATA ORGANIZATION

The data are presented in three parts. Part I is a world review of the current agricultural situation and the overall economy. Part II is a regional review of developed and developing countries. Part III deals with water policies and resources management. There are 10 exhibits, 20 boxes, 9 tables, and 12 figures illustrating the tables. Special issues discussed include food access and nutrition, commodity prices and exports, forestry, fishing, and biotechnology in agriculture.

METHODOLOGY

The publication is designed to provide data-driven analysis on which agricultural policymakers can base their decisions.

CONTENTS

Part I

World Review

I. Current Agricultural Situation - Facts and Figures

1. Crop and Livestock Production in 1992
2. Per Caput Food Production in 1992
3. Agricultural Production by Major Commodities
4. Food Shortages and Emergencies
5. Current Cereal Supply, Utilization, and Stocks
6. Cereal Trade Prospects for 1993/94
7. External Assistance to Agriculture
8. Food Aid Flows in 1992/93
9. Fisheries Catch, Disposition, and Trade
10. Forestry Production and Trade in 1992

II. Overall Economic Environment and Agriculture

Economic Overview

The Economic Outlook and Prospects for Agriculture

Prospects for Developing Countries' Agriculture

Prospects for Economies Heavily Dependent on Agriculture

Selected Issues

Meeting the Goals of the International Conference on Nutrition

Past Achievements and Current Challenges

Nutrition at the Center of Development

Action to Improve Nutrition

Decline in Agricultural Commodity Real Prices and Exporters' Earnings

Uruguay Round of Multilateral Trade Negotiations

Current Issues in Fisheries Management

Coastal Zone Fisheries and Local Involvement in Management

High Sea Fishing

Current Issues in Forestry

Recycling in Forest Industries

Forests and Forest Industries in Countries in Economic Transition

Trade and Sustainable Forest Management

Biotechnology: Challenges and Opportunities for the 1990s

Application and Potential

Challenges and Issues

Part II

Regional Review

I. Developing Country Regions

Sub-Saharan Africa

Regional Overview

Ethiopia

The Country: General Characteristics

The Economy

Economic Policies Affecting Agriculture

Agricultural Sector Policies

The Impact of Policies on Agriculture

Current Issues in Agricultural Development

Asia and the Pacific

Regional Overview

Growing Intraregional Trade and Investment Flows

The Challenges of Economic Transition

The Environment and Sustainable Agriculture

Sectoral Policies Following Macroeconomic and Structural Reforms

Bangladesh

The Agricultural Sector

Rice and Foodgrain Policies

Sri Lanka

The Agricultural Sector

The Small Farm Sector

The Estate Sector

Latin America and the Caribbean

Regional Overview

The Agricultural Sector

Agricultural Policies

Mexico
Overview
Economic Setting
The New Policy Framework and Economic
  Performance
The Economic Role of Agriculture
Agricultural Reform
Outstanding Issues and Prospects for Agriculture

Near East and North Africa
Regional Overview
Policy Developments
Implications of Agricultural Policy Reforms

Egypt
Agriculture's Role in the Economy
Economic Policy Reform
Agricultural Strategy in the 1990s
Implications for Agricultural Performance

Syrian Arab Republic
Economic Overview
The Role of Agriculture
Irrigation Development

II. Developed Country Regions
  Central and Eastern Europe
  Economies in Transition

Bulgaria
The Agricultural Sector
Policy Reform
The Impact of Agricultural Reform
Prospects and Policy Issues

Romania
The Agricultural Sector
Policy Reform
The Impact of Economic Reform
Prospects and Policy Issues

The Russian Federation
Food Supply
Agricultural Production in 1992/93
Agricultural Policies
Barter Operations and Foreign Trade
Prospects for Agriculture

OECD Countries
Overview

United States
The Budget Deficit and its Impact on
  Agricultural Policy
The Recent Situation and Policy Developments

European Economic Community
Common Agricultural Policy Reform
Farm Production
Farm Incomes and Farm Structures
CAP Reform and the Environment
What the CAP Reform Does Not Do

Japan
An Agriculture in Transition
The Agricultural Sector
Agricultural Marketing Policy

Agriculture and the Environment
New Policy Directions

III. Water Policies and Agriculture

I. Water Resource Issue and Agriculture
Introduction and Overview
Purpose and Scope
World Water Resources
Water Scarcity
World Water Use
Water and Health
Water as a Strategic Resource
The Water Sector and Natural Resource Policy

II. Water Resources: Economics and Policy
Linking the Water Sector with the National
  Economy
The Social, Physical, and Economic Nature of
  Water
Physical Attributes of Water
Economic Attributes of Water Use
Economic Organization of the Water Sector:
  Markets or Governments?
Market Failures
Government Failures
Economic Structure and Irrigation

III. Water Policies and Demand Management
Institutions and Water Policy
Water Allocation Systems
Property Rights Systems and Surface Water
  Allocation
Prices and Surface Water Allocation
Coordinating Groundwater Extraction
Conjunctive Groundwater and Surface Water
  Management
Preserving Water Quality
Non-Point Pollution Control Options

IV. Policy Issues in Irrigated Agriculture
Irrigation in the 1990s and Beyond
Trends in Irrigated Areas
Crop Prices and Construction Costs
Irrigation and Land Degradation
Irrigation: Good Government and Good
  Management
Irrigation Management: Water User Associations
  and NGOs
Future Directions in Water Management Policy

Exhibits
1. Changes in Agricultural Production, 1989-1992
2. Rates of Change in per Caput Food Production
   by Country, 1991-1992
3. Agricultural Production by Major Commodities,
   1991-1992
4. Food Supply Shortfalls Requiring Exceptional
   Assistance
5. Supply/Utilization Trends in Cereals
6. World Trade in Cereals, by Region
7. Commitments and Disbursements of External
   Assistance to Agriculture
8. Shipments of Food Aid in Cereals

WORLD CROP AND LIVESTOCK STATISTICS

FACTS AT A GLANCE

Number of Pages: 756

Periodicity: Irregular

Publisher: Food and Agriculture Organization (FAO)

PURPOSE AND SCOPE

World Crop and Livestock Statistics is the first issue in the Statistical Processes Series which provides time series data on food, agriculture, rural development, and related socio-economic subjects. The purpose of the series is to provide data useful for research on current and emerging issues in food and agriculture.

DATA ORGANIZATION

World Crop and Livestock Statistics presents data on the production of 237 agricultural commodities in 170 countries. It continues the work of the *World Crop Statistics* published by the Food and Agriculture Organization (FAO) in 1966, but also adds data on livestock products.

METHODOLOGY

Data are assembled by FAO from national agricultural organizations as well as by the statistical data bases maintained by the FAO.

CONTENTS

1. Crops
Cereals, total. Wheat. Rice, paddy. Barley. Maize. Rye. Oats. Millet and sorghum. Mixed grain. Roots and tubers, total. Potatoes. Sweet potatoes. Cassava. Pulses, total. Dry beans. Dry broad beans. Dry peas. Chick-peas. Lentils. Cow peas. Pigeon peas. Vetch. Lupins. Soybeans. Groundnuts, in shell. Castor beans, Sunflower seed, Rapeseed. Sesame seed. Linseed. Safflower seed. Coconuts. Copra. Palm kernels. Palm oil. Olives. Olive oil. Seed cotton. Cottonseed. Oil crops (oil equivalent). Oil crops (cake equivalent). Vegetables, total. Cabbages. Artichokes. Tomatoes. Cauliflowers. Dry onions. Green beans. Green peas. Cantaloupes and other melons. Watermelons. Fruits and berries, total.

Grapes. Wine. Raisins. Bananas. Oranges.
Tangerines and mandarins. Lemons and limes.
Grapefruits and pomelos. Apples. Pears. Apricots.
Sour cherries. Cherries. Peaches and nectarines.
Plums. Figs. Dates. Pineapples. Strawberries.
Raspberries. Currants. Nuts, total. Cashew nuts.
Chestnuts. Almonds. Walnuts. Hazelnuts. Sugar
cane. Sugar beets. Centrifugal sugar (raw value).
Non-centrifugal sugar. Coffee. Cocoa. Tea. Hops.
Tobacco leaves. Natural rubber. Flax fibre and tow.
Sisal, jute, and jute-like fibres. Cotton (lint).

2. Livestock Products

Meat, total. Beef and buffalo meat. Mutton and goat
meat. Pig meat. Poultry meat. Milk, total. Cow milk.
Buffalo milk. Sheep milk. Goat milk. Hen eggs.
Honey. Wool, greasy. Fresh cocoons.

AIR TRANSPORT

WORLD AIR TRANSPORT STATISTICS

FACTS AT A GLANCE

Number of Pages: 106

Periodicity: Annual

Publisher: International Air Transport Association (IATA)

PURPOSE AND SCOPE

This annual compiled by the Industry Automation
and Financial Services Department of the
International Air Transport Association is designed as
a compendium of selected statistics covering the air
transport and aviation industry.

DATA ORGANIZATION

World Air Transport Statistics is divided into four sections. Section I is a review of air transport developments; Section II reviews developments in airport operations and airline finances; and Section III provides statistics on safety, personnel, finances, operations, and operational fleet.

METHODOLOGY

The statistics are collected by the International Air
Transport Association directly from its members
through questionnaires.

CONTENTS

Section I: Review of Air Transport Development in 1993

Section II: World Air Transport

Section III: IATA Industry Statistics

ALCOHOL

WORLD DRINK TRENDS: INTERNATIONAL BEVERAGE, ALCOHOL CONSUMPTION, AND PRODUCTION TRENDS

FACT AT A GLANCE

Number of Pages: 122

Periodicity: Annual

Publisher: NTC Publications/Produktshap voor
Gedistilleeerde Draanken

PURPOSE AND SCOPE

World Drink Trends is an expanded English language
edition based on the original 28th edition of the
Dutch-language Hoeveel alcoholhoudende dranken
worden er in de wereld gedronken?.

DATA ORGANIZATION

The publication provides data on consumption and
production of spirits, beer, wine, and total alcohol by
country and the changes in production. The data
cover 46 countries.

METHODOLOGY

Production and consumption data are based on information collected from producers and distributors in the countries covered.

CONTENTS

Section 1: World Alcohol Consumption Data
Spirits Consumption by Country (1987-89)
Change in Spirits Consumption (1969-89)
Beer Consumption by Country (1987-89)
Change in Beer Consumption (1969-89)
Wine Consumption by Country (1987-89)
Change in Wine Consumption (1969-89)
Total Alcohol Consumption by Country (1987-89)
Change in Total Alcohol Consumption (1969-89)
Total Alcohol Consumption in Europe (1989) (Map)
Change in Total Alcohol Consumption in the EC (1961-89) (Chart)
Total Alcohol Consumption by World Region (1980-89)
Change in Total Alcohol Consumption by World Region (Chart)

Section 2: World Alcohol Production Data
Spirits Production by Country
Beer Production by Country (1987-89)
Change in Beer Production (1980-89)
Total World Beer Production
Total World Beer Production (1969-89) (Chart)
Wine Production by Country (1987-89)
Change in Wine Production (1980-89)
Total World Wine Production
Total World Wine Production (mid 1969-mid 1989) (Chart)

Section 3: Alcohol Consumption Data by Country

For Each Country:
Consumption Per Capita (1961-89);
Indices of Alcohol Consumption (Chart);
Relative Importance by Sector (1961-89) (Chart)

Index of Countries Covered
Algeria
Argentina
Australia
Austria
Belgium
Brazil
Bulgaria
Canada
Chile
Colombia
Cuba
Cyprus
Czechoslovakia
Denmark
Finland
France
Germany - DR
Germany - FR

Greece
Hungary
Iceland
Republic of Ireland
Israel
Italy
Japan
Luxembourg
Mexico
Morocco
Netherlands
New Zealand
Norway
Paraguay
Peru
Poland
Portugal
Romania
South Africa
Spain
Sweden
Switzerland
Tunisia
United Kingdom
Uruguay
United States of America
Venezuela
Yugoslavia

ASIA—GENERAL

ASIA-PACIFIC IN FIGURES

FACTS AT A GLANCE

Number of Pages: 42

Periodicity: Annual

Publisher: United Nations

PURPOSE AND SCOPE

Asia-Pacific in Figures provides basic information on the economic and social trends and developments in East Asia.

DATA ORGANIZATION

Asia-Pacific in Figures covers 42 countries in the region and presents data on demographics, health, and education.

METHODOLOGY

The publication uses primarily official data, but when these are incomplete or lacking, it uses data published by the United Nations and related organizations.

CONTENTS

Introduction

Explanatory Notes

Population Statistics

Social Statistics

KEY INDICATORS OF DEVELOPING ASIAN AND PACIFIC COUNTRIES

FACTS AT A GLANCE

Number of Pages: 393

Periodicity: Annual

Publisher: Asian Development Bank (ADB)

PURPOSE AND SCOPE

The purpose of the publication is to provide key indicators on development for Pacific Rim countries. It is part of the Asian Development Bank's effort to monitor the performance of the economies of the region and the creditworthiness of its countries.

DATA ORGANIZATION

The focus of the tables is on the national economies. With this goal in mind, the tables examine population, GDP, trade, agriculture, industry, debt, public finance, net financial flows, and also ADB's loan approvals and disbursements.

METHODOLOGY

ADB performs a regional role similar to the global role of the World Bank. The publication is based on its collection of economic data from member countries designed to help it to perform that role more effectively.

CONTENTS

Part 1 - Developing Asia/Pacific and World Tables

Part 2 - Regional Tables

19. Yield of Paddy and Maize
20. Coconut Production
21. General Index of Agricultural Production
22. General Index of Per Capita Agricultural Production
23. Mining Production Index
24. Manufacturing Production Index
25. Electricity Production Index
26. Petroleum and Petroleum Products Imports
27. Consumer Price Index
28. Wholesale Price Index
29. Prices of Selected Primary Commodities
30. Money Supply Index
31. Central Government Expenditures and Taxes
32. Merchandise Exports, f.o.b.
33. Merchandise Imports, c.i.f.
34. Annual Growth Rates of Merchandise Exports and Imports
35. Composition of Exports
36. Composition of Imports
37. Direction of Trade: Merchandise Exports
38. Direction of Trade: Merchandise Imports
39. Terms of Trade
40. Current Account Balance
41. Current Account Balance as Percent of GNP
42. Workers Remittances
43. Foreign Direct Investment
44. Ratio of International Reserves to Imports
45. International Reserves
46. Foreign Exchange Rates
47. Total External Debt
48. Debt Service on Long-Term External Debt
49. Selected Debt Indicators
50. Selected Debt Ratios
51. Interest Rates of New Commitments from All Creditors
52. Maturity Period of New Commitments from All Creditors
53. Grace Period of New Commitments from All Creditors
54. Grant Element of New Commitments from All Creditors
55. Total Net Flows of Financial Resources from All Sources to DMCs
56. Net Official Flows from All Sources to DMCs
57. Official Development Assistance Flows from All Sources to DMCs
58. Net Private Flows from DAC Countries to DMCs
59. Official Development Assistance Commitments from All Sources to DMCs
60. Borrowing of DMCs in International Capital Markets
61. ADB Net Flows to DMCs
62. ADB Loan Approvals by Country and Source of Funds
63. ADB Loan Disbursements by Country and Source of Funds
64. ADB Loan Approvals by Sector and by Source of Funds
65. ADB Technical Assistance to DMCs

Part 3 - Country Tables
Afghanistan, Republic of
Bangladesh
Bhutan
China, People's Republic of
Cook Islands
Fiji
Hong Kong
India
Indonesia
Kiribati
Korea, Republic of
Lao, People's Democratic Republic of
Malaysia
Maldives
Mongolia
Myanmar
Nepal
Pakistan
Papua New Guinea
Philippines
Singapore
Solomon Islands
Sri Lanka
Taipei, China
Thailand
Tonga
Vanuatu
Viet Nam, Socialist Republic of
Western Samoa

STATISTICAL INDICATORS FOR ASIA AND THE PACIFIC

FACTS AT A GLANCE

Number of Pages: 96

Periodicity: Monthly

Publisher: United Nations

PURPOSE AND SCOPE

Statistical Indicators for Asia and the Pacific provides monthly data assessing demographic and economic trends.

DATA ORGANIZATION

The publication is divided into two parts: The first part contains regional tables focusing on population, vital statistics, education, industry, agriculture, gross domestic product, and trade. The second part contains country tables.

METHODOLOGY

The regional tables are more complete than the country tables where there are significant gaps.

CONTENTS

Part I - Regional Tables

Part II - Country/Area Tables

STATISTICAL YEARBOOK FOR ASIA AND THE PACIFIC

FACTS AT A GLANCE

Number of Pages: 502

Periodicity: Annual

Publisher: United Nations (UN)

PURPOSE AND SCOPE

Each of the regional UN economic (and social) commissions publishes an annual statistical yearbook providing detailed information on its region. The *Statistical Yearbook for Asia and the Pacific* is the flagship publication of the United Nations Economic and Social Commission for Asia and the Pacific.

DATA ORGANIZATION

The *Statistical Yearbook for Asia and the Pacific* is new to the *United Nations Statistical Yearbook* format and covers a wide variety of subjects. Two summary tables, entitled Regional Statistical Indicators, appear in the book.

METHODOLOGY

In most cases, data are published in the form in which they are available, but in a few cases they have been grouped to achieve a degree of consistency. Index numbers have been given a uniform base year in order to facilitate comparison.

CONTENTS

Introduction

General Explanatory Notes

World and ESCAP Region

ESCAP Region

Developing ESCAP Region

Afghanistan
Australia
Azerbaijan
Bangladesh
Bhutan
Brunei Darussalam
Cambodia
China
Commonwealth of the Northern Mariana Islands
Cook Islands
Democratic People's Republic of Korea
Fiji
Guam
Hong Kong
India
Indonesia
Iran, Islamic Republic of
Japan
Kazakhstan
Kiribati
Kygyzstan
Lao, People's Democratic Republic of
Macau
Malaysia
Maldives
Marshall Islands
Micronesia
Mongolia
Myanmar
Nauru
Nepal
New Zealand
Niue
Pakistan
Papua New Guinea
Philippines
Republic of Korea
Republic of Palau
Samoa
Singapore
Solomon Islands
Sri Lanka
Tajikistan
Thailand
Tonga
Turkmenistan
Tuvalu
Uzbekistan
Vanuatu
Viet Nam

Annexes

I. Principal Sources
II. Conversion Coefficients and Factors

BALANCE OF PAYMENTS

BALANCE OF PAYMENTS STATISTICS YEARBOOK

FACTS AT A GLANCE

Number of Pages: Part One: 791; Part Two: 109

Periodicity: Annual

Publisher: International Monetary Fund (IMF)

PURPOSE AND SCOPE

The *Balance of Payments Statistics Yearbook* (BPY) is the official record maintained by the IMF on the international financial transactions based on trade in merchandise and invisibles.

DATA ORGANIZATION

The *BPY* comprises two parts: Part I contains country sections presenting aggregated transactions data (Table 1), detailed transactions data (Table 2), and detailed stock data (Table 3). Table 1A presents unadjusted quarterly data and Table 1B presents seasonally adjusted data. The standard components of the *Balance of Payments* are classified into six standard groups. Part II aggregates data given in Part I by balance of payments category. For each category you will find data on countries, country groups, and the world. Table 1, Summary of International Transactions, provides an area summary. Table 2, Summary of Balances of Current Account, gives a disaggregation of the current account showing global balances for each of the main standard components. To the extent that global balances are not zero, they reflect statistical discrepancies.

METHODOLOGY

The tables are based on data reported to IMF or estimated by IMF staff, or drawn from published sources. All data are rearranged or amended by the IMF staff for the sake of consistency. The present edition has enhanced the data in the country sections in two important ways. The first way being that the data on transactions in other goods, services, and income are presented in greater detail, identifying services and income separately. Secondly, data on total change in reserves are replaced by transactions in reserves.

CONTENTS

Part I.

Country sections are composed of an aggregated presentation containing transactions data (Table 1); a detailed presentation containing transactions data (Table 2); and for some countries, a detailed presentation containing stock data (Table 3); and notes. If quarterly transactions data are available, they are given in an aggregate format in Table 1A. A few countries report quarterly transactions data that are seasonally adjusted. For these countries, Table 1A presents unadjusted quarterly data, and Table 1B presents the seasonally adjusted data. The seasonal element shown in Table 1B is the difference between the current account totals in the two tables. Data are shown for the eight or nine most recent periods available for each country and, unless indicated otherwise, are reported in terms of the Gregorian calendar.

The aggregated presentation has been enhanced in two important ways: (1) the data on transactions in other goods, services, and income (credit and debit) are presented in greater detail, identifying services and income separately; and (2) data for total change in reserves are replaced by data on transactions in reserves. In addition, total changes in reserves along with revaluation items (valuation changes in reserves, monetization or demonetization of gold, and SDR allocations) appear as memorandum items.

The standard components of the balance of payments are classified into six standard groups considered relevant for analyzing the international economic relationship of the reporting countries in a uniform manner. The selected groups, however, do not necessarily reflect the Fund's recommendations about the analytic approach that would be appropriate for countries to adopt for their own purposes. Moreover, the balances that have been drawn in the presentation may be affected by special circumstances that must be taken into account when interpreting the figures that purport to measure a given concept of imbalance. Finally, the aggregated presentation should be read in the light of other developments in the national and world economic situation that also have a bearing on the surpluses and deficits that can be compiled from the standard components.

Part II.

Part 2 of the *Balance of Payments Statistics Yearbook*, aggregates data given in Part 1 by balance of payments category. For each category, data for countries, country groups, and the world are provided. The tables cover data for international organizations and for a number of countries not covered in Part 1. This is because the latter countries did not report data in sufficient detail or because they did not report data for all or some of the years covered by Part 1. Data were estimated for these countries. However, the estimates, which are included in regional totals, are not shown for the individual countries concerned. Owing to the nonavailability of information for publication, no data are shown in the line for the category "Other countries n.i.e." The list of country codes given on page viii of this volume refers to countries that are included in Part 1 (of either the current issue or earlier volumes). The totals shown in the tables cover transactions of countries and inter-national organizations that have been either reported or estimated by Fund staff. Data on Fund transactions—for example, transactions in SDRs and of the Fund's General Resources Account—are obtained from Fund sources.

Table 1, Summary of Balances of International Transactions, provides an area summary of selected balances on international transactions. In Tables A-1 through A-11, each of the balances given in Table 1 is shown with a breakdown for international organizations, by country group, and by country. Tables B-1 through B-4 show gross flows of goods, services, income, unrequited transfers, and net transactions and changes in financial assets and liabilities underlying Tables A-1 through A-11. Capital flows are usually recorded on a net basis, with inflows netted against outflows in each category. Therefore, Table B-4 shows only net credits or net debits for specified assets and liabilities. Tables C-1 through C-38 provide details, by item, country group, and country, of the amounts shown in Tables B-1 through B-4. With the exception of data in Tables C-23, C-24, C-26, C-27, C-29, and C-30, capital flows shown in Tables C-16 through C-38 are on a net basis; net inflows and net outflows are shown as credits and debits, respectively. The notation "n.i.e." is used in table headings and stubs to indicate that the data exclude exceptional financing, or liabilities constituting foreign authorities' reserves, or both.

Table 2, Summary of Balances of Current Account, n.i.e., gives a disaggregation of the current account, showing global balances for each of the main standard components. To the extent that global balances are not zero, they reflect statistical discrepancies (after taking into consideration minor amounts of exceptional financing included in official unrequited transfers). The discrepancies measure net errors and omissions and inconsistencies in reported and estimated data. Countries' recording practices vary in statistical coverage, data collection, and estimation. Although the number of countries that have adopted the compilation recommendations of the Fund's *Balance of Payments Manual* (fourth edition) has increased, differences remain in the recording of international transactions. In a continuing effort to achieve consistency and international comparability, the Fund adjusts national data to conform to the *Manual* to the extent possible.

Annex I

Detailed Presentation

Current Account

Goods, Services, and Income
Total Credit
Total Debit
1. Merchandise: Exports f.o.b.
2. Merchandise: Imports f.o.b.
3. Shipment: Credit
4. Shipment: Debit
5. Passenger Services: Credit
6. Passenger Services: Debit
7. Other Transportation: Credit
8. Other Transportation: Debit
9. Travel: Credit
10. Travel: Debit
11. Reinvested Earnings on Direct Investment Abroad
12. Reinvested Earnings on Direct Investment in (Reporting Economy)
13. Other Direct Investment Income: Credit
14. Other Direct Investment Income: Debit
15. Other Investment Income of Resident Official, including Interofficial: Credit
16. Other Investment Income of Resident Official, including Interofficial: Debit
17. Other Investment Income of Foreign Official, excluding Interofficial: Credit
18. Other Investment Income of Foreign Official, excluding Interofficial: Debit
19. Other Investment Income: Credit
20. Other Investment Income: Debit
21. Interofficial, n.i.e: Credit
22. Interofficial, n.i.e: Debit
23. Other Resident Official, n.i.e: Credit
24. Other Resident Official, n.i.e: Debit
25. Other Foreign Official, n.i.e: Credit
26. Other Foreign Official, n.i.e: Debit
27. Labor Income, n.i.e: Credit
28. Labor Income, n.i.e: Debit
29. Property Income, n.i.e: Credit
30. Property Income, n.i.e: Debit
31. Other Goods, Services, and Income: Credit
32. Other Goods, Services, and Income: Debit

Unrequitted Transfers
Total Credit
Total Debit
33. Migrants' Transfers: Credit
34. Migrants' Transfers: Debit
35. Workers' Remittances: Credit
36. Workers' Remittances: Debit
37. Other Private Transfers: Credit
38. Other Private Transfers: Debit
39. Interofficial Transfers: Credit
40. Interofficial Transfers: Debit
41. Other Transfers of Resident Official: Credit
42. Other Transfers of Resident Official: Debit
43. Other Transfers of Foreign Official: Credit
44. Other Transfers of Foreign Official: Debit

Capital Account

Capital, Excluding Reserves

Direct Investment Abroad
45. Equity Capital
46. Reinvestment of Earnings
47. Other Long-term Capital
48. Short-term Capital

Direct Investment in (Reporting Economy)
49. Equity Capital
50. Reinvestment of Earnings
51. Other Long-term Capital
52. Short-term Capital

Portfolio Investment

Public Sector Bonds
53. Assets
54. Liabilities Constituting Foreign Authorities' Reserves
55. Other Liabilities

Other Bonds
56. Assets
57. Liabilities Constituting Foreign Authorities' Reserves
58. Other Liabilities

Corporate Equities
59. Assets
60. Liabilities Constituting Foreign Authorities' Reserves
61. Other Liabilities

Other Long-term Capital of Resident Official Sector
62. Drawings on Loans Extended
63. Repayments on Loans Extended
64. Other Assets
65. Liabilities Constituting Foreign Authorities' Reserves
66. Drawings on Other Loans Received
67. Repayments on Other Loans Received
68. Other Liabilities

Other Long-term Capital of Deposit Money Banks
69. Drawings on Loans Extended
70. Repayments on Loans Extended
71. Other Assets
72. Liabilities Constituting Foreign Authorities' Reserves Denominated in National Currency
73. Liabilities Constituting Foreign Authorities' Reserves Denominated in Foreign Currency
74. Drawings on Other Loans Received
75. Repayments on Other Loans Received
76. Other Liabilities

Other Long-term Capital of Other Sectors
77. Drawings on Loans Extended
78. Repayments on Loans Extended
79. Other Assets
80. Liabilities Constituting Foreign Authorities' Reserves
81. Drawings on Other Loans Received
82. Repayments on Other Loans Received
83. Other Liabilities

Other Short-term Capital of Resident Official Sector
84. Loans Extended
85. Other Assets
86. Liabilities Constituting Foreign Authorities' Reserves
87. Other Loans Received
88. Other Liabilities

Other Short-term Capital of Deposit Money Banks
89. Assets
90. Liabilities Constituting Foreign Authorities' Reserves Denominated in National Currency

91. Liabilities Constituting Foreign Authorities' Reserves Denominated in Foreign Currency
92. Other Liabilities

Other Short-term Capital of Other Sectors
93. Loans Extended
94. Other Assets
95. Liabilities Constituting Foreign Authorities' Reserves
96. Other Loans Received
97. Other Liabilities

Reserves

Monetary Gold
98. Total Change in Holdings
99. Counterpart to Monetization/Demonetization
100. Counterpart to Valuation Changes

Special Drawing Rights
101. Total Change in Holdings
102. Counterpart to Allocation/Cancellation
103. Counterpart to Valuation Changes

Reserve Position in the Fund
104. Total Change in Holdings
105. Counterpart to Valuation Changes

Foreign Exchange Assets
106. Total Change in Holdings
107. Counterpart to Valuation Changes

Other Claims
108. Total Change in Holdings
109. Counterpart to Valuation Changes

Use of Fund Credit and Loans
110. Total Change in Holdings
111. Counterpart to Valuation Changes

CATHOLIC CHURCH, ROMAN

STATISTICAL YEARBOOK OF THE CHURCH

FACTS AT GLANCE

Number of Pages: 441

Periodicity: Annual

Publisher: Vatican Secretariat - Central Statistics Office

PURPOSE AND SCOPE

The *Statistical Yearbook of the Church* is the most significant and only available collection of statistics on the Roman Catholic Church worldwide.

DATA ORGANIZATION

The book is divided into seven chapters. The first chapter gives data on the area and population of the

2,776 ecclesiastical jurisdictions under the Holy See. Chapter II provides data on the Workforce for the Apostolate, including cardinals, archbishops, bishops and priests, and religious men and women. Chapter III provides information on Catholic seminaries and other educational institutions and their staff and students. Chapter IV gives tables on the practice of religion, including baptisms, marriages, confirmations, and other rites. Chapter V gives information on welfare institutions including hospitals. Chapter VI gives information on monasteries and other institutions for consecrated men and women. The final chapter gives information on diocesan and regional tribunals, especially those that deal with marriages.

METHODOLOGY

The *Annuario,* as the *Statistical Yearbook* is commonly called, is one of the most respected statistical publications in the world but its limitations are expressed in a series of caveats in the introduction. The data are collected through indirect surveys. Because some of these ecclesiastical jurisdictions are in countries hostile to the Catholic Church, the returns are often incomplete. The Holy See is in communication with only 2,616 out of a total of 2,776 jurisdictions. The totals and subtotals represent only these 2,616 jurisdictions with which the Statistical Office is in contact.

CONTENTS

CHILD MORTALITY

CHILD MORTALITY IN DEVELOPING COUNTRIES

FACTS AT A GLANCE

Number of Pages: 127

Periodicity: Irregular

Publishers: United Nations

PURPOSE AND SCOPE

The present volume is a follow up of the 1985 study of socio-economic differentials in child mortality in developing countries undertaken in cooperation with the World Health Organization. Like the 1985 study, it assesses trends in child mortality differentials in developing countries. The study also identifies categories of children at high risk of child mortality and determines how patterns of child mortality have changed over time.

DATA ORGANIZATION

The study is limited to six developing countries: Kenya, Costa Rica, Honduras, Paraguay, Jordan, and Thailand.

METHODOLOGY

The study was prepared in cooperation with the United Nations regional commissions. Estimates of the probability of child deaths are made by regression coefficients and other mathematical procedures.

Contents

35. Socio-economic Indicators, Thailand, 1970 and 1980
36. Probability of Dying by Age 5, by Mother's Education, Thailand, 1970, 1980, and 1987
37. Distribution of the Population at Risk, by Socio-Economic Characteristics, Thailand, 1970 and 1980
38. Probability of Dying by Age 5 and Relative Risks of Child Mortality, by Socio-economic Characteristics, Thailand, 1970 and 1980 Census
39. Multivariate Coefficients of Child Mortality, by Socio-Economic Characteristics, Thailand, 1970 and 1980 Censuses
40. Child Mortality Risks Groups, by Place of Residence, Mother's Occupation, and Father's and Mother's Education, Thailand, 1970 Census
41. Child Mortality Risks Groups, by Place of Residence, Mother's Occupation, and Father's and Mother's Education, Thailand, 1980 Census

Figures
I. Trends in the Probability of Dying by Age 5, Kenya, 1950-1989
II. Trends in Infant Mortality, Costa Rica, 1970-1984
III. Child Mortality and Distribution of Births According to Risk Groups, Costa Rica, 1968 and 1979
IV. Age Patterns of Child Mortality as Observed by the 1976 Jordan Fertility Survey, Compared with Patterns from the Coale and Demeny Model Life-tables, Jordan
V. Estimates of the Probability of Dying by Age 5, Jordan
VI. Trends in the Probability of Dying by Age 5, Thailand, 1960-1985
VII. Probability of Dying by Age 5, by Place of Residence, Thailand, 1965-1987

COAL

ANNUAL BULLETIN OF COAL STATISTICS FOR EUROPE

FACTS AT A GLANCE

Number of Pages: 135

Periodicity: Annual

Publisher: United Nations (UN)

PURPOSE AND SCOPE

The purpose of the *Annual Bulletin of Coal Statistics for Europe* is to provide basic data on developments and trends in the field of solid fuels in European countries, Canada, and the United States.

DATA ORGANIZATION

The data refer to production, stocks, inland availabilities, deliveries, trade, employment, and labor productivity.

METHODOLOGY

The statistics are presented in the form of time series. Additional reports on the coal situation are published by the UN Economic Commission for Europe.

CONTENTS

Graphs
1. Production of Hard Coal, Brown Coal, and Coke in the World and in the ECE Region, 1970-1991
2. Production of Hard Coal and Brown Coal in the ECE Region, 1970-1991
3. Hard Coal Consumption by User Sectors in the ECE Region in 1991
4. Production of Electricity by Fuel in the ECE Region in 1980 and 1991
5. Production of Electricity by Fuel for ECE Regions in 1991
6. Main Hard Coal Exporters: Part of Production Exported in 1991
7. Main Hard Coal Importers: Part of Consumption Imported in 1991

Tables
1. Balance Sheet of Solid Forms of Energy
2. Hard Coal Mines. Structure of Production, Employment, and Productivity of Labour
3. Brown Coal Mines. Structure of Production, Employment, and Productivity of Labour
4. Imports of Solid Fuels, by Country
5. Exports of Solid Fuels, by Country
6. Average Net Calorific Value of Processed Coal Products

Table Notes by Country

COAL INFORMATION

FACTS AT A GLANCE

Number of Pages: 514

Periodicity: Annual

Publisher: Organization for Economic Cooperation and Development (OECD)

PURPOSE AND SCOPE

Coal Information, published annually since 1983, is intended to provide both OECD member countries and coal industry specialists with information on current world coal market trends and long-term prospects. It includes information on coal prices, demand, trade, supply, productive capacity, transport, environmental issues, coal ports, coal-fired power stations, and coal used in non-OECD countries.

DATA ORGANIZATION

Part I provides an overview of the world coal market developments and prospects based on historical data collected by the IEA or obtained from outside sources, and projections of trends in coal supply, demand, and trade submitted by individual OECD member countries. Part I has five annexes: a list of coal ports; a list of OECD and non-OECD coal importers and coal-fired power stations; worldwide hard coal supply and end-use statistics; coal balance and coal trade for major non-OECD coal exporters and importers; and data on emission limits for coal-fired boilers. Part II provides, in tabular and graphic form, a more detailed and comprehensive picture of coal developments, prices, and future prospects for the OECD by regions and countries.

METHODOLOGY

Coal Information is published each July and compiled from the International Energy Agency (IEA) Coal Information System. It is guided by the Coal Industry Advisory Board's Standing Committee of Coal Information. Additional information included in this edition are tables on coke production and consumption, pulverized injection coals, coal stocks, resources of the major coal fields of the world, and seaborne coal trade. Information on coal production and productive capacity as well as representative coal costs is brought together in Chapter 6. Chapter 7, dealing with environmental issues, has been considerably expanded. Data on Germany have been revised to integrate East and West German figures from 1970.

CONTENTS

Part I. Summary of World Coal Developments

Part II. OECD Coal Data and Projections

COCOA

QUARTERLY BULLETIN OF COCOA STATISTICS

FACTS AT A GLANCE

Number of Pages: 69

Periodicity: Quarterly

Publisher: International Cocoa Organization (ICO)

PURPOSE AND SCOPE

The *Quarterly Bulletin of Cocoa Statistics* is a global summary of cocoa production, consumption, trade, and prices.

DATA ORGANIZATION

Each monthly issue contains 3 charts and 30 tables. Three tables deal with production, 11 with trade, 5 with prices, and the remaining 11 with main cocoa importing countries.

METHODOLOGY

The data are compiled from reports supplied directly to the International Cocoa Organization by member and non-member countries and supplemented by other official sources. Estimates are provided by the ICO statisticians.

CONTENTS

7. Exports of Cocoa Powder and Cake
8. Exports of Cocoa Paste/Liquor
9. Exports of Chocolate and Chocolate Products
10. Imports of Cocoa Beans
11. Imports of Cocoa Butter
12. Imports of Cocoa Powder and Cake
13. Imports of Cocoa Paste/Liquor
14. Imports of Chocolate and Chocolate Products

Prices
15a. Monthly Averages of Daily Prices of Cocoa Beans
15b. ICCO Daily Prices of Cocoa Beans
16. Monthly and Annual Averages of Daily Prices of Cocoa Beans
17. Cocoa Bean Prices of International Significance, London and New York

Cocoa Consumption, 1985/86-1992/93
18. Cocoa Consumption (by Final Consumer) by Country
19. Per Caput Cocoa Consumption by Country

Origin of Imports and Destination of Exports for Individual Main Cocoa-importing Countries, 1990/91-1993/94
20. Belgium/Luxembourg
21. Canada
22. France
23. Germany
24. Italy
25. Japan
26. Netherlands
27. Switzerland
28a. USSR
28b. Russian Federation
29. United Kingdom
30. United States of America

THE WORLD COCOA MARKET

FACTS AT A GLANCE

Number of Pages: 175

Periodicity: Irregular

Publisher: International Cocoa Organization

PURPOSE AND SCOPE

The World Cocoa Market analyzes recent trends in the world cocoa economy and forecasts likely developments within the next decade.

DATA ORGANIZATION

The publication contains seven chapters of which the first is the Introduction. Chapter II is a summary review of major developments in the world cocoa market. Chapter III describes the structure and relationships that operate in the cocoa market with particular reference to production, consumption, and price. Chapter IV contains projections of selected variables for the principal cocoa-producing countries and regions. Chapter V describes trends in consumption and makes appropriate projections. Chapter VI contains projections relating to stock and price. Chapter VII presents conclusions. There are two annexes of which Annex A presents statistical time series. The statistical annex is accompanied by 43 charts and 22 tables.

METHODOLOGY

The study is produced by the International Cocoa Organization based on its own internal resources.

CONTENTS

Charts and Tables

I. Introduction

II. Review of Recent Developments
  A. Global Cocoa Supply/Demand Balance
  B. Cocoa Production
  C. Cocoa Consumption
  D. Cocoa Stocks
  E. Cocoa Prices
    (1) Cocoa Bean Prices
    (2) Cocoa Product Prices
    (3) Cocoa Derived Export Earnings
  F. Cocoa Exports and Imports

III. Fundamental Relationships in the World Cocoa Market
  A. Basic Market Relationships
  B. Models of Cocoa Production
  C. Models of Cocoa Consumption
  D. The Cocoa Market Price Model

IV. Estimation Results and Projection of Cocoa Production
  A. Production in Africa
    (1) Cote d'Ivoire
    (2) Ghana
    (3) Nigeria
    (4) Cameroon
    (5) Other Africa
  B. Production in the Americas
    (1) Brazil
    (2) Ecuador
    (3) Other Americas
  C. Production in Asia and Oceania
    (1) Malaysia
    (2) Indonesia
    (3) Other Asia and Oceania
  D. World Cocoa Production

V. Estimation Results and Projections of Cocoa Consumption
  A. Consumption in Western Europe
  B. Consumption in Eastern Europe and the Former USSR
  C. Consumption in Africa
  D. Consumption in the Americas

39.
   A. Composition of World Cocoa Consumption by Region
   B. Regional Shares of World Cocoa Consumption
40. World Cocoa Market Scenario with Low Consumption Growth (Localized Consumption Model)
41. World Cocoa Market Scenario with High Consumption Growth (Global Consumption Model with Price-Level Effects)
42.
   A. Forecasts of World Cocoa Production with High or Low Consumption Growth
   B. Forecasts of World Cocoa Consumption with High or Low Consumption Growth
43.
   A. Forecasts of World Cocoa Market Stocks with High or Low Consumption Growth
   B. Forecasts of World Cocoa Market Prices with High or Low Consumption Growth

Tables
1. Global Supply/Demand Balance in the World Cocoa Market
2. Evolution of World Cocoa Stocks in Relation to World Grindings, 1981/82-1990/91
3. Age-Specific Yield Profile of Immature Cocoa Trees
4. Globally-Adjusted Apparent Final Consumption of Cocoa by Region and Major Consuming Country from 1961/62 to 1990/91
5. Cote d'Ivoire Cocoa Areas and Production
6. Ghana Cocoa Areas and Production
7. Nigeria Cocoa Areas and Production
8. Cameroon Cocoa Areas and Production
9. Brazil Cocoa Areas and Production
10. Ecuador Cocoa Areas and Production
11. Malaysia Cocoa Areas and Production
12. Indonesia Cocoa Areas and Production
13. Projected Production by Origin for the Period 1991/92 - 2000/01: Low-Consumption-Growth Scenario
14. Projected Production by Origin for the Period 1991/92 - 2000/01: High-Consumption-Growth Scenario
15. Annual Plantings of Cocoa and Total Tree-Stocks in Major Producing Countries in Five-Year Periods
16. Equivalent Mature Areas and Yields of Cocoa in Major Cocoa-Producing Countries in Five-Year Periods
17. Estimated Elasticity Coefficients of Apparent Final Consumption of Cocoa
18. Projections of Final Consumption of Cocoa on the Basis of Localized Consumption Models
19. Projections of Shares of World Consumption of Cocoa Using Localized Consumption Models
20. Preliminary Estimates of Current and Potential CBE Usage in the EC Chocolate Industry
21. World Cocoa Market Development through to 2000/01; Scenario Based Upon the Localized

Consumption Models (Low-Consumption-Growth Scenario)
22. World Cocoa Market Development through to 2000/01; Scenario Based Upon the Global Consumption Model with Price-Level Effects (High-Consumption-Growth Scenario)

COCONUTS

COCONUT STATISTICAL YEARBOOK

FACTS AT A GLANCE

Number of Pages: 277

Periodicity: Annual

Publisher: Asian and Pacific Coconut Community

PURPOSE AND SCOPE

The *Coconut Statistical Yearbook* is the only compilation of statistics on the subject of coconuts.

DATA ORGANIZATION

The publication presents 58 tables dealing with production, consumption, supply and demand, exports and imports, and prices of coconuts, copra, coconut oil, copra meal, and coir fiber.

METHODOLOGY

Much of the data are derived from reports from member organizations and countries in Asia and the Pacific.

CONTENTS

Foreword

List of Tables

World
1.1 Production of Coconuts in Nut Equivalent, 1989-1993
1.2 Production of Coconuts in Copra Equivalent, 1989-1993
1.3 Area of Coconuts, 1989-1993
1.4 Production of Copra, 1989-1993
1.5 Supply and Demand Balance of Coconut Oil, 1989-1993
1.6 Estimated Consumption of Coconut Oil, 1989-1993
1.7 End-Month Stocks of Coconut Oil in Selected Consuming Countries, 1989-1993
1.8 Supply and Demand of Copra Meal, 1989-1993
1.9 Estimated Consumption of Copra Meal, 1989-1993
1.10 Estimated Consumption of Desiccated Coconut by Selected Countries, 1989-1993

COMMODITIES

COMMODITY TRADE AND PRICE TRENDS

FACTS AT A GLANCE

Number of Pages: 98

Periodicity: Annual

Publisher: World Bank and The Johns Hopkins University Press

PURPOSE AND SCOPE

The purpose of *Commodity Trade and Price Trends* is to present basic international trade and price statistics for both developing and industrial countries with a focus on primary commodities.

DATA ORGANIZATION

Section I provides general information regarding changes in the present edition and the classification system for countries and regions. World totals now cover all economies including oil exporters. At the end of Section I is a list that cross references all commodity names used in *Commodity Trade and Price Trends* and their equivalents in the United Nations Standard International Trade Classification (SITC) Codes. Section II provides an overview of commodity price trends and Section III presents international trade statistics. Tables 1 and 2 provide external trade values for broad commodity groups by economic region over the last two decades with annual data for the past four years. Tables 3 and 4 present time series of trade volume, value, and unit value indices by economic region as well as by terms of trade indices. Tables 5 and 6 present time series on the direction of trade by economic regions. Also included in Section III are detailed commodity trade matrices. Tables 7 and 9 provide country profiles of the primary commodity export composition for the Lower Middle Income Countries (LMIC) as well as for each country's share in world exports, subtotals for the regional groups, and totals for the high income groups and for the world. Tables 7 to 9 highlight five additional commodities: fisheries, soybeans, oilseed cake and meal, alumina, and nickel. Tables 10 to 13 present time series of LMIC exports and imports by commodity; Tables 14 to 17 present the same series for high income Organization for Economic Cooperation and Development (OECD) countries. Tables 18 to 19 present direction of trade data by commodity for high income OECD countries. Section IV contains a selection of general price indices, including the Manufacturing Unit Value (MUV) Index, that can be used as an inflation index. Table 21 presents purchasing power indices of primary commodities exported by developing countries and subcategory commodity indices for food, beverages, cereals, fats and oils, agricultural non-food raw materials, timber, metals and minerals, and petroleum. The section ends with a list of selected ocean freight rates. Section V reports market quotations for 55 commodities in current or nominal dollars and constant or real dollars, deflated using the MUV Index. Prices are generally freight on board.

For some commodities more than one price series is shown, as when different grades or varieties command significantly different market prices. In other cases, as in non-ferrous metals, market forces, such as trade barriers, transportation costs, or consumer preferences, result in two or more prominent trading markets. As markets shift some price series become unavailable. The discontinued series are presented alongside the new series. For the current edition, four new price series have been added: Brazilian cocoa, white pepper, and two steel products. The series on U.S. steel carbon plates has been deleted. All price data are accompanied by charts to reflect their rates of growth over time.

METHODOLOGY

Price quotations are compiled from international commodity organizations or information sources that monitor specific commodity markets. In previous editions, trade statistics were compiled using United Nations data. The current edition is the first to use the International Economics, Commodities, and International Trade (IECIT) Database, based on the UN COMTRADE.

CONTENTS

Cereals

Rice, Thai, f.o.b. Bangkok
Rice, U.S., f.o.b. Mills
Grain Sorghum, U.S., f.o.b. Gulf Ports
Maize, Argentine, c.i.f. Rotterdam
Maize, U.S., No. 2, f.o.b. Gulf Ports
Wheat, U.S., Soft Red Winter, f.o.b. Atlantic Ports
Wheat, Canadian, Western Red Spring, Basis in
    Store, Thunder Bay

Sugar

Sugar, World, Raw, f.o.b. Caribbean Ports
Sugar, London, Raw, c.i.f. UK

Meat

Beef, U.S. Import, Frozen, c.i.f. Port of Entry
Beef, Argentine, f.o.b. Unit Value of Exports to EEC
Lamb, New Zealand, London Market

Fruits and Spices

Bananas, Ecuadorian, Fresh, c.i.f. Hamburg
Bananas, any Origin, Fresh, c.i.f. U.S. Port of Entry
Pepper, Black, any Origin, Spot New York
Pepper, White, Spot New York

Oilseeds, Oils, Cakes, and Meals

Copra, Philippines, c.i.f. European Ports
Coconut Oil, Philippines/Indonesia, c.i.f.
    Rotterdam
Groundnut Meal, Indian, c.i.f. European Ports
Groundnut Oil, Nigerian, c.i.f. European Ports
Linseed, Canadian No. 1, c.i.f. European Ports
Linseed Oil, Argentine, c.i.f. Europe
Palm Kernels, Nigerian, c.i.f. European Ports
Palm Oil, Malaysian, c.i.f. European Ports
Soybeans, U.S., c.i.f. Rotterdam
Soybean Oil, U.S., any Origin, f.o.b. Ex-mill
Soybean Meal, U.S., c.i.f. Rotterdam
Fishmeal, Peruvian/Other Origins, c.i.f Hamburg

Non-Foods

Fibers

Cotton, U.S., c.i.f. Liverpool
Cotton, Egyptian, c.i.f. Liverpool
Cotton, "A" Index, c.i.f. North Europe
Burlap, U.S., Spot New York
Jute, Bangladesh, White C, c.i.f. Dundee
Jute, Bangladesh, White D, f.o.b.
    Chittagong/Chalna
Sisal, East African, UG, c.i.f. European Ports
Sisal, Kenyan/Tanzanian, c.i.f. London
Wool, New Zealand, 56's, Dominion Auction, c.i.f.
    UK

Rubber

Rubber, Natural, RSS 1, Spot London
Rubber, Natural, RSS 1, Spot New York

Timber

Logs, Philippines, Lauan, Average Wholesale Price
    in Japan
Logs, Malaysian, Meranti, Sales Price Charged by
    Importers in Japan
Logs, West African, Sapelli, f.o.b. Cameroon
Plywood, Philippines, Lauan, Spot Tokyo
Sawnwood, Malaysian, c.i.f. French Ports

Tobacco

Tobacco, Indian, Export Unit Value

Fuels, Metals, and Minerals

Fuels

Coal, U.S., Bituminous, f.o.b. U.S. Ports
Petroleum, Average OPEC Official Selling Price
Petroleum, Average OPEC Spot Price
Petroleum Products, Gasoline
Petroleum Product, Jet Fuel Kerosene
Petroleum Product, Gas Oil
Petroleum Product, Fuel Oil

Non-Ferrous Metals

Aluminum, Minimum 99.5 Percent Ingot, c.i.f.
    Europe
Aluminum, Minimum 99.5 Percent Ingot, LME
Bauxite, Jamaican, U.S. Import Reference Price
Copper, Electrolytic Wirebar, LME
Copper, Electrolytic Wirebar, New York
Lead, Soft Pigs, LME
Lead, Pig, Desilverized, New York
Tin, Standard, LME
Tin, Straits, Kuala Lumpur Tin Market (KLTM)
    Settlement Price
Tin, Pig, Straits, New York
Zinc, Good Ordinary Brands, LME
Zinc, Prime Western Grade, New York

Other Metals and Minerals

Iron Ore, Brazilian, f.o.b. Tubarao
Iron Ore, Swedish, f.o.b. Narvik
Manganese Ore, Indian, 46-48 Percent Minimum.,
    c.i.f. U.S. ports
Nickel, Canadian, f.o.b. Shipping Point
Nickel, U.S. Spot, f.o.b. New York
Steel, Japanese, re-bar, f.o.b.
Steel, Japanese, Hot-rolled Sheet, f.o.b.
Steel, German, Bessemer Bar, Producer Price

Fertilizers

Phosphate Rock, Moroccan, f.a.s. Casablanca
Diammonium Phosphate (DAP), U.S., f.o.b. Gulf
    Ports
Potassium Chloride, Canadian, f.o.b. Vancouver
Triple Superphosphate (TSP), U.S., f.o.b. Gulf Ports
Urea, any Origin, f.o.b. Europe

COMMODITY YEARBOOK

FACTS AT A GLANCE

Number of Pages: 412

Periodicity: Annual

Publisher: United Nations

PURPOSE AND SCOPE

The *Commodity Yearbook* provides disaggregated data at the global, regional, and country levels for the production, trade, and consumption of selected agricultural primary commodities and minerals, ores, and metals.

DATA ORGANIZATION

The data are presented in three parts: Part I presents trade values and shares of commodity aggregates and direction and value of commodity exports and imports. Six tables cover share of primary commodities in merchandise trade and gross domestic product. Part II shows trade in selected agricultural commodities by regions and selected countries, volume and value, volume of production, and volume of consumption. Part III gives minerals, ores, metals, and crude petroleum statistics by regions and countries.

METHODOLOGY

The *Yearbook* is based on background data collected regularly by the United Nations in conjunction with the Conference on Trade and Development.

CONTENTS

Part One

Trade Values and Shares of Commodity Aggregates, Direction of Commodity Exports

Part Two

Trade in Selected Agricultural Commodities by Regions and Selected Countries, Volume and Value, Volume of Production, Volume of Consumption, 1986 to 1991

B. Agricultural Raw Materials

2.27.1 Value of Exports of Hides, Skins, and Furskins, Undressed (1970, 1975, 1982-1991)

2.27.2 Value of Imports of Hides, Skins, and Furskins, Undressed (1970, 1975, 1982-1991)

2.27.3 Production of Cattle and Buffalo Hides, Fresh (1970, 1975, 1982-1991)

2.27.4 Apparent Availability of Bovine Hides and Skins (1970, 1975, 1980-1989)

2.28.1 Production of Natural Rubber (1970, 1975, 1982-1991)

2.28.2 Exports of Natural Rubber, Quantity and Value

2.28.3 Imports of Natural Rubber, Quantity and Value

2.28.4 Consumption of Natural Rubber (1970, 1975, 1982-1991)

2.29.1 Production of Non-coniferous Industrial Roundwood (1970, 1975, 1982-1991)

2.29.2 Exports of Non-coniferous Wood, Quantity and Value

2.29.3 Imports of Non-coniferous Wood, Quantity and Value

2.30.1 Value of Exports of Natural Textile Fibres (1970, 1975, 1982-1991)

2.30.2 Value of Imports of Natural Textile Fibres (1970, 1975, 1982-1991)

2.31.1 Estimated Value of Exports of Cotton and Cotton Yarn (1970, 1975, 1982-1991)

2.31.2 Estimated Value of Imports of Cotton and Cotton Yarn (1970, 1975, 1982-1991)

2.31.3 Production of Cotton (1970, 1975, 1982-1991)

2.31.4 Exports of Cotton, Quantity and Value

2.31.5 Imports of Cotton, Quantity and Value

2.31.6 Production of Cotton Yarn (1970, 1975, 1982-1991)

2.31.7 Quantity of Exports of Cotton Yarn (1970, 1975, 1982-1991)

2.31.8 Quantity of Imports of Cotton Yarn (1970, 1975, 1982-1991)

2.31.9 Consumption of Cotton (1970, 1975, 1982-1991)

2.32.1 Estimated Value of Exports of Jute and Jute Products (1970, 1975, 1982-1991)

2.32.2 Estimated Value of Imports of Jute and Jute Products (1970, 1975, 1982-1991)

2.32.3 Production of Jute (1970, 1975, 1982-1991)

2.32.4 Exports of Jute, Quantity and Value

2.32.5 Imports of Jute, Quantity and Value

2.32.6 Production of Jute Goods (1970, 1975, 1982-1991)

2.32.7 Quantity of Exports of Jute Products (1970, 1975, 1982-1991)

2.32.8 Quantity of Imports of Jute Products (1970, 1975, 1982-1991)

2.32.9 Consumption of Jute (1970, 1975, 1982-1991)

2.33.1 Estimated Value of Exports of Hard Fibres and Hard Fibres Manufactures (1970, 1975, 1982-1991)

2.33.2 Estimated Value of Imports of Hard Fibres and Hard Fibres Manufacturers (1970, 1975, 1982-1991)

2.33.3 Quantity of Exports of Hard Fibres Manufactures (1970, 1975, 1982-1991)

2.33.4 Quantity of Imports of Hard Fibres Manufactures (1970, 1975, 1982-1991)

2.33.5 Production of Sisal (1970, 1975, 1982-1991)

2.33.6 Exports of Sisal, Quantity and Value

2.33.7 Imports of Sisal, Quantity and Value

2.33.8 Production of Abaca (1970, 1975, 1982-1991)

2.33.9 Exports of Abaca, Quantity and Value

2.33.10 Imports of Abaca, Quantity and Value

2.34.1 Production of Wool Greasy (1970, 1975, 1982-1991)

2.34.2 Value of Exports of Total Wool (1970, 1975, 1982-1991)

2.34.3 Value of Imports of Total Wool (1970, 1975, 1982-1991)

2.34.4 Quantity of Exports of Wool Greasy and Wool Degreased

2.34.5 Quantity of Imports of Wool Greasy and Wool Degreased

2.34.6 Consumption of Wool (1970, 1975, 1982-1991)

Part Three

Minerals, Ores, Metals, and Crude Petroleum Statistics by Regions and Countries, 1986 to 1991

I. Aluminum

3.1.1 Production of Bauxite

3.1.2 Value of Exports of Bauxite (1980 to 1991)

3.1.3 Quantity of Exports of Bauxite

3.1.4 Value of Imports of Bauxite (1980 to 1991)

3.1.5 Quantity of Imports of Bauxite

3.1.6 Production of Alumina (1980 to 1991)

3.1.7 Exports of Alumina, Quantity and Value

3.1.8 Imports of Alumina, Quantity and Value

3.1.9 Production of Aluminum (1980 to 1991)

3.1.10 Exports of Aluminum, Quantity and Value

3.1.11 Imports of Aluminum, Quantity and Value

3.1.12 Consumption of Primary Aluminum (1980 to 1991)

3.1.13 Total Consumption of Aluminum (Primary and Secondary) (1980 to 1991)

II. Copper

3.2.1 Production of Copper Ore (1980 to 1991)

3.2.2 Exports of Copper Ore, Quantity and Value

3.2.3 Imports of Copper Ore, Quantity and Value

3.2.4 Production of Unrefined Copper (1980 to 1991)

3.2.5 Exports of Unrefined Copper, Quantity and Value

3.2.6 Imports of Unrefined Copper, Quantity and Value

3.2.7 Production of Refined Copper (1980 to 1991)

3.2.8 Production of Secondary Refined Copper (1980 to 1991)

3.2.9 Exports of Refined Copper, Quantity and Value

COMPETITIVENESS

NATIONAL COMPETITIVENESS REPORT

FACTS AT A GLANCE

Number of Pages: 214

Periodicity: Annual

Publisher: World Economic Forum

PURPOSE AND SCOPE

The *National Competitiveness Report* presents competitiveness profiles of 41 major industrial powers.

DATA ORGANIZATION

The report discusses factors that make some industries and nations more competitive than others. It also provides statistical tables to illustrate national profiles.

METHODOLOGY

The report includes detailed notes on methodology and data sources, and it provides an index to criteria.

CONTENTS

Is Competitiveness Unfair?

Executive Summary and Key Results

Methodology

Zooming Inside Factors of Competitiveness

National Competitiveness Profiles

Competitiveness in Perspective
  Claude Smadja, Senior Adviser to the World
  Economic Forum

  Thomas E. Vollmann, Professor of Manufacturing
  Management, IMD

Statistical Tables

Data Processing Methodology

Appendix I: Notes to Tables

Appendix II: Data Sources

Appendix III: Index to Criteria

National Competitiveness Profiles
  Argentina
  Australia
  Austria
  Belgium/Luxembourg
  Brazil
  Canada
  Chile
  Colombia
  Czech Republic
  Denmark
  Finland
  France
  Germany
  Greece
  Hong Kong
  Hungary
  India
  Indonesia
  Ireland
  Italy
  Japan
  Korea (Republic of)
  Malaysia
  Mexico
  Netherlands
  New Zealand
  Norway
  Philippines
  Poland
  Portugal
  Singapore
  South Africa
  Spain
  Sweden
  Switzerland
  Taiwan
  Thailand
  Turkey
  United Kingdom
  United States
  Venezuela

COTTON

COTTON: WORLD STATISTICS

FACTS AT A GLANCE

Number of Pages: 59

Periodicity: Annual

Publisher: International Cotton Advisory Committee

PURPOSE AND SCOPE

Cotton: World Statistics is one of a series of statistical publications of the International Cotton Advisory Committee providing annual statistics on the production and consumption of and trade in cotton worldwide.

DATA ORGANIZATION

The tables concentrate on world cotton supply and use with additional data on yield, exports, imports, stocks, and prices.

METHODOLOGY

The publication is based on official and private sources in member and nonmember countries. Cotton in the tables refers to ginned lint or raw cotton. It does not include seed cotton, linters, cotton mill waste, or cotton fibers subject to non-gin processes.

CONTENTS

Supply and Use Tables
World Cotton Supply and Use
Supply and Distribution of Cotton
Supply of Extra-Fine Cotton
1990/91 Supply and Use of Cotton by Country
1991/92 Supply and Use of Cotton by Country
1992/93 Supply and Use of Cotton by Country
1993/94 Supply and Use of Cotton by Country
1994/95 Supply and Use of Cotton by Country
1995/96 Supply and Use of Cotton by Country
Production of Cotton, All Types
Area
Yield
Consumption
Imports
Exports
Ending Stocks
Ratios of Ending Stocks to Use

Prices
Prices of Cotton, c.i.f. North Europe
Prices of Polyester
New York Cotton Futures Prices

INTERNATIONAL COTTON INDUSTRY STATISTICS

FACTS AT A GLANCE

Number of Pages: 28

Periodicity: Annual

Publisher: International Textile Manufacturers Federation

PURPOSE AND SCOPE

International Cotton Industry Statistics presents data on the productive capacity, machinery utilization, and raw materials consumption in the mill sector of textile industries in virtually all of the textile producing countries of the world.

DATA ORGANIZATION

Each of the three main sections—Spinning, Weaving, and Raw Materials Consumption—begins with a graphic illustration of the most salient features of the tables.

METHODOLOGY

The data are derived from reports from the major textile manufacturers of the world.

CONTENTS

Section 1: Spinning Machinery
Installed Capacities, 1992
Changes in Installed Capacities, 1982-1992
Tables: Installed Machinery and Its Utilization, 1992
Africa
The Americas
Asia and Oceania
Europe

Section 2: Weaving Machinery
Installed Capacities, 1992
Changes in Installed Capacities, 1982-1992
Tables: Installed Machinery and Its Utilization, 1992
Africa
The Americas
Asia and Oceania
Europe

Section 3: Raw Materials Consumption
Raw Materials Consumption, 1992
Changes in Raw Materials Consumption, 1982-1992
Tables: Raw Materials Consumption, 1992
Africa
The Americas
Asia and Oceania
Europe

WORLD COTTON TRADE

FACTS AT A GLANCE

Number of Pages: 89

Periodicity: Annual

Publisher: International Cotton Advisory Committee (ICAC)

PURPOSE AND SCOPE

World Cotton Trade is the most important source of data on cotton trade among members of the International Cotton Advisory Committee.

DATA ORGANIZATION

The preliminary chapter reviews developments during the year in world cotton trade, followed by data on global cotton exports and imports and trade by countries of origin and destination.

METHODOLOGY

The data are based on reports from ICAC member countries.

CONTENTS

CRIME

INTERNATIONAL CRIMINAL STATISTICS

FACTS AT A GLANCE

Number of Pages: 191

Periodicity: Biennial

Publisher: INTERPOL

PURPOSE AND SCOPE

INTERPOL has been publishing crime statistics since 1950. The purpose of this biennial publication is to present comparative tables of crime and criminal activity and police systems based on available data.

DATA ORGANIZATION

The statistics cover 91 countries only and they are listed in the French alphabetical order. In its usual multilingual format, data are presented in French, English, German, and Arabic. The decimal point is represented by a comma after the continental fashion.

METHODOLOGY

The INTERPOL Secretariat limits its work to reproducing the questionnaire forms mailed to the member countries. Reporting countries use their own definitions of offenses in filling these forms and sometimes adopt different methods of calculation. Some countries have an interest in underreporting crimes. There is also the problem that the percentage of unreported crimes varies from country to country.

CONTENTS

DEBT, EXTERNAL

EXTERNAL DEBT STATISTICS

FACTS AT A GLANCE

Number of Pages: 32

Periodicity: Annual

Publisher: Organization for Economic Cooperation and Development (OECD)

PURPOSE AND SCOPE

This annual review presents comprehensive statistics on the external debt of developing countries and territories, Central and Eastern Europe, and other non-OECD countries.

DATA ORGANIZATION

Section I contains notes and summary tables. Section II gives basic data on long-term debt and amortization payments for 151 countries and territories.

METHODOLOGY

The major sources of the data are the Creditor Reporting System operated by the OECD and the joint OECD-BIS Survey of Bank and Trade-Related Non-Bank External Claims with further information drawn from the Debtor Reporting System operated by the World Bank and the banking statistics of the International Monetary Fund.

CONTENTS

WORLD DEBT TABLES

FACTS AT A GLANCE

Number of Pages: 534

Periodicity: Annual

Publisher: World Bank

PURPOSE AND SCOPE

The *World Debt Tables* is the complete record of the Debt Reporting Service (DRS) maintained by the World Bank. It presents summaries of the amount of debt of each of the 129 developing countries, the repayments, interest payments, and current disbursements.

DATA ORGANIZATION

The *World Debt Tables* consists of two volumes. Volume I contains analysis and commentary on recent developments in international finance for developing countries, together with summary statistical tables on groups comprising 148 developing countries. Volume II contains statistical tables showing the external debt of the 129 countries reporting to the DRS. For the first time the tables include the countries of the former Soviet Bloc. Some of the tables are also presented as charts showing the relation between debt stock and its components, net flow, net resource flows, net transfers, and the relation between net resource flows and balance of payments.

METHODOLOGY

Several new features have been introduced in the current edition including:

All aggregate tables in Volume I present data on the external debt of all low- and middle-income countries, including 19 countries that do not report to the DRS.

Data on portfolio equity flows are included in aggregate net flows and net transfers in individual country data in Volume II and aggregate data in Volume I.

Arrears of principal and arrears of interest have been disaggregated to show amounts owed to official creditors and private creditors separately.

Two new sections have been introduced in the individual country data in Volume II and aggregate tables in Volume I. Section 6 provides information on the currency composition of the long-term debt, (i.e., whether they are in U.S. dollars, yen, francs, or

SDRs). Section 8 reconciles the stock and flow data on total external debt for each year beginning with 1988. It illustrates changes in stock due to five factors: net flow, net change in interest arrears, capitalization of interest, debt forgiveness, and cross-currency valuation effects.

CONTENTS

Part I. External Finance for Developing Countries

Summary
The Rise in Flows from Private Sources
The Stagnation in Flows to Low Income Countries
Debt Overhang for SILICs
Foreign Direct Investment: Fast Growth in the Services Sector

1. Financial Flows to Developing Countries: Developments and Issues

   Recent Developments
   Trends and Issues in Official Flows
   Trends and Issues in Private Financing

2. Developments and Trends in External Debt

   Debt Trends in 1992 and 1993
   Progress in Implementing Debt Strategies
   The Special Debt Problem of the SILICs

Part II. Special Features

3. Trends in Foreign Direct Investment for Developing Countries

   Global Pattern of Inward and Outward FDI
   Developments in Recipient Countries
   Sectoral and Industry Trends: The Growth of Services
   Sectoral and Industry Trends: The Growth of Services
   Regional Economic Integration and Prospects for FDI

Appendixes

1. Debt Burden Indicators and Country Classification
2. External Debt Restructuring: October 1992-September 1993
3. Debt Conversion Programs
4. Portfolio Investment in Developing Countries
5. The Evolution of the External Debt in the Former Soviet Union, 1992-93
6. World Bank and OECD Measures of Resource Flows: Reconciling the Differences

Part III. Summary Tables

Methodology

Sources and Definitions

Groups of Reporters

Non-DRS Economies

Summary Tables
  All Developing Countries
  Africa, South of the Sahara

East Asia and Pacific
Europe and Central Asia
Latin America and the Caribbean
North Africa and the Middle East
South Asia
Severely Indebted Low-Income Countries
Severely Indebted Middle-Income Countries
Moderately Indebted Low-Income Countries
Moderately Indebted Middle-Income Countries
Other Countries
Low-Income Countries
Middle-Income Countries
Eastern Europe and Former Soviet Union
Special Program of Assistance

DEVELOPMENT

DEVELOPMENT COOPERATION

FACTS AT A GLANCE

Number of Pages: 240

Periodicity: Annual

Publisher: Organization for Economic Cooperation and Development (OECD)

PURPOSE AND SCOPE

Development Cooperation is the annual report of the Development Assistance Committee (DAC), a group of developed donor nations administering aid programs for developing nations.

DATA ORGANIZATION

The data are organized in a complex system supported by tables, charts, and boxes. The 20 Annex tables deal with disbursements and composition of financial resources. Ten additional tables examine the official overseas development assistance (ODA) performance of DAC members, total disbursed debt, net resource flows, financial terms of ODA commitments, and ODA from non-OECD members. They are supported by seven charts. Six boxes explore aid in transition, strategic challenges to main developing regions, DAC work in progress in meeting those challenges, trends in resource flows, trends in the volume and allocation of ODA, and trends in DAC performance and policies. Part III consists of an independent statistical annex with 11 sections as follows:
  Section A: Basic Resource Flows
  Section B: Aid Performance by DAC Members
  Section C: Detailed Data on Financial Flows from
    DAC Countries
  Section D: Multilateral Aid
  Section E: Sectoral Allocation of ODA
  Section F: Terms and Conditions

Section G: Technical Cooperation
Section H: Geographical Distribution of ODA
Section I: Aid by Arab Donors
Section J: Key Reference Indicators for Developing Countries
Section K: Key Reference Indicators for DAC Countries

METHODOLOGY

The report incorporates a revised list of developing countries and an adjustment of the definition of ODA. The report also includes a report on financial flows to Eastern Europe and the new independent states of the former Soviet Union.

CONTENTS

Annex Tables

Table 1: Composition of Total Net Disbursements to CEECs/NIS and Multilateral Organizations in 1991-92
Table 2: Official Aid Disbursements to CEECs/NIS and Multilateral Organizations in 1990-92
Table 3: Composition of Official Aid Disbursements to CEECs/NIS in 1992
Table 4: Composition of Official Aid Disbursements to CEECs/NIS in 1991
Table 5: Bilateral Official Net Aid Disbursements to CEECs in 1992
Table 6: Bilateral Official Net Aid Disbursements to CEECs in 1991
Table 7: Bilateral Official Net Aid Disbursements to NIS in 1992
Table 8: Bilateral Official Net Aid Disbursements to NIS in 1991
Table 9: Composition of Other Official and Private Net Flows to CEECs/NIS in 1992
Table 10: Composition of Other Official and Private Net Flows to CEECs/NIS in 1991
Table 11: Other Official and Private Net Disbursements to CEECs in 1992
Table 12: Other Official and Private Net Disbursements to CEECs in 1991
Table 13: Other Official and Private Net Disbursements to NIS in 1992
Table 14: Other Official and Private Net Disbursements to NIS in 1991
Table 15: Total Net Official and Private Flows to CEECs/NIS and Multilateral Organizations in 1991-92
Table 16: Total Net Disbursements of Financial Resources to CEECs in 1992
Table 17: Total Net Disbursements of Financial Resources to CEECs in 1991
Table 18: Total Net Disbursements of Financial Resources to NIS in 1992
Table 19: Total Net Disbursements of Financial Resources to NIS in 1991
Table 20: Net Disbursements from Multilateral Organizations to CEECs/NIS in 1991-92

List of Tables, Charts, and Boxes

Tables

Table II-1: Projected Population Growth
Table IV-1: Total Net Resource Flows to Developing Countries
Table IV-2a: Total Disbursed Debt of Developing Countries During 1984-92 by Source and Terms of Lending
Table V-1: ODA Performance of DAC Countries, 1991 and 1992
Table V-2: Comparative ODA Performance of DAC Countries, 1981/82-1991/92
Table V-3: Regional Allocation of Aid
Table V-4: ODA by Income Groups, 1991
Table V-5: Financial Terms of ODA Commitments of DAC Members
Table V-6: ODA from Non-OECD Donors, Net Disbursements
Table V-7: Main Recipients of Arab Bilateral Aid

Charts

Chart IV-1: Structure of Main Categories of Resource Flows by Selected Regions
Chart IV-2: Total External Debt and Debt Service by Region, 1982-92
Chart IV-3: Total Disbursed Debt by Source and Terms of Lending, 1992
Chart IV-4: Number of Paris Club Agreements and Amounts of Developing Country Debt Rescheduled, 1956-92
Chart IV-5: Changes in Debt Service Ratios by Income Groups, 1982-91
Chart V-3: ODA Disbursements of United Nations Agencies
Chart V-4: Total Multilateral ODA Disbursements by Region
Chart V-5: Bilateral and Multilateral Disbursements by Income Group
Chart V-6: DAC Members' Net Multilateral ODA and Net ODA to LICs in 1990-91
Chart V-7: ODA from DAC Members and Multilateral Institutions to LLDCs and Low- and Middle-Income Countries
Chart V-8: Total Bilateral Tied Aid Commitments, 1989-91 Average

Boxes

I. Aid in Transition: Building Security in a Changed World

Aid to South Africa
The New DAC List of Aid Recipients

II. Strategic Challenges in Major Developing Regions

Sub-Saharan Africa
The Maghreb
The Middle East
Central Asian Republics
South Asia
South-East and East Asia
Indochina

THE LEAST DEVELOPED COUNTRIES: A STATISTICAL PROFILE

FACTS AT A GLANCE

Periodicity: Irregular

Publisher: United Nations (UN)

PURPOSE AND SCOPE

This work presents in one sheet, key indicators of development in the least developed countries as a group and individually.

DATA ORGANIZATION

The data are presented for 42 countries identified as "least developed" by the United Nations.

METHODOLOGY

All the data are taken from other publications of the UN system.

CONTENTS

Forty-two countries have been identified as "least developed" by the United Nations General Assembly. These countries are: Afghanistan, Bangladesh, Benin, Bhutan, Botswana, Burkina Faso, Burundi, Cape Verde, Central African Republic, Chad, Comoros, Djibouti, Equatorial Guinea, Ethiopia, Gambia, Guinea, Guinea-Bissau, Haiti, Kiribati, Lao People's Democratic Republic, Lesotho, Liberia, Malawi, Maldives, Mali, Mauritania, Mozambique, Myanmar, Nepal, Niger, Rwanda, Samoa, Sao Tome and Principe, Sierra Leone, Somalia, Sudan, Togo, Tuvalu, Uganda, United Republic of Tanzania, Vanuatu, and Yemen.

DISABILITY

DISABILITY STATISTICS COMPENDIUM

FACTS AT A GLANCE

Number of Pages: 350

Periodicity: Irregular

Publisher: United Nations (UN)

PURPOSE AND SCOPE

This unique work is the first international compendium of disability statistics. It is based on a microcomputer database called DISTAT, prepared in 1988 as mandated by the International Year of Disabled Persons (1981) and the World Programme of Action Concerning Disabled Persons (1982).

DATA ORGANIZATION

DISTAT contains detailed national data on 12 major topics regarding disabled persons including age, sex, residence, educational attainment, economic activity, marital status, household characteristics, causes of impairment, and special aids used. The original database covered 55 countries.

METHODOLOGY

As may be expected in a pioneering work, much of the data is fragmentary. There are few guidelines or recommendations on how to produce disability statistics, and hence the data are exploratory. Nevertheless, the compendium provides valuable information which may pave the way to a new edition with broader coverage and better data. The conceptual framework of the publication was supported by the World Health Organization and the UN Centre for Social Development and Humanitarian Affairs.

CONTENTS

I. Introduction
    A. United Nations Programme on Global Monitoring of Disablement
    B. General Socio-economic and Demographic Framework
    C. International Disability Statistics Database (DISTAT)

II. Overview

    A. Data Collection Strategies

    1. Three Types of Data Collection Programmes
      a. Population and Housing Censuses
      b. Sample Surveys
      c. Administrative Reporting Systems

    2. Identifying Disabled Persons: Screening Techniques
      a. Example of a Disability (D Code) Survey Screen
      b. Example of an Impairment Screen
    3. Survey Estimates of Disability
      a. Percentage of Disabled
      b. Choosing Between I Codes or D Codes for Identifying Disabled Groups
      c. Consequences of Screening Techniques

    B. Illustrative Examples

    1. Demographic Characteristics
      a. Population Aging and Disablement
      b. Geographical Area, Residence, and Disability
    2. Socio-economic Assessment of Disablement
      a. Educational Attainment and School Attendance
      b. Labour Force Participation and Employment Opportunities
      c. Marital Status and Family Formation; Living Arrangements
    5. Population, Disabled Persons, and Disabilities by Type of Impairment or Disability, and Prevalence Rate by Age, Sex, and Urban/Rural Residence
    6. Educational Characteristics of Disabled Persons, by Age, Sex, and Type of Impairment or Disability
    7. Employment Characteristics of Disabled Persons, by Age, Sex, and Type of Impairment or Disability
    8. Marital Status of Disabled Persons, by Age, Sex, and Type of Impairment or Disability
    9. Family Characteristics of Disabled Persons, by Age, Sex, and Type of Impairment or Disability
    10. Housing Characteristics of Disabled Persons, by Age, Sex, and Type of Impairment or Disability
    11. Causes of Impairments of Disabled Persons by Age, Sex, and Type of Impairment or Disability
    12. Aids Used for Reducing Disabilities of Disabled Persons, by Age, Sex, and Type of Impairment or Disability

Annexes

I. National References

II. Conditions of Use and Order Forms for the United Nations Disability Statistics Database on Microcomputer Diskettes (DISTAT)

List of Tables

    I.1 Topics Covered in National Publications and Reports Concerning Disability by Type of Data Collection Programme
    II.1 Percentage Disabled by Sex, Year, and Type of Data Collection Programme
    II.2 Population Surveyed and Disabled Persons by Age Group
    II.3 Geographical Disaggregation Available in Censuses and Surveys Covering Disabled Persons, Selected Countries and Areas

ECONOMICS

COUNTRY FORECASTS

FACTS AT A GLANCE

Number of Pages: 37

Periodicity: Quarterly

Publisher: Economist Intelligence Unit

PURPOSE AND SCOPE

Country Forecasts provides five-year macroeconomic
forecasts for the world's top 55 economies. Updated
quarterly, each report covers one country and provides detailed analysis based on common global
assumptions.

DATA ORGANIZATION

The time horizon of *Country Forecasts* is the immediate
future. It brings together the various elements of the
economic environment to present data-driven predictions. The predictions cover the economy, politics
and government, business, demographics, income,
inflation, finance, and trade. Historical and forecast
summaries are provided, and changes from base periods are highlighted.

METHODOLOGY

Country Forecasts are compiled by the Economist
Intelligence Unit and draw on the resources of The
Economist.

CONTENTS

Fact Sheet

Executive Summary

  Political Outlook
  Party Politics
  Political Reform
  Election Watch
  Foreign Relations

  Economic Forecast
  Forecast Summary
  Global Outlook
  Domestic Policy Outlook
  Economic Growth
  Wage and Price Inflation
  Financial Markets
  External Sector
  Ten-year Growth Outlook

  Demographic and Social Trends
  Demographic Trends
  Social Trends

  The Business Environment
  General Business Outlook
  Policy Towards Foreign Investment
  Foreign Trade and Exchange Controls
  Policy Towards Industry
  Taxes
  Infrastructure
  Environmental Issues

Data Sources and Definitions

  Tables
  Historical Summary
  Forecast Summary
  Historical Summary

  Real Percent Change
  GDP
  Private Consumption
  Government Consumption
  Gross Fixed Investment
  Exports of Goods and Services
  Imports of Goods and Services
  Change in Stocks (as percent of GDP)

  Population and Income
  GDP ($ billion)
  Population (million)
  GDP per Head ($)
  Real GDP per Head (percent change)

  Inflation (percent)
  Consumer Prices
  Monthly Earnings in Manufacturing

Financial Indicators
Exchange Rate
Y:$
Commercial Bank Prime Rate (year-end, percent)

External Trade ($ billion)
Merchandise Exports
Merchandise Imports
Trade Balance
Invisibles Credits
Invisibles Debits
Invisibles Balance
Net Transfer Payments
Current-account Balance

Memorandum Item

Current Account Balance (as percent of GDP)

Forecast Summary

Real Percent Change
GDP
Private Consumption
Government Consumption
Gross Fixed Investment
Exports of Goods and Services
Imports of Goods and Services
Change in Stocks (percent of GDP)

Population and Income
GDP ($ billion)
Population (million)
GDP per Head ($)
Real GDP per Head (percent change)

Inflation (percent)
Consumer Prices
Monthly Earnings in Manufacturing

Financial Indicators

Exchange Rate
Y:$
Commercial Bank Prime Rate (year-end, percent)

External Trade ($ billion)
Merchandise Exports
Merchandise Imports
Trade Balance
Invisibles Credits
Invisibles Debits
Invisibles Balance
Net Transfer Payments
Current Account Balance

Memorandum Item

Current Account Balance (as percent of GDP)

COUNTRY REPORTS

FACTS AT A GLANCE

Number of Pages: 33
Periodicity: Quarterly
Publisher: Economist Intelligence Unit

PURPOSE AND SCOPE

Country Reports monitor and analyze recent political and economic developments and give two-year outlooks for over 180 countries every quarter.

DATA ORGANIZATION

The primary focus of *Country Reports* is on the economy which is analyzed under nine sectoral headings: National Income, Industrial Production, Construction, Employment, Retail Trade, Wages and Prices, Money, Foreign Trade, and Exchange Holdings.

METHODOLOGY

Country Reports are prepared by the Economist Intelligence Unit and draw on the resources of The Economist.

CONTENTS

Quarterly Indicators of Economic Activity

National Income

GDP
Personal Consumption
Private Fixed Investment

Industrial Production

General

Manufacturing
Total
Durable
Non-durable
Mining
Utilities
New Orders, Net Total
Unfilled Orders

Inventories
Book Value
Manufacturing
Wholesale
Retail

Construction
Completed
Housing Starts, Private

Employment
Civil Employment
Manufacturing
Unemployment

Actual
Ratio

Retail Trade

Retail Sales
Total
Automotive Group
Apparel
Food
General Merchandise

Consumer Credit
Outstanding

Wages and Prices

Wages, Gross
Manufacturing

Consumer Prices
Change Year-on-Year

Producer Prices
General
Farm Products and Processed Foods
Industrial Goods

Share Prices, Common Stock

Money
M1 Change Year-on-Year
M2
M3

Discount Rate
NYFR Bank

Treasury Bond Rate
Long-term

Foreign Trade and Payments
Exports FAS
Imports CIF
Balance on Current Account

Exchange Holdings

Gold Reserves

Exchange Rate

Market Rate

THE COUNTRY RISK SERVICE

FACTS AT A GLANCE

Number of Pages: 17

Periodicity: Quarterly

Publisher: Economist Intelligence Unit

PURPOSE AND SCOPE

The purpose of *The Country Risk Service* (CRS) is to provide full, internationally comparable and regularly updated macroeconomic country risk analysis on 82 developing countries with external debt problems.

DATA ORGANIZATION

A report is written on one of the 82 CRS countries every three months. Of the four annual reports, two are main reports and two are update reports. A short subset of countries have only one main report and three updates because of the unavailability of data and/or lack of investment opportunities.

CRS Reports are published according to a standard format. The six monthly main reports are divided into three separate parts, including:

Summary and Country Risk Ratings. This is a resume of the current state of the country's foreign debt situation, key economic policies, and the main features of its political and economic climate. The first page includes credit risk ratings and a statistical summary of the external financial ratios. The second page contains a structural review.

Text and Short-term Forecasts. This section summarizes political and credit risks. The analysis is complemented by two-year projections for growth and inflation, external account, financing requirements, and external debt.

Data Supplement. This section provides a complete and up-to-date selection of the economic statistics used for country risk analysis and debt management.

METHODOLOGY

Whenever possible, estimates are made for unpublished data. These estimates are based on *The Economist's* own resources, movements in closely related trends, or information published by national or international bodies. Annual data are presented as a five-year run together with 10-year historical summaries. In the final table of the database, quarterly data are presented for the most recent six quarters. (Diskettes provide historical data for the past 11 years and 11 quarters for the quarterly series).

A subset of country reports are formatted slightly differently. These countries include the former Soviet Union and former Yugoslav republics.

CONTENTS

A. Summary and Country Risk Ratings

B. Text and Short-Term Forecasts

C. Data Supplement

Table B.1: Quarterly Indicators

Exchange Rate (per US$)
Average
End-Period

Domestic Indicators (percent pa)
Consumer Prices

Energy Indicators
Petroleum Production ('000 b/d)

Trade Balance ($ million)

Exports (f.o.b. $ million)

Imports (c.i.f. $ million)

Commercial Banks Foreign Assets ($ million)

Assets with BIS Reporting Banks ($ million)

Liabilities with BIS Reporting Banks ($ million)

Use of IMF Credit (net $ million)

Bank Loans ($ million)

Bond Issues ($ million)

Table B.2: Economic Structure

Nominal GDP ($ million)
Nominal GDP (Syrian pounds million)
Real GDP (1985 Syrian pounds million)

Real Sector (percent growth rates)
Demand: GDP
Private Consumption
Public Consumption
Gross Fixed Investment
Exports, Goods and Services
Imports, Goods and Services
Origin: Agriculture

Industry of Which: Manufacturing Services

Ratios (percent)
Agriculture/GDP
Industry/GDP
Services/GDP
Fixed Investment/GDP
Exports/GDP
Imports/GDP
Savings/Investment

Energy Indicators
Petroleum Production ('000 b/d)
Petroleum Reserves (m barrels)

Policy Indicators
Money Supply - M1 (percent pa)
Money Supply - M2 (percent pa)

Prices and Exchange Rates
Interest Rates (percent)
CPI (average percent pa)
Exchange Rate/US$ (average)
Exchange Rate/US$ (end-period)

Population (million)
Population Growth (percent pa)
Labor Force (million)
Per Capita GDP ($)

Table B.3: Foreign Payments ($ million)

Current-Account Balance
Merchandise Exports
Merchandise Imports

Trade Balance

Invisibles Inflows
Interest, Profits, and Dividends
Other Services

Invisibles Outflows
Interest, Profits, and Dividends of Which: Interest
Other Services

Net Public Transfers

Net Private Transfers

Principal Repayments

Financing Requirement
M and LT Debt Inflows
Net Direct Investment
Net Portfolio Investment (net of bonds)
Use of IMF Credit (net)
Increase in Interest Arrears (if any)
Other Capital Flows (net)
Change in Reserves

International Reserves
Foreign Reserves
Gold - National Valuation
Commercial Banks Foreign Assets

Ratios (percent)
Trade Balance/GDP
Exports/Imports
Current-Account Balance/GDP
Import Cover (months)

Memorandum Items
Export Credits (net)
Capital Flight (net)

Table B.4: External Debt ($ million)

Total Foreign Indebtedness
Public, Medium, and Long-Term
Private, Medium, and Long-Term
Short-Term
IMF
Interest Arrears
Principal Arrears
Memorandum Item: Export Credits

Official Creditors
Percent of Total Debt
Bilateral
Multilateral

Commercial Creditors
Percent of Total Debt

Debt Owed to BIS Banks
0-1 Year
1-2 Years
Over 2 Years

Total Debt/GDP (percent)

Total Debt/Exports (percent)

Debt per Capita ($)

Total Foreign Debt Service
Public Debt Service
Private Debt Service
Short Term Interest Payments
Debt Service/GDP (percent)

Total Interest Payments
Official Creditors
Commercial Creditors

Percentage of Total Debt Service

Percentage of GDP

Percentage of Exports

Principal Repayments
Official Creditors
Commercial Creditors

Effective Interest Rate (percent)
Effective Maturity (years)

Table B.5: External Trade

Total Exports (f.o.b $ million) of Which, Major
Exports:
Crude Petroleum
Cotton

Tourism Receipts ($ million)

Total Imports (c.i.f. $ million) of Which, Major
Imports:
Immediate Goods
Capital Goods
Consumer Goods

Volume and Prices
Export Volume of Goods (percent pa)
Import Volume of Goods (percent pa)
Export Prices (percent pa)
Import Prices (percent pa)
Terms of Trade (1985=100)

Table B.6: Trade Structure

Principal Export Markets (percent share)
USSR
France
Italy
Germany

Principal Import Suppliers (percent share)
France
Germany
Turkey
Italy

Major Exports (percent share)
Crude Petroleum
cotton

Major Imports (percent share)
Intermediate Goods
Capital Goods
Consumer Goods

HANDBOOK OF INTERNATIONAL ECONOMIC STATISTICS

FACTS AT A GLANCE

Number of Pages: 197

Periodicity: Annual

Publisher: Central Intelligence Agency (CIA)

PURPOSE AND SCOPE

The *Handbook* provides basic statistics for comparing worldwide economic performance, but focuses particularly on Russia, Eastern Europe, the Organization for Economic Cooperation and Development (OECD) member countries, and the newly industrializing countries.

DATA ORGANIZATION

In general, the data are for 1970, 1980, and for individual years from 1985 to 1992. Data have been adjusted to achieve some comparability. The edition under review is a transitional one, as the regional economic groupings have changed following the collapse of the Soviet Union. For most tables the major groupings are: OECD, Eastern Europe, and Other. The last group includes Organization of Petroleum Exporting Countries and newly industrializing countries of the Pacific Rim. New tables cover energy, environment, regional trade flows, and aid. A number of tables in the previous editions have been omitted.

METHODOLOGY

The methodology is explained in the footnotes. The base year for the average annual rate of growth is the year prior to the stated period. The data given for the most recent year is provisional and subject to revision. Where official data do not exist, the CIA makes estimates or draws on other published sources.

CONTENTS

I. Figure and Table Listing

II. Economic Profile

Gross domestic product per capita, 1992 (in 1992 U.S. dollars) Europe, China: special economic zones. World gross domestic product and population, 1992. Selected world statistics. Selected OECD countries: economic profile, 1992. Selected east European countries: economic profile, 1992. Newly industrializing economies: economic profile, 1992.

Selected countries: economic profile, 1992. Organization of petroleum exporting countries: economic profile, 1992.

III. Aggregate Trends

Selected OECD countries: real gross domestic product comparisons, 1973-92. Selected OECD countries: aggregate inflation trends, 1971-92. United States and selected countries: growth indicators. Estimated real gross domestic product. Real gross domestic product growth. Real gross domestic product per capita growth. Defense expenditures as a share of gross domestic product. Agricultural prices. World crude oil prices. Metal prices. Eastern Europe: debt, by source. Selected countries: economic indicators. Population. Labor force. Agricultural labor force. Agricultural labor force. Non-agricultural labor force. Industrial employment.

IV. OECD Country Trends

Selected OECD countries: percent change in value of currencies relative to the U.S. dollar. Selected OECD countries: government budget balance as a share of GDP, 1970-92. Big seven: comparative tax burden, 1990. United States, Germany, Japan: real long-term interest rates. Big seven: economic indicators. Selected OECD countries: comparative tax burden. Big seven: unemployment rates. Big seven: personal savings rates.

V. Independent Republics of the Former Soviet Union

Independent republics of the former Soviet Union. Independent republics of the former Soviet Union: economies at a glance. Independent republics of the former Soviet Union: economic, energy, and social indicators. Russia: selected economic indicators. Ukraine: selected economic indicators. Belarus: selected economic indicators. Moldova: selected economic indicators. Kazakhstan: selected economic indicators. Kyrgyzstan: selected economic indicators. Tajikistan: selected economic indicators. Turkmenistan: selected economic indicators. Uzbekistan: selected economic indicators. Armenia: selected economic indicators. Azerbaijan: selected economic indicators. Georgia: selected economic indicators. Estonia: selected economic indicators. Latvia: selected economic indicators. Lithuania: selected economic indicators.

VI. Energy

Selected OECD countries: measures of energy efficiency, 1975-91. Primary energy consumption. Primary energy production. Primary energy production, by type. Crude oil refining capacity. Oil consumption. Crude oil production. Major exporters of oil. Selected importers of oil. Imports of crude oil and refined products by the OECD countries, 1992. Oil revenues of selected exporters. Oil costs of selected importers. Natural gas production. Hard coal production. Brown coal and lignite production. Proved reserves of crude oil and natural gas. Electricity production. Selected countries: electricity generated, by type of fuel. Installed nuclear electricity generating capacity.

VII. Agriculture

Selected countries: food consumption as a share of total household expenditures. Grain yields. Total grain production. Soybean production. Wheat production. Coarse grain production. Rice production. Sugar production. Coffee production.

VIII. Mineral and Metals

Selected countries: iron ore production. Selected countries: bauxite production. Selected countries: pig iron production. Selected countries: crude steel production. Selected countries: rolled steel production. Selected countries: refined copper production. Selected countries: primary aluminum production. Selected countries: cobalt production. Selected countries: platinum-group metals production. Selected countries: gold production.

IX. Chemicals and Manufactured Goods

Selected countries: nitrogen fertilizer production, nutrient content. Selected countries: phosphate fertilizer production, nutrient content. Selected countries: potassium fertilizer production, nutrient content. Worldwide sales of data processing equipment and services, by region. Worldwide sales of telecommunications equipment and services, by region. Worldwide sales of semiconductors by U.S., Japanese, and west European firms. Machine tool production. Selected countries: installed industrial robots. Selected countries: installed robots per 10,000 persons in the manufacturing industry. Selected countries: passenger automobile production. Selected countries: truck and bus production.

X. Foreign Trade and Aid

Vulnerable single-commodity-dependent countries. Regional trade blocs in perspective. The scale of world trade within and between major regions, 1991. Regionalization of trade: nonfuel imports originating within region. Global trade flows: microelectronics and automobiles, 1992. Global trade flows: steel and textile/clothing, 1992. Global trade flows: grains and non-oil commodities, 1992. Big seven: direction of trade. Big seven: exports, by commodity. Big seven: imports, by commodity. United States: exports to other North American countries. United States: exports to Japan. United States: exports to western Europe. United States: exports to Latin America. United States: exports to east Asian rim and Oceania. United States: trade with China. United States: imports from China, 1992. United States: exports to China, 1992. United States: exports to south Asia. Japan: exports to North America. Japan: exports to western Europe. Japan: exports to Latin America. Japan: exports to east Asian rim and Oceania. Japan: exports to south Asia. European Community: exports to North America. European Community: exports to Japan. European Community: exports to other west European countries. European Community: exports to Latin America. European Community: exports to east Asian rim and Oceania. European Community: exports to south Asia. Newly industrializing economies: exports to North America. Newly industrializing economies: exports to North America. Newly industrializing economies: exports to Japan. Newly industrializing economies: exports to western Europe. Newly industrializing economies: exports to Latin America. Newly industrializing economies: exports to east Asia and Australia. Newly industrializing economies: exports to south Asia. Newly industrializing economies: trade with the big seven. Newly industrializing economies: trade with the United States. China: exports. China: imports. Cuba: exports. Cuba: imports. Share of global exports of high technology products. Worldwide market for data processing equipment, by region. Selected countries: exports of machine tools. Selected countries: imports of machine tools. Former Soviet Union: economic support from the international community, 1990-92. Economic support to the former Soviet Union, 1990-91. Former Soviet republics: outstanding aid pledged by the international community. Western countries: total economic aid to selected LDCs, by recipient. United States: economic aid commitments to selected LDCs, by recipient. United States: military deliveries to selected LDCs, by recipient.

XI. Environmental Topics

Selected greenhouse gas emissions by source, 1989. CFC emissions and consumption, 1989. Selected countries: comparison of public and private sector pollution-control expenditures. Major importers and exporters of unprocessed, processed, and finished wood products, 1990. Selected countries: wood exports as a share of total exports. Newly green countries: pollution-control standards. Moderately tough countries: pollution-control standards. Stringent countries: pollution-control standards. Operational soviet-designed nuclear power plants. Radiation hotspots resulting from the Chernobyl nuclear power plant accident. Selected developing countries: access to sanitation services and safe drinking water. Selected OECD countries: hazardous waste generation, trade and disposal. OECD: waste generated. Selected countries: land area, forested area, and average annual deforestation and reforestation. OECD countries: imports of tropical wood, 1990. Selected countries: plywood production. OECD countries: nitrogen oxide emissions. Carbon dioxide emissions. OECD countries: sulfur dioxide emissions. Selected countries: participation in major international environmental agreements. Selected OECD countries: government R&D expenditures for environmental protection, 1988-89. Selected countries: debt-for-nature swaps. Selected countries: paper production, consumption, and waste-paper recovery.

XII. Index and Conversion Factors

Index. Conversion factors. The GATT system: spectrum of country relationships. Regional trade arrangements: country affiliations, December 1992.

ANNUAL BULLETIN OF ELECTRIC ENERGY STATISTICS FOR EUROPE

FACTS AT A GLANCE

Number of Pages: 138

Periodicity: Annual

Publisher: United Nations

PURPOSE AND SCOPE

The purpose of the *Annual Bulletin of Electric Energy Statistics for Europe* is to provide basic data on developments and trends in the field of electric energy in European Union member states.

DATA ORGANIZATION

The data refer to the capacity of plants, production, consumption, supplies to consumers, consumption of fuels, and corresponding production of electricity, heat, trade, and international exchanges.

METHODOLOGY

This publication is purely statistical in character.

CONTENTS

Explanatory Notes

Graphs
1. Total Gross Consumption of Electric Energy in the World and ECE, 1960-1991
2. Average Per Capita Consumption of Electric Energy in the ECE Member Countries, 1980-1991
3. Share of Electric Energy in Final Energy Consumption in the ECE Member Countries, 1980-1991
4. Production of Electricity by Fuel in the ECE Member Countries, 1980-1991
5. Net Imports and Exports of Electric Energy in 1991
6. Exchanges of Electricity in 1991

Tables
1. Production, Imports, Exports, and Supplies to Consumers
2. Electricity Consumption
3. Maximum Net Electrical Capacity of Plants in Continuous Operation by Type
4. Net Maximum Electrical Capacity of Conventional Thermal Power Plants
5. Consumption of Fuels and Corresponding Production of Electricity and Heat
6. Imports and Exports of Electric Energy

Table Notes by Country

Annexes
  I. List of ECE Periodic Reviews in the Field of Electric Energy
  II. Definitions and General Notes

ELECTRIC POWER IN ASIA AND THE PACIFIC

FACTS AT A GLANCE

Number of Pages: 127

Periodicity: Biennial

Publisher: United Nations

PURPOSE AND SCOPE

This work provides data on electric power production, consumption, and trade in the Economic and Social Commission for Asia and the Pacific region.

DATA ORGANIZATION

Data are organized under 17 topical sections. Section 1 and 2 deal with installed generating capacity by ownership and by prime mover (hydro, steam, internal combustion, gas turbine, nuclear, geothermal, and new and renewable sources); Section 3, with major power plants of public electric utilities completed during the period under review; Sections 4 and 5, with voltages and frequencies; Section 6, with transmission systems completed during the period under review; Sections 7 and 8, with generation of electric power; Section 9, with fuel consumption; Section 10, with energy used and losses in transmission; Section 11, with electric power supply in relation to area and population; Section 12, with electric power demand by category of consumers; Section 13, with revenues and personnel; Section 14, with power development projects under construction; Section 15, with water power potentials; Section 16, with comparative electricity bills; and Section 17, with rural electrification.

METHODOLOGY

With the exception of Section 1, the format in this edition is unchanged from the last edition.

CONTENTS

Statistical Tables
  Public Electric Utilities and Self-generating Industries: Statistical Summary and Graphs for 1989 and 1990
  1. Installed Generating Capacity of Public Utilities and Self-generating Industries by Ownership, 1989-1990
  2. Installed Generating Capacity of Public Electric Utilities and Self-generating Industries by Ownership and Type of Prime Mover, 1989 and 1990
     a. Hydro (Generators Driven by Water-wheels)
     b. Steam (Generators Driven by Steam Engines and Turbines)
     c. Internal Combustion (Generators Driven by Diesel Engines, Gas Engines, etc.)
     d. Gas Turbine (Generators Driven by Gas Turbines)
     e. Nuclear (Generators Driven by Nuclear Power)
     f. Geothermal (Generators Driven by Geothermal Power)
     g. New and Renewable Sources of Energy (Generators Driven by New and Renewable Sources of Energy, excluding Hydro and Geothermal)
  3. Major Power Plants of Public Electric Utilities or their Extensions Completed During 1989 and 1990 (Installed Generating Capacity)
     a. Hydro Plants (Generators Driven by Water-wheels)
     b. Steam (Generators Driven by Steam Engines and Turbines)
     c. Internal Combustion (Generators Driven by Diesel Engines, Gas Engines, etc.)
     d. Gas Turbine (Generators Driven by Gas Turbines)
     e. Nuclear (Generators Driven by Nuclear Power)
     f. Geothermal (Generators Driven by Geothermal Power)
  4. Voltages and Frequencies Employed in Public Supply Systems, 1990
  5. Length and Voltage of Transmission, Subtransmission, and Distribution Lines, 1990
  6. Major Transmission Systems or Extensions Completed During 1989 and 1990
  7. Generation in Public Electric Utilities and Self-generating Industries by Ownership, 1986-1990
  8. Generation in Public Electric Utilities and Self-generating Industries by Ownership and Type of Plant, 1989 and 1990
     a. Hydro (Generators Driven by Water-wheels)
     b. Steam (Generators Driven by Steam Engines and Turbines)
     c. Internal Combustion (Generators Driven by Diesel Engines, Gas Engines, etc.)
     d. Gas Turbine (Generators Driven by Gas Turbines)
     e. Nuclear (Generators Driven by Nuclear Power)
     f. Geothermal (Generators Driven by Geothermal Power)
     g. New and Renewable Sources of Energy (Generators Driven by New and Renewable Sources of Energy, excluding Hydro and Geothermal)
  9. Fuel Consumption by Thermal Power Stations (Steam, Internal Combustion, and Gas Turbine) of Public Electric Utilities, 1989 and 1990

a. Steam

b. Internal Combustion Engines and Gas Turbines

10. Energy Used by Station Auxiliaries and Losses in Transmission and Distribution in Public Electric Utilities, 1989 and 1990

11. Electric Power Supply in Relation to Area and Population (Public Utilities plus Self-generating Industries)

12 a. Electric Power Demand by Category of Consumers, 1989 and 1990 (Number of Customers and Supply)

b. Details of Electric Power Demand by Category of Consumers

13. Revenue by Class of Service and Number of Employees of Public Electric Utilities, 1990

14. Power Development Projects under Construction and/or Consideration

15. Water Power Potential and Development, 1990

16. Comparative Electricity Bills, 1990

a. Domestic Consumers

b. Commercial Consumers

c. Industrial Consumers

17. Status of Rural Electrification at the End of 1990

Annex

List of Organizations and Authorities which Supplied Information to the ESCAP Secretariat for the Compilation of this Publication

EMPLOYMENT AND UNEMPLOYMENT

EMPLOYMENT AND UNEMPLOYMENT: AGGREGATES

FACTS AT A GLANCE

Number of Pages: 55

Periodicity: Annual

Publisher: European Communities

PURPOSE AND SCOPE

Employment and Unemployment Aggregates, formerly *Employment and Unemployment,* provides a comprehensive view of the labor market by presenting its main representative aggregates.

DATA ORGANIZATION

This edition is the first to be divided into three volumes: Volume I contains data on the active population, unemployment, and employment. Volume II contains data on employees by International Standard Industrial Classification, and Volume III contains data on working time and labor relations.

METHODOLOGY

The methodology used in preparing the data are outlined in *Employment Statistics: Methods and Definitions.* Readers are advised to consult the *Community Labor Force Survey* which harmonizes statistics produced at the national level.

CONTENTS

1. Selected Indicators

Global activity rates by sex (percent). Activity rates for the population aged 15 or over, by sex (percent). Proportion of women employed in each sector of economic activity (percent). Proportion of employees in each sector of economic activity (percent). Proportion of sectors of economic activity in total employment (percent).

2. Population and Active Population

Total population by sex (1000). Total active population by sex (1000). Civilian active population by sex (1000).

3. Employment

Total employment by sex (1000). Civilian employment by sex (1000). Total employment by sector of economic activity, males and females (1000). Total employment by sector of economic activity, females (1000). Employers, self-employed, and family workers by sex (1000). Employees by sex (1000). Employers, self-employed, and family workers by sector of economic activity, males and females (1000). Employers, self-employed, and family workers by sector of economic activity, females (1000). Employees by sector of economic activity, males and females (1000). Employees by sector of economic activity, females (1000). Unemployment rates by sex and age category, annual averages (percent). Unemployment by sex and age category, annual averages (1000). Unemployment by sex and age category at time of survey (1000). Unemployment of one or more years duration as a proportion of total unemployment by sex and age category at time of survey (percent). Unemployment of two or more years duration as a proportion of total unemployment by sex and age category at time of survey (percent). Persons registered at employment offices by sex and age category, annual averages (1000).

EMPLOYMENT OUTLOOK

FACTS AT A GLANCE

Number of Pages: 198

Periodicity: Annual

Publisher: Organization for Economic Cooperation and Development (OECD)

PURPOSE AND SCOPE

The *Employment Outlook* provides an annual assessment of labor market developments and prospects in OECD member countries.

DATA ORGANIZATION

The *Employment Outlook* consists of two parts. The first part contains an overall analysis of labor market trends and short-term forecasts. Part Two deals with key labor market issues and social policies and is accompanied by 65 tables. A Statistical Annex contains 21 special focus tables.

METHODOLOGY

The *Employment Outlook* is based on OECD labor market databases.

CONTENTS

Part One: Monitoring Labour Market Prospects and Developments

Part Two: Key Issues for Labour Market and Social Policies

List of Tables

ENERGY

ANNUAL BULLETIN OF GENERAL ENERGY STATISTICS FOR EUROPE

FACTS AT A GLANCE

Number of Pages: 189

Periodicity: Annual

Publisher: United Nations

PURPOSE AND SCOPE

The purpose of the *Annual Bulletin* is to provide basic data on the energy situation in European countries, Canada, and the United States.

DATA ORGANIZATION

The scope of the statistics comprises production of energy by form, overall energy balance sheets, and deliveries of petroleum products for domestic consumption. While fewer details are given for solid and gaseous fuels than in previous editions, more information is given for liquid fuels and nuclear, hydro-, and geothermal energy.

METHODOLOGY

Data in the *Bulletin* are compiled from responses to questionnaires prepared by the United Nations (UN) Economic Commission for Europe and supplemented by data from the UN Statistical Division, Statistical Office of the European Union.

CONTENTS

Explanatory Notes

Tables

I. Production of Energy by Form

1.   Solid Fuels
     Hard coal. Brown coal and lignite. Other primary solid fuels. Patent fuel. Coke-oven coke. Gas coke. Brown coal coke. Brown coal briquettes.

2.   Liquid Fuels
     Crude petroleum. Other inputs to petroleum refineries. Aviation and motor gasoline. Jet fuel. Kerosene. Naphthas. Gas (diesel) oil. Residual fuel oil. Other petroleum products.

3.   Gaseous Fuels
     Natural gas. LPG produced at crude petroleum and natural gas sources. Gasworks gas. Coke-oven gas. Blast furnace gas. Substitute natural gas. LPG, excluding that produced at crude petroleum and natural gas sources.

4a. Electric Energy—Gross Production
     Geothermal electric energy. Hydro-electric, excluding that resulting from pumping. Nuclear electric energy. Thermo-electric energy. Hydro-electric energy resulting from pumping. Electric energy produced by public power plants. Electric energy produced by self-producers.

4b. Electric Energy—Net Production
     Geothermal electric energy. Hydro-electric energy, excluding that resulting from pumping. Nuclear electric energy. Thermo-electric energy. Hydro-electric energy resulting from pumping. Electric energy produced by public power plants. Electric energy produced by self-producers.

5.   Steam and Hot Water
     From geothermal sources. From public thermal power plants for combined generation of electric energy and heat.

II. Overall Energy Balance Sheet

III. Deliveries of Petroleum Products for Inland Consumption

Annex

Definitions and General Notes

BP STATISTICAL REVIEW OF WORLD ENERGY

FACTS AT A GLANCE

Number of Pages: 37

Periodicity: Annual

Publisher: British Petroleum (BP)

PURPOSE AND SCOPE

The *BP Statistical Review of World Energy* is a data compendium on the primary forms of energy: oil, natural gas, coal, nuclear, and hydroelectric.

DATA ORGANIZATION

The summary tables deal with production, consumption, trade, reserves, prices, and refinery capacities and throughput for oil, natural gas, coal, nuclear, and hydro.

METHODOLOGY

British Petroleum is one of the seven sisters, or major international energy producers and distributors. It collects for its internal use an enormous mass of data on which the *Review* is based.

CONTENTS

Oil
Reserves
Production
Consumption
Regional Consumption - by Product Group
Crude Oil Prices
Refinery Capacities
Refinery Throughputs
Trade Movements

Natural Gas
Reserves
Production
Consumption
Trade Movements
Gas Prices

Coal
Reserves
Production
Consumption

Nuclear Energy
Consumption

Hydroelectricity
Consumption

Primary Energy
Consumption
Consumption - by Fuel
Fossil Fuel R/P Ratios
Energy Consumption Per Capita

ENERGY BALANCES AND ELECTRICITY PROFILES

FACTS AT A GLANCE

Number of Pages: 484

Periodicity: Irregular

Publisher: United Nations

PURPOSE AND SCOPE

The purpose of *Energy Balances and Electricity Profiles* is to present energy data for selected developing countries and areas in a format which shows the overall energy production, consumption, and conversion. The data are useful for assessing and analyzing production and consumption patterns on an internationally comparable basis. The work complements the *Energy Statistics Yearbook*, but focuses more on the demand structure of energy.

DATA ORGANIZATION

The level of detail disaggregates the energy sector and final demand, but covers the main sectors only because of the limitations in the quantity and quality of currently available information. The data accommodate the whole spectrum of national energy and are compatible with the existing balance formats set by the United Nations Regional Commissions.

METHODOLOGY

The book includes a section of charts for selected countries designed to graphically present the consumption patterns. The first group of charts (stacked bar charts) presents the final consumption data for the latest year for each country by sector (such as industry, transport, and household) and includes a breakdown of the consumption by component energy sources. The charts highlight the role of traditional fuels in many of these countries. The second group of pie charts illustrates electricity profiles. For each selected country, the first chart presents production by plant type and the second shows fuel input to thermal power plants.

CONTENTS

Introduction

Concepts and Definitions

Table Notes

Abbreviations and Symbols

Conversion Factors

Energy Balances (1987-1990)
Argentina
Bangladesh
Barbados
Bolivia
Brazil

Chile
Colombia
Costa Rica
Cote d'Ivoire
Cuba
Cyprus
Ecuador
Egypt
El Salvador
Fiji
Gabon
Honduras
Hong Kong
India
Indonesia
Israel
Jamaica
Jordan
Kenya
Korea, Republic of
Kuwait
Malawi
Malaysia
Morocco
Nepal
Nicaragua
Niger
Nigeria
Pakistan
Papua New Guinea
Peru
Philippines
Qatar
Singapore
Solomon Islands
Sri Lanka
Thailand
Trinidad and Tobago
Tunisia
Uruguay
Venezuela
Zambia
Zimbabwe

Electricity Profiles (1985-1990)
Algeria
Argentina
Bangladesh
Barbados
Belize
Benin
Bolivia
Botswana
Brazil
Brunei Darussalam
Burundi
Central African Republic
Chad
Chile
Colombia
Costa Rica
Cote d'Ivoire

Cuba
Cyprus
Dominican Republic
Equador
Egypt
El Salvador
Ethiopia
Fiji
French Guiana
Gabon
Ghana
Grenada
Guatemala
Haiti
Honduras
Hong Kong
India
Indonesia
Israel
Jamaica
Jordan
Kenya
Korea, Republic of
Kuwait
Madagascar
Malwi
Malaysia
Mali
Mauritius
Mexico
Morocco
Myanmar
Nepal
Nicaragua
Niger
Nigeria
Pakistan
Papua New Guinea
Philippines
Puerto Rico
Qatar
Rwanda
St. Pierre and Miquelon
Senegal
Seychelles
Singapore
Solomon Islands
South Africa Customs Union
Sri Lanka
Sudan
Thailand
Trinidad and Tobago
Tunisia
Uruguay
Venezuela
Zaire
Zambia
Zimbabwe

Graphs

ENERGY BALANCES OF OECD COUNTRIES

FACTS AT A GLANCE

Number of Pages: 216

Periodicity: Biennial

Publisher: Organization for Economic Cooperation and Development (OECD)

PURPOSE AND SCOPE

Energy Balances of OECD Countries contains current data on the supply and consumption of solid fuels, oil, gas, electricity, and heat as well as historical tables for 1991-1992, summarizing key energy and economic indicators.

DATA ORGANIZATION

The publication provides standardized energy balance sheets expressed in a common unit for each OECD country and for the following regions: OECD total, OECD North America, OECD Pacific, OECD Europe, and the European Community. The energy balance is a presentation of the basic supply and demand data for all fuels in a manner which shows the main fuels together in a common physical unit and also separately.

METHODOLOGY

The publication complements *Energy Statistics of OECD Countries*. The historical data is cumulated in *Energy Balances of OECD Countries, 1960-1979* and *Energy Balances of OECD Countries, 1980-89*.

CONTENTS

I.   **Introduction**

II. **Explanatory Notes**
     a. Unit
     b. Conversion from Original Unit to Toe
     c. Layout

III. **Conversion Factors**

IV. **Notes Relating to Individual Countries**

V.   **Geographical Coverage**

VI. **Energy Indicators and Energy Balance Sheets, 1991-1992**

ENERGY POLICIES OF OECD COUNTRIES

FACTS AT A GLANCE

Number of Pages: 528

Periodicity: Annual

Publisher: Organization for Economic Cooperation and Development (OECD)

PURPOSE AND SCOPE

The report reviews the energy policies of 23 OECD member countries and recent developments in the international energy scene, focusing particularly on demand, conservation, efficiency, supply, environment, technology, and research and development.

DATA ORGANIZATION

Member countries' energy policies are reviewed in depth on a three-year cycle. In the present edition, the in-depth reviews cover Australia, Belgium, New Zealand, Norway, and Turkey. The profiles of the other 18 members are updated from previous editions and summarized. There is a summary of the *World Energy Outlook to 2010*. The publication also contains a general report highlighting major developments in non-OECD countries.

METHODOLOGY

Annexes II and III provide specific energy data on government energy research and development budgets.

CONTENTS

Foreword

Part I: General Report on the 1992 Review of National Energy Policies of International Energy Agency (IEA) Countries

Executive Summary

I.   **Introduction**

II. **Energy Demand and Efficiency Developments**
     Energy Intensity
     Sectoral Developments
     Industry
     Residential/Commercial
     Transport
     Energy Efficiency Funding and Policy
     Funding
     Policy Developments
     Standards and Regulations
     Market Incentive Activities
     Information and Technology Transfer
     Pricing and Taxes
     Data and Evaluation Methods

III. **Energy, Production, Supply, and Distribution**
     Introduction
     Oil
     Natural Gas
     Coal and Other Solid Fuels
     Electricity
     Industry Structure and Regulations
     Regulation
     Trends in Generation Capacity
     Nuclear Power
     Hydroelectricity
     Non-Hydro Renewable Energy Sources
     Combined Heat and Power

IV. Energy and the Environment
International Cooperation
Global Environment
Global Climate Change
Other Policy Developments
Regional Progress
National Progress

V. Transport Energy Use and the Environment
Emission Standards
Fuel Quality
Fuel Economy
Fuel Switching

VI. Emergency Response Measures

VII. Technology, Research, and Development
Government Policies for Energy Technology and R&D
Government Expenditure on Energy R&D
Opportunities and Directions for Collaboration

VIII. Energy Developments in Non-OECD Countries
Former Soviet Union
Overview
Russia
Reforms in the Energy Sector
Energy Supply
Energy Demand
Energy Trade
Other Republics
Pipeline Developments
Foreign Assistance and Investment
Eastern Europe
Asia
Latin America
Middle East and Africa

IX. World Energy Outlook

Part II: The Country Reports
Introduction and List of Rapporteurs
Australia (In-Depth Review)
Austria
Belgium (In-Depth Review)
Canada
Denmark
Finland
France
Germany
Greece
Ireland
Italy
Japan
Luxembourg
Netherlands
New Zealand (In-Depth Review)
Norway (In-Depth Review)
Portugal
Spain
Sweden
Switzerland
Turkey (In-Depth Review)
United Kingdom
United States

Annex I: Communiqué of the Meeting of the Governing Board at Ministerial Level (including IEA Shared Goals)

Annex II: Key Indicator Tables and Energy Balances

Annex III: Government Energy R&D Budgets

Annex IV: Measurement of Financial Support for Coal Production Using a Producer Subsidy Equivalent Calculation (PSE)

Annex V: Glossary and List of Abbreviations

Annex VI: Footnotes to Country Energy Balances and Key Indicators

General Report: List of Tables and Figures

Tables
1. Public Sector Budgets for Improving End-Use Efficiency
2. Public Sector Activity for Improving End-Use Efficiency - Residential/Commercial/Industrial Sectors
3. Public Sector Activity for Improving End-Use Efficiency - Transport Sector
4. IEA Estimates of Total Producer Subsidy Equivalent (PSE) for Coal Production in Selected IEA Countries
5. IEA Member Countries' Participation in Implementing Agreements, 1992

Figures
1. TPES, TFC, GDP, and Energy Prices, OECD, 1980-1991
2. Energy Intensity, OECD, 1973-1991
3. TPES and TFC, by Energy Type, 1973 and 1991
4. Industrial Sector Energy Intensity, 1973-1991
5. Industrial Sector Consumption, by Energy Type, 1973 and 1991
6. Electricity Generation, by Fuel, OECD, 1960-2010
7. Development of Nuclear Capacity, 1960-2000
8. Nuclear Power in Electricity Generation, OECD, 1960-2005
9. Nuclear Intensity in Selected OECD Countries, 1991
10. OECD Energy Supply, GDP, and Emissions, 1970-1991
11. Effects of Stated OECD Policies on OECD CO2 Emission Forecasts
12. Energy Supply and GDP, Eastern Europe, 1988-1992

ENERGY STATISTICS OF OECD COUNTRIES

FACTS AT A GLANCE

Number of Pages: 230

Periodicity: Annual

Publisher: Organization for Economic Cooperation and Development (OECD)

PURPOSE AND SCOPE

Energy Statistics of OECD Countries is a compilation of energy supply and consumption data in original units for oil, coal, gas, and electricity.

DATA ORGANIZATION

The publication contains current data as well as historical data. Production is shown for other solid fuels such as wood, heat, and waste.

METHODOLOGY

Each issue includes definitions as well as explanatory notes on individual countries and sources of energy.

CONTENTS

I. Introduction

II. General Notes

III. Notes Regarding Each Source of Energy

IV. Notes Relating to Individual Countries

V. Geographical Coverage

VI. Annual Tables 1991-1992

VII. Summary Tables

VIII. Other Solid Fuels

IX. Heat

X. Electricity

ENERGY STATISTICS YEARBOOK

FACTS AT A GLANCE

Number of Pages: 492

Periodicity: Annual

Publisher: United Nations

PURPOSE AND SCOPE

The *Energy Statistics Yearbook* is the United Nations flagship publication on energy. It presents a comprehensive collection of statistics on the international energy situation in time series format. Its principal objective is to provide a global framework of comparable data on long-term trends in the supply of mainly commercial primary and secondary forms of energy.

DATA ORGANIZATION

Data for each type of fuel and aggregate data for the total mix of commercial fuels are shown for individual countries and areas and are summarized in regional and world totals. In addition to basic tables showing production, trade, stock changes, bunkers, and consumption, information is also provided on: principal importers and exporters of crude petroleum and natural gas; capacity of petroleum refineries, natural gas liquids, and electricity generating plants; and new and renewable sources of energy such as fuelwood, charcoal, bagasse, peat, solar, wind, tide wave, and geothermal.

METHODOLOGY

Data are compiled primarily from annual questionnaires. Where official data are not available or are inconsistent, estimates are made by the United Nations based on available information and analysis of current energy events. Cumulative data are available from 1950. Monthly and quarterly updates of the data may be found in the *Monthly Bulletin of Statistics*.

CONTENTS

I. Coal Equivalent Coefficients

II. Specific Gravities of Crude Petroleum

III. Specific Gravities of Petroleum Products

IV. Conversion Factors for Crude Petroleum and Petroleum Products

V. Heat Values of Gases

Commercial Energy - Production, Trade, and Consumption

1. Coal Equivalent
2. Oil Equivalent
3. Terajoules
4. Total Energy Requirement (Terajoules)

Solid Fuels

5. Production, Trade, and Consumption of Solids
6. Production, Trade, and Consumption of Hard Coal
7. International Trade of Hard Coal (Principal Importers and Exporters), 1991 and 1992
8. Production, Trade, and Consumption of Lignite
9. Production, Trade, and Consumption of Coke
10. Production, Trade, and Consumption of Hard Coal Briquettes
11. Production, Trade, and Consumption of Briquettes of Lignite and Peat
12. Production, Trade, and Consumption of Peat
13. Selected Series of Statistics on Fuelwood, Charcoal, and Bagasse

Liquid Fuels

14. Production, Trade, and Consumption of Crude Petroleum

15. International Trade of Crude Petroleum (Principal Importers and Exporters), 1991 and 1992
16. Refinery Distillation Capacity, Throughput, and Output
17. Production, Trade, and Consumption of Liquefied Petroleum Gas
18. Production, Trade, and Consumption of Aviation Gasoline
19. Production, Trade, and Consumption of Motor Gasoline
20. Production, Trade, and Consumption of Kerosene
21. Production, Trade, and Consumption of Jet Fuels
22. Production, Trade, and Consumption of Gas-diesel Oils
23. Production, Trade, and Consumption of Residual Fuel Oil
24. Production, Trade, and Consumption of Energy Petroleum Products
25. Production of Non-energy Products from Refineries - by Type
26. Production of Energy Products from Refineries - by Type
27. Capacity and Production of Natural Gas Liquid Plants - by Type

Gaseous Fuels

28. Production, Trade, and Consumption of Natural Gas
29. International Trade of Natural Gas (Principal Importers and Exporters), 1991 and 1992
30. Production of Other Gases - by Type
31. Production, Trade, and Consumption of Gases

Electricity and Heat

32. Net Installed Capacity of Electric Generating Plants - by Type
33. Utilization of Installed Electric Generating Capacity - by Type
34. Production of Electricity - by Type
35. Production, Trade, and Consumption of Electricity
36. Production of Heat

Nuclear Fuels

37. Production of Uranium (Uranium Content)

Energy Resources

38. Fossil Fuel, Nuclear, and Hydraulic Resources

Graphs

INTERNATIONAL ENERGY ANNUAL

FACTS AT A GLANCE

Number of Pages: 196

Periodicity: Annual

Publisher: Energy Information Administration (EIA)

PURPOSE AND SCOPE

The *International Energy Annual* presents an overview of key international energy topics, as well as current data and trends for production, consumption, imports, and exports of primary energy commodities in more than 100 countries and territories. Also included are prices for crude oil and petroleum products in selected countries. Renewable energy resources covered include hydroelectric power, geothermal power, and alcohol for fuel.

DATA ORGANIZATION

The *International Energy Annual* begins with an overview of international energy developments. The next two chapters deal with world primary energy production and consumption. Chapter 3 deals with petroleum; Chapter 4, with natural gas; Chapter 5, with coal; and Chapter 6, with electricity. The final chapter deals with world energy reserves. The text is backed by 48 tables.

METHODOLOGY

The data presented are largely derived from published sources and reports submitted by U.S. Embassy personnel in foreign posts. All data have been converted to units of measurement and thermal values used in the United States. For most industrialized countries, EIA obtains statistical data from official reports and documents as well as from secondary sources. These sources are cross checked against secondary sources from international organizations such as the United Nations, the International Energy Agency, the World Bank, and others. The EIA also uses industry reports, academic studies, and trade publications. Few developing countries regularly publish energy statistics. In such cases, EIA makes educated estimates by seeking expert opinions and reviewing available data and comparing them with data from related or comparable countries. In addition, the data are checked for reasonableness through the development of time series and supply and demand balances for primary fuels.

CONTENTS

1992 International Energy Developments

1. World Primary Energy Production
   Crude oil. Natural gas plant liquids. Dry natural gas. Coal. Hydroelectric power. Nuclear electric power. Key organizations.

2. World Primary Energy Consumption
   Petroleum. Natural gas. Coal. Hydroelectric power. Nuclear electric power. Key organizations.

3. World Petroleum Supply, Disposition, and Refining Capacity
   Oil production. Crude oil imports. Crude oil exports. Refinery production. Refined product imports. Refined product exports. Refined product consumption. OECD stocks. Refining capacity.

4. World Natural Gas Supply and Disposition
Gross production. Vented and flared. Reinjected. Dry gas production. Imports and consumption. Exports and production. Consumption.

5. World Coal Supply and Disposition
Production. Consumption. Imports. Exports.

6. World Electricity Supply, Consumption, and Capacity - by Type
Electricity supply. Consumption. Capacity. 1992 worldwide commercial nuclear power.

7. World Energy Reserves
Crude oil. Natural gas. Coal. Oil, natural gas, and coal reserve trends: qualifying reserve estimates; crude oil reserves; natural gas reserves; coal reserves.

Appendices

World primary energy production and consumption in British Thermal Units. World primary energy production and consumption in Joules. Primary energy sources by selected country groups. Production of crude oil, NGL, other liquids, and refinery gain. International energy prices. Conversions. Regions and organization. Energy chronology. Glossary.

Tables

INTERNATIONAL ENERGY OUTLOOK

FACTS AT A GLANCE

Number of Pages: 42

Periodicity: Annual

Publisher: Energy Information Administration (EIA)

PURPOSE AND SCOPE

The purpose of the *International Energy Outlook* is to assess the long-term outlook for international energy markets.

DATA ORGANIZATION

The report is the international counterpart of the survey of the U.S. energy market in *Annual Energy Outlook*. The projections in the *International Energy Outlook* extend to world oil prices for every year until 2010.

METHODOLOGY

Projections for the United States use the Intermediate Future Forecasting System. Projections of foreign oil production and consumption and prices of world oil were prepared using the Oil Market Simulation model. Assumptions about total energy requirements of projected economic growth and fuel shares making up the total are incorporated in the World Energy Projection System. Projections of foreign nuclear power consumption are based on EIA's World Nuclear Capacity and Fuel Cycle Requirements. Uncertainties associated with the assumptions used to create a base case projection are presented through a set of uncertainty ranges rather than alternative scenarios.

CONTENTS

Highlights

1. World Oil Market

Long-term price trends. World oil consumption. OPEC production. Energy vulnerability. Kuwaiti and Iraqi production. Non-OPEC production potential. Comparison of international oil projections.

2. World Energy Consumption

Energy intensity. Prospects for natural gas. Prospects for coal. Nuclear and other energy sources. Environmental considerations.

References

Appendix

Analytical Methods

Tables

Figures

ENGINEERING

STATISTICS ON WORLD TRADE IN ENGINEERING PRODUCTS

FACTS AT A GLANCE

Number of Pages: 570

Periodicity: Annual

Publisher: United Nations

PURPOSE AND SCOPE

The purpose of *Statistics of World Trade in Engineering Products* is to show the flow of engineering products in world trade. Data given in this edition cover the exports of 34 countries. The commodity breakdown is based on SITC Revision 3 which replaced Revision 2 used in the previous issues.

DATA ORGANIZATION

Engineering products are defined as including machinery and transport equipment; manufactures of metal, professional, scientific, and controlling instruments and apparatus; photographic apparatus and optical goods; and watches and clocks. The materials are divided into 82 commodity groups and cover 127 countries and 12 regions. For some countries and groups only totals are shown. For all countries, summary tables show total trade. Summary tables include data for countries for which a distribution by country of destination and/or region is not available. Table 7 includes exporting countries whose total exports of engineering products are over $30 million.

METHODOLOGY

Data are compiled from responses to questionnaires supplied by various countries, or from official national sources. The United Nations Economic Commission for Europe handled data from Eastern Europe and Russia and the United Nations Statistical Office processed other country data.

CONTENTS

1. Explanatory Notes
2. List of Countries included in the Statistical Tables
3. Names of Commodities included in the Statistical Tables for Countries Applying SITC, Rev. 3
4. Names of Commodities included in the Statistical Tables for Countries Applying SITC, Rev. 2

A. Tables

1. Total Exports of Engineering Products (Section 7) by Exporter
2. Total Trade of Engineering Products (Section 7) Between Geographical and/or Economic Regions
3. Total Trade of Engineering Products (Section 7) Between Countries in the EEC Region
4. Total Exports of Engineering Products (Section 7), by Region and Country of Destination
5a. Total Exports of Engineering Products, by Main Exporter and by Commodity Group (SITC, Rev. 3)
5b. Total Exports of Engineering Products, by Main Exporter and by Commodity Group (SITC, Rev. 2)
6a. Total Exports of Engineering Products of Main Exporters by Destination (SITC, Rev. 3)
6b. Total Exports of Engineering Products of Main Exporters by Destination (SITC, Rev. 2)
7. Exports of Engineering Products, by Region and Country of Destination
8. Exports of Manufactures of Metal n.e.s. (Division 69), by Region and Country of Destination
9. Exports of Professional, Scientific, and Controlling Instruments and Apparatus; Photographic Apparatus and Equipment; Optical Goods; Watches and Clocks (Division 87, Groups 881, 884, 885), by Region and Country of Destination

ENVIRONMENT

ENVIRONMENTAL INDICATORS

FACTS AT A GLANCE

Number of Pages: 77

Periodicity: Annual

Publisher: Organization for Economic Cooperation and Development (OECD)

PURPOSE AND SCOPE

Environmental Indicators focuses on sets of indicators integrating environmental and economic data, assessing and monitoring the state of the environment, and detecting changing conditions and trends. It is published with and supplements the OECD State of the Environment.

DATA ORGANIZATION

Environmental Indicators presents 18 strictly environmental indicators followed by seven key indicators on economics and population that impinge on the environment. Some indicators relate to environmental quality itself (river quality, nature protection, etc.), some to national environmental goals (controlling waste generation, etc.), and some to international environmental agreements and issues (greenhouse emissions, trade in forest products, etc.). It includes three types of indicator sets: (1) Those that measure environmental performance and quality and reveal basic trends in air and water quality and other factors affecting health and well being; (2) Sectoral indicators showing environmental efficiency and the linkages between economic policies and trends in key sectors and the environment; (3) Indicators on pioneering methods of environmental accounting at the macro level, particularly auditing natural resources.

METHODOLOGY

The work is based on the OECD SIREN database and the OECD environmental data compendia published since 1984. Data are generally shown in terms of volume, per unit of gross domestic product, and per capita.

CONTENTS

1. Introduction
   The demand for environmental indicators. The OECD response. The short term: a preliminary set of indicators. The medium-term perspectives.

2. Environmental Indicators
   CO_2 emissions. Greenhouse gas emissions. Sox emissions. Nox emissions. Use of water resources. River quality. Wastewater treatment. Land use changes. Protected areas. Use of nitrogenous fertilizers. Use of forest resources. Trade in tropical wood. Threatened species. Fish catches. Waste generation. Municipal waste. Industrial accidents. Public opinion. Growth of economic activity. Energy intensity. Energy supply. Industrial production. Transport trends. Private final consumption. Population.

3. Technical Annex

OECD ENVIRONMENTAL DATA

FACTS AT A GLANCE

Number of Pages: 324

Periodicity: Biennial

Publisher: Organization for Economic Cooperation and Development (OECD)

PURPOSE AND SCOPE

This compendium is a biennial OECD publication which has been regularly published since 1985. It presents the best available data on the environment. It is designed to help incorporate environmental concerns in decision making, promote sustainable development, and evaluate national environmental performances.

DATA ORGANIZATION

The publication relates data on pollution and natural resources to such areas of economic activity as energy, transport, industry, and agriculture. The data are organized from three perspectives including: the state of the environment (Sections 2 to 9); pressures upon it (Sections 10 to 13); and environmental management (Sections 14 and 15).

METHODOLOGY

The compendium supplements other OECD work on environmental indicators. The current edition has expanded data and geographical coverage.

CONTENTS

1. Introduction

Part I. The State of the Environment

2. Air
3. Inland Waters
4. Land
5. Forest
6. Wildlife
7. Waste
8. Risks
9. Noise

Part II. Pressures on the Environment

10. Energy
11. Transport
12. Industry
13. Agriculture

Part III. Managing the Environment

14. Responses
15. General Data

THE STATE OF THE ENVIRONMENT

FACTS AT A GLANCE

Number of Pages: 297

Periodicity: Annual

Publisher: Organization for Economic Cooperation and Development (OECD)

PURPOSE AND SCOPE

The State of the Environment reviews the state of the environment and assesses the progress achieved by OECD members in the past two decades. It also identifies the remaining problems concerning global atmospheric issues, air, inland waters, the marine environment, land, forest, wildlife, solid waste, and noise.

DATA ORGANIZATION

The report focuses on the state of the environment in OECD member countries, but it places analysis in the context of world economic and ecological interdependence. OECD countries represent only 16 percent of the world's population and 24 percent of its land area, but they represent 72 percent of gross global product (GGP), 78 percent of road vehicles, 50 percent of energy use, 76 percent of world trade, and they provide 95 percent of bilateral assistance.

METHODOLOGY

The report draws on OECD's environmental database and national environmental yearbooks, where available. The report received the support and cooperation of the OECD Environment Committee.

CONTENTS

List of Insets

Global Atmospheric Issues
Potential sea-level rise in relation to climate change: a Dutch case study (Netherlands). Saving atmospheric ozone: the Montreal protocol (Canada).

Air
Forecasting emissions to air (Norway). Her Majesty's Inspectorate of Pollution (United Kingdom). Controlling air pollution in Osaka (Japan). Air pollution and art (Italy).

Inland Waters
Reducing lead in drinking water (United States). Restoring the Mersey Basin (United Kingdom). Groundwater contamination and management in Prince Edward Island (Canada). Pollution and reclamation of Lake Orta (Italy).

Marine Environment
Controlling TBT anti-fouling paints (United Kingdom). Contaminants in the Arctic Ocean (Canada). Toxic algae blooms in the North Sea (Norway). Coastal zone management in Tasmania (Australia). Monitoring of coastal bathing water (France). The Venice Lagoon (Italy).

Land
Louisiana's vanishing coastal wetlands (United States). Acidification of soil and water (Sweden). radon in houses (United Kingdom). The landslide of Valtellina (Italy). Soil erosion and management: the Portuguese case (Portugal).

Forest
Preserving a unique Finnish forest: Seitseminen National Park (Finland). Decline in Canada's sugar maple stands (Canada). New Zealand's policy on indigenous forests (New Zealand). Forest management (Portugal).

Wild Life
The North American waterfowl management plan (Canada/United States). Japan's green census (Japan). Causes of plant species decline (Germany). Using seed banks to conserve biodiversity (United States).

Solid Waste
The PCB storage site fire at St. Basile Le Grand (Canada). Incinerator ash management (Japan).

Noise
Zurich: monitoring aircraft noise (Switzerland). Reducing noise from motor vehicles (Australia). Lille: noise abatement in public buildings (France).

Agriculture
Fur farming (Finland). Protecting environmentally sensitive areas (United Kingdom). Pesticide monitoring (United States). Over-fertilization and eutrophication (Netherlands).

Industry
OECD world related to accidents involving hazardous substances (OECD). Reducing hazardous waste generation with low-waste technologies (Germany).

Transport
Transport and the Los Angeles air quality maintenance plan (United States). International lorry traffic transit through austria (Austria).

Energy
Electricity production and district heating in Helsinki (Finland). The management of radioactive wastes (OECD).

Socio-Demographic Changes
Coastal population growth (United States).

Economic Responses
Environment-economic integration (Finland). The polluter pays principle (OECD). Environmental dimensions of the 1992 European Community internal market (European Commission).

International Responses
Information exchange related to the export of hazardous chemicals (OECD). International cooperation and the Rhine River (OECD). Trade in wildlife (IUCN). Swapping debt for conservation (OECD).

List of Figures

Introduction
Scope and framework of the report.

Global Atmospheric Issues
Trends in ozone concentrations. Greenhouse effect. Trends in man-made carbon dioxide emissions. Trends in carbon dioxide concentration. Changes in global surface temperature.

Air
Man-made emissions of air pollutants. Man-made emissions of air pollutants per unit of GDP. Trends in man-made sulfur oxide emissions. Trends in man-made nitrogen oxide emissions. Trends in sulphur dioxide concentrations.

Inland Waters
Water withdrawal. Trends in population served by waste water plants. Water quality of selected rivers. Marine Environment
Oil pollution of the seas. Catches of fish, crustaceans, and molluscs.

Land
State of land use. Major protected areas.

Forest
Wooded areas. Demand for selected forest products. Trade in forest industry products.

Wildlife
State of Wildlife.

Solid Waste
Municipal and industrial waste generated. Trends in municipal waste per capita.

Agriculture
Changes in agricultural energy use, farm machinery, manpower, and fertilizer use. Trends in irrigated areas. Application of nitrogenous fertilizers on arable land.

Industry
Trends in industrial production, volume index. Trends in industrial investment. Changes in industrial structure.

Transport
Structural changes in freight and in passenger traffic. Trends in road network length. Trends in road vehicle stocks. Trends in road traffic. Trends in energy consumption by road transport.

Energy
Changes in primary energy requirements, by source. Trends in indigenous energy production. Trends in energy requirements by unit of gdp. Electricity generate by primary energy source. Trends in emissions of selected air pollutants, G7 countries.

Socio-Demographic Changes
Population trends. Private final consumption expenditures. Trends in international tourism.

Economic Responses
Public Opinion: environment protection vs. Growth tradeoff.

List of Tables

Air
Health effects of selected toxic trace air pollutants, organic compounds. Health effects of selected toxic trace air pollutants, metals.

Inland Waters
Major floods and related losses. Trends in public water pollution expenditures.

Marine Environment
Pressures on the marine environment. Selected accidental oil spills, world. Aquaculture.

Land
Major natural disasters of geologic origin, OECD countries.

Forest
Commercial forests: growing stock and efficiency in usage of timber resources. Industrial roundwood balances.

Solid Waste
Recorded exports of hazardous wastes.

Agriculture
Selected environmental effects of agriculture. Agriculture and the environment: selected indicators.

Industry
Environmental effects of selected industrial sectors. Selected accidents involving hazardous substances.

Transport
Selected environmental effects of principal transport modes. Transport and the environment: selected indicators.

Energy
Selected environmental effects of the energy sector. Energy and the environment: selected indicators. Socio-Demographic Changes
Structure of households' consumption expenditures.

Economic Aspects
Pollution abatement and control (PAC) expenditures. Types of charge systems.

International Aspects
List of multilateral conventions. Public opinion on environmental problems.

I. The State of the Environment: Progress and Concerns

1. Global Atmospheric Issues

Stratospheric Ozone Depletion
Background. Global Ozone Trends. Antarctic Ozone Trends. Causes of the Antarctic Ozone Hole. Global Implications. Prediction of Ozone Depletion.

The Greenhouse Effect
The Greenhouse Gases. Global and Regional Climatic Changes. Greenhouse Gas Emissions. Projected Emissions and Temperature Changes. Observed Changes in Globally Averaged Temperature. Effects of Global Warming. Other Global Atmospheric Pollution. Conclusions.

2. Air

Local and Urban Air Pollution
Traditional Air Pollutants. Emissions of Traditional Pollutants. Ambient Concentration Levels of Traditional Pollutants. Expectations in the 1990s. Toxic Trace Pollutants. Assessment of Toxic Trace Pollutant Emissions. Risk of Human Exposure to Toxic Trace Pollutants. Recent Legislation and

Regulations to Limit Exposure to Toxic Air Pollutants and Future Outlook.

Large-Scale Air Pollution

Acid deposition of sulfates and nitrates. Photochemical smog pollution by ozone and nox. Deposition of heavy metals. International policies for combating transboundary air pollution—initiatives and achievements. Conclusions.

3. Inland Waters

Development of Water Resources

Water quantity. Floods and droughts.

Quality of water resources

domestic discharges. Industrial discharges. Diffuse discharges. State of surface waters. State of ground water.

Drinking Water

Sources and structure of distribution systems. Contaminants.

Water Management

Integration of water quality and water quantity management. Interaction among inland waters, oceans, land ,and air. Integration of environmental concerns into economic sectors. Conclusions.

4. Marine Environment

Pressures on the Marine Environment

Waste inputs to the oceans. Nutrients. Sewage. Oil. Synthetic organic compounds. Metals. Radionuclides. Persistent litter and debris. Environmental restructuring. Resource exploitation. Atmospheric change.

The State of the Marine Environment

The North Sea. The Baltic Sea. The Mediterranean Sea. Japan's Marine Environment. North America's marine environment.

Sustainable Use of Living Marine Resources: Fisheries and Aquaculture

Fisheries. Aquaculture. Conclusions.

5. Land

Soils

Natural roles. Soil loss and degradation. Interdependencies with other media.

Land Use

Land use and land cover patterns. Protected areas. Critical areas. Mining and extraction impacts.

Land Use and Natural Disasters

Earthquakes. volcanic eruptions. Landslides. Climatic and meteorological disasters. Land use and the management of natural disasters. Conclusions.

6. Forest

Forests as ecosystem. Different methods of forest exploitation. Economic uses of forests. Social role of forests.

Forest Resources in OECD Countries

Wooded areas. Growing stock and annual increment. Efficient use of forest resources.

Demand for Forest Products

Demand for Industrial roundwood. Supply of industrial roundwood. Industrial roundwood balances.

Environmental Effects of Forestry Management

Effects on the climate and atmosphere. Effects on the soil. Effects on water. Effects on the diversity of wild life. Effects on social uses. Conclusions.

External Pressures on the Forest Resources of OECD Countries

Atmospheric pollution. Climate change and the greenhouse effect. Forest fires. Plant diseases. Changes in land use.

Consequences for the Rest of the World

Trade in forest products. Tropical deforestation. Sustainable development in different regions.

Conclusions

7. Wildlife

Uses and Value of Wildlife

Biological diversity. Environmental value. Economic value. Cultural value.

Conditions and Trends

Wildlife populations. Protected areas. Land use trends and wildlife.

The Impact of Human Activities

Habitat modification. Excessive and illegal exploitation. Pollution and climate change. Species introduction.

Protection and Management

Integration of conservation and development. International cooperation. Conclusions.

8. Solid Waste Production

Municipal waste. Industrial waste. Specific waste.

Waste Disposal

Disposal of municipal waste. Disposal of industrial waste.

Transfrontier Movements of Waste

A reality that must be kept under control. West-east and north-south movements.

Old Landfill Sites

A plethora of "problem sites." The need to step up remedial action.

Recovery, Recycling, and Prevention

Recyclable waste. Recovery and recycling of municipal waste. Recovery and recycling of industrial waste. Towards preventing the generation of waste. Prevention through the use of "clean" technologies. Prevention through the manufacture of "clean" products. Conclusions.

9. Noise

The Effects of Noise
Effects on Health. Effects on Communication. Psychological Annoyance and Effects on Behavior. Noise Abatement Objectives.

The State of the Noise Environment Since the Early 1970s
Exposure to noise from surface and air transport. Main sources of traffic noise. Other sources of noise and neighborhood noise.

The Noise Environment in the 1990s
Noise from road transport. Noise from rail transport. Noise from air transport. New sources and sites of noise and new nuisances. Population and industrial trends, and multi-exposure to noise. Conclusions.

II. A Changing Economic Context

10. Agriculture

Agriculture-environment Relations

Changes in Agriculture: Trends and Prospects
Major changes in agriculture. Structural changes of environmental significance. Prospects.

Environmental Impacts of Agricultural Changes
Effects on soil. Effects on foodstuffs. Other effects of pesticides. Effects on water systems. Effects on flora and fauna. Effects on amenity and life quality. Impact of pollution from other sources on agriculture. Conclusions.

11. Industry

Industry-Environment Relations
Quantitative impact of industry on the environment. The increasing complexity of risks.

Changes in Industry: Trends and Prospects
Deindustrialization is only relative. A continuous and radical redeployment of structures. Development of worldwide industrial markets. Transition to a new technological system. Selective inclusion of environmental considerations in industrial strategy.

Environmental Impact of Industrial Change: Appraisal and Challenges
The consequences of old industrialization in declining regions. The ambivalence of technological progress: opportunities and risks for the environment of the future. Increasing complexity of risk management. Irreversible internationalization of industrial environment problems. Conclusions.

12. Transport

The Interface Between Transport and the Environment

Transport Trends of Environmental Significance
Importance of different transport modes. Transport infrastructures. Increasing motorization and mobility in road transport. Energy consumption by road transport. Emission control for motor vehicles. Conclusions.

13. Energy

Energy Changes: Trends and Projects
Growth in energy requirements and indigenous energy production. The contribution of environmental policies and of public awareness. Improvement in the energy intensity of economies. Structural changes in energy supplies. Development of electricity. Energy "markets."

Environmental Impacts: Appraisals and Challenges
Major achievements. Environmental issues. Future energy supply and demand. Future environmental and energy policies. Conclusions.

14. Socio-Demographic Changes

Socio-Demographic Changes: Trends and Prospects
Slower population growth. Aging of the population and changing household structure. Diverse trends in urban areas. Social values and attitudes. Prospects.

The Environmental Significance of Consumption and Tourism Activities
Consumption patterns: a new focus for environmental protection policies. Tourism: a need for sustainable development.Conclusions.

III. Managing the Environment: Towards Sustainability

15. Economic Responses

Measuring Benefits, Costs, and Economic Impacts of Environmental Policies
Environmental benefits. Environmental control costs. Indirect economic impacts.

Instruments of Environmental Policy
Economic Instruments. Regulatory Instruments.

Sustainable and Integrated Development
Sustainable development. Priority for sustainable development in the 1990s. Conclusions.

16. International Responses

Transfrontier pollution

Global Commons
Atmospheric issues. Marine environment. Outlook for international environmental law.

Trade and the Environment
Trade and environmental regulations. Trade and sustainable development. Broader economic aspects of international trade and the environment.

Aide and the Environment
The problems. Addressing the problems: 1970-1990. Agenda for the future. Conclusions.

Conclusions on the State of the Environment

The Environment Today

Progress. remaining problems. Atmospheric problems. Water. Waste. Noise. Land. Forests. Wildlife.

Towards Sustainable Development

A new challenge for environmental policies. Changes in substances of concern. Better integration within environmental policies. Adjusting economic structures. Industry. Transport. Energy. Agriculture. Forestry. Consumption and time-use patterns. The international context.

List of Members of the Group on the State of the Environment

WORLD RESOURCES

FACTS AT A GLANCE

Number of Pages: 400

Periodicity: Biennial

Publisher: Oxford University Press

PURPOSE AND SCOPE

The sixth edition of *World Resources* is designed to meet the critical need for accessible and accurate information on environment and development. Published by Oxford University Press, itt is a collaborative effort of the United Nations Environment Programme, the United Nations Development Programme, and the World Resources Institute.

DATA ORGANIZATION

The current edition has a special focus on people and the environment. Part I consists of three special chapters that highlight different aspects of people and the environment: natural resource consumption trends and their environmental consequences; the complex interaction between population growth and environmental degradation; and the role of women in sustainable development. Part II examines particular regions in more detail—in this case China and India. Part III reports on basic conditions and trends, key issues, major problems, and the efforts to resolve them, and recent developments in principal resource categories from agriculture to water. All data tables are found in this part. Among the special areas explored in the data sets are tropical forests, greenhouse gas emissions, air pollution in megacities, and climate change.

METHODOLOGY

New data sets include purchasing power parity rates, flow of trade between the north and south, status of the megacities, value of agricultural production, status of natural habitats, value of mineral reserves, large lakes, and budgets of international organizations. Historical data are cumulated in the World Resources Database which contains 20-year data on diskette.

CONTENTS

Part I. People and the Environment

Introduction to Part I

1. Natural Resource Consumption
2. Population and the Environment
3. Women and Sustainable Development

Part II. Regional Focus

4. China
5. India

Part III. Conditions and Trends

6. Food and Agriculture
7. Forests and Rangelands
8. Biodiversity
9. Energy
10. Water
11. Atmosphere and Climate
12. Industry
13. International Institutions
14. National and Local Policies and Institutions

Part IV. Data Tables

Introduction to Part IV

15. Basic Economic Indicators
15.1 Gross National and Domestic Product Estimates, 1980-91
15.2 Official Development Assistance and External Debt Indicators, 1979-91
15.3 Defense Expenditures, Military Personnel, and Refugees, 1985-92
15.4 World Commodity Indexes and Prices, 1975-92
15.5 International Trade Flows, 1965-90

16. Population and Human Development
16.1 Size and Growth of Population and Labor Force, 1950-2025
16.2 Trends in Births, Life Expectancy, Fertility, and Age Structure, 1970-95
16.3 Mortality and Nutrition, 1970-95
16.4 Access to Safe Drinking Water, Sanitation, and Health Services, 1972-90
16.5 Education and Child Health, 1970-91
16.6 World's Women, 1970-92

17. Land Cover and Settlements
17.1 Land Area and Use, 1979-91
17.2 Urban and Rural Populations, Transport, and Labor Force, 1965-95
17.3 Twenty-one Megacities

18. Food and Agriculture
18.1 Food and Agricultural Production, 1980-92
18.2 Agricultural Inputs, 1979-91
18.3 Livestock Populations and Grain Consumed as Feed, 1972-92
18.4 Food Trade and Aid, 1979-91
18.5 Agricultural Productivity, Research Personnel, and Expenditures, 1961-90

BASIC STATISTICS OF THE COMMUNITY

FACTS AT A GLANCE

Number of Pages: 397

Periodicity: Annual

Publisher: European Communities (EC)

PURPOSE AND SCOPE

Basic Statistics of the Community is one of the EC's most important publications, bringing together a wealth of statistics on all significant sectors of the European Union (EU) member countries.

DATA ORGANIZATION

Data are organized under eight macrosectors including:

Section 1: General Statistics

Section 2: Economy, National Accounts, Balance of Payments, and Finance

Section 3: Population and Social Conditions, including Labor, Education, Social Protection, Wages and Salaries, and Quality of Life

Section 4: Energy and Industry

Section 5: Agriculture, Forestry, and Fisheries

Section 6: Foreign Trade

Section 7: Services and Transport, including Tourism

Section 8: Environment

There is a statistical supplement on Liechtenstein.

METHODOLOGY

The data are derived from the Eurostat Data Bank based on reports received from EU member governments.

CONTENTS

1. General Statistics

Illustrations

1.1   Area, Population, Density per Square Kilometer, see Table 3.1
1.2   Gross Domestic Product per Head, Volume (PPS)
1.3   Volume Index of GDP per Head
1.4   Civilian Employment, see Table 3.17
1.5   Evolution of Unemployment Levels, see Table 3.21

HISTORICAL STATISTICS

FACTS AT A GLANCE

Number of Pages: 170

Periodicity: Annual

Publisher: Organization for Economic Cooperation and Development (OECD)

PURPOSE AND SCOPE

This annual publication accompanies the mid-year issue of the *OECD Economic Outlook* and contains the same kind of data in a time series format.

DATA ORGANIZATION

The data are intended to display the movements of certain major economic variables or, alternatively, the structure or composition of certain economic aggregates. There are two kinds of statistics in this arrangement—percentage rates of change and percentage ratios or shares. The format is designed to facilitate inter-country and inter-year comparisons with annual country data appearing in the rows of tables and longer time series data in the columns. Part III consists of a series of graphs illustrating the principal changes in OECD economies. The first shows how gross domestic product (GDP) growth in money terms is fueled by increases in the prices of goods and services rather than their volume. The second shows how the various components of government expenditure have tended to increase relative to GDP. The third shows the cyclical behavior of output and other aggregates. Annual percentage rates of change are given for a wide range of economic variables from population to GDP, labor force, and money supply. Annual rates of change are shown for individual years from 1976 to 1989 and also for a 30-year period from 1960.

Historical Statistics provides the background data against which to evaluate recent developments in the OECD economies described in *The Economic Outlook*—the two publications are complementary. In addition to time series data on rates of change for a number of variables, *Historical Statistics* gives percentage shares or ratios, such as the percentage of the population economically active, the percentage of the labor force unemployed, the percentage of GDP devoted to capital formation, the percentage of GDP originating in manufacturing, and so on. Averages are also given for these structural statistics for the entire period from 1967 to 1989. The benchmark data for 1989 are expressed in absolute terms. Examples are the first three tables on GDP at current prices, the fourth table on the labor force, and actual value of imports and exports in Section 12.

METHODOLOGY

Almost all the data in *Historical Statistics* are derived from the following regular OECD publications: *Labor Force Statistics* (annual and quarterly), *National Accounts* (annual), *Main Economic Indicators* (monthly), *Monthly Statistics of Foreign Trade, Foreign Trade by Commodities* (annual), and *Indicators of Industrial Activity* (quarterly).

CONTENTS

Introduction

I. Benchmark Data for 1989 and Exchange Rates, 1960-1989
National accounts in national currency. National accounts in U.S. dollars based on exchange rates. National accounts in U.S. dollars based on PPPs. Population and labor force. Exchange rates.

II. Analytical Tables
Growth of population and labor force. Structure of population and labor force. Growth of real GDP and productivity. Growth of real final expenditure. Industrial structure of GDP. Structure of final demand, government outlays, and saving. Profit shares. Price movements. Movements of wages and labor costs. Internal finance and interest rate. Foreign trade and official reserves. Value of foreign

trade by SITC section. Foreign trade by partner country group. Foreign trade by SITC sections.

III. Graphs
The evolution and cyclical behavior of OECD economies.

FERTILIZER

FERTILIZER YEARBOOK

FACTS AT A GLANCE
Number of Pages: 147

Periodicity: Annual

Publisher: Food and Agriculture Organization (FAO)

PURPOSE AND SCOPE
The *Fertilizer Yearbook* is an annual review of world production, trade, consumption, and prices of fertilizers.

DATA ORGANIZATION
The *Yearbook* presents 34 tables organized in five sections: Tables 1 through 6 make up Section I and present summary tables for nitrogenous, phosphate, and potash fertilizers. Tables 7 through 9 make up Section II and deal with rock phosphate; Tables 10 through 13 make up Section III and deal with ammonia; and Tables 14 through 29 make up Section IV and provide country-specific data on production, consumption, and exports. Tables 30 through 34 make up Section V and present data on prices.

METHODOLOGY
Data are derived from FAO data archives.

CONTENTS

I. Summary Tables
1. World Production, Trade, Consumption, and Available Supply of Fertilizers
2. Nitrogenous Fertilizers: Production, Trade, and Consumption by Economic Classes and Regions
3. Phosphate Fertilizers: Production, Trade, and Consumption by Economic Classes and Regions
4. Potash Fertilizers: Production, Trade, and Consumption by Economic Classes and Regions
5. Estimated Production of Technical Grade Potash
6. Potash Re-exports in the Form of Complex Fertilizers

II. Rock Phosphate
7. Production of Rock Phosphate
8. Imports of Rock Phosphate
9. Exports of Rock Phosphate

III. Ammonias and Phosphoric Acid
10. Imports of Ammonia
11. Exports of Ammonia
12. Imports of Phosphoric Acid
13. Exports of Phosphoric Acid

IV. Fertilizers by Country
14. Production of Nitrogenous Fertilizers
15. Imports of Nitrogenous Fertilizers
16. Exports of Nitrogenous Fertilizers
17. Consumption of Nitrogenous Fertilizers
18. Production of Phosphate Fertilizers
19. Imports of Phosphate Fertilizers
20. Exports of Phosphate Fertilizers
21. Consumption of Phosphate Fertilizers
22. Production of Potash Fertilizers
23. Imports of Potash Fertilizers
24. Exports of Potash Fertilizers
25. Consumption of Potash Fertilizers
26. Total Production of Nitrogenous, Phosphate, and Potash Fertilizers
27. Total Imports of Nitrogenous, Phosphate, and Potash Fertilizers
28. Total Exports of Nitrogenous, Phosphate, and Potash Fertilizers
29. Total Consumption of Nitrogenous, Phosphate, and Potash Fertilizers

V. Prices

Index Numbers of Prices
30. Index Numbers of Prices Received by Farmers for Crops and Prices Paid by Farmers for Fertilizers

Prices Paid by Farmers
31. Nitrogenous Fertilizers
32. Phosphate Fertilizers
33. Potash Fertilizers
34. Mixed and Complex Fertilizers

FINANCE

INTERNATIONAL FINANCIAL STATISTICS YEARBOOK

FACTS AT A GLANCE

Number of Pages: 772

Periodicity: Annual

Publisher: International Monetary Fund

PURPOSE AND SCOPE

The *International Financial Statistics Yearbook* (IFSY) is the standard authority on international and national financial transactions of all members of the International Monetary Fund. It cumulates the data appearing in the monthly *International Financial Statistics* (IFS). Historical financial statistics from 1948 are maintained in the IFS Economic Information System.

DATA ORGANIZATION

IFSY consists of country tables and world tables. The country tables show major economic aggregates, such as exchange rates, international liquidity, money and banking, interest rates, production, prices, international transactions, government accounts, and national accounts. World data in this edition cover 30 years from 1963 to 1992.

The principal elements of the country data are:

1. Exchange Rates expressed in U.S. dollars per national currency, and a single rate for Special Drawing Rights (SDR). The exchange rates are classified as official rate, market rate, and multiple rates.

2. Fund Accounts. Details of the members' positions in the Fund are presented in eight world tables and cover all transactions within the General Resources Account (GRA), Structural Adjustment Facility (SAF), Enhanced Structural Adjustment Facility (ESAF), and Trust Fund Loans.

3. International Liquidity shows the U.S. dollar value of monetary authorities' holdings of SDR, reserve position in the Fund, Foreign Exchange, the sum of the items, total reserves minus gold, and official holdings of gold in millions of fine troy ounces and U.S. dollars.

4. International Banking Statistics Based on Reports From International Banking Centers. These statistics are presented in eight tables: The first two tables summarize data on foreign accounts of financial institutions other than monetary authorities. The remaining six tables recast the available details of the deposit banks' external accounts plus accounts of monetary authorities with nonresident deposit banks. These eight tables present a comprehensive picture of international banking activity by residence of creditor or debtor. Two tables on crossborder interbank accounts report on the accounts of monetary authorities and deposit banks with nonresident banks. Two tables on international bank credit to nonbanks report on the claims of deposit banks on nonresident nonbanks, and two tables on the international bank deposits of nonbanks report on the liabilities of deposit banks to nonresident nonbanks.

5. Money and Banking. Sections 10 through 50 of the country pages give statistics on money and banking. The Banking Survey consolidates monetary authorities and other banking institutions and provides a broad measure of monetary liabilities, generally called M3. For a few countries additional data are given on nonbank financial

institutions such as insurance companies and pension funds.

6. Interest Rates. The country pages report up to five groups of interest rates. The Discount Rate or the Bank Rate (the rate at which monetary authorities lend or discount eligible paper for deposit money banks); short term Money Market Rate, also known as the Treasury Bill Rate; Bank Deposit Rate, governing time and savings accounts and certificates of deposit; Bank Lending Rate, governing business loans; and Government Bond Yields. A subsidiary table gives international interest rates comprising the London interbank rate on deposits denominated in SDRs, U.S. dollars, French francs, German Deutschemarks, Japanese yen, and Swiss francs and Paris interbank rate for deposits denominated in pounds sterling.

7. Prices, Wages, Production, and Employment statistics are given in lines 62 through 67.

8. International Transactions are given in lines 70 through 79. They cover values, volumes, and unit values of external trade, prices for exports and imports, and balance of payment.

9. Government Finances are given in Section 80. They cover consolidated central government operations.

10. National Accounts. The summary data for national accounts reported in Section 90 are compiled in accordance with the United Nations System of National Accounts (SNA).

11. World Tables bring these country data together. Also included are series on wholesale prices and unit values of principal world trade commodities.

METHODOLOGY

Sections 1 through 10 provide general information on methodologies used in the compilation of data. Sections 11 through 16 deal with computational and presentational issues such as the calculation of area and world aggregates, charts, codes, symbols, and abbreviations. The individual country pages have notes on deviations from standard methodologies and discontinuities in the data. Arithmetic means are used for unit values of exports and imports and are reported in U.S. dollars. Geometric means are used for money and consumer prices and are reported in national currencies.

CONTENTS

1. **Exchange Rates and Exchange Rate Arrangements**
2. **Fund Accounts**
3. **International Liquidity**
4. **International Banking**
   Eight World Tables

5. **Money and Banking**
   Banking Survey
   Nonbank Financial Institutions
6. **Interest Rates**
   World Table on International Interest Rates
7. **Prices, Wages, Production, and Employment**
8. **International Transactions**
9. **Government Finance**
10. **National Accounts and Population**
11. **World Tables**
   Area and World Indices
   Individual World Tables Described
   International Reserves
   Deposit Banks' Foreign Assets
   Deposit Banks' Foreign Liabilities
   Cross-Border Interbank Accounts (two tables)
   Cross-Broder Bank Credit to Nonbanks (two tables)
   Cross-Border Bank Deposits of Nonbanks (two tables)
   Reserve Money, Money, and Money plus Quasi-Money
   Ratio of Reserve Money to Money plus Quasi-Money
   Income Velocity of Money plus Quasi-Money
   Real Effective Exchange Rate Indices
   Industrial Production
   Wages
   Employment
   Wholesale Prices and Consumer Prices
   Exports and Import
   c.i.f./f.o.b. Factor
   Export Unit Values and Import Unit Values
   Terms of Trade
   Balance of Payments
   Government Finance
   GDP (or GNP) Deflator
   Consumption as Percent of GDP (or GNP)
   Investment as Percent of GDP (or GNP)
   Commodity Prices

FISHERIES

FAO FISHERY STATISTICS YEARBOOK: CATCHES AND LANDINGS

FACTS AT A GLANCE

Number of Pages: 639

Periodicity: Annual

Publisher: Food and Agriculture Organization (FAO)

PURPOSE AND SCOPE

This book presents annual global statistics on nominal catches of fish, crustaceans, molluscs, and other aquatic animals by types and classes of fishing vessels operating in inland fresh water, brackish, inshore, offshore, and high sea fishing areas.

DATA ORGANIZATION

Data are organized under 5 sections.

METHODOLOGY

The data are derived from FAO archives and reports from national fishery authorities.

CONTENTS

FAO FISHERY STATISTICS YEARBOOK: COMMODITIES

FACTS AT A GLANCE

Number of Pages: 396

Periodicity: Annual

Publisher: Food and Agriculture Organization (FAO)

PURPOSE AND SCOPE

The *FAO Fishery Statistics Yearbook* presents annual and global statistics on the production and international trade in fishery commodities.

DATA ORGANIZATION

The data are organized globally and by type of fishery product. Global summaries present world catch, imports and exports, international trade by principal exports, and importers by seven fishery commodity groups. The remaining tables provide data on the various fish commodity groups by countries and methods of preparation (salted, dried, frozen, etc.).

METHODOLOGY

Food balance sheets for fish and fishery products have been updated with provisional data. A table of exports and imports by country and by seven fishery commodity groups has been reintroduced.

CONTENTS

E1.   Production, by Countries or Areas and by Products
E1-1. Fish Products and Preparations, whether or not in Airtight Containers: Production, by Countries or Areas
E1-2. Salmons Canned
E1-3. Herrings, Sardines, Anchovies, etc., Canned
E1-4. Tunas, Bonitos, Billfishes, etc., Canned
E1-5. Miscellaneous Fish Products, Canned
E1-6. Fish Products in Airtight Containers
E1-7. Fish Preparations, not in Airtight Containers
E2.   Imports and Exports, by Countries or Areas
E2-1. Fish Products and Preparations, whether or not in Airtight Containers

F.   Crustacean and Mollusc Products and Preparation, whether or not in Airtight Containers
F1.   Production by Countries or Areas and by Products
F1-1. Crustacean and Mollusc Products and Preparations, whether or not in Airtight Containers: Production, by Countries or Areas
F1-2. Crustacean Products, Canned
F1-3. Mollusc Products, Canned
F1-4. Crustaceans and Mollusc, Prepared for Preserved, n.e.I.
F1-5. Crustacean and Molluscs Preparations, not in Airtight Containers
F2.   Imports and Exports, by Countries or Areas
F2-1. Crustacean and Mollusc Products and Preparations, whether or not in Airtight Containers

G.   Oils and Fats, Crude or Refined, of Aquatic Animal Origin
G1.   Production, by Countries or Areas and by Products
G1-1. Oils and Fats, Crude or Refined, of Aquatic Animal Origin: Production, by Countries or Areas
G1-2. Fish Liver Oils
G1-3. Fish Oils and Fats (other than Fish Liver Oils)
G1-4. Oils and Fats of Marine Mammals
G1-5. Oils and Fats of Aquatic Animals, n.e.i.
G2.   Imports and Exports, by Countries or Areas
G2-1. Oils and Fats, Crude or Refined, of Aquatic Animal Origin

H.   Meals, Solubles, and Similar Animal Feedingstuffs, of Aquatic Animal Origin
H1.   Production, by Countries or Areas and by Products
H1-1. Meals, Solubles, and Similar Animal Feedingstuffs, of Aquatic Animal Origin: Production, by Countries or Areas
H1-2. Fish Meals from 'White Fish' ('Ground Fish')
H1-3. Fish Meals from Oily Fish

H1-4. Miscellaneous Meals of Aquatic Animal Origin
H1-5. Solubles from Fish and Marine Mammals
H2.   Imports and Exports, by Countries or Areas
H2-1. Meals, Solubles, and Similar Animal Feedingstuffs, of Aquatic Animal Origin

I.   Fish and Fishery Products - Provisional Food Balance Sheets

J.   Appendix

Selected Fishery Commodities: Imports and Exports, by Countries or Areas

Notes

Notes on Individual Countries or Areas

REVIEW OF FISHERIES IN OECD MEMBER COUNTRIES

FACTS AT A GLANCE

Number of Pages: 360

Periodicity: Annual

Publisher: Organization for Economic Cooperation and Development (OECD)

PURPOSE AND SCOPE

The annual review of the OECD Committee for Fisheries describes major developments affecting the commercial fisheries of the OECD countries, including production, processing, marketing, and international trade.

DATA ORGANIZATION

Data are organized in 215 tables.

METHODOLOGY

The annual follows the same format as in previous editions except for a special survey on Poland.

CONTENTS

General Survey

Tables to General Survey

STATISTICAL BULLETIN (TUNA)

FACTS AT A GLANCE

Number of Pages: 184

Periodicity: Annual

Publisher: International Commission for the Conservation of Atlantic Tuna

PURPOSE AND SCOPE

The *Statistical Bulletin* is the statistical record of tuna fishing in the Atlantic and the Mediterranean.

DATA ORGANIZATION

The volume is divided into five parts: The first part presents total catches by species and by country. Part II presents data on catches by species, subdivided by fishery gear, area, and country. Part III presents data on number of fishing boats by type, size, country, and year. Part IV presents detailed data on landings by country. Part V presents data on billfish catches.

METHODOLOGY

Some of the data are the best estimates of scientists. They are supplemented by data collected directly from fleets at the landing ports and also by data supplied by the Fishery Information, Data, and Statistics Service of the Food and Agriculture Organization.

CONTENTS

Part I. Cumulative Tuna Catch, By Ocean and by Country/Total
By Ocean
By Country

Part II. Atlantic and Mediterranean Cumulative Tuna Catch by Species, by Fishery (Gear), by Area and Fishery, and by Country/Total
BFT
SBF
YFT
ALB
BET
BLF
LTA
SKJ
BON
FRI
BOP
WAH
SSM
KGM
SAI
BLM
BUM
WHM
SWO
SPF
BIL
KGX
MAW
CER
BLT
BRS
OTH

Part III. Fishing Power
By Year
By Country

Part IV. Statistics by Country

Part V. Atlantic Billfish Catched, by Species, Region, Country, and Fishery
SAI
BUM
WHM
SPF
BIL

FOREIGN AID

GEOGRAPHICAL DISTRIBUTION OF FINANCIAL FLOWS TO DEVELOPING COUNTRIES

FACTS AT A GLANCE

Number of Pages: 340

Periodicity: Annual

Publisher: Organization for Economic Cooperation and Development (OECD)

PURPOSE AND SCOPE

The *Geographical Distribution of Financial Flows to Developing Countries* is the latest in a series presenting the volume and sources of external financial resources provided to individual developing countries and territories. The data show the transactions of each recipient country with Development Assistance Committee (DAC) member countries, multilateral agencies, and OPEC members. DAC members are Australia, Austria, Belgium, Canada, Denmark, Finland, France, Germany, Ireland, Italy, Japan, Luxembourg, the Netherlands, New Zealand, Norway, Portugal, Spain, Sweden, Switzerland, the United Kingdom, and the United States. Financial flows from Arab countries are shown as a combined total for Algeria, Iraq, Kuwait, Libya, Qatar, Saudi Arabia, and the United Arab Emirates.

DATA ORGANIZATION

The report consists of two sections:

Section A
This section contains eight tables covering the period 1986 to 1992. They show the receipts of each developing country or territory.

Two tables show the receipts of each developing country of net disbursements of concessional assistance ("multilateral ODA") and total net disbursements from multilateral agencies combined. Each table in this section contains a recapitulation of the resource receipts of selected developing country groups. These data are also illustrated graphically.

Section B

The tables in this section treat each developing country individually showing its resource receipts by type. Commitments by CEEC countries are shown under "Other Aggregates." These tables are followed by tables of identical format showing the same information for groups of developing countries. Population and GNP per capita data can be found at the end of each table.

METHODOLOGY

Reported totals usually include unallocated components which include administrative costs and research costs incurred in the donor country on behalf of the recipients. The totals do not reflect confidential financial flows where the identity of the donor or partner country is not revealed. Unallocated amounts are too small to be significant in the case of transactions by DAC members and multilateral organizations, but they are significant in the case of concessional flows from Arab donor countries, where the data do not account for vast amounts of ODF going for the propagation of Islam, the promotion of terrorism, and other causes. Some distortions also occur in reports from donor countries when investment flows are not allocated by country but only reported as regional and global totals.

CONTENTS

Section A

Basic Summary Tables
Official Development Assistance (ODA)
Net Disbursements
Net Disbursements of ODA by DAC Countries Combined, to Individual Recipients, 1986 to 1992.
Net Disbursements of ODA from All Sources Combined, to Individual Recipients, 1986 to 1992.

Flows from Multilateral Agencies
Net Disbursements
Net Disbursements of Concessional Assistance by Multilateral Agencies Combined, to Individual Recipients, 1986 to 1992
Total Net Disbursements from Multilateral Agencies Combined, to Individual Recipients1986 to 1992

Total Resource Flows
Net Disbursements
Total Net Disbursements of Financial Flows by DAC Countries Combined, to Individual Recipients, 1986 to 1992

Total Net Disbursements of Financial Flows from All Sources Combined, to Individual Recipients, 1986 to 1992

Official Development Assistance (ODA)
Commitments
Commitments of ODA by DAC Countries Combined, to Individual Recipients, 1986 to 1992
Commitments of ODA from All Sources Combined, to Individual Recipients, 1986 to 1992

Section B

Detailed Tables for Individual Recipients by Origin of Resources

1. Total Receipts Net (6 + Private)
2. ODA Loans Gross
3. Total Official Gross (7 + 9)
4. Total ODA Net (5 + 8)
5. ODA Loans Net
6. Total Official Net (4 + 12)
7. Total ODA Gross (2 + 8)
8. Grants (including 11)
9. Total OOF Gross
10. ODA Commitments
11. Technical Cooperation Grant Disbursements (included in 8)
12. Total OOF Net
13. ODF Commitments by Purpose PERCENT
14. Grant Element of ODA PERCENT
15. Other Aggregates (including private)

FORESTS

FORESTRY STATISTICS

FACTS AT A GLANCE

Number of Pages: 117

Periodicity: Irregular

Publisher: European Communities

PURPOSE AND SCOPE

The purpose of *Forestry Statistics* is to provide basic data on forests and forestry in the European Union.

DATA ORGANIZATION

The volume focuses on area, ownership, tree species, wood production, raw wood balances, trade in wood products and raw wood, wood consumption, and forest fires.

METHODOLOGY

Data are based on Eurostat data archives and reports from national forestry organizations in member countries.

CONTENTS

YEARBOOK OF FOREST PRODUCTS

FACTS AT A GLANCE

Number of Pages: 335

Periodicity: Annual

Publisher: Food and Agriculture Organization (FAO)

PURPOSE AND SCOPE

The *Yearbook of Forest Products* contains annual data on the production and trade of forest products and the direction of trade.

DATA ORGANIZATION

The tables are arranged in three parts: Part I deals with the volume of production and the volume and value of trade. Part II deals with the direction of trade. Part III shows unit values in trade for some commodities obtained by dividing total value by total volume traded. The tables in the first part present data for 12 years from 1980. The tables for each commodity are presented in sequence.

METHODOLOGY

Because the commodity subdivisions for production and for trade statistics differ, not all commodities carry both production and trade data. In general, tables for roundwood are followed by those for sawnwood, panel products, pulp, and paper, in that order. The direction of trade statistics shown in the second part are based on export data.

CONTENTS

Production and Trade

Roundwood
Production
Imports, quantity
Imports, value
Exports, quantity
Exports, value

Roundwood (C)
Production
Roundwood (NC)
Production

Fuelwood + Charcoal
Production
Imports, quantity
Imports, value
Exports, quantity
Exports, value

Fuelwood (C)
Production

Fuelwood (NC)
Production

Fuelwood
Imports, quantity
Imports, value
Exports, quantity
Exports, value

Charcoal
Production
Imports, quantity
Imports, value
Exports, quantity
Exports, value

Industrial Roundwood
Production
Imports, quantity
Imports, value
Exports, quantity
Exports, value

Industrial Roundwood (C)
Production

Industrial Roundwood (NC)
Production

Sawlogs and Veneer Logs
Production
Imports, quantity
Imports, value
Exports, quantity
Exports, value

Sawlogs + Veneer logs (C)
Production
Imports, quantity
Imports, value
Exports, quantity
Exports, value

Sawlogs + Veneer logs (NC)
Production
Imports, quantity
Imports, value
Exports, quantity
Exports, value

Pulpwood + Particles
Production
Imports, quantity
Imports, value
Exports, quantity
Exports, value

Pulpwood (C)
Production

Pulpwood (NC)
Production

Pulpwood
Imports, quantity
Imports, value
Exports, quantity
Exports, value

Chips + Particles
Imports, quantity
Imports, value
Exports, quantity
Exports, value

Wood Residues
Imports, quantity
Imports, value
Exports, quantity
Exports, value

Other Industrial Roundwood Production
Imports, quantity
Imports, value
Exports, quantity
Exports, value

Other Industrial Roundwood (NC)
Production

Sawnwood
Production
Imports, quantity
Imports, value
Exports, quantity
Exports, value

Sawnwood (C)
Production
Imports, quantity
Imports, value
Exports, quantity
Exports, value

Sawnwood (NC)
Production
Imports, quantity
Imports, value
Exports, quantity
Exports, value

Wood-based Panels
Production
Imports, quantity
Imports, value
Exports, quantity
Exports, value

Veneer Sheets
Production
Imports, quantity
Imports, value
Exports, quantity
Exports, value

Plywood
Production
Imports, quantity
Imports, value
Exports, quantity
Exports, value

Particle Board
Production

Imports, quantity
Imports, value
Exports, quantity
Exports, value

Fiberboard
Production
Imports, quantity
Imports, value
Exports, quantity
Exports, value

Fibreboard, (C)
Production
Imports, quantity
Imports, value
Exports, quantity
Exports, value

Fibreboard, (NC)
Production
Imports, quantity
Imports, value
Exports, quantity
Exports, value

Wood Pulp
Production
Imports, quantity
Imports, value
Exports, quantity
Exports, value

Mechanical Wood Pulp
Production
Imports, quantity
Imports, value
Exports, quantity
Exports, value

Semi-Chemical Wood Pulp
Production
Imports, quantity
Imports, value
Exports, quantity
Exports, value

Chemical Wood Pulp
Production
Imports, quantity
Imports, value
Exports, quantity
Exports, value

Unbleached Sulphite Pulp
Production
Imports, quantity
Imports, value
Exports, quantity
Exports, value

Bleached Sulphite Pulp
Production
Imports, quantity
Imports, value

Exports, quantity
Exports, value

Unbleached Sulphate Pulp
Production
Imports, quantity
Imports, value
Exports, quantity
Exports, value

Bleached Sulphate Pulp
Production
Imports, quantity
Imports, value
Exports, quantity
Exports, value

Dissolving Wood Pulp
Production
Imports, quantity
Imports, value
Exports, quantity
Exports, value

Other Fibre Pulp
Production
Imports, quantity
Imports, value
Exports, quantity
Exports, value

Paper + Paperboard
Production
Imports, quantity
Imports, value
Exports, quantity
Exports, value

Newsprint
Production.
Imports, quantity
Imports, value
Exports, quantity
Exports, value

Printing + Writing Paper
Production
Imports, quantity
Imports, value
Exports, quantity
Exports, value

Other Paper + Paperboard
Production
Imports, quantity
Imports, value
Exports, quantity
Exports, value

Household and Sand Paper
Production
Imports, quantity
Imports, value
Exports, quantity
Exports, value

Wrapping + Packing Paper + Board
Production
Imports, quantity
Imports, value

Paper + Paperboard (n.e.s.)
Production
Imports, quantity
Imports, value
Exports, quantity
Exports, value

Forest Products
Imports, value
Exports, value

Direction of Trade
Sawlogs + Vlogs (C)
Sawlogs + Vlogs (NC)
Pulpwood
Chips + Particles
Sawnwood (C)
Sawnwood (NC)
Veneer Sheets
Plywood
Particle Board
Fibreboard
Wood Pulp
Newsprint
Paper + Board + Newsprint

Unit Value

Sawlogs + Vlogs (C)
Imports
Exports

Sawlogs + Vlogs (NC)
Imports
Exports

Pulpwood + Particles
Imports
Exports

Sawnwood (C)
Imports
Exports

Sawnwood (NC)
Imports
Exports

Plywood
Imports
Exports

Particle Board
Imports
Exports

Wood Pulp
Imports
Exports

Newsprint
Imports
Exports

Printing + Writing Paper
Imports
Exports

Other Paper + Paperboard
Imports
Exports

GAS, NATURAL

ANNUAL BULLETIN OF GAS STATISTICS FOR EUROPE

FACTS AT A GLANCE

Number of Pages: 132
Periodicity: Annual
Publisher: United Nations

PURPOSE AND SCOPE

The purpose of the *Annual Bulletin of Gas Statistics for Europe* is to provide basic data on developments and trends in the field of gaseous fuels in European Union member states.

DATA ORGANIZATION

The data cover production, stocks, inland availabilities, deliveries, trade, and length of pipelines.

METHODOLOGY

Each table is followed by explanatory notes. Definitions and general notes are found at the end of the book.

CONTENTS

Graphs
1. Production of Natural Gas in the World 1980, 1985, and 1991
2. Natural Gas, Consumption in the World and ECE in 1991
3. Natural Gas, Consumption by Main User Sectors in the ECE in 1991
4. Main Importing and Exporting Countries of Natural Gas in 1991
5. Production of LPG in the World 1980, 1985, and 1991

Tables
1. Production, Imports, Exports, and Consumption of Gas
2. Imports of Gas by Country of Origin
3. Exports of Gas by Country of Destination
4. Length of Mains for Transport and Distribution of Gas

Table Notes, by Country

Annexes

I. List of ECE Periodic Reviews in the Field of Electric Energy

II. Definitions and General Notes

BP REVIEW OF WORLD GAS

FACTS AT A GLANCE

Number of Pages: 29

Periodicity: Annual

Publisher: British Petroleum (BP)

PURPOSE AND SCOPE

BP Review of World Gas is an annual survey of natural gas operations and output worldwide and a summary of key data relating to the gas industry.

DATA ORGANIZATION

BP Review of World Gas provides data on reserves, production, consumption, trade, and prices, for both natural gas and liquefied petroleum gas (LPG).

METHODOLOGY

For the first time in this edition, LPG figures for the United States have been revised downward by removing LPG consumed by refineries for further processing.

CONTENTS

Foreword

Summary of Gas and LPG Production and Consumption

Primary Energy

Consumption

Natural Gas
Reserves
Production
Consumption
International Trade
Gas and Oil Prices
LNG Project and Contract Summary

LPG
Production
Consumption
International Trade
Shipping
Prices

General

Conversion Factors and Definitions

BP's Gas Activities

HEALTH

NATIONAL HEALTH DATA REFERENCE GUIDE

FACTS AT A GLANCE

Number of Pages: 109

Publisher: National Center for Health Statistics

PURPOSE AND SCOPE

The main purpose of the *National Health Data Reference Guide* is to provide health-related information not readily available in published form. A secondary purpose is to develop a common framework for international comparisons.

DATA ORGANIZATION

The guide focuses on the availability of selected national hospital and health manpower resources and population-based health survey statistics. Additionally, the book includes health surveys citing the title, responsible agency or ministry, objective, scope, collection method, data content, frequency, and availability of data. Also included is a matrix of the data variables from the surveys. The data cover 40 nations.

METHODOLOGY

Information was obtained from official health agencies.

CONTENTS

Vital Statistics

Natality

Mortality

Marriage and Divorce

Hospital Statistics

Facility

Discharge

Health Manpower Statistics

National Population-Based Surveys

Profile of National Population-based Surveys

General Topics Covered in Health Surveys, by Country

NATIONAL HEALTH SYSTEMS OF THE WORLD

FACTS AT A GLANCE

Number of Pages: 660

Periodicity: Irregular

Publisher: Oxford University Press

PURPOSE AND SCOPE

National Health Systems of the World is a global survey of the characteristics of national health systems. The survey is data-rich and documents the statistical dimensions of the health systems adequately.

DATA ORGANIZATION

The book is divided into two parts. The first part (Chapters 1-4) is an overview of the principal characteristics of the health systems, their determinants and components, the health needs of various societies, resources, the organization of programs, management, and the delivery of services. The second part (Chapters 5-18) is a country-specific survey divided by types of societies: industrialized, transitional, socialist, very poor, and oil-rich. The book ends with a summary of the primary trends in health system developments and their impact on society.

METHODOLOGY

The data in the book are derived from World Health Organization (WHO) files which in turn are based on national reports.

CONTENTS

Delivery of Services
Economic Support

People's Republic of China
Historical Background
Imperial China (Before 1911)
The Kuomintang Years, 1912-1949
Early Postliberation China, 1949-1965
The Cultural Revolution, 1965-1975
Post-Mao Modernizations, 1976-1989
Health Resources in China
Organizational Structure
Economic Support
Health System Management
Delivery of Health Services
Some Health Status Outcomes

Taiwan A Note
Health System Structure and Resources
Economic Support, Health Services, and Trends

Summary Comment

References

Part Five: Commentary

Chapter Eighteen
Health Systems of Oil-Rich Developing Countries

Gabon
Libya
Saudi Arabia
Kuwait

Summary Comment

References

Chapter Nineteen
Health Systems in Society

Overview

Social Trends and Their Impacts
Urbanization
Industrialization
Education
Government Structure
International Trade
Demographic Changes

Health System Developments
General System Organization
Resource Expansion
Increased Utilization of Health Services
Rising Expenditure
Collectivized Financing
Cost-control Strategies
Improving System Efficiency
Higher Technology
Prevention and Primary Health Care
Quality Assurance
Scope of Public Responsibilities
Popular Participation in Policy Determination

Public/Private Dynamics in Health Systems
Historical Background
Private/Public Sector Expenditures
Private/Public Mixes of Resources
Patterns of Health Service Delivery
A Privatization Movement
A General Theory of Health System Development?
Previous Approaches
Sociopolitical Functionalism?

Health Systems and Human Health
Life Expectancy in Countries
Some Contrasting Health Systems
Influences on Life Expectancy

Health Care and Human Rights

References

WORLD HEALTH STATISTICS ANNUAL

FACTS AT A GLANCE

Number of Pages: 555

Periodicity: Annual

Publisher: World Health Organization (WHO)

PURPOSE AND SCOPE

The *World Health Statistics Annual* is the flagship statistical publication of the WHO and presents key indicators of health status, causes of death, medical facilities and personnel, and vital statistics.

DATA ORGANIZATION

The first part describes methods developed in China and India to generate reliable statistics on causes of death and vital events in the absence of a system of universal vital registration. The second part presents health and demographic data in three tables on population and growth rate, natality and mortality, women and children, and health personnel. The final and most extensive part presents vital statistics and life tables for a large number of countries. It also sets out detailed data on causes of death by sex and age. Also included are country-specific statistics on life expectancy and the chances of dying from eight major causes by sex and age.

METHODOLOGY

The data are oriented toward the WHO goals in the field of health and healthcare. They, therefore, focus on certain key health issues designed to help health policymakers formulate their responses.

CONTENTS

Section A/B
Cause of Death Statistics and Vital rates, Civil Registration Systems and Alternative Sources of Information

Section C: Health and Demographic Date
Table C.1: Population, Growth Rate, Natality and Mortality

Table C.2: Health-Related Demographic Data on Women and Children: Fertility, Mortality of Women and Children and Child-Dependency Ratio

Table C.3: Health Personnel by Selected Category, 1988-1991
Notes

Section D: Causes of Death, Life Tables, and Mortality Trends
Table D.1: Causes of Death, by Sex and Age

WHO African Region
Mauritius 1992

WHO Region of the Americas
Argentina 1990
Brazil 1988
Brazil 1989
North and North-East 1987
North and North-East 1988
North and North-East 1989
South, South-East, and Central West 1987
South, South-East, and Central West 1988
South, South-East, and Central West 1989
Canada 1991
Colombia 1987
Colombia 1988
Colombia 1989
Colombia 1990
Costa Rica 1990
Costa Rica 1991
Mexico 1991
Nicaragua 1988
Nicaragua 1989
Sweden 1990
Switzerland 1992
United Kingdom 1992
United Kingdom
    England and Wales 1992
    Northern Ireland 1992
    Scotland 1992

WHO Western Pacific Region
Australia 1989
Australia 1990
Australia 1991
Australia 1992
China 1990
    Selected Rural Areas
    Selected Urban Areas
Hong Kong 1990
Hong Kong 1991
Japan 1992

New Zealand 1990
New Zealand 1991
Republic of Korea 1988
Republic of Korea 1989
Republic of Korea 1990
Republic of Korea 1991
Singapore 1991

Table D.2: Causes of Infant Deaths, by Sex and Age

Table D.3: Life Expectancy, Number of Survivors and Chances per 1000 of Eventually Dying from Specified Causes, at Selected Ages, by Sex, Latest Available Years

Table D.4: Age-Standardized Death Rates for Selected Causes, by Sex, Latest Available Year

Table D.5: Trends in Maternal Mortality, 1950-54 to 1985-89

Table D.6: Trends in Mortality for Selected Causes, by Sex, 1950-54 to 1985-89

Annexes
I. Users' Guide to Standardized Computer-Tape Transcripts
II. List of Member States of WHO, by Region

HOUSING

ANNUAL BULLETIN OF HOUSING AND BUILDING STATISTICS FOR EUROPE

FACTS AT A GLANCE
Number of Pages: 173

Periodicity: Annual

Publisher: United Nations

PURPOSE AND SCOPE
The purpose of the *Annual Bulletin of Housing and Building Statistics for Europe* is to provide annual data on trends in the fields of housing and building in European countries, Canada, and the United States. The publication is purely statistical.

DATA ORGANIZATION
The data cover dwelling stock; structure of dwelling construction; dwellings completed by type of investor; dwellings completed by type of material; energy consumption per household; consumer price and rent indices; value of construction put in place; indices of employment and unemployment in the construction industry; structure of the building industry; input and output price indices for housing construction; production and wholesale price indices of building materials and production; trade; and apparent consumption of cement.

Methodology

The current edition has been enlarged and revised in accordance with the recommendations of the Meeting on Housing Statistics. The main changes include: (1) the deletion of former Tables 17 and 19; (2) the replacement of former Table 18 with Table 2; (3) the enlargement of former Table 10; and the (4) consolidation of former tables 4, 5, and 6 into new Table 8. Three new Tables (3, 4, and 5) have been added.

Contents

Tables

Part I. Population and Housing Statistics

1. Estimates of Mid-year Population and its Range of Change
2. Dwelling Stock
3. Size, Facilities, and Period of Construction in Dwellings, by Tenure
4. Dwellings by Number of Persons and Number of Rooms
5A. Number of Persons in a Household, by Tenure and Useful Floor Space
5B. Number of Persons in a Household, by Tenure and Living Floor Space
6. Energy Consumption by Households
7. Consumer Price and Rent Indices

Part II. Building Statistics

8. Dwellings Completed
9. Gross Fixed Capital Formation in Western European Countries, Canada, and the United States
10. New Non-residential Buildings Completed
11. Value of Construction Put in Place
12. Investments in Central and Eastern European Countries
13. Indices of Employment and Unemployment in the Construction Industry
14. Structure of the Building Industry
15. Production of Building Materials

Tables

16. Production, Imports, Exports, and Apparent Consumption of Cement
17. Input and Output Price Indices for Housing Construction
18. Wholesale Price Indices of Building Materials

Annexes

I. List of ECE Reports in the Field of Housing, Building, and Planning
II. Sources of Data
III. Definitions and General Notes
IV. List of the Main National Publications on Housing and Building Statistics

HUMAN SETTLEMENTS

HUMAN SETTLEMENTS: BASIC STATISTICS

Facts at a Glance

Number of Pages: 214

Periodicity: Irregular

Publisher: United Nations

Purpose and Scope

Human Settlements: Basic Statistics is a compendium of data relating to human settlements worldwide.

Data Organization

The book includes data culled from various United Nations sources on settlement patterns arranged by countries and regions.

Methodology

The data are incomplete in many respects because of the lack of primary statistics and the absence of any major international organization devoted to the collection of such statistics.

Contents

Note: Table of Contents not available.

INDUSTRY

INDUSTRIAL STRUCTURE STATISTICS

Facts at a Glance

Number of Pages: 338

Periodicity: Annual

Publisher: Organization for Economic Cooperation and Development (OECD)

Purpose and Scope

Industrial Structure Statistics is prepared by the Economic Analysis and Statistics Division of the Directorate for Science, Technology, and Industry in the OECD Secretariat. The time series show data for the preceding 10 years (five in the case of number of establishments and hours worked).

DATA ORGANIZATION

Data are classified by ISIC and presented in two sections. The first contains data derived directly from industrial surveys and foreign trade data. The second gives estimates from national accounts disaggregated by industry.

METHODOLOGY

Industrial surveys are sample surveys conducted by national statistical organizations. Since the sampling procedures vary, data presented in Section 1 are more suitable for cross-sectional intra-country analyses than for inter-country comparisons. Foreign trade statistics are drawn from customs reports and are product-based—the classification of products varies from country to country. In the economy-wide national accounts estimates in Section 2, figures for individual industries are derived by using a "top-down" approach whereas industrial surveys use a "bottoms-up" approach. The print version corresponds to the magnetic tape, Information System on Industrial Structures.

CONTENTS

Foreword

Note to Readers

1. Industrial Survey and Foreign Trade Statistics

2. Disaggregated National Accounts by Industry

3. Currency Abbreviations and Other Signs Used

4. Definitions of ISIC

Annex 1. Sources and Definitions

Annex 2. Exchange Rates and Purchasing Power Parities

WORLD INDUSTRY DEVELOPMENT INDICATORS

FACTS AT A GLANCE

Periodicity: Irregular

Publisher: United Nations

PURPOSE AND SCOPE

World Industry Development Indicators presents data on growth in manufacturing output and capacity in 117 countries based on the United Nations Industrial Development Organization (UNIDO) Database of Industrial Statistics.

DATA ORGANIZATION

The first part of *World Industry Development Indicators* consists of page-length reports on 100 countries. This is a sample subset of 117 countries used to derive the

sectoral forecasts of manufacturing value added (MVA) for 28 industrial branches. Each page includes a diagram of industrial structural change and graphs of gross domestic product (GDP) and MVA growth rates. The second part consists of short tables for the remaining countries.

The diagram of industrial structural change is based on the value added in 1985 deflated prices. The box on the upper right shows the average annual growth rate for 1975-90, and the index of structural change for the same period.

METHODOLOGY

The industrial data are drawn from the UNIDO Database of Industrial Statistics, *National Accounts Statistics*, and the population data from United Nations (UN) Demographic Statistics Division and the *Monthly Bulletin of Statistics*. Estimates and forecasts of GDP and MVA are derived from *National Accounts Statistics*. Two figures are reported for manufacturing value added. One is based on the national income accounts definition and the other on the industrial census definition. Included in the former but not in the latter, are small establishments with less than five or 10 employees. The former classifies output as industrial based on the product and the latter classifies establishments by the nature of the operations.

CONTENTS

Note: Table of Contents not available.

JEWS

WORLD JEWISH POPULATION: TRENDS AND POLICIES

FACTS AT A GLANCE

Number of Pages: 327

Periodicity: Irregular

Publisher: The Institute of Contemporary Jewry

PURPOSE AND SCOPE

The *World Jewish Population* is a report examining the demographic and social trends among Jewish populations in various countries.

DATA ORGANIZATION

The book is organized into four parts. Part I deals with the global trends; Part II, with special aspects of Jewish demographics, including country studies; Part III examines family and community, family education, and the social implications of demographic changes; and Part IV examines population policies in Israel and the Diaspora. The book provides information not easily available elsewhere on Jewish populations.

METHODOLOGY

Nearly 100 scholars on contemporary Jewry have contributed the essays which make up the book.

CONTENTS

Part I. Opening and Closing Addresses

World Jewish Population: Trends and Policies
Roberto Bachi

Part II. Jewish Population Trends

World Jewish Population in the 1980s: A Short Outline

U.O. Schmetz

The Demographics of American Jewry

Sidney Goldstein

Recent Trends in Jewish Marriage

Sergio DellaPergola

The Fertility of the Jewish People: A Contemporary Overview

Paul Ritterband

The Geographic Expansion of Jewish Communities and Its Implication for Social Cohesion and Community Organization

Stanley Waterman

A 1990 National Jewish Population Study: Why and How

Sidney Goldstein

Recent Demographic Trends: Country Reports

Marlena Schmool, Doris Bensimon, Susana Lerner, Allie A. Dubb, W.D. Rubinstein, Sergio DellaPergola, Janos Gonda, Reuven Foux, Moshe Sicron

Socio-demographic Processes: Significance and Implications

Egon Mayer, Rosa N. Geldstein, Joelle Allouche-Benayoun, Steven M. Cohen, Harold S. Himmelfarb, Vivian Z. Klaff, Jack Habib

Jewish Fertility in Israel

Shlomo Kupinsky and Eric Peritz, Ilana Ziegler, Ariela Keysar, U.O. Schmetz

Sources of Jewish Population Data: Present and Future

Sergio DeltaPergola, Peter Friedman, Steven Huberman, Bruce A. Philips, Barry A. Kosmin, Alice Goldstein, Michel Louis Levy, U.O. Schmetz

Part III. Jewish Population Prospects and Policies in the Diaspora

Jewish Family and Community in Historical Perspective

Yaakov Katz, Robert Cohen, David Sidorsky, Rabbi Rene Sbmuel Sirat, Haim Avni

Promoting the Jewish Family in the Diaspora

Steven Bayme, Susan Mizrachi, Donald Feldstein, Alice Shalvi, Judith Kandel, Rabbi Rene Shmuel Sirat

Forms of Jewish Education in the Diaspora

Harold S. Himmelfarb, Brenda Katten, Carol Diamond, Michael Rosenak, Mordechai Bar-On, Bella Burstein, Gideon Shimoni, Norman Zissblatt, Yosef Meleze-Modrzejewski

Jewish Family Education

Stephen G. Donshik, Rabbi Shlomo Riskin, Hertzel Fishman, Yitzbak Halbrecht, Guggy Graham, Ines Lumir, Michael Zmorah Cohen

Jewish Community Services and Jewish Continuity

David Saada, Kalman Sultanik, Fritz Hollander, Emanuel Tennenbaum, Leon Kovalivker, Rabbi Bernard Caspar, Barry A. Kosmin, Peter Friedman, Rabbi Bent Melchior, Ernest Krausz

Increasing Public Awareness of Demographic Trends and Their Implications

Daniel Elazar, Daniel Thurz, Stella Rozan, Belle Simon, Rabbi Wolf Kelman, Stephen Roth, Nicole Goldmann, David Singer, Rela Geffen Monson, Doris Bensimon, Charlotte Jacobson, Roberto Bachi, Sidney Goldstein, Daniel Elazar

Part IV. Jewish Population Policies in Israel and in the Diaspora: Background Papers and Recommendations

Population Trends and Policies in Israel

The Demographic Center, Ministry of Labor and Social Affairs

Some Suggestions on Possible Demographic Policies in the Diaspora

Conference Organizing Committee

Fertility Trends and Policies in Low Fertility Countries and Their Applicability to Israel

Shlomo Kupinsky

Results of the Fertility Study Relevant to a Population Policy in Israel

Shlomo Kupinsky

Resolutions of the Conference on theWorld Jewish Population, Jerusalem, October 1987

Excerpts from the Decisions of the Government of Israel on Demographic Trends within the Jewish People, May 1986

Summary of Proposals, Submitted to the National Conference on Jewish Population Growth, New York, 1983

The American Jewish Committee, The W. Petuschek National Family Center

LABOR

LABOUR FORCE SAMPLE SURVEY

FACTS AT A GLANCE

Number of Pages: 52

Periodicity: Irregular

Publisher: European Communities

PURPOSE AND SCOPE

The *Labor Force Sample Survey* is a report on the contents and the methodological characteristics of the Community Sample Survey on the Labor Force held annually in the European Union member countries.

DATA ORGANIZATION

The volume provides data on employment and unemployment and covers the main technical features of the survey, the basic concepts and definitions, and explanatory notes. There is also a section on sampling and adjustment methods used by each member state.

METHODOLOGY

The main objective of the *Survey* was to guarantee a high degree of data comparability. To do so, the tables skew closely to the recommendations of the 13th International Conference of Labor Statisticians held in October 1982.

CONTENTS

1. **Introduction**

2. **Technical Features of the Survey**
   Organization of the survey. Reference period. Field of survey. Unit of measurement. Reliability of the results. Comparability of the results from country to country. Comparability between the results of successive surveys. Basic concepts and definitions.

3. **Sampling Methods and Adjustment Procedures by Member State**

4. **Community List of Questions**

Annexes

I - Regional Codes for Level I and Level II of the Nomenclatures of Territorial Units

II - Codes for Divisions and Classes of the General Industrial Classification of Economic Activities within the European Communities (NACE)

   Explanatory Notes to the Community List of Questions

5. **National Experts of the Working Party on the Labour Force Sample Survey Since 1982**

6. **Bibliographical Note**

LABOUR FORCE STATISTICS

FACTS AT A GLANCE

Number of Pages: 509

Periodicity: Annual

Publisher: Organization for Economic Cooperation and Development (OECD)

SCOPE AND PURPOSE

Labour Force Statistics contains historical time series on the evolution of the population and the labor force for the 24 OECD member states.

DATA ORGANIZATION

The book is divided into three parts: Parts I and II were prepared by the Economic Statistics and National Accounts Division of the Statistics Directorate. Part I contains general tables on the main aggregates from 1968 to 1991 and graphs showing labor force trends since 1972. Part II contains data broken down by country, with five basic pages and one or more pages of notes for each. The data cover a 20-year period from 1971 to 1991. Part III, compiled by the Central Analysis Division of the Directorate for Education, Employment, Labour, and Social Affairs, contains time series for participation rates and unemployment rates by age and sex for 16 member countries covering the period from 1962 to 1992.

METHODOLOGY

All series conform to the international definitions adopted by ILO/OECD in 1982. But important differences persist among countries regarding concepts, classifications, and the methods used for collecting data. Because of these differences, OECD has made numerous adjustments to reduce the inconsistencies among the various time series and maintain the homogeneity of the long-term data structure. Where it was not possible to adjust these differences, breaks have resulted in the time series.

SPECIAL FEATURES

Since August 1975, the *Quarterly Labour Force Statistics* has updated the information contained in this book, using the same definitions and coverage.

CONTENTS

Definitions

Symbols Employed

Source

1. General Tables and Graphs

Total population. Total population: from 15 to 64 years. Total labor force. Total labor force as percentage of total population. Total employment. Armed forces. Civilian labor force. Unemployment: total. Civilian employment: total. Civilian employment by sector. Civilian employment by sector (percentages). Crude birth rates. Total labor force as percentage of total population. Evolution of civilian employment by sector. Unemployment as percentage of total labor force.

2. Country Tables

3. Participation Rates and Unemployment Rates

General Tables and Graphs

YEARBOOK OF LABOUR STATISTICS

FACTS AT A GLANCE

Number of Pages: 125

Periodicity: Annual

Publisher: International Labour Organisation (ILO)

PURPOSE AND SCOPE

The *Yearbook of Labour Statistics* is one of the oldest global statistical publications in the world, going back to the *International Labour Review* of 1921. After the *International Labour Review* became the *ILO Yearbook* in 1930, statistics were included as a separate volume until 1935-36, when a separate *Yearbook of Labour Statistics* was created. The number of countries covered increased steadily through the 1950s and 1960s as new nations became independent.

The current edition presents a summary of the principal labor statistics for 180 countries, areas, and territories. Whenever possible, the data cover the last 10 years.

DATA ORGANIZATION

The data are organized in nine chapters. Chapter I presents the total and economically active population; Chapter II, employment levels by industry and occupation; Chapter III, unemployment; Chapter IV,

hours of work; Chapter V, wages; Chapter VI, labour cost; Chapter VII, consumer prices; Chapter VIII, occupational injuries; and Chapter IX, strikes and lockouts. There are 31 tables in the book, some of them further subdivided into subtopical tables.

CONTENTS

Chapter 1: Total And Economically Active Population

Explanatory Notes

Synoptic Table

Sources and Coverage of the Data in Total and Economically Active Population

Table 1: Total and Economically Active Population by Sex and Age Group

Table 2: Economically Active Population
A. By Industry (Major Divisions), by Status in Employment, and by Sex
B. By Occupation (Major Groups), by Status in Employment, and by Sex
C. By Industry (Major Divisions), by Occupation (Major Groups), and by Sex

Notes to Tables 1 to 2C

Chapter II: Employment

Explanatory Notes

Table 3: Employment
A. General Level
B. By Industry (Major Divisions)
C. By Occupation (Major Groups)

Table 4: Paid Employment in Non-Agricultural Activities

Table 5 : Paid Employment in Manufacturing
A. All Industries
B. By Industry (Major Groups)

Table 6: Paid Employment in Mining and Quarrying

Table 7: Paid Employment in Construction

Table 8: Paid Employment in Transport, Storage, and Communication

Chapter III: Unemployment

Explanatory Notes

Table 9: Unemployment
A. General Level
B. By Sex and Age Group

Table 10: Unemployed by Work Experience
A. General Level
B. By Industry (Major Divisions)
C. By Occupation (Major Groups)

Chapter IV: Hours of Work
Explanatory Notes

Table 11: Hours of Work per in Non-Agricultural Activities

Table 12: Hours of Work per Week in Manufacturing
A. All Industries
B. By Industry (Major Groups)

Table 13: Hours of Work per Week in Mining and Quarrying

Table 14: Hours of Work per Week in Construction

Table 15: Hours of Work per Week in Transport, Storage, and Communication

Chapter V: Wages

Explanatory Notes

Table 16: Wages in Non-Agricultural Activities

Table 17: Wages in Manufacturing
A. All Industries
B. By Industry (Major Groups)

Table 18: Wages in Mining and Quarrying

Table 19: Wages in Construction

Table 20: Wages in Transport, Storage, and Communication

Table 21: Wages in Agriculture

Chapter VI: Labour Cost

Explanatory Notes

Table 22: Labour Cost in Manufacturing
A. All Industries
B. By Industry (Major Groups)

Chapter VII: Consumer Prices

Explanatory Notes

Table 23: General Indices

Table 24: General Indices Excluding Shelter

Table 25: Food Indices

Table 26: Fuel and Light Indices

Table 27: Clothing Indices

Table 28: Rent Indices

Chapter VIII: Occupational Injuries

Explanatory Notes

Table 29: Persons Injured and Work-Days Lost by Industry (Major Divisions)

Table 30: Rates of Fatal Injuries by Industry (Major Divisions)

Chapter IX: Strikes and Lockouts

Explanatory Notes

Table 31: Strikes and Lockouts
A. General Level

B. By Industry (Major Divisions)

Appendix

Classifications Used in the Year Book

International Standard Industrial Classification of All Economic Activities (ISIC-1968)

International Standard Classification of Occupations (ISCO-1968)

International Classification by Status by Employment (ICSE)

International Standard Classification of Occupations (ISCO-88)

References and Sources
A. References
B. Sources

Order of Arrangement of Countries, Areas, and Territories

Index (Countries, Areas, or Territories included in Each Table)

LATIN AMERICA—GENERAL

STATISTICAL YEARBOOK FOR LATIN AMERICA AND THE CARIBBEAN

FACTS AT A GLANCE
Number of Pages: 778
Periodicity: Annual
Publisher: United Nations

PURPOSE AND SCOPE
This edition of the *Statistical Yearbook for Latin America and the Caribbean* updates the main statistical series on economic and social trends in Latin America and the Caribbean.

DATA ORGANIZATION
No major structural changes have been made in the presentation of data since the 1991 edition. Part One consists of derived socioeconomic indicators (growth rates, ratios, and coefficients) useful for specialized analyses and evaluations of the developmental process. Part Two provides historical series in absolute figures. The majority of the tables focus on a single topic organized to facilitate comparisons.

METHODOLOGY
Although 33 countries are members of the United Nations Economic Commission for Latin America and

the Caribbean, the tables are limited to 25. The Caribbean statistics are far from complete and the regional coverage varies according to the subject. In most tables, the countries appear in the Spanish alphabetical order. The indicators in Part One correspond generally to 1970, 1980, and the seven years from 1985 through 1991. Some of the indicators based on census information relate only to the years that the census was taken. Data are given in Part Two for the years 1970, 1980, 1982, and the eight years from 1984 through 1991.

CONTENTS

Part I. Indicators of Economic and Social Development in Latin America and the Caribbean

1. Social Development and Welfare

Total population growth. Demographic dependency. Growth of the population of active age. Urbanization. Urban population. Urban concentration. Urban population growth. Natality. Mortality. Life expectancy at birth. Fertility. Size of private households. Participation in economic activity, by sex. Participation in economic activity, by sex and age, 1970. Participation in economic activity, by sex and age, 1980. Participation in economic activity, by sex and age, 1985. Economically active population, by sex and sector of economic activity, 1960. Economically active population by sex and sector of economic activity, 1970. Economically active population, by sex and sector of economic activity, 1980. Sectoral growth of employment, by sex, 1970-1980. Urban unemployment. Incidence of poverty. Growth of per capita private consumption. Calories and proteins available. Physicians. Infant mortality. Medical assistants. Hospital beds. Public expenditure on health. Illiteracy. Enrollment, by education level. Teachers, by education level. Enrollment, by age group and sex. Public expenditure on education. Persons per room in the urban area. Occupied private dwelling units, by type of services available.

2. Economic Growth

Growth of gross domestic product, at constant market prices. Growth of per capita gross domestic product, at constant market prices. Growth of real gross national disposable income, at constant market prices. Growth of quantum of imports of goods and services. Coefficients of imports of goods and services. Growth of quantum exports of goods and services. Coefficients of gross domestic investment. Growth of agriculture, forestry, hunting, and fishing. Share of agriculture, forestry, hunting, and fishing in the generation of the product. Eleven main products: area harvested. Growth of food production. Mechanization. Agricultural exports. Growth of mining production. Per capita consumption of hydrocarbons. Growth of total consumption of hydrocarbons. Per capita consumption of electric energy. Growth of total consumption of electric energy. Share of hydroelectric power in generation of electricity. Growth of manufacturing. Share of manufacturing in the generation of the product. Growth of per capita manufacturing, product at constant market prices. Industrial concentration. Share of industrial output produced by the metal manufactures and machinery industry.

3. Domestic Prices

Variations in the consumer prices index. Investment in construction. Investment in machinery and equipment. Coefficients of gross domestic saving. Share of gross domestic saving in investment financing. Coefficients of gross national saving. Share of gross national saving in investment financing.

4. External Trade

Exports of primary products. Exports of manufactures. Latin America: exports of the ten leading products by their percentage share each year. Argentina: exports of the ten leading products by their percentage share each year. Barbados: exports of the ten leading products by their percentage share each year. Bolivia: exports of the ten leading products by their percentage share each year. Brazil: exports of the ten leading products by their percentage share each year. Columbia: exports of the ten leading products by their percentage share each year. Costa Rica: exports of the ten leading products by their percentage share each year. Chile: exports of the ten leading products by their percentage share each year. Ecuador: exports of the ten leading products by their percentage share each year. El Salvador: exports of the ten leading products by their percentage share each year. Guatemala: exports of the ten leading products by their percentage share each year. Honduras: exports of the ten leading products by their percentage share each year. Mexico: exports of the ten leading products by their percentage share each year. Nicaragua: exports of the ten leading products by their percentage share each year. Panama: exports of the ten leading products by their percentage share each year. Paraguay: exports of the ten leading products by their percentage share each year. Peru: exports of the ten leading products by their percentage share each year. Trinidad and Tobago: exports of the ten leading products by their percentage share each year. Uruguay: exports of the ten leading products by their percentage share each year. Venezuela: exports of the ten leading products by their percentage share each year. Intra-regional exports. Intra-regional imports. Income from transport and insurance. Expenditure on transport and insurance. Travel income. Travel expenses.

5. External Financing

Balance on current account with respect to exports. Balance on current account with respect to imports. Contribution of net external financing to gross domestic investment. Coefficients of net external financing. Remittances for payments of profits and interest. Annual changes in international reserves.

Part Two: Statistical Series for Latin America and the Caribbean

1. Population

Total population. Projections of total population. Estimated population, by sex and age group, 1991. Population, by size of locality. Population in private households, by size of household.

2. National Accounts

Latin America and the Caribbean: gross domestic product, by type of expenditure, at constant market prices. Latin America and the Caribbean: gross domestic product, by kind of economic activity, at constant market prices. Latin America and the Caribbean: relations among main national accounts aggregates, at constant prices. Total gross domestic product, at constant market prices. Per capita gross domestic product, at constant market prices. Gross domestic product of agriculture, at constant market prices. Gross domestic product of industrial activities, at constant market prices. Gross domestic product of basic services, at constant market prices. Gross domestic product of other services, at constant market prices. Total consumption, at constant market prices. Gross fixed capital formation, at constant market prices. Investment in construction, at constant market prices. Investment in machinery and equipment, at constant market prices. Real gross national disposable income, at constant market prices. Gross domestic saving. Gross national saving. Effect of the terms of trade. Net factor income paid to the rest of the world. Antigua and Barbuda: gross domestic product, by kind of economic activity, at factor cost. Argentina: gross domestic product, by type of expenditures, at market prices. Argentina: relations among main national accounts aggregates. Argentina: gross domestic product by kind of economic activity, at market prices. Bahamas: gross domestic product, by type of expenditure, at market prices. Bahamas: relations among main national accounts aggregates. Bahamas: income and outlay of the general government. Barbados: gross domestic product, by type of expenditure, at market prices. Barbados: gross domestic product by kind of economic activity, at factor cost. Belize: gross domestic product by type of expenditure, at market prices. Belize: relations among main national accounts aggregates. Belize: gross domestic product, by kind of economic activity, at factor cost. Bolivia: gross domestic product, by type of expenditure, at market prices. Bolivia: gross domestic product, by kind of economic activity, at market prices. Bolivia: income and outlay of the general government. Brazil: gross domestic product, by type of expenditure, at market prices. Brazil: relations among main national accounts aggregates. Brazil: gross domestic product, by kind of economic activity, at factor cost. Brazil: income and outlay of the general government. Colombia: gross domestics product, by type of expenditure, at market prices. Colombia: relations among main national accounts aggregates. Colombia: gross domestic product, by kind of economic activity, at market prices. Colombia: income and outlay of households, including private unincorporated non-financial enterprises. Colombia: income and outlay of the general government. Costa Rica: gross domestic product, by type of expenditure, at market prices. Costa Rica: relations among main national accounts aggregates. Cost Rica: gross domestic product, by kind of economic activity, at market prices. Cost Rica: income and outlay of the general government. Cuba: creation and use of national income. Cuba: net material product. Cuba: gross social product. Chile: gross domestic product, by type of expenditure, at market prices. Chile: relations among main national accounts aggregates. Chile: gross domestic product, by kind of economic activity, at market prices. Dominica: gross domestic product, by type of expenditure, at market prices. Dominica: gross domestic product, by kind of economic activity, at factor cost. Ecuador: gross domestic product, by type of expenditure, at market prices. Ecuador: relations among main national accounts aggregates. Ecuador: gross domestic product, by kind of economic activity, at market prices. Ecuador: income and outlay of household, including private unincorporated non-financial enterprises. Ecuador: income and outlay of the general government. El Salvador: gross domestic product, by type of expenditure, at market prices. El Salvador: relations among main national accounts aggregates. El Salvador: gross domestic product, by kind of economic activity, at market prices. Grenada: gross domestic product, by type of expenditure, at market prices. Grenada: gross domestic product, by kind of economic activity, at factor cost. Guatemala: gross domestic product, by type of expenditure, at market prices. Guatemala: relations among main national accounts aggregates. Guatemala: gross domestic product, by kind of economic activity, at market prices. Guyana: relations among main national accounts aggregates. Guyana: gross domestic product, by kind of economic activity, at factor cost. Haiti: gross domestic product, by type of expenditure, at market prices. Haiti: relations among main national accounts aggregates. Haiti: gross domestic product, by kind of economic activity, at market prices. Honduras: gross domestic product, by type of expenditure, at market prices. Honduras: relations among main national accounts aggregates. Honduras: gross domestic product, by kind of economic activity, at factor cost. Jamaica: gross domestic product, by type of expenditure, at market prices. Jamaica: relations among main national accounts aggregates. Jamaica: gross domestic product,, by kind of economic activity, at market prices. Jamaica: income and outlay of households, including private unincorporated non-financial enterprises. Jamaica: income and outlay of the general government. Mexico: gross domestic product, by type of expenditure, at market prices. Mexico: relations among main national accounts aggregates. Mexico: gross domestic product, by kind of economic activity, at market prices. Nicaragua: gross domestic product, by type of expenditure, at market prices. Nicaragua: gross domestic product, by kind of economic activity, at market prices. Panama: gross domestic product, by type of expenditure, at market prices. Panama: relations among main national accounts aggregates. Panama: gross domestic product, by kind of economic activity, at market prices. Panama: income and outlay of the general government. Paraguay: gross domestic product, by type of expenditure, at market prices. Paraguay: relation among main national accounts aggregates. Paraguay: gross domestic product, by kind of economic activity, at market prices. Paraguay: income and outlay of households, including private unincorporated non-financial enterprises. Paraguay: income and outlay of the general government. Peru: gross domestic product, by type of expenditure, at market prices. Peru: relations among main national accounts aggregates. Peru: gross domestic product, by kind of economic activity, at market prices. Peru: income and outlay of households, including private unincorporated non-financial enterprises. Peru: income and outlay of the general government. Dominican Republic: gross domestic product, by type of expenditure, at market prices. Dominican Republic: relations among main national accounts aggregates. Dominican Republic: gross domestic product, by kind of economic activity, at market prices. Saint Kitts and Nevis: gross domestic product, by type of expenditure, at market prices. Saint-Kitts and Nevis: gross domestic product, by kind of economic activity, at factor cost. Saint Lucia: gross domestic product, by kind of economic activity, at factor cost. Saint Vincent and the Grenadines: gross domestic product, by type of expenditure, at market prices. Saint Vincent and the Grenadines: gross domestic product, by kind of economic activity, at factor cost. Suriname: gross domestic product, by type of expenditure, at market prices. Suriname: relations among main national accounts aggregates. Suriname: gross domestic product, by kind of economic activity, at factor cost. Trinidad and Tobago: gross domestic product, by type of expenditure, at market prices. Trinidad and Tobago: relations among main national accounts aggregates. Trinidad and Tobago: gross domestic product, by kind of economic activity, at market prices. Trinidad and Tobago: income and outlay of the general government. Uruguay: gross domestic product, by type of expenditure, at market prices. Uruguay: relations among main national accounts aggregates. Uruguay: gross domestic product, by kind of economic activity, at market prices. Uruguay: income and outlay of households, including private unincorporated non-financial enterprises. Uruguay: income and outlay of the general government. Venezuela: gross domestic product, by type of expenditure, at market prices. Venezuela: relations among main national accounts aggregates.

Venezuela: gross domestic product, by kind of economic activity, at market prices. Venezuela: income and outlay of households, including private unincorporated non-financial enterprises. Venezuela: income and outlay of the general government.

3. Domestic Prices

Implicit prices of gross domestic product, at market prices. General annual wholesale price indexes. Annual consumer price indexes.

4. Balance of Payments

Latin America and the Caribbean. Latin America and the Caribbean: non-oil exporting countries. Latin America and the Caribbean: oil-exporting countries. Argentina. Bahamas. Barbados. Bolivia. Brazil. Colombia. Costa Rica. Chile. Ecuador. El Salvador. Guatemala. Grenada. Guyana. Haiti. Honduras. Jamaica. Mexico. Nicaragua. Panama. Paraguay. Peru. Dominican Republic. Suriname. Trinidad and Tobago. Uruguay. Venezuela.

5. External Financing

Interest paid and outstanding. Profits paid. Net transfer of resources. Net direct investment. International reserves (stocks).

6. External Indebtedness

Total disbursed external debt.

7. External Trade

Indexes of volume of exports of goods. Indexes of units value of exports of goods, FOB. Indexes of merchandise terms of trade FOB/CIF. Indexes of volume of imports of goods, FOB. Indexes of unit value of imports of goods, FOB. Indexes of purchasing power of exports of goods. Value of exports of goods. Total exports (FOB) by products groups. Value of imports of goods. Imports of goods by broad economic categories. Exports of goods by sector of economic activity. Total intra-regional trade in goods, 1970. Total intra-regional trade in goods, 1980. Total intra-regional trade in goods, 1982. Total intra-regional trade in goods, 1983. Total intra-regional trade in goods, 1984. Total intra-regional trade in goods, 1985. Total intra-regional trade in goods, 1986. Total intra-regional trade in goods, 1987. Total intra-regional trade in goods, 1988. Total intra-regional trade in goods, 1989. Total intra-regional trade in goods, 1990. Total intra-regional trade in goods, 1991.

8. Natural Resources and Production of Goods

Quantum indexes of agricultural production. Quantum indexes of agricultural crops. Quantum indexes of livestock production. Quantum indexes of food production. Quantum indexes of per capita food production. Agricultural area. Seed cotton, area harvested. Rice, area harvested. Coffee, area harvested. Sugar cane, area harvested. Dry beans, area harvested. Sunflower seed, area harvested. Maize, area harvested. Cassava, area harvested. Soybeans, area harvested. Sorghum, area harvested. Wheat, area harvested. Production of seed cotton.

Production of rice. Production of bananas and plantains. Production of green coffee. Production of sugar cane. Production of dried beans. Production of sunflower. Production of maize. Production of cassava. Production of soybeans. Production of sorghum. Production of wheat. Total consumption of fertilizers. Number of tractors. Quantum indexes of mining production. Bauxite production. Coal production. Copper production. Tin production. Iron production. Petroleum production. Zinc production. Production of tires. Paper pulp production. Newsprint production. Caustic soda production. Production of television receivers. Cement production. Gasoline production. Production of passenger motor vehicles. Production of commercial vehicles. Production of fertilizers. Production of wire rod. Production of pig iron. Production of steel. Production of flat rolled products. Production of non-flat rolled products. Production of electricity. Production of electricity by type of plant. Installed capacity. Estimate of economically exploitable hydroelectric potential.

9. Infrastructure Services
Total length of the road network. Total length of the railway network. Railway traffic. Merchant fleets, 1991. Air traffic.

10. Employment
Economically active population. Economically active population, by sex and sector of economic activity, 1960. Economically active population, by sex and sector of economic activity, 1970. Economically active population, by sex and sector of economic activity, 1980. Economically active population by occupation. Economically active population, by category of employment.

11. Social Conditions
Hospital beds. Physicians. Medical assistants. Enrollment in first level. Teachers in first level. Enrollment in second level. Teachers in second level. Enrollment in third level. Teachers in third level. Occupied dwelling units, by type of occupation, in urban and rural areas. Occupied dwelling units, by number of rooms. Dwelling units, occupied, by number of occupants. Dwelling units, occupied, by type of services available, in urban and rural areas.

Annex
Latin America and the Caribbean: growth of total gross domestic product. Latin America and the Caribbean: growth of per capita gross domestic product. Latin America and the Caribbean: urban unemployment. Latin America and the Caribbean: variations in consumer price index. Latin America and the Caribbean: exports of goods, FOB. Latin America and the Caribbean: imports of goods, FOB. Latin America and the Caribbean: terms of trade (goods) FOB/FOB. Latin America and the Caribbean: purchasing power of exports of goods. Latin America and the Caribbean: trade balance (goods). Latin America and the Caribbean: balance of payments. Latin America and the Caribbean: total disbursed external debt. Latin America and the Caribbean: net capital inflow and transfer of resources. Latin America and the Caribbean: total interest due as a percentage of exports of goods and services. Latin America and the Caribbean: total disbursed external debt as a percentage of exports of goods and services.

LEAD AND ZINC

LEAD AND ZINC STATISTICS

FACTS AT A GLANCE
Number of Pages: 63

Periodicity: Monthly

Publisher: International Lead and Zinc Study Group

PURPOSE AND SCOPE
Lead and Zinc Statistics is a compendium of industry-wide data on the production, consumption, stocks, and prices of lead and zinc.

DATA ORGANIZATION
For both lead and zinc, separate tables are presented with data on world production, consumption, prices, trade, and stocks, along with country tables for 10 top lead and zinc industry leaders. The tables are accompanied by 13 graphs and diagrams.

METHODOLOGY
The data are compiled on the basis of reports from member countries and organizations.

CONTENTS

Tables

Lead
Current Trends

13. Trade with Eastern European and Socialist
    Countries
14. Australia
15. Canada
16. France
17. Germany, F.R.
18. Italy
19. Japan
20. Mexico
21. Peru
22. United Kingdom
23. United States

Long Term Trends
24. Annual Production and Consumption

Zinc

Current Trends
25. Western World: Supply and Demand
26. Production and Consumption
27. Stocks of Metal
28. Metal Prices

Detailed Tables
29. Mine Production
32. Stocks of Metal
33. Production and Consumption: Eastern
    European and Socialist Countries
34. Secondary Recovery of Zinc
35. Concentrates: Principal Imports and Exports
36. Refined Zinc: Principal Imports and Exports
37. Trade with Eastern European and Socialist
    Countries

Country Tables
38. Australia
39. Canada
40. France
41. Germany
42. Italy
43. Japan
44. Mexico
45. Peru
46. United Kingdom
47. United States

Long Term Trends
48. Annual Production and Consumption

Graphs and Diagrams
A. Lead: Metal Production and Consumption:
   Main Areas
B. Lead: Metal Production and Consumption:
   Main Aeas
C. Lead: Stocks
D. Lead: Price Trends
E. Lead: Mine Production
F. Lead: Metal Production
G. Lead: Metal Consumption
H. Zinc: Metal Production and Consumption
I. Zinc: Metal Production and Consumption: Main
   Areas
J. Zinc: Stocks

K. Zinc: Price Trends
L. Zinc: Mine Production
M. Zinc: Metal Production
N. Zinc: Metal Consumption

Symbols Employed

LIBRARIES

NORDIC RESEARCH LIBRARY STATISTICS

FACTS AT A GLANCE

Number of Pages: 42

Periodicity: Annual

Publisher: Nordic Statistical Secretariat

PURPOSE AND SCOPE

Nordic Research Library Statistics reports library data
from Norway, Sweden, Finland, Denmark, and
Iceland.

DATA ORGANIZATION

The tables provide annual data on stocks, additions,
withdrawals, loans, staff, and economics.

METHODOLOGY

Swedish data remains a problem in this edition.
Swedish libraries use a fiscal year commencing July,
while other Nordic countries use a calendar year.

CONTENTS

Tables
Main Figures from the Tables

1. Stock 31.12.1990
National Libraries

2. Additions 1990
National Libraries
University Libraries
Special Libraries

3. Withdrawals 1990
National Libraries
University Libraries
Special Libraries

4. Local Loans 1990
National Libraries
University Libraries
Special Libraries

5. Inter-Library Loans 1990
National Libraries
University Libraries
Special Libraries

6. Documentation 1990
National Libraries
University Libraries
Special Libraries

7. Staff 1990
National Libraries
University Libraries
Special Libraries

8. Economy 1990
National Libraries
University Libraries
Special Libraries

LITERACY

COMPENDIUM OF STATISTICS ON ILLITERACY

FACTS AT A GLANCE

Periodicity: Irregular

Publisher: United Nations Educational, Scientific, and Cultural Organization (UNESCO)

PURPOSE AND SCOPE

The *Compendium of Statistics on Illiteracy* is a worldwide survey on the state of literacy. It replaces the first edition of the same title published in 1988.

DATA ORGANIZATION

The first part presents revised estimates of the number of illiterates and illiteracy projections by region and by country. The second part presents statistics on illiteracy by country since 1960. The number of countries covered is 150.

METHODOLOGY

The compendium maintains the same format as the first edition. The data are based on UNESCO data files.

CONTENTS

Introduction

Data Sources

Definitions

Part One: Estimates and Projections of Illiteracy

Preliminary Remarks

Classification of Countries

Trends and Prospects at the World and Regional Level

Trends and Prospects by Country

Part Two: Illiteracy by Country, Censuses, and Surveys Since 1960

MATERNAL MORTALITY

MATERNAL MORTALITY: A GLOBAL FACTBOOK

FACTS AT A GLANCE

Number of Pages: 595

Periodicity: Irregular

Publisher: World Health Organization (WHO)

PURPOSE AND SCOPE

The purpose of the *Factbook*, prepared by WHO as part of its Maternal Health and Safe Motherhood Programme, is to assemble facts regarding maternal mortality.

DATA ORGANIZATION

The data measure maternal mortality both globally and nationally. The country profiles show the number of maternal deaths, their causes, the circumstances surrounding them, and the social and cultural factors that contribute to their incidence. The data also deal with maternal care and obstetric procedures that reduce the number of maternal deaths.

METHODOLOGY

The organization of the materials is explained in the Notes and Definitions section.

CONTENTS
1. Introduction

2. The Global Picture
2.1 Dimensions of the Problem
2.2 The Causes of Maternal Death
2.3 Coverage of Maternity Care
2.4 References

3. Measuring Maternal Mortality
3.1 Definitions
3.2 How Reliable are "Official" Rates?
3.3 Community Studies
3.4 Health Service Records
3.5 Indirect Indicators and Other Measures
3.6 References

4. How to Read the Country Profiles
4.1 Geographic Coverage
4.2 How the Information is Organized
4.3 Notes, Definitions, and Explanations
4.4 Abbreviations

5. General Resource Materials

MIDDLE EAST—GENERAL

STATISTICAL ABSTRACT OF THE REGION OF THE ECONOMIC AND SOCIAL COMMISSION FOR WESTERN ASIA

FACTS AT A GLANCE

Number of Pages: 524

Periodicity: Irregular

Publisher: United Nations (UN)

PURPOSE AND SCOPE

Each of the UN regional economic (and social) commissions publish statistical yearbooks that provide, in slightly more detail, the kind of statistical information found in the *United Nations Statistical Yearbook.* This is the yearbook that covers Western Asia.

DATA ORGANIZATION

Data are organized under nine principal headings: (1) Population; (2) Social; (3) National Accounts; (4) Agriculture, Forestry, and Fishing; (5) Industry; (6) Energy; (7) Foreign Trade; (8) Finance; and (9) Transport, Communication, and Tourism.

METHODOLOGY

Much of the data are derived from national publications supplemented from UN data files.

CONTENTS

I. Population
Population Estimates
Demographic Indicators
Population by Age and Sex
Economically Active Population by Economic Activity

II. Social Statistics
Educational Expenditure
Number of Students by Level of Education
Number of Students in Universities by Field of Study
Number of Graduates from Universities by Field of Study
Teaching Staff
Number of Schools, Institutes, and Universities by Level of Education
Number of Persons Engaged in the Medical and Related Professions
Number of Hospitals, Hospital Beds, and Other Health Centers

III. National Accounts
Gross Domestic Product and Expenditure at Current Prices
Gross Domestic Product by Kind of Economic Activity in Producers' Values at Current Prices

IV. Agriculture, Forestry, and Fishing
Index Numbers of Agricultural Production
Land Use
Production of Principal Crops
Number of Livestock
Fish Catches
Meat, Milk, and Eggs Production
Forestry Production
Means of Agricultural Production

V. Industry
Index Numbers of Industrial Production
Mining Production
Value of Industrial Outputs

VI. Energy
Production and Consumption of Electric Energy

VII. Foreign Trade
Value of Imports, Exports, and Balance of Trade
Foreign Trade Index Numbers
Geographical Distribution of Imports
Geographical Distribution of Exports
Imports by SITC Sections
Exports by SITC Sections

VIII. Finance
Currency and Banking
Balance of Payments
Government Receipts
Government Expenditure
Price Index Numbers

IX. Transport, Communication, and Tourism
Railways
Roads and Motor Vehicles
Sea-borne Shipping
Air Traffic
Communication
Arab Arrivals by Nationalities
Tourism

MILITARY

WORLD MILITARY EXPENDITURES AND ARMS TRANSFERS

FACTS AT A GLANCE

Number of Pages: 148

Periodicity: Annual

Publisher: U.S. Arms Control and Disarmament Agency

PURPOSE AND SCOPE

World Military Expenditures and Arms Transfers presents statistical data on the world military situation at the start of a new era. In one sense, it depicts the final years of a passing world order dominated by U.S.-Soviet competition and the Cold War. The momentous events of 1990-1991, the collapse of the Soviet Union, the victory of the Allies in the Gulf War, democracy's sweep through Eastern Europe, the dissolution of the Warsaw Pact, and the conclusion of far-reaching East-West arms control agreements, including the CEE and START treaties, make this edition different from the previous ones.

DATA ORGANIZATION

The data follow the same format as the earlier editions, but they tell a different story. The decline in superpower competition has led to a decline in global military spending to levels unmatched since World War II. The trade in arms, however, continues unabated, and the number of arms exporters has grown. New features in this edition include a set of tables ranking the countries of the world by each variable since 1989 and a new data series on U.S. arms exports.

METHODOLOGY

World Military Expenditures and Arms Transfers is based on the data files of the U.S. Arms Control and Disarmament Agency.

CONTENTS

1. Highlights
Military expenditures. Armed forces. Arms transfers: arms import trends; arms export trends. Military burden and other relative indicators.

2. Briefs
Big Five initiative on arms transfers and proliferation restraints. Recent steps towards transparency in arms.

3. Statistical Notes

4. Country Rankings: 1989

5. Main Statistical Tables
Military expenditures, armed forces, GNP, central government expenditures, and population, 1979-1989, by region, organization, and country. Arms transfer deliveries and total trade, 1979-1989, by region, organization, and country. Arms transfer deliveries, cumulative 1985-1989, by major supplier and recipient country. Arms transfer deliveries and agreements, 1979-1989, by supplier and recipient region. Number of arms delivered, cumulative 1985-1989, by selected supplier, recipient, developing region, and major weapon type.

MINERALS

MINERALS YEARBOOK

FACTS AT A GLANCE

Number of Pages: Volume One: 495; Volume Two: 582; Volume Three: 1,735

Periodicity: Annual

Publisher: U.S. Bureau of Mines

PURPOSE AND SCOPE

The *Minerals Yearbook* discusses the performance of the worldwide minerals and metals industry and provides background information to assist in interpreting this performance.

DATA ORGANIZATION

Volume I contains chapters on virtually all metallic and industrial mineral commodities important to the U.S. economy. Chapters on advanced materials, nonrenewable organic materials, and nonferrous metals recycling were added to the series beginning 1989, 1990, and 1991 respectively. A new chapter on materials recycling and another on trends in mining and quarrying have been added to the edition under review. Volume II consists of area reports for all the 50 states, Puerto Rico, and the U.S. possessions. Volume III contains mineral data on more than 175 foreign countries divided into six regions. The reports incorporate location maps, industry structure tables, and an outlook section previously incorporated in the now discontinued *Mineral Perspectives*.

METHODOLOGY

All survey articles are written by Bureau of Mines experts.

CONTENTS
1. Survey Methods and Statistical Summary of Nonfuel Minerals, by Jacqueline McClaskey and Steven D. Smith
2. Mining and Quarrying Trends in the Metals and Industrial Minerals Industries, by Brian T. Brady, Gregory J. Chekan, and Charles V. Jude
3. Abrasive Materials, by Gordon T. Austin
4. Advanced Materials, by William J. McDonough
5. Aluminum, Bauxite, and Alumina, by Patricia A. Plunkert and Errol D. Sehnke
6. Antimony, by Thomas O. Llewellyn
7. Barite, by James P. Searls
8. Boron, by Phyllis Lyday
9. Bromine, by Phyllis Lyday
10. Cadmium, by Thomas O. Llewellyn
11. Cement, by Cheryl Solomon
12. Chromium, by John F. Papp

13. Clays, by Robert L. Virta
14. Columbium (Niobium) and tantalum, by Larry D. Cunningham
15. Copper, by Daniel L. Edelstein
16. Fluorspar, by M. Michael Miller
17. Gemstones, by Gordon T. Austin
18. Germanium, by Thomas O. Llewellyn
19. Gold, by John M. Lucas
20. Graphite, by Harold A. Taylor, Jr.
21. Gypsum, by Lawrence L. Davis
22. Helium, by William D. Leachman
23. Iodine, by Phyllis A. Lyday
24. Iron Ore, by William S. Kirk
25. Iron and Steel, by Gerald W. Houck
26. Iron and Steel Scrap, by Raymond E. Brown
27. Lead, by William D. Woodbury
28. Lime, by M. Michael Miller
29. Lithium, by Joyce A. Ober
30. Magnesium and Magnesium Compounds, by Deborah A. Kramer
31. Manganese, by Thomas S. Jones
32. Metals Recycling, by Arnold O. Tanner
33. Mica, by Lawrence L. Davis
34. Molybdenum, by John W. Blossom
35. Nickel, by Peter H. Kuck
36. Nitrogen, by Raymond L. Cantrell
37. Nonrenewable Organic Materials, by Raymond L. Cantrell and Deborah A. Kramer
38. Peat, by Raymond L. Cantrell
39. Phosphate Rock, by David E. Morse
40. Platinum-Group Metals, by J. Roger Loebenstein
41. Potash, by James P. Searls
42. Rare-Earths, The Lanthanides, Yttrium and Scandium, by James B. Hedrick
43. Recycling Nonferrous Metals, by James F. Carlin, Jr., Daniel Edelstein, James H. Jolly, Janice L. Jolly, John F. Papp, and Patricia A. Plunkert
44. Salt, by Dennis S. Kostick
45. Sand and Gravel, Construction, by Valentin V. Tepordei
46. Sand and Gravel, Industrial, by Wallace P. Bolen
47. Silicon, by Larry D. Cunningham
48. Silver, by Robert G. Reese
49. Slag—Iron and Steel, by Cheryl Solomon
50. Soda Ash, by Dennis S. Kostick
51. Sodium Sulfate, by Dennis S. Kostick
52. Stone, Crushed, by Valentin V. Tepordei
53. Stone, Dimension, by Harold A. Taylor, Jr.
54. Strontium, by Joyce A. Ober
55. Sulfur, by Joyce A. Ober
56. Talc and Pyrophyllite, by Robert L. Virta
57. Tin, by James F. Carlin, Jr.
58. Titanium, by Joseph Gambogi
59. Tungsten, by Gerald R. Smith
60. Vanadium, by Henry E. Hilliard
61. Zinc, by James H. Jolly
62. Zirconium and Hafnium, by Joseph M. Gambogi

MOTOR VEHICLES

WORLD MOTOR VEHICLE DATA

FACTS AT A GLANCE

Number of Pages: 343

Periodicity: Annual

Publisher: American Automobile Manufacturers Association

PURPOSE AND SCOPE

World Motor Vehicle Data is the leading source of information on passenger cars and commercial vehicles worldwide.

DATA ORGANIZATION

The data cover production, imports, exports, registrations, and sales. There is also an interesting breakdown of production figures by principal manufacturers.

METHODOLOGY

The data come from various sources and as a result, the quality of data is uneven. The principal problems are differences in definition, double counting resulting from counting assembled vehicles as production, and basing data on sales or registrations rather than on production or shipments.

CONTENTS

World Data
　Production
　Exports
　Imports
　New Registrations
　Total Registrations

Africa
　African Continent
　Botswana
　Mauritius
　South Africa, Republic of
　Zimbabwe

Asia
　China
　Hong Kong
　India
　Indonesia
　Japan
　Korea, South
　Malaysia
　Pakistan
　Saudi Arabia

Taiwan
Thailand

Europe
Andorra
Austria
Belgium
Denmark
European Community
Finland
France
Germany
Greece
Ireland
Italy
Luxembourg
The Netherlands
Nordic Countries
Norway
Portugal
Spain
Sweden
Switzerland
Turkey
United Kingdom

Eastern Europe
Commonwealth of Independent States
Czechoslovakia
Hungary
Poland
Yugoslavia
Oceania
Australia
New Zealand
Western Hemisphere
Argentina
Brazil
Canada
Mexico
Peru
Puerto Rico
South America
Trinidad and Tobago
United States
Venezuela

NARCOTIC DRUGS

NARCOTIC DRUGS: ESTIMATED WORLD REQUIREMENTS

FACTS AT A GLANCE

Number of Pages: 205

Periodicity: Annual

Publisher: United Nations

PURPOSE AND SCOPE

Narcotic Drugs is designed to serve the control purposes of national drug enforcement agencies and also to meet the needs of researchers. The estimates are particularly valuable for fixing the limits within which the manufacture of and trade in narcotic drugs will be conducted. The summary balance sheets showing the availability and use of narcotic drugs are used by health, police, customs, and justice officials in each country to monitor the progress of efforts to contain and curtail drug trafficking.

DATA ORGANIZATION

The publication consists of five parts: Parts I and II are general. Part III contains two tables: the first table presents the approved official estimates of narcotic drugs which may be produced or consumed in the country legally; the second table presents world estimates for six years. The tables show both the original estimates and the revised ones. Part IV has 14 tables. Tables I and II contain data on the cultivation of papaver somniferum for the production of opium as well as for other uses. Table III shows statistics on the extraction of the alkaloids of opium, such as morphine, codeine, and thebaine. Table IV gives data on the extraction of alkaloids from poppy straw. Table V gives data on the conversion of morphine to codeine, ethylmorphine, and pholcodine. Tables VI and VII show manufacture of narcotic drugs overall and by country. Table VIII presents data on the manufacture of cocaine and production, utilization, import, and export of cocoa leaf. Tables IX and X show consumption of narcotic drugs overall and by country. Certain preparations are exempted from control measures and thus are not required to be reported. Table XI presents consumption data per capita. Table XII presents data on stocks of all narcotic drugs weighing one kilogram or more. Table XIII presents data on international trade in narcotic drugs. Table XIV presents data on seizures of narcotic drugs. Part V is a comparative statement of estimates and statistics.

METHODOLOGY

The data are based on reports that national drug agencies are required to submit to the International Narcotics Control Board.

CONTENTS

Part One: General Remarks
Introduction
Index of Countries and Non-metropolitan Territories
Index of Narcotic Drugs

Part Two: Status of Adherence to International Conventions on Narcotic Drugs and Receipt of Statistics and Estimates

PSYCHOTROPIC SUBSTANCES

FACTS AT A GLANCE

Number of Pages: 236

Periodicity: Annual

Publisher: United Nations

PURPOSE AND SCOPE

The publication interprets statistics reported by governments and identifies trends in the manufacture, import, and export of psychotropic substances.

DATA ORGANIZATION

Table I presents information on parties and non-parties to the 1971 convention. Table II provides receipt of statistics for 1992. Table III contains information on defined daily doses for psychotropic substances. Table IV presents level of consumption for each group of psychotropic substances in defined daily doses per 1,000 inhabitants per day. Table V presents assessments of annual domestic medical and scientific requirements for substances listed in Schedules II, III, and IV of the 1971 Convention on Psychotropic Substances. Table VI contains tables showing the countries of which national legislation requires issuing of import authorizations for the import of substances of Schedules III and IV of the Convention of Psychotropic Substances, 1971.

METHODOLOGY

The statistics are compiled on the basis of reports supplied by national governments to the International Narcotics Control Board. However, not all governments report such data and therefore, the tables present only a partial picture of global manufacture and trade in psychotropic substances.

CONTENTS

Table I. Parties and Non-Parties to the 1971 Convention

Table II. Receipt of Statistics for 1992

Table III. Defined Daily Doses for Psychotropic Substances

Comments on Reported Statistics

Table IV. Levels of Consumption of Groups of Psychotropic Substances in Defined Daily Doses per Thousand Inhabitants per Day

Tables of Reported Statistics for 1988-1992

Substances Listed in Schedule II
Amfetamine
Delta 9-Tetrahydrocannabinol
Dexamfetamine
Fenetylline
Levamfetamine
Levomethamphetamine
Mecloqualone
Metamfetamine
Metamfetamine Racemate
Methaqualone
Methylphenidate
Phencyclidine
Phenmetrazine
Secobarbital

Substances Listed in Schedule III
Amobarbital
Buprenorphine

Butalbital
Cathine
Cyclobarbital
Glutethimide
Pentazocine
Pentobarbital

Substances Listed in Schedule IV
Allobarbital
Alprazolam
Amfepramone
Barbital
Benzfetamine
Bromazepam
Butobarbital
Camazepam
Chlordiazepoxide
Clobazam
Clonazepam
Clorazepate
Clotiazepam
Cloxazolam
Delorazepam
Diazepam
Estazolam
Ethchlorvynol
Ethinamate
Ethylloflazepate
Etilamfetamine
Fencamfamine
Fenproporex
Fludiazepam
Flunitrazepam
Flurazepam
Halazepam
Halazepam
Haloxazolam
Ketazolam
Lefetamine (SPA)
Loprazolam
Lorazepam
Lormetazepam
Mazindol
Medazepam
Mefenorex
Meprobamate
Methylphenobarbital
Methyprylon
Midazolam
Nimetazepam
Nordazepam
Oxazepam
Oxazolam
Pemoline
Phendimetrazine
Phenobarbital
Phentermine
Pinazepam
Pipradrol
Prazepam
Provalerone
Secbutabarbital

Temazepam
Tetrazepam
Triazolam
Vinylbital

Table V. Assessments of Annual Domestic Medical and Scientific Requirements for Substances Listed in Schedules II, III, and IV of the Convention on Psychotropic Substances, 1971

Table VI. Table Showing the Countries of which National Legislation Requires Issuing of Import Authorizations for the Import of Substances of Schedules III and IV of the Convention on Psychotropic Substances, 1971

NATIONAL ACCOUNTS

NATIONAL ACCOUNTS

FACTS AT A GLANCE

Number of Pages: 151

Periodicity: Annual

Publisher: Organization for Economic Cooperation and Development (OECD)

PURPOSE AND SCOPE

The purpose of *National Accounts* is to give consolidated national accounts on which gross domestic product (GDP) is based for each country.

DATA ORGANIZATION

National Accounts is divided into two volumes. Volume I presents the main aggregates for each country, divided into eight parts. Part One contains graphs showing growth in real terms of gross domestic product and expenditure. Parts Two and Three present these aggregates in U.S. dollars and national currencies respectively. Parts Four and Five give the main components of the final expenditure. Part Six gives a set of comparative tables and Part Seven contains a series of comparative tables based on purchasing power parities. Part Eight gives three tables on basic indicators.

Volume II contains detailed national accounts for each country. The first five tables present private final consumption expenditures, gross fixed capital formation, and total government outlays. Tables 6 through 15 show accounts for four levels of government, accounts for social security funds, accounts for financial and non-financial institutions, accounts for households, private unincorporated enterprises, and private nonprofit institutions, external transactions, capital finance accounts, GDP by kind of activity, cost components of value added, profit shares, and employment.

METHODOLOGY

The data are compiled by OECD from questionnaires completed by national monetary and fiscal authorities on the basis of the System of National Accounts.

CONTENTS

Volume I
Note: Table of Contents not available.

Volume II
1. Main Aggregates
2. Private Final Consumption Expenditure by Type and Purpose (Current And Constant Prices)
3. Gross Fixed Capital Formation by Kind of Activity of Owner (Current And Constant Prices)
4. Gross Fixed Capital Formation by Type of Good and Owner (Current And Constant Prices)
5. Total Government Outlays by Function and Type
6. Accounts for General Government
6.1 Accounts for Central Government
6.2 Accounts for State or Provincial Government
6.3 Accounts for Local Government
6.4 Accounts for Social Security Funds
7. Accounts for Non-financial and Financial Corporate and Quasi-Corporate Enterprises
7.1 Accounts for Non-financial Corporate and Quasi-Corporate Enterprises
7.2 Accounts for Financial Institutions
8. Accounts for Households and Private Unincorporated Enterprises
9. Accounts for Private Non-profit Institutions Serving Households
10. External Transactions, Current and Capital Accumulation Accounts
11. Capital Finance Accounts
12. Gross Domestic Product by Kind of Activity (current and constant prices)
13. Cost Components of Value Added by Kind of Activity
14. Profit Shares and Rates of Return on Capital
15. Employment by Kind of Activity

NATIONAL ACCOUNTS STATISTICS: MAIN AGGREGATES AND DETAILS

FACTS AT A GLANCE

Number of Pages: 2,122

Periodicity: Annual

Publisher: United Nations

PURPOSE AND SCOPE

This book provides detailed national accounts for 178 countries and areas. *National Accounts Statistics: Main Aggregates and Detailed Tables* was prepared by the Statistical Division of the Department for Economic and Social Information and Policy Analysis in cooperation with national statistical services. The book is complemented by the *Trends in International Distribution of Gross World Product.*

DATA ORGANIZATION

National accounts estimates are shown for each of the following tables:

Part I: Summary Information

Part II: Final Expenditures on Gross Domestic Product: Detailed Breakdowns

Part III: Institutional Sector Accounts for general government, corporate and quasi-corporate enterprises, households and private unincorporated enterprises, private non-profit institutions, external transactions, and production by kind of activity. For countries whose data are in terms of the System of Material Product Balances, separate estimates are shown.

METHODOLOGY

The form and concepts of the tables conform to the recommendations in *A System of National Accounts, Studies in Methods,* Series F. No. 2, Rev 3. or, in the case of countries using MPS, *Basic Methodological Principles Governing the Compilation of the System of Statistical Balances of the National Economy,* Series F. No.17, Rev. 1. The data are collected from the national statistical services on the basis of questionnaires.

CONTENTS

Part I.
Introduction

I. System of National Accounts (SNA)

II. System of Material Product Balances (MPS)

III. Country Tables
Afghanistan
Albania
Algeria
Angola
Anguilla
Antigua and Barbuda
Argentina
Armenia
Australia
Austria
Bahamas
Bahrain
Bangladesh
Barbados

Belarus
Belgium
Belize
Benin
Bermuda
Bhutan
Bolivia
Botswana
Brazil
British Virgin Islands
Brunei Darussalam
Bulgaria
Burkina Faso
Burundi
Cameroon
Canada
Cape Verde
Cayman Islands
Central African Republic
Chad
Chile
China
Colombia
Congo
Cook Islands
Costa Rica
Cote d'Ivoire
Cuba
Cyprus
Czech Republic
Czechoslovakia (Former)
Denmark
Djibouti
Dominica
Dominican Republic
Ecuador
Egypt
El Salvador
Equatorial Guinea
Estonia
Ethiopia
Fiji
Finland
France
French Polynesia
Gabon
Gambia
Germany, Federal Republic of
Ghana
Greece
Grenada
Guadeloupe
Guatemala
Guinea-Bissau
Guyana
Haiti
Honduras
Hong Kong
Hungary
Iceland
India

Indonesia
Iran (Islamic Republic of)
Iraq
Ireland
Israel
Italy
Jamaica
Japan
Jordan
Kenya
Kiribati
Korea, Republilc of
Kuwait

Part II.
Introduction

I. System of National Accounts (SNA)

II. System of Material Product Balances (MPS)

III. Country Tables
Latvia
Lebanon
Lesotho
Liberia
Libyan Arab Jamahiriya
Lithuania
Luxembourg
Madagascar
Malawi
Malaysia
Maldives
Mali
Malta
Martinique
Mauritania
Mauritius
Mexico
Mongolia
Montserrat
Morocco
Mozambique
Myanmar
Nepal
Netherlands
Netherlands Antilles
New Caledonia
New Zealand
Nicaragua
Niger
Nigeria
Norway
Oman
Pakistan
Panama
Papua New Guinea
Paraguay
Peru
Philippines
Poland
Portugal
Puerto Rico

Qatar
Republic of Moldova
Reunion
Romania
Russian Federation
Rwanda
Saint Kitts and Nevis
Saint Lucia
Saint Vincent and the Grenadines
Sao Tome and Principe
Saudi Arabia
Senegal
Seychelles
Sierra Leone
Singapore
Slovakia
Slovenia
Solomon Islands
Somalia
South Africa
Spain
Sri Lanka
Sudan
Suriname
Swaziland
Sweden
Switzerland
Syrian Arab Republic
Tajikistan
Thailand
Togo
Tonga
Trinidad and Tobago
Tunisia
Turkey
Uganda
Ukraine
United Arab Emirates
United Kingdom
United Republic of Tanzania
United States
Uruguay
USSR (Former)
Vanuatu
Venezuela
Viet Nam
Yemen
Yugoslavia (Former)
Zaire
Zambia
Zimbabwe

NORDIC COUNTRIES

YEARBOOK OF NORDIC STATISTICS

FACTS AT A GLANCE

Number of Pages: 431

Periodicity: Annual

Publisher: Nordic Statistical Secretariat

PURPOSE AND SCOPE

The *Yearbook of Nordic Statistics* provides key statistics on various social conditions in the five Nordic countries: Denmark, Finland, Norway, Sweden, and Iceland.

DATA ORGANIZATION

The data are organized in 291 tables, 13 charts, and 7 maps. They are grouped in sections covering: Area, Climate, and Environment; Population and Families; Trade; Transport and Communication; Wages, Prices, and Consumption; Personal Income; Credit Markets; Public Finance; Social Welfare and Public Health; Crime and Justice; Research and Development; Cultural Life and Mass Media.

In addition, regional statistics are presented for the Oresund and Nordkalott Areas.

METHODOLOGY

The *Yearbook* is the annual summary of data collected by the Nordic Statistical Secretariat.

CONTENTS

Tables

Area, Climate, and Environment
General Note
1. Total Area
2. Principal Administrative Divisions
3. Precipitation
4. Temperature
5. Emissions to Air by Source
6. Sulphur Dioxide Concentration in Air in Some Large Cities
7. Estimated Depositions of Sulphur and Nitrogen and the Relations Between Depositions and Emissions
8. Consumption of Fertilizers
9. Sales of Pesticides
10. Water Consumption from Public Water Works
11. Public Wastewater Treatment Works Serving at Least 200 Persons
12. Land Under Conservation and Protection, End of Year

Population and Families
General Note
13. Population by Sex, 1800-1992
14. Mean Population by Sex and Age
15. Population by Sex and Age
16. Population by Sex and Marital Status
17. Native-Born and Foreign-Born by Sex and Age
18. Population by Sex, Citizenship and Age
19. Population by Citizenship
20. Aliens by Sex and Marital Status
21. Population Projections by Sex and Age, End of 1995-2030
22. Population by Sex, Urban/Rural Residence, and Density
23. Population of the Biggest Municipalities
24. Family Units by Living Arrangements and Number of Children Under 18 Years of Age
25. Children Under 18 Years of Age by Living Arrangement, Age, and Number of Brothers and Sisters
26. Vital Statistics
27. Vital Statistics Per 1000 of Mean Population
28. Live Births and Stillbirths by Sex
29. Live Births by Age of Mother
30. Adopted Children
31. Live Births and Infant Mortality
32. Stillbirths and Infant Mortality
33. Age-Specific Fertility Rates and Reproduction Rates
34. Deaths by Sex and Age
35. Death Rates Per 1,000 Mean Population by Sex and Age
36. Expectation of Life at Specified Ages by Sex
37. Survivors of 100,000 Live Births by Sex
38. Marriages
39. Divorces
40. Aliens Naturalized in the Nordic Countries
41. Immigrants
42. Emmigrants
43. Immigrants and Emigrants by Country
44. Asylum Applicants, Quota Refugees, and Residence Permits Granted for Refugees, etc.

Labour Market
General Note
45. Population by Activity, Sex, and Age 1992, Relative Distribution
46. Population Between 15/16 to 74 Years of Age by Activity
47. Labour Force Rates and Unemployment Rates
48. Employed and Unemployed by Sex and Age
49. Employed by Industry and Sex
50. Employed by Industry and Sex, 1992
51. Employed by Sex and Age, 1992
52. Stoppages of Work

Agriculture
General Note
53. Land Utilization
54. Use of Arable Land
55. Agricultural Holdings by Size of Arable Land
56. Crop Farming: Total Harvest

57. Crop Farming: Harvest of Grain
58. Crop Farming: Average Yield
59. Agricultural Holdings with and without Cattle
60. Livestock, Mid-year Estimates
61. Agricultural Production, Quantum Index
62. Production of Milk and Eggs
63. Farm Machinery

Forestry
General Note
64. Productive Forest Area by Owner Groups
65. Growing Stock and Annual Recorded Growth by Tree Species
66. Estimated Annual Removals
67. Hunting

Fisheries
General Note
68. Quantity of Catch
69. Value of Catch
70. Quantity and Value of Catch by Species
71. Fisherman
72. Fishing Vessels

Mining and Manufacturing
General Note
73. Manufacturing, Mining, and Quarrying, etc. by Branches of Industry
74. Manufacturing, Mining, and Quarrying by the Nordic Standard Industrial Classification
75. Volume Index of Industrial Production
76. Establishments in Manufacturing Industry According to Size by Number of Persons Engaged
77. Industrial Investments
78. Foreign-owned Industrial Enterprises
79. Merchant Vessels Under Construction
80. Merchant Vessels Launched
81. Patents Valid at End of Year
82. Patent Applications
83. Patents Granted

Energy
General Note
84. Gross Inland Supply of Energy
85. Final Inland Energy Consumption
86. Capacity of Crude Oil Refineries
87. Final Inland Consumption by Energy Sources
88. Balance Sheet of Energy Sources for Denmark
89. Balance Sheet of Energy Sources for Finland
90. Balance Sheet of Energy Sources for Iceland
91. Balance Sheet of Energy Sources for Norway
92. Balance Sheet of Energy Sources for Sweden
93. Overall Energy Balances for Denmark
94. Overall Energy Balances for Finland
95. Overall Energy Balances for Iceland
96. Overall Energy Balances for Norway
97. Overall Energy Balances for Sweden
98. Electric Energy: Installed Capacity and Corrresponding Average-year Production by

Installed Hydro-power and Windpower
99. Elecric Energy: Electricity Production, Gwh

Housing and Households

General Note

100. Housing Construction: Completed Dwellings
101. Dwellings by Type of House and Size
102. Dwellings by Period of Construction and Type of House
103. Dwelling Households by Number of Occupants and Size of Dwelling
104. Dwelling Households and Occupants by Size of Dwelling
105. Dwelling Households by Number of Members
106. Dwelling Households by Number of Children

Internal Trade

General Note

107. Retail Trade: Sales Establishments by Size
108. Retail Trade Value Index

External Trade

General Note

109. Value of External Trade, in Millions of National Currency Units
110. Value of External Trade, in Millions of U.S. Dollars
111. Quantity of External Trade, in Thousand Tons
112. Imports and Exports 1992 by Sections and Divisions of the SITC
113. Value of Imports, 1992 by Countries and Regions of Origin
114. Value of Exports, 1992 by Countries and Regions of Consumption/Consignment
115. Nordic Countries Trade, 1992 with Regions and by Sections and Divisions of the SITC
116. Intra-Nordic Trade: Value of Imports
117. Intra-Nordic Trade: Value of Exports
118. Intra-Nordic Trade: Value of Imports, 1992 by Sections of the SITC
119. Intra-Nordic Trade: Value of Exports, 1992 by Sections of the SITC
120. Intra-Nordic Trade: Imports and Exports, 1992 by Sections and Divisions of the SITC
121. Value of Imports, 1992 from the Faroe Islands: Analysis by SITC Sections
122. Value of Exports, 1992 to the Faroe Islands: Analysis by SITC Sections
123. Value of Imports, 1992 from Greenland: Analysis by SITC Sections
124. Value of Exports, 1992 to Greenland: Analysis by Sections SITC
125. Unit Value and Quantum Indexes of Imports and Exports, and Terms of Trade

Transport and Communication

General Note

126. International Goods Transport by Various Modes of Transport
127. Merchant Fleets
128. Merchant Fleets by Type of Vessel
129. Merchant Fleets by Size and Age
130. International Sea-borne Shipping: Vessels Entered and Cleared
131. International Sea-borne Shipping: Goods Loaded and Unloaded
132. Ships Totally or Partially Lost at Sea and Loss of Life
133. Railways: Length of Lines and Rolling Stock
134. Railways: Passenger Traffic
135. Railways: Goods Traffic
136. Registered Motor Vehicles and Trailers
137. New Registrations of Motor Vehicles and Trailers
138. Public Roads
139. Road Traffic Accidents: Persons Killed or Injured by Age
140. Road Traffic Accidents: Persons Killed or Injured by Category of Road Users
141. Road Traffic Accidents with Personal Injury: Traffic Units Involved
142. Civil Aviation: Engine-driven Aircraft
143. Civil Aviation: Embarking and Disembarking Passengers
144. Traffic of Finnair
145. Traffic of Icelandair
146. Traffic of Scandinavian Airlines System (SAS)
147. Domestic Conveyance of Passengers by Means of Transportation
148. Domestic Freight Transport by Means of Transportation
149. Number of Hotels, Hotel Beds, Guest Rights by Nationality, and Camping Sites
150. Volume of Mail
151. Telephone Services
152. Telegraph and Telex Services

Wages, Prices, and Consumption

General Note

153. Wages in Manufacturing and Construction by Branches of Industry
154. Wages in Manufacturing: All Industries
155. Wages for Full-time Employees
156. Retail Prices of Selected Food Products
157. Wholesale Price Index
158. Consumer Price Index
159. Consumer Prices: Annual Percentage Change
160. Steel Consumption
161. Consumption of Newsprint
162. Supply of Coffee, Tea, Cocoa, and Tobacco
163. Consumption Expenditure of Households
164. Per Capita Consumption of Food
165. Consumption of Alcoholic Beverages

Personal Income

General Note

166. Income Earners, Income, and Taxes
167. Tax Payers
168. Income Earners and Average Income by Sex and Age
169. Deciles for Income Earners
170. Income Shares in Decile Groups and Equalization Percentage

Credit Market

General Note

171. Foreign Exchange Reserves
172. Money Supply - Percentage: Annual Change
173. Central Bank Discount Rate

OIL

ANNUAL STATISTICAL BULLETIN

FACTS AT A GLANCE

Number of Pages: 143

Periodicity: Annual

Publisher: Organization for Petroleum Exporting Countries (OPEC)

PURPOSE AND SCOPE

The *Annual Statistical Bulletin* is the principal statistical publication issued by the OPEC consolidating the data collected from member countries on production, trade, and prices of petroleum and natural gas.

DATA ORGANIZATION

Data are organized under five sections. Section 1 provides summary tables and basic indicators. Section 2 presents oil and gas data, including exploration and reserves, production, share of production by company, refining, consumption, exports, and imports. Section 3 provides data on transportation, including pipelines, tanker fleets, and freight rates. Section 4 presents data on prices and the final section profiles the major oil companies and provides data on their principal operations, revenues, and capital expenditures.

METHODOLOGY

The publication is based on information collected by the OPEC from its member countries and reflects as closely as possible, the state of their petroleum and natural gas sectors.

CONTENTS

Section 1
Summary Tables and Basic Indicators

Tables

FACTS AND FIGURES

FACTS AT A GLANCE

Number of Pages: 34

Periodicity: Annual

Publisher: Organization of Petroleum Exporting Countries

PURPOSE AND SCOPE

After missing a year, *Facts and Figures* returns with this edition, which includes current data on world energy trends covering the five major commercial energy sources: oil, gas, coal, hydro, and nuclear.

DATA ORGANIZATION

Facts and Figures has six sections. The first three present a global perspective. Sections I and II focus on production and consumption trends in primary energy generally and oil and gas specifically, while Section III examines the energy resource base. Sections IV and V deal with the energy markets and economics. The last section makes broad global comparisons.

METHODOLOGY

This new edition marks a departure from the previous editions in some respects. The opening map of the world shows the flows of the Organization of Petroleum Exporting Countries' (OPEC) crude and refined oil excludes Ecuador (which left OPEC in 1992), and includes a table showing average daily output for the four major OPEC regions: Africa, Far East, Latin America, and the Middle East. Information is given on: OPEC's share of world oil output in Graph 6; recoverable conventional energy for Eastern Europe and the former Soviet Union in Graph 13; and a recalculation of OPEC's spot reference basket from 1982 in Graph 25.

CONTENTS

World Primary Energy Trends

World Oil and Gas Trends

World Energy Resources

OPEC Flows and Volumes

OPEC Prices and Values

Economic Comparisons

OIL AND GAS INFORMATION

FACTS AT A GLANCE

Number of Pages: 581

Periodicity: Annual

Publisher: Organization for Economic Cooperation and Development (OECD)

PURPOSE AND SCOPE

The fifth edition of *Oil and Gas Information* provides comprehensive statistics on the production and consumption of and trade in oil and natural gas principally in OECD countries, but also in other selected countries of the world.

DATA ORGANIZATION

The data are organized in three parts: Part I provides summary tables of world oil and market developments as a time series from the early 1970s. Parts II and III provide in tabular form, a more detailed picture of oil and gas supply and demand for the OECD region and its member countries.

METHODOLOGY

Statistics for OECD countries are based on data submissions from national energy administrations. Statistics up to 1991 are from the Annual Oil Statistics and Annual Gas Statistics databases while oil data for 1992 are based on the Monthly Oil and Gas Statistics database. Monthly statistics submitted by member governments are historically lower than annual statistics as they exclude demand for certain products, such as petroleum coke in some countries. To make the data compatible with the time series, they are adjusted upward to make up for the underreporting. Data for non-OECD countries are primarily from the International Energy Agency (IEA) database on World Energy Statistics. They cover supply and demand for all forms of energy for over 88 non-OECD countries. The data are collected from national statistical publications, other international organizations, and the energy industry.

CONTENTS

Part I: World Oil and Gas Developments

   Introduction

   Definitions

   Geographical Coverage

   Country Notes
   Oil
   Gas

   Conversion Factors

   Tables and Graphs for Part I
   OECD Energy Consumption, Oil Demand, and Economic Indicators
   World Oil Demand by Country
   World Demand by Main Product Group
   World Crude Oil and NGL Production
   World Refinery Output and Capacity
   World Oil Ports
   World Trade of Crude Oil and Products
   IEA Oil Prices, Crude Imports, and Product Prices
   World Natural Gas Production, Consumption, and Trade

Part II: OECD Oil Data

Part III: OECD Gas Data

PAPER

THE PULP AND PAPER INDUSTRY

FACTS AT A GLANCE

Number of Pages: 99

Publisher: Organization for Economic Cooperation and Development (OECD)

PURPOSE AND SCOPE

The purpose of *The Pulp and Paper Industry* is to present the best available statistics on the pulp and paper industry in the principal paper producing countries of the world.

DATA ORGANIZATION

The report provides an overview of developments in the pulp and paper industry in OECD member countries, focusing on production, consumption, exports and imports, and waste.

METHODOLOGY

The report follows the same format as other OECD publications dealing with industrial sectors.

CONTENTS

I. General Statistics
   1. Pulp Production, 1991
   2. Paper and Paperboard Production, 1991
   3. Comparison Between Industrial Production and Production of Pulp and Paper, 1987-1991
   4. Production and Consumption of Woodpulp, 1984-1991
   5. Production and Consumption of Paper and Board, 1984-1991
   6. Production Capacity Utilization, 1990-1991
   7. Paper and Board Consumption Per Capita, 1985-1991
   8. Production Capacity of Woodpulp, 1983-1996
   9. Production Capacity of Paper and Board, 1983-1996

II. Definition of Products

III. Imports-Exports 1991
   1-11. Pulp
   12. Waste Paper
   13-33. Paper and Paperboard

POPULATION

DEMOGRAPHIC YEARBOOK

FACTS AT A GLANCE

Number of Pages: 567

Periodicity: Annual

Publisher: United Nations (UN)

PURPOSE AND SCOPE

The *Demographic Yearbook* is a comprehensive collection of international demographic statistics prepared by the UN Statistical Division. Each edition focuses on a special topic. The topic of the current edition is ageing and the situation of elderly persons.

DATA ORGANIZATION

The tables in the *Yearbook,* presented in two volumes, begin with a world summary of basic demographic statistics, followed by tables presenting data on the size, distribution, and trends in population, natality, fetal mortality, infant and maternal mortality, general mortality, nuptiality, and divorce. Many of the tables present separate data for urban and rural inhabitants.

METHODOLOGY

The data merges official statistics received from national statistical services with estimates prepared by the Population Division of the UN Department of Economic and Social Development. The use of these estimates makes it possible to present complete tables for all countries and areas using a base year of reference.

The current *Demographic Yearbook* must be read along with the *Demographic Yearbook: Historical Supplement* covering a 30-year period from 1948 to 1978.

CONTENTS

World Summary

1. Population, Rate of Increase, Birth and Death Rates, Surface Area and Density for the World, Macro Regions and Regions: Selected Years
2. Estimates of Population and its Percentage Distribution, by Age and Sex, and Sex Ratio for all Ages for the World, Macro Regions and Regions: 1990
3. Population by Sex, Rate of Population Increase, Surface Area and Density for each Country or Area of the World: Latest Census, and Mid-year Estimates for 1985 and 1991
4. Vital Statistics Rates, Natural Increase Rates, and Expectation of Life at Birth: Latest Available Year

Population

5. Estimations of Mid-year Population: 1982-1991
6. Urban and Total Population by Sex: 1982-1991
7. Population by Age, Sex, and Urban/Rural Residence: Latest Available Year, 1982-1991 by Urban/Rural Residence
8. Population of Capital Cities and Cities of 100,000 and More Inhabitants: Latest Available Year

Natality

9. Live Births and Crude Live-birth Rates by Urban/Rural Residence: 1987-1991
10. Live Births by Age of Mother, Sex, and Urban/Rural Residence: Latest Available Year by Urban/Rural Residence
11. Live-birth Rates Specific for Age of Mother, by Urban/Rural Residence: Latest Available Year by Urban/Rural Residence

Fetal Mortality

12. Late Fetal Deaths and Late Fetal Death Ratios, by Urban/Rural Residence: 1986-1990

Legally Induced Abortion

13. Legally Induced Abortions: 1982-1990
14. Legally Induced Abortions by Age and Number of Previous Live Births of Woman: Latest Available Year

Infant and Maternal Mortality

15. Infant Deaths and Infant Mortality Rates by Urban/Rural Residence: 1987-1991 by Urban/Rural Residence
16. Infant Deaths and Infant Mortality Rates by Age, Sex, and Urban/Rural Residence: Latest Available Year by Urban/Rural Residence
17. Maternal Deaths and Maternal Mortality Rates: 1981-1990

General Mortality

18. Deaths and Crude Death Rates, by Urban/Rural Residence: 1987-1991 by Urban/Rural Residence
19. Deaths by Age, Sex, and Urban/Rural Residence: Latest Available Year by Urban/Rural Residence
20. Death Rates Specific for Age, Sex, and Urban/Rural Residence: Latest Available Year by Urban/Rural Residence
21. Deaths and Death Rates by Cause: Latest Available Year
22. Expectation of Life at Specified Ages for each Sex: Latest Available Year

Nuptiality

23. Marriages and Crude Marriages Rates, by Urban/Rural Residence: 1987-1991 by Urban/Rural Residence
24. Marriages by Age of Groom and Age of Bride: Latest Available Year
25. Divorces and Crude Divorce Rates: 1987-1991

Index

Subject Matter Index

THE SEX AND AGE DISTRIBUTION OF THE WORLD POPULATION

FACTS AT A GLANCE

Number of Pages: 399

Periodicity: Irregular

Publisher: United Nations

PURPOSE AND SCOPE

This report presents data on estimated sex and age distributions for the 40-year period from 1950 to 1990 and high-, medium-, and low-variant projections for 1995 to 2025. Projections for the constant-fertility variant are not included in this publication but are found in the electronic version. The publication supplements the wall chart entitled "World Population" and the report entitled *World Population Prospects, 1992 Revision*.

DATA ORGANIZATION

The report summarizes the results of the 13th round of population projections and estimates published in 1992. Data are presented for countries with a population of at least 200,000 in 1990. Data for smaller countries are included in the regional population totals but not presented separately. One set of estimates covers 1950 to 1990 followed by four variants for 1990 to 2025. The major differences among the variants are the assumed fertility levels (low, medium, high, constant) and future patterns of migration.

METHODOLOGY

Most of the estimates are derived from available national data that have been evaluated and, whenever necessary, adjusted for deficiencies and inconsistencies. All estimates are consistent with past censuses and surveys and in line with estimated past trends of fertility, mortality, and migration.

CONTENTS

Population by Sex and Age, for the World, Major Areas and Regions, 1950-2025, Estimates and Medium-, High,- and Low-Variant Projections

World Total

More Developed Regions

Less Developed Regions

Africa
Eastern Africa
Middle Africa
Northern Africa
Southern Africa
Western Africa

Asia
Eastern Asia
Southeastern Asia
Southern Asia
Western Asia

Europe
Eastern Europe
Northern Europe
Southern Europe
Western Europe

Latin America
The Caribbean
Central America
South America

Northern America

Oceania
Australia-New Zealand
Melanesia
Micronesia
Polynesia

USSR (former)

Special Groups
Less Developed Regions, Excluding China
Least Developed Countries

Sub-Saharan Africa

Economic Commission for Africa (ECA)

Economic Commission for Europe (ECE)

Economic Commission for Latin America and the Caribbean (ECLAC)

Economic and Social Commission for Western Asia (ESCWA)

THE STATE OF WORLD POPULATION

FACTS AT A GLANCE

Number of Pages: 66

Periodicity: Annual

Publisher: United Nations (UN)

PURPOSE AND SCOPE

The *State of World Population* is the annual statistical review that summarizes the basic facts about global population and demography.

DATA ORGANIZATION

The data are standard elements that measure population growth and change. Certain social elements are added, including adult literacy, school enrollment ratio, gross national product per capita, agricultural density, access to safe water, and food production per capita.

METHODOLOGY

The data are derived from the UN Population Fund's data files.

CONTENTS

Population (millions)
1994

Population (millions)
2025

Average Growth Rate
1990-95

Birth Rate per 1,000
1990-95

Death Rate per 1,000
1990-95

Life Expectancy
1990-95

Infant Mortality
1990-95

Percent Urban
1992

Urban Growth Rate (percent)
1990-95

Fertility Rate/Women
1990-95

Adult Literacy M/F
1990

Secondary School Enrollment M/F
1986-91

Births Attended by Health Workers (percent)
1983-92

Family Planning Users (percent)
1975-93

Access to Health Services (percent)
1985-92

Access to Safe Water (percent)
1985-92

Food Production Per Capita (1979-81=100)
1991

Agricultural Pop/ha/Arable Land
1989

Capita (US$)
1991

GNP Per Capita (US$)
1991

Percent of Central Government Expenditure - Education and Health
1991

WORLD POPULATION PROFILE

FACTS AT A GLANCE

Number of Pages: 142

Periodicity: Biennial

Publisher: U.S. Bureau of the Census

PURPOSE AND SCOPE

The *World Population Profile* presents updates of U.S. Census Bureau's population estimates and projections for all countries and regions of the world. It includes information on population composition, population growth, fertility, mortality, and the use of contraception. A special chapter focuses on AIDS. The report is accompanied by a set of maps illustrating the data.

DATA ORGANIZATION

The *World Population Profile* includes summary demographic information for the world, regions, and all countries and territories with a population of at least 5,000 in 1994. Detailed tables backing up the charts and text are presented in Appendix A. The tables cover 225 countries and territories, reflecting the new countries born out of the breakup of the Soviet Union, Yugoslavia, and Czechoslovakia. In the tables, data for countries are aggregated into regional totals. Countries and territories are further classified by development status according to categories used by the United Nations.

METHODOLOGY

The methodology and assumptions used for making the population estimates and projections are given in Appendix B. Detailed notes and documents on the methodological procedures may be obtained from the Chief, Population Studies Branch, Center for International Research, U.S. Bureau of the Census, Washington, DC 20233-3700.

CONTENTS

Highlights

Introduction

1. Population Size and Growth
World population and average annual rates of growth per decade, by development category: 1950 to 2020. Population of major world regions by development category: 1970, 1994, and 2020. Average annual rates of population growth for world regions: 1950 to 2020. Population in 1994 and population to be added from 1994 to 2020, for world regions. Population added each hour for world regions: 1994. Distribution of world population by country: 1994. Population and average annual growth rate, for today's most populous countries:

1950 to 2020. Countries ranked by land area and by population: 1994. Countries ranked by population and by land area: 1994. Population density of the ten most populous countries: 1994. Demographics of the former soviet union: 1994.

2. Population Composition
Population, by age, sex, and development category: 1994 and 2020. Distribution of world population in selected ages by development category: 1994. Percent of population under age 15 years by region: 1994 and 2020. Median age by development category: 1994 to 2020. Percent of population ages zero to four years and 60 years and over: 1994 and 2020. Percent change in number of women of child bearing ages by region: 1990 to 2020. Growth rate of school age, working age, and elderly population by region: 1990 to 2020.

3. Components of Change
World births, deaths and natural increase by development category: 1994. Share of world population, births, and deaths by development category: 1994. Crude birth rates by region: 1994. Average number of seconds between births by region: 1994. Distribution of world population by level of crude birth rate: 1994. Distribution of world births by country: 1994. World births and total fertility rates: 1994 to 2020. Number of countries and population represented by level of total fertility rate: 1994. Ten countries with largest fertility decline: 1985 to 1994. Crude death rates by development category and region: 1994. Life expectancy at birth by sex and region: 1994. Infant mortality rates by sex and region: 1994. Infant deaths as a proportion of all deaths by region: 1994. Percent distribution of world infant deaths by country/region: 1994. Distribution of countries with high infant mortality rates by region: 1994. Net migration rate and rate of natural increase, for selected countries: 1994.

4. Contraceptive Prevalence
Contraceptive prevalence rate for large countries: 1985 or later. Contraceptive prevalence rate for selected countries by region: 1985 or later. Contraceptive prevalence rates for selected countries by urban/rural residence: latest year. Percent of married women using contraception by method for selected countries: latest year. Trends in contraceptive prevalence rates for selected countries or areas: 1965 to 1993. Trend in percent of married women using traditional and modern methods of contraception. Contraceptive prevalence rates for selected countries by age: 1991 or later. Trends in contraceptive prevalence rates for selected countries by age. Contraceptive prevalence rate for Bangladesh by age and urban/rural residence: 1991. Total fertility rate and contraceptive prevalence rate, for selected countries: 1967 or later. Unmet need for family planning among currently married women for selected countries: 1985 or later.

5. Focus on HIV/AIDS
Reported cumulative AIDS cases by region: January 1993. Estimated cumulative HIV seroprevalence in adults by region: mid 1993. Adult AIDS cases for Europe and the United States by mode of transmission: 1992. HIV infected for Sub-Saharan Africa and Latin America by mode of transmission: 1992. HIV seroprevalence among commercial sex workers for selected urban areas in Africa: 1983 to 1992. HIV seroprevalence among pregnant women for selected urban areas in Africa: 1985 to 1992. HIV-1 seroprevalence among low-risk urban populations in Africa: circa 1992 . HIV-2 seroprevalence among low-risk urban populations in Africa: circa 1992. HIV seroprevalence among commercial sex workers in Bombay, India: 1986 to 1992. HIV seroprevalence among commercial sex workers in Thailand by region: 1990 to 1992. Illustrative impact of HIV on age-specific mortality rates at approximately 20 percent adult prevalence. Survivors per 100,000 births with and without AIDS by age. AIDS and non-AIDS deaths, for 13 African countries: 1985 to 2010. Vital rates with and without AIDS, for 13 African countries: 1985 to 2010. Crude death rate with and without AIDS, for selected countries: 2010. Infant mortality rate with and without AIDS, for selected countries: 2010. Child mortality rate with and without AIDS, for selected countries: 2010. Life expectancy at birth with and without AIDS, for selected countries: 2010. Population growth rates with and without AIDS, for selected countries: 2010. Population size with and without AIDS, for selected countries: 2020. Population of Zambia, Kenya, and Zaire, with and without AIDS: 2010.

Appendix A: Detailed Tables
World population and average annual rates of growth by region and development category: 1950 to 2020. Population, vital events, and rates by region and development category: 1994. Population by country or area: 1950 to 2020. Population, vital events, and rates, by country or area: 1994. All women and currently married women of reproductive age (15 to 49 years) by country or area: 1990 to 2000. Population by region, development category and age: 1994 to 2020. Total fertility rates by country or area: 1985 to 2020. Infant mortality rates and life expectancy of birth by country or area and sex: 1994. Percent of currently married women using contraception by method: all available years. Percent of currently married women using contraception by age: all available years.

Appendix B: Population Projections and Availability of Data

1. Making Population Projections

2. Population Projections Incorporating AIDS
Empirical seroprevalence data for selected countries by urban/rural residence. Empirical trend in HIV seroprevalence among urban pregnant women for selected countries: 1985 to 1992. Three scenarios

and empirical trend of urban female HIV seroprevalence. Three scenarios and empirical trend of total female HIV seroprevalence. Projected HIV seroprevalence among adults for selected countries: 1990 to 2010.

3. Recency of the Data Base for the Projections

Distribution of countries and of population by region, and recency of reliable data on population size. Distribution of countries and of population by region, and recency of reliable data on fertility. Distribution of countries and of population, by region, and recency of reliable data on mortality.

4. Information on Contraceptive Prevalence

Distribution of countries and of population by region, and recency of reliable data on contraceptive prevalence.

Appendix C: References

Appendix D: Glossary

WORLD POPULATION PROSPECTS

FACTS AT A GLANCE

Number of Pages: 677

Periodicity: Biennial

Publisher: United Nations

PURPOSE AND SCOPE

World Population Prospects is the record of the 13th round of global demographic estimates and projections.

DATA ORGANIZATION

The data present estimates and projections for: (1) the world; and (2) more developed and less developed regions, 7 major areas, 22 regions, and 211 countries. Short term projections and estimates are also presented for the 12 countries of the former Soviet Union. The population estimates have been influenced by two new factors: large migratory movements across borders and the AIDS pandemic. For the first time, regional estimates include child mortality by sex and age patterns of fertility.

METHODOLOGY

The bottom limit of the population size for countries has been lowered to 200,000. As a result, six new countries have been included in the tables: Brunei, Maldives, Bahamas, Solomon Islands, Guam, and French Polynesia. Most of the estimates are derived from available national data, evaluated and adjusted for deficiencies and inconsistencies. For countries where the data are lacking or deficient, the estimates correspond to reasonable assumptions.

CONTENTS

Asia
Eastern Asia
Southeastern Asia
Southern Asia
Western Asia

Europe
Eastern Europe
Northern Europe
Southern Europe
Western Europe

Latin America
The Caribbean
Central America
South America

Northern America

Oceania
Australia-New Zealand
Melanesia
Micronesia
Polynesia

USSR (former)

Less Developed Regions, Excluding China
Least Developed Countries

Sub-Saharan Africa

ECA

ECE

ECLAT

ESCAP

ESCWA

A.19 Demographic Indicators, by Country

1. World Population Size, Medium, High, and Low Variants
2. Growth Rates: More Developed and Less Developed Regions and Least Developed Countries
3. Growth Rate Difference Between More Developed and Less Developed Regions
4. Growth Rates: Africa, Latin America, Asia, Northern America, and Europe
5. Annual Increment: Major Areas of the World, 1985-1990
6. Distribution of Population, 1950-2025
7. Distribution of World Population, 1992
8. Crude Birth Rate: World, More Developed and Less Developed Regions, 1950-1995
9. Annual Births: More Developed and Less Developed Regions and Least Developed Countries, 1950-1995 to 2020-2025
10. Distribution of Births, by Major Area
11. Total Fertility Rates: World, More Developed and Less Developed Regions and Least Developed Countries, 1950-2025
12. Total Fertility Rate, by Major Area

13. (A) Total Fertility Rate; (B) Number of Births: Africa
14. (A) Total Fertility Rate; (B) Number of Births: Asia
15. (A) Total Fertility Rate; (B) Number of Births: Latin America
16. (A) Total Fertility Rate: Europe and Northern America: (B) Number of Births: Europe
17. Age-Specific Fertility Rate, Percentage of Births, by Age of Mother; Distribution of Births, by Age of Mother: World, More Developed and Less Developed Regions, 1985-1990
18. Age-Specific Fertility Rate; Percentage of Births, by Age of Mother; Distribution of Births, by Age of Mother: Less Developed Regions
19. Age-Specific Fertility Rate; Percentage of Births, by Age of Mother; Distribution of Births, by Age of Mother: More Developed Regions
20. Crude Death Rates: World, More Developed and Less Developed Regions and Least Developed Countries, 1950-2025
21. Average Annual Deaths: World, More Developed and Less Developed Regions, and Least Developed Countries, 1950-2025
22. Average Annual Deaths: Major Areas, 1950-2025
23. Life Expectancy: World, More Developed and Less Developed Regions, and Least Developed Countries, 1950-1995
24. Life Expectancy: Major Areas, 1950-1995
25. (A) Life Expectancy; (B) Number of Deaths: Africa
26. (A) Life Expectancy; (B) Number of Deaths: Asia
27. (A) Life Expectancy; (B) Number of Deaths: Latin America
28. (A) Life Expectancy: Europe and Northern America; (B) Number of Deaths: Europe
29. Deaths, by Age: World, More Developed and Less Developed Regions
30. Deaths, by Age: Major Areas, 1985-1990
31. Infant Mortality Rate: World, More Developed and Less Developed Regions, 1950-1995
32. Infant Mortality Rate: Africa, Asia, Latin America, and Oceania
33. Infant Mortality Rate: Europe, Northern America, and USSR (former)
34. Child Mortality Estimates: Major Areas and Regions, 1985-1990
35. Sex Differentials in Life Expectancy: World, More Developed and Less Developed Regions, 1950-1995
36. Sex Differentials in Life Expectancy: Major Areas
37. Sex Differentials in Child Mortality: Major Areas and Regions, 1985-1990
38. Decline in Population Due to the Aids Epidemic, 1980-2005
39. Impact of Aids on the Number of Deaths, 1975-2005

POSTAL SERVICES

POSTAL STATISTICS

FACTS AT A GLANCE

Number of Pages: 508

Periodicity: Annual

Publisher: Universal Postal Union

PURPOSE AND SCOPE

Postal Statistics has been published in one form or another since 1875. The statistical publication under review was begun in 1964, and it presents the most complete range of statistical information on postal communications and systems.

DATA ORGANIZATION

The publication is divided into two parts: Part I presents data for the past five years for each country or territory. Part II presents the same information thematically under several appropriate headings.

METHODOLOGY

The new edition represents a break with the format of past editions. First, the information is presented not only by country, but also by topic. Second, time series data are presented in place of the former annual data. The total number of topical headings has been reduced, a few have been deleted and others added.

CONTENTS

General Remarks
Area of Territory (km2)
Population (millions)
Statistical Period Covered
Financial Period Covered
Rate of Exchange (national currency for one SDR)

Staff
Number of Full-time Staff
Number of Part-time Staff
Total Number of Staff

Postal Establishments
Post Offices Open to the Public
Permanent Post Offices
Number of Offices Offering a Full Range of
    Services
Number of Secondary Offices Staffed by
    Administration Officials
Number of Secondary Offices Staffed by People
    from Outside the Administration
Total Number of Permanent Offices
Average Area Covered by a Permanent Office (km2)

Average Number of Inhabitants Served by a
    Permanent Office

Mobile Post Offices
Number of Mobile Offices (road, river, etc.)
Number of Rural Postmen Providing the Services of
    a Permanent Office
Number of Localities Served by Mobile Post Offices
Number of Post Offices (permanent and mobile)
    Accepting Financial Transactions

Post Offices Not Open to the Public
Number of Sorting Offices
Number of Offices of Exchange with Abroad
Number of Travelling Post Offices (rail, road, river,
    etc.)
Technical Means
Number of Letter-boxes
Number of Post Office Boxes
Number of Aircraft
Number of Trucks and Automobiles
Number of Motorcycles, Scooters, and Mopeds
Number of Bicycles
Number of Automatic Vending Machines for
    Postage Stamps or Prepayment Labels
Number of Franking Machines
Number of Machines for Facing Letter-post Items
Number of Canceling Machines
Number of Machines Combining Facing and
    Canceling
Number of Letter-sorting Machines
Number of Machines for Sorting Packets and
    Parcels
Number of Sorting Machines with Automatic
    Address Reading

Financial Results
Total Receipts (SDR)
Total Operating Expenditure (SDR)
Expenditure on Investments (SDR)

Delivery
Average Number of Deliveries per Day in Urban
    Areas
Average Number of Deliveries per Week in Rural
    Areas
Percentage of Items Delivered Through Post Office
    Boxes
Percentage of the Population Having Mail Delivered
    at Home
Percentage of the Population Having to Collect Mail
    from a Postal Establishment
Percentage of the Population without Postal
    Delivery

Letter Post: Total Traffic
Total Number of Letter Post Items
Domestic Service
International Service - Dispatch
International Service - Receipt
Average Number of Letter-post Items Posted per
    Inhabitant

LC (letters and cards) or Priority Items

Domestic Service

International Service - Dispatch

PRICES AND EARNINGS

PRICES AND EARNINGS AROUND THE GLOBE

FACTS AT A GLANCE

Number of Pages: 29

Periodicity: Annual

Publisher: Union Bank of Switzerland

PURPOSE AND SCOPE

The standard international sourcebook on price and salary comparisons compiled by the Economic Research Department of the Union Bank of Switzerland. Individual surveys were carried out by correspondent banks of the Union Bank of Switzerland.

DATA ORGANIZATION

The survey is based on a questionnaire containing 141 questions on prices and 96 questions on salaries, salary deductions, and hours worked in 12 different professions. A total of 52 cities were covered, including three added for this edition: Frankfurt, Nairobi, and Nicosia.

METHODOLOGY

All prices and wages are converted into a uniform currency and are thus subject to fluctuations in currency rates. International price and salary comparisons depend on a basket of selected goods and services, weighted in the same manner for all cities.

CONTENTS

Most Expensive Cities: Tokyo, Oslo, Helsinki, and Stockholm

Swiss and Scandinavian Cities Boast Highest Hourly Earnings

Long Workweeks in Far East, Short Working Hours in Europe

Earnings in Los Angeles Buy Most

Inflation Dominated by Exchange Rate Developments

Purchasing Power Parities Higher than Floating Exchange Rates

International Price Comparison

Basis of Calculation

Price Differences Between Categories of Goods

Foodstuffs Priced Highest in Japan, Scandinavia, and Switzerland

Low-Cost Apparel in Manila

Rents in Some Areas Exorbitant

Furnished 4-Room Apartments Range from $360 to $9,500

3-Room Apartments from $180 to $6,000

Typical Low Cost Rents from $40 to $1,430

Household Appliances Cost Less in America

Public Transportation Cheap in South America and the Far East

Automobiles: Buy One in North America and Drive it in South America

Hotel Overnight Stays in Africa Reasonably Priced

Short Stays in Major European Cities Can be Costly

Service Charges in Line with Earnings

Wages and Salaries Around the World

Top Earners in Switzerland, America, West Germany, and Scandinavia

No Taxes and Social Insurance Contributions in Abu Dhabi and Jakarta

Working Year Averages 1,966 Hours

Over Four Weeks of Vacation...and a Workweek of Under 43 Hours

PUBLIC FINANCE

GOVERNMENT FINANCE STATISTICS YEARBOOK

FACTS AT A GLANCE

Number of Pages: 701

Periodicity: Annual

Publisher: International Monetary Fund (IMF)

PURPOSE AND SCOPE

The *Government Finance Statistics Yearbook* is the principal IMF publication on public finance and budgets and other related financial transactions of all countries.

DATA ORGANIZATION

The current edition, like its predecessors, is divided into three parts: World Tables, Statistical Tables for Individual Countries, and Institutional Tables 1-3 for individual countries. World Tables permits international comparisons of the structure and relative magnitude of government operations. Data for each central government are calculated as a percentage of total revenue or expenditure or as a percentage of gross domestic product (GDP). The nations are divided into industrial and developing, and the latter are again subdivided by continents or regions. Four world tables present composite items for central governments as percentages of total revenue, total expenditure, and total expenditure and lending minus repayments. Thirty three tables show individual central government items as percentages of total expenditure, total revenue, and total expenditure and lending minus repayments. Eight tables present the major aggregates and defense expenditures as percentages of GDP.

The statistical tables for individual countries are presented on central government revenue, expenditure, lending minus repayments, financing, and debt for 114 countries. For many countries additional, though less detailed, data are presented for state and local governments. Summary tables show consolidated budgetary, social security, and extrabudgetary accounts of central government. Tables A through G show the details of principal aggregates which are cross referenced in the summary tables.

METHODOLOGY

Information for the *Yearbook* is obtained primarily by means of a detailed questionnaire distributed to government finance statistics correspondents usually working in each country's respective finance ministry or central bank. Statistics on some Organization for Economic Cooperation and Development countries are obtained directly from its Committee on Fiscal Affairs.

CONTENTS

World Tables

Central Government: Tables for Composite Items, Most Recent Years Available

Major Components as Percentages of Total Expenditure and Lending Minus Repayments (S.6)

Types of Revenue as Percentages of Total Revenue (S.2)

Expenditures by Function as Percentages of Total Expenditure (S.7)

Expenditures by Economic Type as Percentages of Total Expenditure and Lending Minus Repayments (S.6)

Central Government: Tables for Individual Items, 1986-1993

Overall Deficit/Surplus (S.15) as a Percentage of Total Expenditure and Lending MinusRepayments (S.6)

Domestic Financing (S.18) as a Percentage of Total Expenditure and Lending Minus Repayments(S.6)

Foreign Financing (S.17) as a Percentage of Total Expenditure and Lending Minus Repayments (S.6)

Financing from Monetary Authorities (S.18.3) as a Percentage of Total Expenditure and Lending Minus Repayments (S.6)

Financing from Deposit Money Banks (S.18.2) as a Percentage of Total Expenditure and Lending Minus Repayments (S.6)

Domestic Debt (F.ll) as a Percentage of Total Expenditure and Lending Minus Repayments (S.6)

Foreign Debt (F.lll) as a Percentage of Total Expenditure and Lending Minus Repayments (S.6)

Taxes on Income and Profits (A.1) as a Percentage of Total Revenue (S.2)

Social Security Contributions (A.2) as a Percentage of Total Revenue (S.2)

Taxes on Domestic Goods and Services (A.5) as a Percentage of Total Revenue (S.2)

Taxes on International Trade and Transactions (A.6) as a Percentage of Total Revenue(S.2)

Nontax Revenue (S.3.2) as a Percentage of Total Revenue (S.2)

Grants (S.5) as a Percentage of Total Revenue (S.2)

Expenditure on Defense (B.2) as a Percentage of Total Expenditure (S.7)

Expenditure on Social Security and Welfare (B.6) as a Percentage of Total Expenditure (S.7)

Expenditure on Education (B.4) as a Percentage of Total Expenditure (S.7)

Expenditure on Health (B.5) as a Percentage of Total Expenditure (S.7)

Expenditure on Housing and Community Amenities (B.7) as a Percentage of Total Expenditure (S.7)

Expenditure on Economic Affairs and Services (B.9-13) as a Percentage of Total Expenditure (S.7)

Expenditure on Mining, Manufacturing, and Construction (B.11) as a Percentage of Total Expenditure (S.7)

Expenditure on Other Economic Affairs and Services (B.13) as a Percentage of Total Expenditure (S.7)

Expenditure on Fuel and Energy (B.9) as a Percentage of Total Expenditure (S.7)

Expenditure on Agriculture, Forestry, Fishing, and Hunting (B.10) as a Percentage of Total Expenditure (S.7)

Expenditure on Road Transport (B.12.1) as a Percentage of Total Expenditure (S.7)

Expenditure on Other Transportation and Communication (B.12.2-8) as a Percentage of Total Expenditure (S.7)

Current Expenditure on Goods and Services (C.1) as a Percentage of Total Expenditure and Lending Minus Repayments (S.6)

Subsidies and Other Current Transfers (C.3) as a
Percentage of Total Expenditure and
Lending Minus Repayments (S.6)

Current Expenditure on Wages and Salaries
(C.1.1) as a Percentage of Total Expenditure
and Lending Minus Repayments (S.6)

Other Current Purchases of Goods and Services
(C.1.3) as a Percentage of Total Expenditure
and Lending Minus Repayments (S.6)

Interest Payments (C.2) as a Percentage of Total
Expenditure and Lending Minus Repayments
(S.6)

Transfers to Other Levels of National
Government (C.3.2 plus C.7.1.1) as a
Percentage of Total Expenditure and
Lending Minus Repayments (S.6)

Capital Expenditure (S.9) as a Percentage of
Total Expenditure and Lending Minus
Repayments (S.6)

Lending Minus Repayments (S.10) as a
Percentage of Total Expenditure and
Lending Minus Repayments (S.6)

**Central Government: Tables for Individual Items,
1982-1993**

Overall Deficit/Surplus (S.15) as a Percentage of
Gross Domestic Product

**Overall Deficit/Surplus without Grants (S.15 minus
S.5) as a Percentage of Gross Domestic Product**

Current Account Surplus with Current Grants
(S.12) as a Percentage of Gross Domestic
Product

Current Account Surplus without Grants (S.11)
as a Percentage of Gross Domestic Product

Total Revenue (S.2) as a Percentage of Gross
Domestic Product

Total Expenditure (S.7) as a Percentage of Gross
Domestic Product

Expenditure on Defense (B.2) as a Percentage of
Gross Domestic Product

Total Expenditure and Lending Minus
Repayments (S.6) as a Percentage of Gross
Domestic Product

REVENUE STATISTICS OF
OECD MEMBER COUNTRIES

FACTS AT A GLANCE

Number of Pages: 265

Periodicity: Annual

Publisher: Organization for Economic Cooperation
and Development (OECD)

PURPOSE AND SCOPE

The purpose of this annual bulletin is to provide
internationally comparable data on tax levels and
structures in OECD member countries.

DATA ORGANIZATION

The material is organized in eight parts. Part I consists of an introduction and a series of comparative
graphs showing differences between countries regarding tax levels and structures. Part II contains standardized OECD classifications of taxes. Part III consists of three sets of statistical tables for the period
from 1965 through 1991. Part IV presents, in somewhat less disaggregated form, estimates of 1992 tax
revenues for all countries. Part V presents data for
1955 and 1960 for all OECD countries except France,
Greece, Ireland, Luxembourg, and Spain. Part VI
shows tax revenues received by general government
from the following sectors: supranational, central,
state, local, and social security funds. Part VII presents data on non-tax revenues, capital revenue, and
grants. Part VIII provides an overview of tax revenues, non-tax revenues, and grants. A special supplement provides data on tax revenues for Bulgaria,
the Czech Republic, Slovakia, Hungary, Poland, and
Romania.

METHODOLOGY

The data, supplied by delegates to the OECD
Committee on Fiscal Affairs, are presented in a standardized format based on the "OECD Classification of
Taxes and Interpretative Guide." The OECD classification system is not materially different from the SNA
(the United Nations System of National Accounts)
and the ESA (European System of Integrated
Economic Accounts of the European Communities).
Non-tax revenues are presented separately.

CONTENTS

Introduction

I. Comparative Graphs
Total tax revenue as percentage of GDP, 1991. Tax
revenue of main headings as percentage of total tax
revenues, 1991. Taxes on income and profits
(1,000) as percentage of GDP, 1965-1991. Social
Security contributions (2,000) as percentage of
GDP, 1965-1991. Taxes on goods and services
(5,000) as percentage of GDP, 1965-1991. Tax structures in OECD member countries as percentage of
total tax revenues, 1965-1991.

II. The OECD Classification of Taxes and
Interpretative Guide
Coverage. Basis of reporting. General classification
criteria. Commentaries on the items of the list.
Relation to national accounting systems. Relation of
OECD classification of taxes to the IMF system.
Comparison of the OECD classification of taxes with
other international classifications. Attribution of tax
revenues by sub-sector of general government.

III. The Statistical Tables (1965-91)
Comparative tables on tax revenues. Country tables
on tax revenues. Country tables on the financing of
social security benefits. Country tables on social

security contributions and payroll taxes paid by government. Country tables on compulsory loans collected through the tax system.

IV. Estimates of 1992 Tax Revenues

V. Tax Revenues for 1955 and 1960

VI. The Attribution of Tax Revenues by Sub-sector of General Government (1975, 1985, 1991)

VII. Non-tax Revenue, Capital Revenue, and Grants
Introduction. Definitions of the components of current non-tax revenue, capital revenue, and grants. Country tables on current non-tax revenue, capital revenue, and grants.

VIII. Tax Revenues, Non-tax Revenues, and Grants: An Overview
Special Feature. Statistics on central and eastern European countries.

List of Tables

A. List of Comparative Tables
1. Total Tax Revenue as Percentage of GDP (1991)
2. Total Tax Revenue (excluding Social Security) as Percentage of GDP 1991
3. Total Tax Revenue as Percentage of GDP (1965-1991)
4. Total Tax Revenue (excluding Social Security) as Percentage of GDP (1965-1991)
5. Total Tax Revenue as Percentage of GDP-3 Year Moving Average (1965-1991)
6. Tax Revenue of Main Headongs as Percentage of GDP (1991)
7. Tax Revenue of Main Headings as Percentage of Total Taxation (1991)
8. Taxes on Income and Profits (1000) as Percentage of GDP
9. Taxes on Income and Profits (1000) as Percentage of Total Taxation
10. Taxes on Personal Income (1100) as Percentage of GDP
11. Taxes on Personal Income (1100) as Percentage of Total Taxation
12. Taxes on Corporate Income (1200) as Percentage of GDP
13. Taxes on Corporate Income (1200) as Percentage of Total Taxation
14. Social Security Contributions (1200) as Percentage of Total Taxation
15. Social Security Contributions (2000) as Percentage of GDP
16. Employee's Social Security Contributions (2100) as Percentage of GDP
17. Employee's Social Security Contributions (2100) as Percentage of Total Taxation
18. Employer's Social Security Contributions (2200) as Percentage of GDP
19. Employer's Social Security Contributions (2200) as Percentage of Total Taxation
20. Taxes on Payroll and Workforce (3000) as Percentage of GDP
21. Taxes on Payroll and Workforce (3000) as Percentage of Total Taxation
22. Taxes on Property (4000) as Percentage of GDP
23. Taxes on Property (4000) as Percentage of Total Taxation
24. Taxes on Goods and Services (5000) as Percentage of GDP
25. Taxes on Goods and Services (5000) as Percentage of Total Taxation
26. Consumption Taxes (5100) as Percentage of GDP
27. Consumption Taxes (5100) as Percentage of Total Taxation
28. Taxes on General Consumption (5110) as Percentage of GDP
29. Taxes on General Consumption (5110) as Percentage of Total Taxation
30. Taxes on Specific Goods and Services (5120) as Percentage of GDP
31. Taxes on Specific Goods and Services (5120) as Percentage of Total Taxation
32. Total Tax Revenue in Million Dollars
33. Tax Revenue of Individual Countries as Percentage of Total OECD Tax Revenue
34. Tax Revenue in Dollars Per Capita
35. Annual Percentage Change in Total Tax Revenue (National Currencies)
36. GDP at Market Prices - Billions of National Currency Units
37. Exchange Rates Used - National Currency Units per Dollar

B. Country Tables on Tax Revenues of General Government
38. Australia
39. Austria
40. Belgium
41. Canada
42. Denmark
43. Finland
44. France
45. Germany
46. Greece
47. Iceland
48. Ireland
49. Italy
50. Japan
51. Luxembourg
52. The Netherlands
53. New Zealand
54. Norway
55. Portugal
56. Spain
57. Sweden
58. Switzerland
59. Turkey
60. United Kingdom
61. United States

C. Country Tables on the Financing of Social Security Benefits
62. Australia

148. Sweden
149. Switzerland
150. Turkey
151. United Kingdom
152. United States

C. Non-tax Revenue, Capital Revenue, and Grants
153. Australia
154. Austria
155. Belgium
156. Canada
157. Denmark
158. Finland
159. France
160. Germany
161. Greece
162. Iceland
163. Ireland
164. Italy
165. Japan
166. Luxembourg
167. The Netherlands
168. New Zealand
169. Norway
170. Portugal
171. Spain
172. Sweden
173. Switzerland
174. Turkey
175. United Kingdom
176. United States

Tax Revenues, Non-tax Revenues, and Grants
177. Revenues Received by General Governments
178. Revenues Received by State and Local Governments

RAILWAYS

INTERNATIONAL RAILWAY STATISTICS

FACTS AT A GLANCE

Number of Pages: 101

Periodicity: Annual

Publisher: International Union of Railways

PURPOSE AND SCOPE

International Railway Statistics is the only compendium of statistics on railways worldwide. It covers the physical and economic aspects of the rail industry.

DATA ORGANIZATION

The data are organized under three broad groups: Composition and Resources (covering the infrastructure, such as lines, tractive stock, freight transport and passenger transport stock, personnel, and train movements); Technical Operations and Traffic (covering rolling stock movements and freight passengers carried); and Finance and Economics.

METHODOLOGY

The data are compiled by the International Union of Railways through direct questionnaires and reports submitted by member railways.

CONTENTS

Composition and Resources of the Railway
11. Lines
21. Tractive stock
22. Passenger transport stock
23. Freight transport stock
31. Staff
41. Train movements
42. Gross hauled tonne-kilometers of trains

Technical Operating Movements Results
43. Rolling stock
51. Revenue-earning passenger traffic
61. Freight traffic
71. Balance sheet

Financial Results
72. Specific costs and revenue. Operating and general results for the financial year.

RESEARCH AND DEVELOPMENT

RESEARCH AND DEVELOPMENT: ANNUAL STATISTICS

FACTS AT A GLANCE

Number of Pages: 191

Periodicity: Annual

Publisher: European Communities

PURPOSE AND SCOPE

Research and Development: Annual Statistics (formerly known as *Government Financing of Research and Development*) is part of a series of annuals providing statistical information on research and development in the European Union.

DATA ORGANIZATION

The focus in the first 14 tables is on government budgetary appropriations for research and development. Table 15 deals with the business enterprise sector, and Table 17 with the higher education sector. There is new information on scientists and engineers in research and development.

METHODOLOGY

Some restructuring has been done in the current edition involving the deletion of some tables and the addition of others. Data are derived from statistical information received from member states.

CONTENTS

ROADS

WORLD ROAD STATISTICS

FACTS AT A GLANCE

Number of Pages: 193

Periodicity: Annual

Publisher: International Road Federation

PURPOSE AND SCOPE

World Road Statistics is the premier statistical reporter on statistics relating to roads, motor vehicles and road traffic, and related subjects.

DATA ORGANIZATION

World Road Statistics deals primarily with roads but it also provides data on road construction, production and exports of motor vehicles, vehicles in use, road traffic, road accidents, fuels, and road taxes and expenditures.

METHODOLOGY

The International Road Federation is a major statistical collection agency on roads and road networks and collects data directly from its members, including public transportation officials in member countries.

CONTENTS

Diagrams
1. Road Expenditures as a Percentage of State Receipts
2. Number of Four-Wheel Vehicles Per Kilometer of Road
3. Production and Exports of Motor Vehicles (Excluding 2-Wheeled Vehicles)
4. First Registrations of Four-Wheeled Vehicles Per 1000 Persons
5. Percentage Growth of the Number of Cars in Use Between 1987 and 1991
6. Percentage Changes in the Total of Injury Accidents Between 1987 and 1991
7. Examples of Average Annual Taxation on a Private Car of 1500 cc Consuming 1500 Liters of Petrol
8. Road Taxes as a Percentage of State Receipts
9. Road Expenditure as a Percentage of Road Taxes
10. Comparison of Number of Killed Persons per 1 Million with Numbers of Cars per 1000 Persons

I. Road Networks
II. Production and Exports of Motor Vehicles
III. First Registration and Imports of Motor Vehicles
IV. Vehicles in Use
V. Road Traffic

VI. Motor Fuels
VII. Road Accidents
VIII. Rates and Basis of Assessments of Road User Taxes
IX. Examples of Average Annual Taxation
X. Annual Receipts from User Taxation
XI. Road Expenditure

ROBOTS

WORLD INDUSTRIAL ROBOT STATISTICS

FACTS AT A GLANCE

Number of Pages: 120

Periodicity: Annual

Publisher: United Nations (UN)

PURPOSE AND SCOPE

World Industrial Robot Statistics presents statistics on the growth and extent of use of industrial robots. Robots are the most advanced form of industrial automation and they form the centerpiece of computer-integrated manufacturing systems. Industrial robots not only improve productivity, but also help to obtain more consistent product quality. They play an increasingly important role in rationalization of production techniques and reduction of hazards in the workplace, such as exposure to heat, gases, and chemicals. They can replace human workers in work environments requiring the lifting of heavy weights or repetitious and monotonous physical movements.

Worldwide stock of robots is estimated at 600,000 units. Spurred by advances in semiconductor and computer technologies, robots are found not only in industry, but also in construction, hospitals (especially in surgery), hotels, and laboratories. The annual is a joint effort of the UN/ECE (Economic Commission for Europe) Working Party on Engineering and Automation and the International Federation of Robotics.

DATA ORGANIZATION

Part I is a global overview of the stock of robots by major application areas and industrial branches. Part II focuses on 22 countries with the highest density of robots.

METHODOLOGY

The publication is based on the statistical files of the International Federation of Robotics and the ECE Working Party on Engineering Industries and Automation.

CONTENTS

1. Worldwide Robot Diffusion in 1992 - An Overview

Worldwide diffusion and growth in 1992. Analysis of the development of robot density in selected countries. Analysis of the stock and supply of robots in 1992 by major application areas. Analysis of the stock and supply of robots in 1992 by major industrial branches. Analysis of the stock supply of robots in 1992 by major industrial branches.

2. The Diffusion of Robots in Individual Countries in 1991 and 1992

Introduction. Australia. Austria. Benelux. Denmark. Finland. France. Germany. Hungary. Italy. Japan. Norway. Poland. Russian Federation. Singapore. Slovak Republic. Slovenia. Spain. Sweden. Taiwan (province of China). United Kingdom. United States.

RUBBER

KEY RUBBER INDICATORS

FACTS AT A GLANCE

Number of Pages: 90

Periodicity: Annual

Publisher: International Rubber Study Group (IRSG)

PURPOSE AND SCOPE

Key Rubber Indicators is based on the World Rubber Database maintained by the International Rubber Study Group.

DATA ORGANIZATION

The first part presents detailed data on total and per capita consumption, imports, exports, prices, and export unit values. The second part presents data on rubber-based products and vehicles.

METHODOLOGY

The data are derived from reports from member organizations and governments.

CONTENTS

Notes

List of IRSG Member Governments and Members of the Panel of Associates

Sources of Information

  Supplementary Rubber Statistics
  Total Rubber Consumption Per Capita, 1960-1992
  Natural Rubber Consumption Per Capita, 1960-1992
  Synthetic Rubber Consumption Per Capita, 1960-1992

Gross Natural Rubber Imports by Type, 1988-1992
Canada, U.S.A., France
Germany, Italy, U.K.
Japan, Republic of Korea, Taiwan
Imports and Exports of Synthetic Rubber by Type, 1988-1992
Styrene-Butadiene (SBR) Latex
Styrene-Butadiene (SBR) Solid
Polybutadiene (BR)
Isobutene-Isoprene (IIR)
Halo-Isobutene-Isoprene (CIIR/BIIR)
Chlorobutadiene (CR) Latex
Chlorobutadiene (CR) Solid
Acrylonitrile-Butadiene (NBR) Latex
Acrylonitrile-Butadiene (NBR) Solid
Polyisoprene (IR)
Ethylene-Propylene Non-Conjugated Diene (EPDM) Masterbatch
Kuala Lumpur Natural Rubber Prices, 1984-1992
Synthetic Rubber Export Unit Values, 1980-1992
Styrene-Butadiene (SBR) Latex
Styrene-Butadiene (SBR) Solid
Butadiene (BR)
Isobutene-Isoprene (IIR), Halo-Isobutene-Isoprene (CIIR/BIIR), Chlorobutadiene (CR) Latex and Solid
Acrylonitrile-Butadiene (NBR) Latex and Solid
Isoprene (IR), Ethylene-Propylene Non-conjugated Diene (EPDM)

Rubber Good Statistics
Car Tire Production: 1975-1992
Commercial Vehicle Tyre Production, 1975-1992
Car Tire Exports of Major Countries, 1975-1992
Commercial Vehicle Tyre Exports of Major Countries, 1975-1992
Production of General Rubber Products, 1975-1992
Hose and Tubing
Belting
Crepe and Foam Rubber
Hygienic and Pharmaceutical Articles
Floor Covering
Rubberized Cloth
Soling, Soles, and Heels
Glues, Solutions, and Dispersions
Sports Goods and Toys
Ebonite Goods
Other Rubber Products

Vehicle-related Statistics
Car Production and Assemblies, 1975-1992
Commercial Vehicle Production and Assemblies, 1975-1992
Cars in Use, 1960-1992
Commercial Vehicles in Use, 1960-1992
Cars in Use per Thousand Population, 1960-1992
Commercial Vehicles in Use per Thousand Population, 1960-1992

Traffic Volume, 1975-1992
Cars
Commercial Vehicles

Average Annual Distance, 1975-1992
Cars
Commercial Vehicles

Fuel Consumption, 1975-1992
Cars
Commercial Vehicles

RUBBER STATISTICAL BULLETIN

FACTS AT A GLANCE

Number of Pages: 47

Periodicity: Monthly

Publisher: International Rubber Study Group (IRSG)

PURPOSE AND SCOPE

The purpose of the *Rubber Statistical Bulletin* is to update the *World Rubber Statistics Handbook* and *Key Rubber Indicators*.

DATA ORGANIZATION

The *Bulletin* follows the same format as the *Statistics Handbook* but adds several data elements on current rubber production.

METHODOLOGY

The *Bulletin* is based on reports received by IRSG from member organizations and governments.

CONTENTS

List of IRSG Member Governments and Members of the Panel of Associates

Current Publications and Prices

Summary Tables
Table 1. Production, Consumption, and Stocks of Natural Rubber
Table 2. Production, Consumption, and Stocks of Synthetic Rubber
Table 3. Consumption of Natural and Synthetic Rubber
Table 4. Percentage Consumption of Synthetic Rubber
Table 5. Reported Stocks of Natural Rubber in Consuming Areas
Table 6. Reported Stocks of Synthetic Rubber

Natural Rubber
Table 7. Production of Natural Rubber
Table 8. Technically Specified Rubber
Table 9. Net Exports of Natural Rubber (including latex data)
Table 10. Gross Exports of Sheet Rubber by Grade
Table 11. Gross Exports of Technically Specified Rubber by Grade

Table 12. Net Imports of Natural Rubber
Table 13. Consumption of Natural Rubber
Table 14. Consumption of Natural Rubber in Producing Countries
Table 15. Stocks of Natural Rubber in Producing Countries
Table 16. Current Rubber Position in Peninsular Malaysia and Malaysian Rubber Exports
Table 17. Current Rubber Position in Singapore
Table 18. Current Rubber Position in Indonesia
Table 19. Current Rubber Position in Thailand
Table 20. Current Rubber Position in Sri Lanka
Table 21. Gross Imports of Natural Rubber into Major Non-producing Countries

Natural Rubber Latex
Table 22: Net Imports of Natural Rubber Latex
Table 23: Consumption of Natural Rubber Latex

Synthetic Rubber
Table 24: Production of Synthetic Rubber
Table 25: Gross Exports of Synthetic Rubber
Table 26: Exports of Synthetic Rubber by Destinations
Table 27: Net Imports of Synthetic Rubber
Table 28: Consumption of Synthetic Rubber

Current Rubber Positions
Tables 29-32: United States of America, Brazil, France, and Germany
Tables 33-36: United Kingdom, Australia, India, and Japan

Major Sectors and End Products
Table 37: Rubber Consumption by Major Sectors
Table 38: Production of Car and Truck Tires
Table 39: Tire Production [Car + Truck]
Table 40: Tire Exports of Major Countries
Table 41: Tire Imports of Major Countries
Table 42: Indices of Rubber Goods Production

General
Table 43: SBR Export Values
Table 44: Natural Rubber Prices
Table 45: Synthetic Rubber List Prices
Table 46: Area Under Plantation Rubber (including 1990 Data Where Available)
Table 47: World Synthetic Rubber Capacities

WORLD RUBBER STATISTICS HANDBOOK

FACTS AT A GLANCE

Number of Pages: 73

Periodicity: Annual

Publisher: International Rubber Study Group

PURPOSE AND SCOPE

The *World Rubber Statistics Handbook* is the principal statistical publication of the International Rubber

Study Group presenting comprehensive statistics on production, consumption, and trade in natural and synthetic rubber.

DATA ORGANIZATION

The book opens with summary tables followed by chapters on natural rubber, synthetic rubber, major sectors and end products, and prices. The next section deals with vehicles which are the largest users of rubber. The final historic section presents data from 1900.

METHODOLOGY

Data are compiled from member organizations and countries and have a high degree of reliability and consistency.

CONTENTS

Summary Tables
Table 1. Production, Consumption, and Stocks of Natural Rubber
Table 2. Production, Consumption, and Stocks of Synthetic Rubber
Table 3. Consumption of Natural and Synthetic Rubber
Table 4. Percentage Consumption of Synthetic Rubber
Table 5. Reported Stocks of Natural Rubber in Consuming Areas
Table 6. Reported Stocks of Synthetic Rubber

Natural Rubber
Table 7: Production of Natural Rubber
Table 8: Net Exports of Natural Rubber (including Latex Data)
Table 9: Gross Exports of Sheet Rubber by Grade
Table 10: Gross Exports of Technically Specified Rubber by Grade
Table 11: Net Imports of Natural Rubber
Table 12: Imports of Natural Rubber into 'Other' Countries
Table 13: Consumption of Natural Rubber
Table 14: Consumption of Natural Rubber in Producing Countries
Table 15: Stocks of Natural Rubber in Producing Countries
Table 16: Net Imports of Natural Rubber Latex
Table 17: Consumption of Natural Rubber Latex
Table 18: Planted Area Under Rubber

Synthetic Rubber
Table 19: Production of Synthetic Rubber
Table 20: Gross Exports of Synthetic Rubber
Table 21: Net Imports of Synthetic Rubber
Table 22: Synthetic Rubber Imports into 'Other' Countries
Table 23: Consumption of Synthetic Rubber
Table 24: World Synthetic Rubber Capacities

Major Sectors and End Products
Table 25: Rubber Consumption by Major Sectors
Table 26: Indices of Rubber Goods Production

Table 27: Production of Car Tires
Table 28: Production of Commercial Vehicle Tires
Table 29: Car Tire Radialisation
Table 30: Commercial Vehicle Tire Radialisation
Table 31: Car Tire Exports of Major Countries
Table 32: Commercial Vehicle Tire Exports of Major Countries
Table 33: Car Tire Imports of Major Countres
Table 34: Commercial Vehicle Tire Imports of Major Countries

Prices
Table 35: Natural Rubber Prices
Table 36: INRO Daily Market Indicator Price
Table 37: Synthetic Rubber List Prices
Table 38: SBR Export Values

Vehicles
Table 39: Car Production
Table 39a: Car Assemblies
Table 40: Commerical Vehicle Production
Table 40a: Commercial Vehicle Assemblies
Table 41: New Car Registrations
Table 42: New Commercial Vehicle Registrations
Table 43: Cars in Use
Table 44: Commercial Vehicles in Use

Historic
Table 45: World Position of Natural Ruber, 1900-1945
Table 46: Natural Rubber Prices, 1900-1960
Table 47: World Rubber Position, 1946-1960

SHIPPING

MARITIME TRANSPORT

FACTS AT A GLANCE

Number of Pages: 184

Periodicity: Annual

Publisher: Organization for Economic Cooperation and Development (OECD)

PURPOSE AND SCOPE

Maritime Transport covers developments and likely future trends in international shipping.

DATA ORGANIZATION

Part I outlines international maritime developments in the context of international shipping policies. It also provides a brief description of developments in shipbuilding policies in the OECD area. Part II considers commercial developments in world shipping including interaction of supply and demand. The statistical annex brings together the principal elements of international sea-borne trade, world fleet, and freight markets.

METHODOLOGY

The data are collected from members of the Maritime Transport Committee, the principal coordinating body responsible for monitoring maritime transport and traffic.

CONTENTS

Part I. International Shipping Developments

Chapter 1. Shipping Policy Developments in Member Countries
Developments within the Organization
General
Treatment of Support Measures
The Open Registry Phenomenon
The Aging of the World Fleet
OECD Shipping Relations with Non-Member Countries
National Shipping Policy Developments

Chapter 2. Shipping Policy Developments Outside the OECD Area
West and Central African States
Latin America
Dynamic Asian Economies
Central and Eastern European Countries

Chapter 3. Maritime Piracy and Armed Robberies
Incidents
Preventive Measures
Further Action

Chapter 4. Developments in the United Nations
United Nations Conference on Trade and Development
Standing Committee on Developing Services
Sectors: Shipping
The United Nations Convention on the Law of the Sea
Status of Conventions

Chapter 5. General Agreement on Tariffs and Trade
Multilateral trade negotiations - General Agreement on Trade in Services (GATS)

Chapter 6. BIAC and TUAC Developments
BIAC
TUAC

Chapter 7. Activities of the International Maritime Organization
General
Maritime Safety Committee (MSC)
International Convention on Standards of Training, Certification, and Watchkeeping for Seafarers, 1978 (STCW 1978)
Facilitation Committee
Working Group on Strategy for Port Interface
Marine Environment Protection Committee (MEPC)
London Dumping Convention, 1972 (LDC)
Legal Committee

Chapter 8. Government Policies in Favor of the Shipbuilding Industry
Negotiations on Competitive Conditions in Shipbuilding
Shipbuilding Policies Pursued by Member Countries

Part II. Commercial Developments in World Shipping Economic Background - 1992 Review

Chapter 9. Demand for Shipping Services
Developments in Shipping Markets
Dry and Liquid Bulk Shipping Markets
Developments in Liner Shipping Markets
Outlook for Shipping Demand

Chapter 10. Supply of Shipping Services
Overall Developments
The World Merchant Fleet by Major Ship Types
Newbuilding Prices
Tonnage Lost and Laid Up
Ship Scrapping

Chapter 11. The Freight Markets
General
Dry Bulk Freight Markets
Tanker Freight Markets
Liner Freight Rates
Bunker Prices

Part III. Transition from a Centrally Planned Economy

Chapter 12. The Maritime Transport Sector Located in Eastern Germany
Introduction
Provisional Legal Framework for the Transition
Adjustment Processes in the MaritimeTransport Sector
Sales/Marketing
Privatization and Rehabilitation
Summary and Conclusions

Annexes

1. Status of UNCTAD Shipping Conventions

2. Statistical Annex

WORLD FLEET STATISTICS

FACTS AT A GLANCE

Periodicity: Annual

Publisher: Lloyd's Register of Shipping

PURPOSE AND SCOPE

World Fleet Statistics is a new publication from Lloyd's Register that replaces the *Statistical Tables* and the *Annual Summary of Merchant Ships Completed*.

DATA ORGANIZATION

World Fleet Statistics contains data on the global fleet of propelled sea-going merchant ships at the end of a calendar year and on ships completed during the calendar year. Two characteristics of the new publication are: one, it is more oriented toward ship-types and, two, tables are continually updated from one issue to the next. Each table gives the number of ships, aggregate gross tonnage, aggregate deadweight tonnage for cargo ships, aggregate gas capacity for liquefied natural gas ships, aggregate twenty-foot equivalent unit capacity for fully cellular container ships, and aggregate insulated capacity in cubic meters for fully refrigerated cargo ships. Where relevant, average age is also included. Tables I and IIA through IIE list world merchant fleets in alpha order of flag states with offshore registries and dependent states shown as sublistings.

METHODOLOGY

The publication excludes pleasure craft, ships of less than 100 tons gross tonnage, naval auxiliaries, and ships restricted to harbor service or river and canal service. The definition of ship-types is based on design functions with hull structure and cargo carrying modes being given due prominence. Supplementary information and analyses are provided in the Statistical Notes section.

CONTENTS

Merchant Fleets - Cargo Carrying Ships/Ships of Miscellaneous Activities
Table Merchant Fleets of the World

Merchant Fleets - Cargo Carrying Ships
Table 2A: Bulk Liquid Cargo
Table 2B: Bulk Dry Cargo
Table 2C: Other Dry Cargo

Merchant Fleets - Ships of Miscellaneous Activities
Table 2D: Fishing and Offshore
Table 2E: Other Activities

Completions During the Year - Cargo Carrying Ships/Ships of Miscellaneous Activities
Table 3: Countries of Build

Completions During the Year - Countries of Build
Table 4A: Bulk Liquid Cargo and Bulk Dry Cargo
Table 4B: Other Dry Cargo
Table 4C: Ships of Miscellaneous Activities

Age Profile of the World Fleet/Completions During the Year
Table 5: Ship-type Categories

Deadweight and Age Profile/Completions During the Year
Table 6: Cargo Carrying Ships

Principal Ship-type Categories - Age Profile/Completions During the Year
Table 7A: Liquefied Gas - Deadweight Ranges
Table 7B: Liquefied Gas - Gas Capacity Ranges
Table 8: Chemical - Deadweight Ranges
Table 9: Oil - Deadweight Ranges
Table 10: Bulk Dry - Deadweight Ranges

Table 11: Bulk Dry/Oil - Deadweight Ranges
Table 12: General Cargo (including Passenger/General Cargo) - Deadweight Ranges
Table 13: Ro-Ro Cargo (including Passenger/Ro-Ro Cargo) - Deadweight Ranges
Table 14A: Container - Deadweight Ranges
Table 14B: Container - TEU Capacity Ranges
Table 15A: Refrigerated Cargo - Deadweight Ranges
Table 15B: Refrigerated Cargo - Insulated Capacity Ranges
Table 16: Passenger - Gross Tonnage Ranges
Table 17: Fish Catching - Gross Tonnage Ranges

Gross Tonnage and Age Profile/Completions During the Year
Table 18: The World Fleet
Time Series - The Previous Five Years
Table 19: Principal Merchant Fleets of the World
Table 20: Principal Cargo Carrying Fleets - by Flag State
Table 21: Completions - by Principal Countries of Build
Table 22: Completions - by Ship-type Category
Table 23: Ship Disposals and Losses - by Principal Flag States
Table 24: Ship Disposals and Losses - by Ship-type Category

SOCIAL

COMPENDIUM OF SOCIAL STATISTICS AND INDICATORS

FACTS AT A GLANCE

Number of Pages: 168

Periodicity: Irregular

Publisher: United Nations

PURPOSE AND SCOPE

The purpose of the *Compendium of Social Statistics and Indicators* is to provide a series of data and indicators on the social situation and economic and social changes in Western Asia.

DATA ORGANIZATION

The data and indicators in the *Compendium* illustrate social and economic changes. These indicators focus on women, children, youth, the disabled, and other disadvantaged groups. The data cover the following topics: population, human settlements, households and families, marital status, education, health and human services, economic activity, income and expenditure, culture and communication, and crime and criminal justice.

METHODOLOGY

The *Compendium* draws on other databases, such as the UNICEF's, Putting Data to Work for Children, the ILO Labour Force Database, the UN Population Database, and the Disability Database developed by the United Nations Statistical Division.

CONTENTS

1. Population Size, Composition, and Change

Population estimates by size, age, and sex. Selected demographic indicators of population change and composition. Estimates of dependency ratios in the ESCWA region, 1990-2015.

2. Human Settlements

Population in urban and rural areas, and in largest city by sex (census rounds). Percentage of population residing in urban areas (estimates 1950-2010). Population of urban agglomerations of one million or more inhabitants in the ESCWA region (estimates 1950-2010). Population of capital cities in the ES region, 1990. Percentage of population with access to safe water, to adequate sanitation and percentages of housing units with electricity, latest available year. Total and per capita consumption of electricity and motor vehicle gasoline. Surface, land area, and land use. Physical features (latitude, normal temperature, and precipitation), capital or other available city.

3. Households and Families, Marital Status

Number of households and average household size. Percentage of never married population in the age group (15-54), and the singulate mean age at marriage. Percentage of currently married by age group and gender, latest available year. Registered divorces and crude divorce rates, 1987-1992. Contraceptive use among currently married women of reproductive age, latest available year.

4. Education

Illiterate population by age group and sex (latest available census). School re-enrollment, annual rate of increase, enrollment ratio, and pupils per teacher (first level). School enrollment, annual rate of increase, enrollment ratio, and pupils per teacher (second level). Enrollment at third level by field of study and sex. Graduates of third level by field of study and sex.

5. Health and Health Services

Selected health indicators (1), 1980-2000. Selected health indicators (2). Health indicators on child nutrition and immunization. Registered deaths by sex and cause of death, latest available year (ICD-9 basic list). Number of reported AIDS cases in the ESCWA region. Prevalence of disability by age group, sex, and type of disability (census rounds).

6. Economic Activity and Population not Economically Active

Economically active population by age groups and sex. Not economically active population by age groups and sex. Economically active population by sex and occupational groups. Estimated economically active population by sex and age group 15+, 1980-2000. Estimates of not economically active population by sex and age group 15+, 1980-2000. Human development index for the ESCWA region.

7. Income and Expenditure

Gross domestic product and per capita, 1980, 1985, 1990, 1991. Government expenditure on education, health, and the military.

8. Culture and Communication

Selected indicators on culture and communication. Annual TV broadcasting hours by type of programs (latest available year). Annual radio broadcasting hours by type of program (latest available year).

9. Crime and Criminal Justice

Recorded crimes by type of crime and category of persons involved. Recorded crimes by persons involved and annual rate of change, 1984-1990.

Index of Graphs

Population pyramid for the ESCWA region. Total fertility rate in the ESCWA region, 1990-1995. Estimated percentages of population residing in urban areas, 1950-1995. Percentage of women currently using contraceptives. Estimates of illiterate population in the ESCWA region, 15 years and under, 1990. School enrollment ratio in the first level for some ESCWA countries, 1980, 1985, and 1990. Infant mortality rate in the ESCWA region, 1990-1995. Number of population per doctor in the ESCWA region, 1984-1989. Participation rate of economically active population in the ESCWA region, latest available year. Human development index for the ESCWA region, 1990. GDP annual growth rate in the ESCWA region, 1985, 1990, and 1991. Annual TV broadcasting hours by type of program for some ESCWA countries (percentage). Number of crimes per 100 thousand inhabitants for some ESCWA countries (1984-1990).

REPORT ON THE WORLD SOCIAL SITUATION

FACTS AT A GLANCE

Number of Pages: 226

Periodicity: Quadrennial

Publisher: United Nations

PURPOSE AND SCOPE

The *Report on the World Social Situation* brings together multidisciplinary data culled from other publications on the world social situation.

DATA ORGANIZATION

The data are presented in 15 chapters: (1) Population; (2) Food; (3) Health; (4) Education; (5) Housing; (6) Employment and Unemployment; (7) Income, Output, and Income; (8) Public Finance; (9) Quality of Life; (10) Government Current Expenditure; (11) Public Welfare; (12) Violence, Ethnic Groups, and Religion; (13) Energy; (14) Environment; and (15) Tobacco and Drugs. Each chapter is accompanied by one or more tables and charts.

METHODOLOGY

The data are derived from a number of other publications dealing with specific topics and subjects covered in the *Report*.

CONTENTS

Tables

SOCIAL INDICATORS FOR THE EUROPEAN COMMUNITY

FACTS AT A GLANCE

Number of Pages: 138

Periodicity: Irregular

Publisher: European Communities

PURPOSE AND SCOPE

This is the third volume of *Social Indicators* produced by the Statistical Office of the European Communities. Its purpose is to provide, by means of indicators and data, the principal features of the social situation in the European Union.

DATA ORGANIZATION

The volume is divided into two parts: the first, comprising five chapters, is devoted to social policies and issues of current concern to the European Union (EU). The second part, comprising two chapters, deals with general social indicators.

METHODOLOGY

Most indicators are derived from statistics which the Eurostat collects through national statistical services in member states and some have been published in other EU publications. Because of the persistence of differences in statistical practices and methodologies, absolute comparisons between countries should be made with caution. However, comparisons within the same country are generally valid and trends in different countries are generally comparable. The volume has explanatory notes and a bibliography to assist the reader in obtaining further clarification and information.

CONTENTS

Introduction

Symbols and Abbreviations

Part A. Indicators for Specific Social Concerns

1. Unemployment.
Commentary. Registered unemployment, EUR 9. Registered unemployment rates, EUR 9 and member states. Number of registered unemployed and breakdown by age. Unemployment rates. Unemployment rates, total and less than 25 years. Age profile of registered unemployed. Duration of registered unemployment. Proportion of unemployed by duration of registration, October 1982. Reasons for unemployment and methods of job search. Unemployment rates by age groups (extended concept).

2. Employment
Commentary. Working population and employment, EUR 10. Working population and employment, member states. Activity rates by sex. Trends in working population. Civilian employment by sector of activity. Total employment by sector of activity. Trends in civilian employment by sector of activity. Trends in total employment by sector of activity. Employees in employment. Civilian employment by status and employees by sector of activity. Activity rates by age groups.

3. The Trend in Employment in Manufacturing Industries
Commentary. Trends in employment in manufacturing industries, 1974-82. Number of employees in selected manufacturing industries. Trends in employment in the ECSC iron and steel industry. Reduction in employment in the ECSC iron and steel industry. Entrants to and leavers from employ-ment in the ECSC iron and steel industry. Employment in the ECSC iron and steel industry.

4. The Position of Women in the Community
Commentary. Women's participation in the education system. Enrollment in full-time education. Marriage, divorce, and childbirth. Average number of children per woman. Composition of household. Households by sex of head. Women at work. Women's activity rates by age groups. Women with a job per 100 men with a job. Percentage of households with children in which the mother is economically active. Women and old age. Additional life expectancy of women aged 60, compared with men.

5. Community Regional Indicators
Commentary. Population density, 1981. Annual rate of change of population, 1975-81. Activity rate, total, 1981. Unemployment rate, total, 1981. Activity rate, women, 1981. Unemployment, women, 1981. Unemployment rate for young people under 25, 1981. Main regional indicators. Gross domestic product per inhabitant, 1980. EUR 10 (PPS)=100.

Part B. General Social Indicators

6. The European Community and the World
Population, employment. Excess of births over deaths per 1,000 inhabitants, 1960-80. Gross domestic product per head of population (ECU). Standard of living, prices, health, education.

7. Miscellaneous Social Indicators
Total population—annual average. Population by sex and age groups. Total population and civilian working population, 1979. Principal demographic indicators. Prices: consumer price indices. Consumer price indices, general index. Exchange rates and purchasing power parities. Comparison of gross domestic product per inhabitant. Earnings. Working time. Public holidays. National accounts: gross domestic product and private consumption. Private consumption per inhabitant. Means of communication and information. Number of pupils and students in full-time education. Social protection: expenditure. Structure of social protection benefits. Medical services: personnel and equipment. Expectation of life at birth. Housing.

Annexes

Explanatory notes

Bibliography

SOCIAL INDICATORS OF DEVELOPMENT

FACTS AT A GLANCE

Number of Pages: 409

Periodicity: Annual

Publisher: World Bank and The Johns Hopkins University Press

PURPOSE AND SCOPE

Social Indicators of Development is the World Bank's primary publication dealing with poverty levels in the world. Priority Poverty Indicators (PPIs) are used in the tables to monitor levels and trends in poverty along with other social data for assessing human welfare.

DATA ORGANIZATION

The publication covers 192 economies, including the newly independent countries of Eastern Europe. The country pages present a selected array of indicators. The left hand page shows selected social and economic conditions and the right hand page shows changes in these conditions. Countries are arranged under regional headings and income groups are listed at the bottom of the page. Only low- and middle-income economies with populations of more than two million are included. The country pages identify poverty trends, the social issues and problems accompanying development, and the role of public policy. In addition to poverty measures, the tables cover wages and prices, health status, access to basic services, and the share of gross domestic product dedicated to social services. The country pages also offer international comparisons by presenting aggregated data mostly weighted by population for reference groups. Three reference groups for each country are the income category in which the economy is classified, the next higher income category, and the geographic region.

METHODOLOGY

The *Social Indicators of Development* apply the Priority Poverty Indicators to monitor changes in social and economic climate. Two thresholds, upper and lower poverty lines, have been established. They are presented along with headcount indexes that report what percentage of a country's population is below each threshold. In general, as countries develop, the poverty lines move up. Income indicators track the income earning opportunities and living standards of the poor. Because the poor spend nearly all their wages on consumption and nearly half of it on food, food prices are also reported disaggregated by urban and rural residence. The tables also track the provision and outcome of social services.

A new feature, Supplementary Poverty Indicators has been introduced in the current edition. These indicators include access to, expenditure on, and coverage of social security for basic public goods such as health care and clean drinking water. They trace the vulnerability of a population to sudden medical emergencies and unemployment. Such vulnerability is higher when there are no safety nets such as national health care and unemployment insurance.

Three charts are included in the PPI page. The first two show changes in population and gross national product (GNP) per capita with the same scale for all countries to make international comparisons easier. The third is a development diamond portraying relationships among four socio-economic indicators—life expectancy, gross primary school enrollment, access to safe water, and GNP per capita—for a given country and comparing them with the average of the country's income group. Each axis presents one indicator connected with a bold line to the others to form a polygon. Any point outside the reference diamond represents a value better than the group average and any point within the reference diamond represents a value below the group average.

The main themes covered in the right hand page are human resources, natural resources, income, expenditure, and investment in human capital.

Social Indicators of Development is issued annually on diskette as well as in print form. The diskette contains time series since 1965.

CONTENTS

I. Population
Population Estimates
Demographic Indicators
Population by Age and Sex
Economically Active Population by Economic Activity

II. Social Statistics
Educational Expenditure
Number of Students by Level of Education
Number of Students in Universities by Field of Study
Number of Graduates from Universities by Field of Study
Teaching Staff
Number of Schools, Institutes, and Universities by Level of Education
Number of Persons Engaged in the Medical and Related Professions
Number of Hospitals, Hospital Beds, and Other Health Centers

III. National Accounts
Gross Domestic Product and Expenditure at Current Prices
Gross Domestic Product by Kind of Economic Activity in Producers' Values at Current Prices

IV. Agriculture, Forestry, and Fishing
Index Numbers of Agricultural Production
Land Use
Production of Principal Crops
Number of Livestock
Fish Catches
Meat, Milk, and Eggs Production
Forestry Production
Means of Agricultural Production

V. Industry
Index Numbers of Industrial Production
Mining Production
Value of Industrial Outputs

VI. Energy
Production and Consumption of Eectric Energy

VII. Foreign Trade
Value of Imports, Exports, and Balance of Trade
Foreign Trade Index Numbers
Geographical Distribution of Imports
Geographical Distribution of Exports
Imports by SITC Sections
Exports by SITC Sections

VIII. Finance
Currency and Banking
Balance of Payments
Government Receipts
Government Expenditure
Price Index Numbers

IX. Transport, Communication, and Tourism
Railways
Roads and Motor Vehicles
Sea-borne Shipping
Air Traffic
Communication
Arab Arrivals by Nationalities
Tourism

STEEL

ANNUAL BULLETIN OF STEEL STATISTICS FOR EUROPE

FACTS AT A GLANCE

Number of Pages: 199

Periodicity: Annual

Publisher: United Nations

PURPOSE AND SCOPE

The purpose of the *Annual Bulletin* is to provide basic data on various aspects of the steel industry including: trade, production, consumption, raw materials, and consumption of energy in the steel industry.

DATA ORGANIZATION

Data are organized in seven sections dealing with production of raw materials, production of finished and semi-finished steel products, deliveries of steel, exports and imports, consumption of raw materials, movements of iron and steel scrap, and consumption of energy by steel producing plants.

METHODOLOGY

An annex provides guidance on nomenclature and classification of steel products.

CONTENTS

Explanatory Notes

List of Countries

Tables
1. Production of Raw Materials and Iron Products
2. Production of Semi-finished and Finished Steel Products
3. Steel Industry Deliveries and Receipts
4. Imports and Exports of Raw Materials and Iron and Steel Products
5. Consumption of Raw Materials in the Steel Industry
6. Movements of Iron and Steel Scrap
7. Consumption of Energy in the Steel Industry

Annexes

Nomenclature with Notes and Definitions

Classification of Energy, Raw Materials, Iron and Steel Products, and Correspondence with SITC Rev. 3 and the Harmonized System (HS)

THE IRON AND STEEL INDUSTRY

FACTS AT A GLANCE

Number of Pages: 48

Periodicity: Annual

Publisher: Organization for Economic Cooperation and Development (OECD)

PURPOSE AND SCOPE

This annual illustrates trends in the iron and steel industry for OECD countries and Mexico.

DATA ORGANIZATION

The statistical tables cover steel production, consumption, trade, employment levels, annual investment expenditures by sector and by country, export prices, domestic prices, and indices for certain iron and steel products.

METHODOLOGY

The data are obtained by OECD from iron and steel producers as well as by national industrial organizations.

CONTENTS

Figures
1. Trend of Actual Investment Expenditures, Production Capacity, and Crude Steel Production in the European Countries Since 1960

2. Continental Producers' Export Prices for Certain Iron and Steel Products

Statistical Tables
1. World Production of Pig Iron and Ferro-Alloys
2. World Production of Crude Steel
3. OECD Production of Pig Iron and Ferro-Alloys
4. OECD Production of Crude Steel
5. Crude Steel Output, Breakdown by Process
6. Total Production of Alloy Steels
7. Production of High Speed Steel and Stainless or Heat Resisting Steel
8. Production of Merchantable Iron Ore
9. Consumption of Iron Ore
10. Manganese Ore Consumption
11. Total National Output of Coke-Oven Coke
12. Coke-Oven Coke Consumption - Total and Blast Furnace
13. Consumption, Imports, and Exports of Scrap
14. Total Imports of Steel
15. Total Exports of Steel
16. Imports of Alloy Steel
17. Exports of Alloy Steel
18. Manpower - Total Numbers and Process Workers
19. Manpower - Average Hours Worked
20. Index of Annual Crude Steel Output per Worker
21. Apparent Home Consumption of Crude Steel
22. Apparent Home Consumption of Certain Rolled Products
23. Annual Investment Expenditure and Percentage Break-down by Sector
24. Actual Investment Expenditure in Relation to Crude Steel Production in the Main OECD Steel-Producing Countries
25. Index of Imported Iron Ore Prices (c.i.f.) for Selected Countries
26. Index of Scrap Prices
27. Basic Home Prices of Certain Iron and Steel Products
28. Continental Producers' Export Prices for Certain Iron and Steel Products
29. Effective Capacity for the Production of Pig Iron in 1990, 1991, and 1992
30. Effective Capacity for the Production of Crude Steel in 1990, 1991, and 1992

Appendices
1. Definition of the Iron and Steel Industry Used in this Report
2. Definition Used for Alloy Steels

STATISTICS OF WORLD TRADE IN STEEL

FACTS AT A GLANCE

Number of Pages: 137

Periodicity: Annual

Publisher: United Nations

PURPOSE AND SCOPE

The purpose of *Statistics of World Trade in Steel* is to provide basic data on exports of semifinished and finished steel products from European and other steel-exporting countries.

DATA ORGANIZATION

There are two summary tables: Table 1 gives total exports of steel products by exporting countries for 1980 and 1985 and from 1990 through 1992. Table 2 relates to the total trade in semi-finished and finished steel products between Economic Commission for Europe (ECE) countries in 1992. Table 3 aggregates country exports by commodity and by region and country of destination.

METHODOLOGY

Data are compiled from the UN COMTRADE database, except in the case of countries that do not report to the database. Information on the latter countries was collected directly. Only ingots and semis are considered as semi-finished products and all others are considered finished. See also the *Annual Bulletin of Steel Statistics for Europe*.

CONTENTS

1. Total Exports of Steel Products by Reporting Countries
2. Total Trade of Steel Products Between Countries in the ECE Region
3. Exports of Steel Products, by Region and Country of Destination in 1992
   Belgium-Luxembourg. Denmark. France. Germany. Greece. Ireland. Italy. Netherlands. Portugal. Spain. United Kingdom. Austria. Finland. Norway. Sweden. Switzerland. Turkey. Bulgaria. Czechoslovakia. Hungary. Poland. Romania. Russian Federation. Canada. United States. Japan . Korea, Republic of. Brazil. Australia. New Zealand.
4. Explanatory Notes
5. List of Countries
6. Classification of Steel Products and Correspondence with SITC Rev. 3 and the Harmonized System (HS)

THE STEEL MARKET IN 1992 AND THE OUTLOOK FOR 1993

FACTS AT A GLANCE

Number of Pages: 37

Periodicity: Annual

Publisher: Organization for Economic Cooperation and Development (OECD)

PURPOSE AND SCOPE

The purpose of the *Steel Market and Outlook* is to present the best available statistics on the steel industry in the principal steel producing countries of the world.

DATA ORGANIZATION

The report provides an overview of the main developments in the steel market illustrated with graphs on consumption, production, trade balances, and employment.

METHODOLOGY

The report follows the pattern of those previous except for the inclusion of Mexico and the exclusion of Central and East European countries.

CONTENTS

Introduction

Notes on the Main Features of the Steel Market in 1992 and 1993

Developments in the Steel Market by Area

Employment in the Steel Industry in OECD Countries

Graphs
1. OECD Apparent Steel Consumption, 1968-1993
2. OECD Crude Steel Capacity and Production, 1968-1993

Tables
1. Apparent Steel Consumption by Area, Selected Years, 1980-1993
2. Steel Trade Balance by Area, Selected Years, 1980-1993
3. Crude Steel Production by Area, Selected Years, 1980-1993
4. The Steel Market by Area in 1991
5. The Steel Market by Area in 1992
6. The Steel Market by Area in 1993
7. Steel Markets in the USA, EC, and Japan, 1990-1993
8. Steel Markets in EC Countries, 1991-1993
9. Steel Markets in Other Western European Countries and in Mexico, 1991-1993
10. Manpower—Average Numbers Employed, Selected Years, 1974-1992

Appendix
1. Data Used for the Present Analysis
2. Definitions

STEEL STATISTICAL YEARBOOK

FACTS AT A GLANCE

Number of Pages: 199

Publisher: International Iron and Steel Institute

PURPOSE AND SCOPE

The *Yearbook* presents a cross-section of steel industry statistics collected by the International Iron and Steel Institute.

DATA ORGANIZATION

The *Yearbook* has seven sections, four of which deal with the four main types: iron, crude steel, finished steel, and raw materials. For each, the data presents tables on production, trade, and consumption.

METHODOLOGY

Data are compiled directly from information supplied to the International Iron and Steel Institute by member countries and producers.

CONTENTS

Section A: Iron
Section B: Crude Steel
Section C: Production of Finished Steel Products
Section D: Trade
Section E: Consumption
Section F: Raw Materials
Section G: Miscellaneous

Annex I: Explanatory Notes
Annex II: Sources

Tables

B-1.   Total Production of Crude Steel

Crude Steel Production by Product:
B-2.   Summary Tables - 1992 and 1993
B-3.   Ingots
B-4.   Continuously-cast Steel
B-5.   Liquid Steel for Castings

Crude Steel Production by Process:
B-6.   Summary Tables - 1992 and 1993
B-7.   Oxygen Blown Converter Production
B-8.   Electric Furnace Production
B-9.   Open Hearth Furnace Production

Crude Steel Production by Quality:
B-10. Summary Tables - 1992 and 1993
B-11. Carbon (non-alloy) Steel
B-12. Alloy Steel of which:
B-13. Stainless Steel
B-14: Monthly Production of Crude Steel 1993 and 1994

C-1:   Railway Track Material
C-2:   Sections of which:

C-3: Heavy Sections (>80mm)
C-4: Light Sections (<80mm)
C-5: Bars of which:
C-6: Concrete Reinforcing Bars
C-7: Other Hot Rolled Bars
C-8: Cold Drawn Bars
C-9: Wire Rod
C-10: Drawn Wire
C-11: Cold Rolled Narrow Strip
C-12: Hot Rolled Narrow Strip
C-13: Electrical Sheet and Strip
C-14: Tinmill Products
C-15: Zinc Coated Sheet and Strip
C-16: Steel Tubes and Fittings of which:
C-17: Seamless Tubes
C-18: Welded Tubes

D-1: Total Exports of Semi-finished and Finished Steel Products
D-2: Total Imports of Semi-finished and Finished Steel Products
D-3: World Steel Trade Summary

Selected Products:
D-4: Exports of Ingots and Semis
D-5: Imports of Ingots and Semis
D-6: Exports of Wire Rod
D-7: Imports of Wire Rod
D-8: Exports of Tinmill Products
D-9: Imports of Tinmill Products
D-10: Exports of Zinc Coated Sheet and Strip
D-11: Imports of Zinc Coated Sheet and Strip
D-12: Exports of Tubes and Tube Fittings of which:
D-13: Exports of Seamless Tubes
D-14: Exports of Welded Tubes
D-15: Imports of Tubes and Tube Fittings of which:
D-16: Imports of Seamless Tubes
D-17: Imports of Welded Tubes

E-1: Apparent Consumption of Crude Steel
E-2: Apparent Consumption of Crude Steel Per Capita
E-3: Apparent Consumption of Finished Steel
E-4: Apparent Consumption of Finished Steel Per Capita
E-5: Steel Intensity of GDP (crude steel)
E-6: Steel Intensity of GDP (finished steel)

F-1: Production of Iron Ore
F-2: Exports of Iron Ore and Concentrates
F-3: Imports of Iron Ore and Concentrates
F-4: Production of Pellets
F-5: Production of Sinter
F-6: Consumption of Scrap
F-7: Exports of Scrap
F-8: Imports of Scrap
F-9: Production of Ferro-alloys
F-10: Exports of Ferro-alloys
F-11: Imports of Ferro-alloys
F-12: Exports of Direct Reduced Iron
F-13: Imports of Direct Reduced Iron
F-14: Production of Coke

G-1: Production of Cement
G-2: Production of Aluminum
G-3: Production of Tin
G-4: Production of Zinc
G-5: Population

WORLD STEEL IN FIGURES

FACTS AT A GLANCE

Number of Pages: 21

Periodicity: Annual

Publisher: International Iron and Steel Institute

PURPOSE AND SCOPE

World Steel in Figures is a publication presenting, in condensed form, basic data on the steel industry worldwide.

DATA ORGANIZATION

The publication includes 21 tables on production, consumption, trade, employment, and investment.

METHODOLOGY

The data are derived from the International Iron and Steel Institute's data bank which is periodically updated on the basis of reports from member countries and organizations.

CONTENTS

World Crude Steel Production, 1950-1993

The Largest Steel-Producing Companies, 1992 and 1993

The Major Steel-Producing Countries, 1992 and 1993

Monthly Crude Steel Production, 67 Reporting Countries, 1990-1993

Crude Steel Production by Process, 1993

Continuously-Cast Steel Output, 1991-1993

Steel Production and Consumption: Geographical Distribution, 1983

Steel Production and Consumption: Geographical Distribution, 1993

World Steel Trade by Area, 1992

The Major Importers and Exporters of Steel, 1992

World Steel Exports, Analysis by Product, 1988-1992

World Trade in Steel Products, 1975-1992

Volume of Trade, Western World, 1980-1992

Iron Ore, 1992

World Iron Ore Trade by Area, 1992

Scrap: Consumption, Trade, and Apparent Domestic Supply, 1992

Pig Iron, 1992 and 1993

Employment in the Steel Industry, 1974 and 1988-1993

Capital Investment Expenditure by the Iron and Steel Industry in Various Countries, 1989-1993

Apparent Steel Consumption Per Capita, 1987-1993

Apparent Steel Consumption, 1987-1993

TEA

ANNUAL BULLETIN OF STATISTICS

FACTS AT A GLANCE

Number of Pages: 133

Periodicity: Annual

Publisher: International Tea Committee

PURPOSE AND SCOPE

The *Annual Bulletin of Statistics* is the International Tea Committee's principal statistical publication providing global data on the production, consumption, trade, and prices of tea.

DATA ORGANIZATION

The preliminary tables give summaries of the world production, exports, and imports of tea, followed by country tables, tables on imports and consumption, stocks, and auctions.

METHODOLOGY

The tables are based on reports from member countries and organizations.

CONTENTS

Index

Chairman's Foreword
ITC - Board of Management
ITC - Members of the Committee
Index to Advertisers

Introduction
General Explanatory Notes
Footnotes to Tables A, B, and Average Yield

Area - Production - Exports
A.   Area Planted with Tea in Various Countries
A1. Extensions, Replacements, and Replantings

Graphs
World Production 1973
World Production 1983
World Production 1993

B.   World Production of Tea 1982-1993
B1. Percentage Share of World Production 1982-1993
B2. Production of Tea - CTC and Orthodox 1988-1993

Graphs
World Exports 1973
World Exports 1983
World Exports 1993

C.   World Exports of Tea 1982-1993
C1. Percentage Share of World Exports 1982-1993

Graphs
World Production-Exports-Retentions 1982-1993
Tea Retained in Producing Countries 1982-1993
Exchange Rates for Selected Countries 1984-1993
Value of Exports of Tea 1982-1993
India-Population/Production/Exports/Consumption 1982-1993

Country Tables - Exports
C2. Bangladesh 1988-1993
C3. India 1988-1993
C4. Sri Lanka 1988-1993
C5. Indonesia 1988-1993
C6. China (Mainland) 1982-1993
C7. Taiwan 1982-1993
C8. Japan 1982-1993
C9. Turkey 1982-1993
C10. Kenya 1988-1993
C11. Malawi 1988-1992
C12. Mauritius 1988-1993
C13. Mozambique 1982-1993
C14. Rwanda 1988-1992
C15. Tanzania 1988-1993
C16. Uganda 1988-1993
C17. Zimbabwe 1988-1992
C18. Argentina 1988-1993
C19. Brazil 1982-1993
C20. Papua New Guinea 1988-1993

Imports and Consumption

Graphs
Imports for Consumption (Net) 1973
Imports for Consumption (Net) 1983
World Net Imports of Tea 1982-1993

D.   Tea Imports for Consumption in Each Country 1982-1993
   1. Europe
   2. North America and West Indies
   3. Latin America
   4. Asia
   5. Africa
   6. Oceania
   7. Major Producing Countries in Asia
   8. Summary

D1.A Percentage of World Tea Imports Retained for Consumption in Major Importing Countries 1982-1993
   1. Europe
   2. North America and West Indies

TELECOMMUNICATIONS

INTERNATIONAL TELECOM STATISTICS

FACTS AT A GLANCE

Number of Pages: 47

Periodicity: Annual

Publisher: Siemens

PURPOSE AND SCOPE

This is an important publication published by a world giant in electronics and telecommunications. It surveys the trends and developments in telecommunications worldwide.

DATA ORGANIZATION

The principal tables show net growth of main lines worldwide, their line capacity, national and international calls, cellular phones, and telex. There are new rankings of the leading public telecom operators, the leading manufacturers in public communication networks, the 10 top local exchange carriers worldwide, the 10 top interexchange carriers worldwide, the 10 top cellular mobile radio operators worldwide, and the 20 top data network operators worldwide. Diagrams show the increase in subscriber numbers from 1990 to 2000, and the dominance of the digital systems which will replace analog technology in the next century.

METHODOLOGY

The annual uses data from the International Telecommunication Union.

CONTENTS

Preface

World: Main Lines Net Growth and Replacement

World Market in Main Lines by Regions

  The Leading Public Telecom Operators
  The Leading Manufacturers in Public
  Communication Networks
  The Top 10 Local Exchange Carriers Worldwide
  The Top 10 Interexchange Carriers Worldwide
  The Top 10 Cellular Mobile Radio Operators
  Worldwide
  The Top 20 Data Network Operators Worldwide

  List of Countries

  Main Lines
  Ratio of Main Lines to GNP
  Line Capacity of Local Public Exchanges
  Local Exchanges

Calls
Local Calls
National Long Distance Calls
International Calls
International Direct Distance Dialing

Public Call Offices
Telex Subscriber Lines
Teletex Subscriber Lines
Videotex Subscriber Lines
Cellular Mobile Telephone Subscribers

Investments in Telecommunications
Main Lines per 100 Inhabitants
Growth of Main Lines per Continent

International Conferences
Abbreviations of International Organizations
Definitions

ITU STATISTICAL YEARBOOK

FACTS AT A GLANCE

Number of Pages: 245

Periodicity: Annual

Publisher: International Telecommunication Union (ITU)

PURPOSE AND SCOPE

The *ITU Statistical Yearbook* is the principal statistical publication on the International Telecommunication Union. It provides data on the telecommunications sector in all member countries and the telecommunications industry, with particular focus on telephone services and providers, traffic, prices, exchanges, lines, equipment, and videotex.

DATA ORGANIZATION

The data are presented in two sections. Network Statistics (37 tables), and Financial Results (25 tables).

METHODOLOGY

The data are based on information provided to the ITU by member countries and operators.

CONTENTS

Preface

  List of Countries

  Table de Matières (French)

  Préface (French)

  Liste de Pays (French)

  Cuadro de Indice (Spanish)

  Prefacio (Spanish)

  Lista de paises (Spanish)

Main Public Telecommunication Operators

Network Statistics

Telephone Stations
Main Telephone Lines
Public Payphones
Private Branch Exchanges (PBX)
Percentage of Telephone Lines Connected to Digital Exchanges
Percentage of Telephone Lines Equipped for Direct International Dialing
Percentage of Residential Telephone Lines
Percentage of Telephone Lines in Urban Areas
Local Public Telephone Switching Exchanges
Capacity of Local Public Telephone Switching Exchanges
Trunk Telephone Circuits
International Telephone Circuits
New Applications for Telephone Lines
Waiting List for Telephone Lines
Trunk (toll) Telephone Traffic
National Telephone Traffic
International Outgoing Telephone Traffic
Percentage of Automatic International Outgoing Telephone Traffic
National Paid Telegrams
International Outgoing Telegrams
Bureaufax Stations
National Bureaufax Traffic
International Outgoing Bureaufax Traffic
Telefax Stations
Telex Subscriber Lines
National Telex Traffic
International Outgoing Telex Traffic
Data Equipment Connected to the Telephone and Telex Networks
Data Equipment Connected to Circuit Switched Data Networks
Data Equipment Connected to Packet Switched Data Networks
Data Equipment Connected to Dedicated Data Networks
Freephone Subscribers
Videotex Subscribers
Videotex Information Providers
MHS F.400/X.400 Mailboxes
Subscribers to Cellular Mobile Telephone Systems
Subscribers to Radiopaging Systems

Financial Results

Income from Telephone Connection Carges
Income from Telephone Annual Rentals
Income from Telephone Calls
Total Income from the Telephone Service
Total Income from the Telegram Service
Total Income from Telex Service
Total Income from Data Transmission Service
Other Income
Total Income fromTelecommunication Services
Total Expenditure for Telecommunication Services
Operational Expenditure
Depreciation

Interest Paid
Taxes
Other Expenditure
Investments in Telecommunications (including land and buildings)
Investments in Telecommunications (excluding land and buildings)
Investments in Telephone Switching Equipments
Investments in External Line Plant
Investments in Transmission Equipments
Telephone Stations per 100 Inhabitants
Telephone Main Lines per 100 Inhabitants
Total Income as a Percentage of GDP
Total Investments as a Percentage of GDP
Number of Inhabitants
Exchange Rate

WORLD TELECOMMUNICATION DEVELOPMENT REPORT

FACTS AT A GLANCE

Number of Pages: 163

Periodicity: Annual

Publisher: International Telecommunication Union (ITU)

PURPOSE AND SCOPE

The ITU *World Telecommunication Development Report* is a survey of the telecommunication industry worldwide and presents the most comprehensive dataset of telecommunication indicators for over 200 countries.

DATA ORGANIZATION

The statistical core of the publication consists of 29 boxes, 47 figures, and 25 tables exploring a variety of issues and developments, including the Internet, privatization, videotex, fax, satellites, networks, convergence, and cellular phones.

METHODOLOGY

ITU has used its enormous data resources in its archives to produce this statistical study.

CONTENTS

TELEPHONES

THE WORLD'S TELEPHONES

FACTS AT A GLANCE

Number of Pages: 227

Periodicity: Annual

Publisher: AT&T

PURPOSE AND SCOPE

The World Telephones presents current data on the telephone systems of the world. It shows global telephone distribution and facilities by country within geographical regions.

DATA ORGANIZATION

The technical data focus on exchange access lines, automated access lines, total access lines, business and residence access lines, service information by type of switching and by type of operation, and telephone traffic. Some of this information is also presented for selected cities. In addition, the annual presents some demographic data for reporting countries.

METHODOLOGY

About one-third of the world's telephone administrations and operating companies supplied data for the current edition. AT&T made no estimates for the non-reporting countries.

CONTENTS

International World Zone Information
The International Telephone World Numbering Zone Plan
Countries by World Zones (Map)
Countries by World Zones

Selected Telephone Statistics for the World and Zones

Growth of Population and Access Line (Graph)

Table 1: Exchange Access Lines per 100 Population; Privately Operated Access Lines: 1990/1991

Table 2: Automatic Access Lines: 1990/1991
Table 3: Total Access Lines in 1990 as Compared to 1985

Total Access Lines in 1991 as Compared to 1986

Countries Reporting Over 1,000,000 Access Lines

Total Access Lines (Millions) (Graph): 1990/1991
Access Lines per 100 Population (Graph): 1990/1991

Table 4: Business and Residence Access Lines: 1990/1991
Table 5: Service Information by Type of Switching: 1990/1991
Table 6: Extension and PBX Access Lines: 1990/1991

All Reporting Countries

Table 7: Service Information by Type of Switching: 1990/1991
Table 8: Service Information by Type of Operation (Private/Government): 1990/1991
Table 9: Total Access Lines by Business and Residence: 1990/1991
Table 10: Total Access Lines by Business Extensions and PBX and by Residence Extensions and PBX: 1990/1991
Table 11: Total Extensions Including PBX by Business and Residence: 1990/1991
Table 12: Total PBX and Centrex Access Lines: 1990/ 1991
Table 13: Coin Box Telephones Including Public Telephone Stations: 1990/1991
Table 14: Most Frequently Called Countries with Number of Messages and Percentage of Total International Calls: 1990/ 1991

Telephone Traffic
Table 15: Local: 1990/1991
Table 16: Long Distance: 1990/1991
Table 17: International Outgoing: 1990/1991

Demographic Characteristics

Population in Descending Order (Graph): 1990/1991

Average Number of Persons/Household in Descending Order (Graph): 1990/1991

Total Households in Descending Order (Graph): 1990/1991

Table 18: Country Population, Number of Households, and Average Number of Persons per Household: 1990/1991

City Data
Table 19: Total Exchange Access Lines in the World's Principal Cities - Total Access Lines and Population: 1990/1991

North American Cities Reporting Over 250,000 Access Lines (Map): 1990/1991

European Cities Reporting Over 250,000 Access Lines (Map): 1990/1991

Japanese Cities Reporting Over 250,000 Access Lines (Map): 1990/1991

Other World Zones Cities Reporting Over 250,000 Access Lines (Map): 1990/1991

Nonreporting Countries

Country Notes

TEXTILES

INTERNATIONAL TEXTILE MACHINERY SHIPMENT STATISTICS

FACTS AT A GLANCE

Number of Pages: 27

Periodicity: Annual

Publisher: International Textile Manufacturers Federation

PURPOSE AND SCOPE

The *International Textile Machinery Shipment Statistics* is published by the principal trade group of textile machinery manufacturers and presents complete data on the shipment of textile machinery worldwide.

DATA ORGANIZATION

The data are complete geographically with the exception of China. The core of the publication is the data on the number of ring spindles, o-e rotors, and looms shipped by manufacturer and by country of destination. Cumulative shipments are shown for the period 1984-93. Each of the two table sections is preceded by introductory graphical summaries.

METHODOLOGY

The annual is compiled with the cooperation of more than 50 textile machinery manufacturers whose combined shipments represent the world total.

CONTENTS

Section 1: Spinning Machinery

List of Participating Companies

Graphical Summaries
Short-staple Spindles
Long-staple Spindles

O-E Rotors

Tables: Spinning Machinery Shipped
To Africa
To the Americas
To Asia and Oceania
To Europe

Section 2: Weaving Machinery

List of Participating Companies

Graphical Summary
Shuttleless Looms

Tables: Weaving Machinery Shipped
To Africa
To the Americas
To Asia and Oceania
To Europe

WORLD TEXTILE DEMAND

FACTS AT A GLANCE

Number of Pages: 121

Periodicity: Annual

Publisher: International Cotton Advisory Committee (ICAC)

PURPOSE AND SCOPE

ICAC publishes the *World Textile Demand* as one of the reports intended to inform member governments of the current situation in the world textile market and its likely evolution in the short-term.

DATA ORGANIZATION

The publication provides primary data on mill consumption, stocks, and production of cotton yarn and production. The book also includes projections of textile fiber demand at the mill level and of yarn and fabric production.

METHODOLOGY

The end-use textile projections and review of world textile demand are based on the ICAC Textile Demand Computer Model. The model is used to adjust mill consumption in supply and utilize accounts of cotton by country. The accounts are the basis of the production, consumption, and stock projections prepared by crop years. Projection of cotton yarn and fabric production are based on a simplified input/output model. The chemical fiber yarn projections are based on historical capacity utilization published by the Fiber Economics Bureau.

CONTENTS

Chapter I: World Economic Outlook
Industrial Countries

Developing Countries
Eastern Europe and the Former USSR

Chapter II: Demand for End-use Products
Current Estimates for 1993
Textile Consumption in 1994-96
Cotton Consumption in 1994-96

Appendix I: Methodology of World Textile Demand Projections

Chapter III: Mill Consumption of Cotton
China (Mainland)
United States
Other Producing Countries
Former COMECON Group
Importing Countries

Appendix II: Mill Consumption of Textile Fibers in Selected Countries

Chapter IV: The Yarn and Fabric Markets
Cotton Yarn and Fabric Production
Chemical Yarn Production

Appendix III: Methodology of Yarn and Fabric Production Projections

Tables
1. Selected Economic Indicators
2. Textile Fiber Consumption (End-use)
3. Textile Fiber Consumption Per Capita (End-use)
4. Impact of Income Growth on Textile Fiber Consumption in 1995
5. Comparison of Most Current Estimates of World Textile Consumption with ICAC Textile Demand Forecasts
6. World Cotton and Non-cotton Textile Fiber Consumption (End-use)
7. Textile Fiber Consumption Per Capita: Regression Results
8. World Cotton and Non-cotton Textile Fiber Consumption Per Capita: Regression Results
9. Real GDP Per Capita Index
10. Prices of Textile Fibers
11. Real GDP Index
12. Population
13. Consumer Price Index
14. World Consumption of Major Textile Fibers
15. Mill Consumption of Cotton
16. Mill Consumption of Textile Fibers in Selected Countries
17. Production of Cotton Yarn
18. Imports of Cotton Yarn
19. Exports of Cotton Yarn
20. Production of Cotton Fabric
21. Imports of Cotton Fabric
22. Exports of Cotton Fabric
23. Production of Chemical Fiber Yarn

Figures
1. World Economic Growth
2. Economic Growth in Selected Countries
3. GDP Per Capita: Developing Countries
4. World Economic Growth by Region

5. World Economic Performance and Textile Fiber Consumption Growth
6. World Textile Fiber Consumption (End-use)
7. World Textile Fiber Consumption Per Capita (End-use)
8. World Textile Fiber Consumption (End-use): Cotton and Non-cotton
9. Relative Cotton Prices
10. Cotton's Share of the World Market
11. Mill Consumption of Cotton
12. Mill Consumption of Cotton: China (Mainland)
13. Mill Consumption of Cotton: USA
14. Mill Consumption of Cotton: Pakistan
15. Mill Consumption of Cotton: Brazil
16. Mill Consumption of Cotton: Japan
17. Mill Consumption of Cotton: European Union
18. Mill Consumption of Cotton: Italy
19. Mill Consumption of Cotton: ASEAN Countries
20. World Cotton Yarn Production
21. Cotton Yarn Production: Industrial Countries
22. Cotton Yarn Production: Asia
23. Cotton Yarn Production: China (Taiwan) and Republic of Korea
24. Cotton Yarn Production: India and Pakistan
25. Cotton Yarn Production: Africa and Latin America
26. World Cotton Fabric Production
27. World Chemical Yarn Production
28. Chemical Yarn Production: Developing Countries
29. Chemical Yarn Production: Industrial Countries

Boxes
1. End-use Textile Demand: Japan
2. Cotton's Non-price Competitiveness

TOURISM

COMPENDIUM OF TOURISM STATISTICS

FACTS AT A GLANCE

Number of Pages: 245

Periodicity: Annual

Publisher: World Tourism Organization (WTO)

PURPOSE AND SCOPE

The *Compendium of Tourism Statistics* provides in a condensed form, basic statistics on domestic and international tourism supply and demand in the countries and regions of the world.

DATA ORGANIZATION

The White Pages contain selected four-year time series for 182 countries and territories. The Blue Pages contain background information on trends in arrivals and international tourism receipts worldwide as a historical time series for 1950-1993 and in the various regions for 1988 - 1992. The Blue Pages also contain the breakdown of total international tourist arrivals and receipts for developed and developing countries and for other selected country economic groupings. Each country table contains 34 selected series.

METHODOLOGY

The tables follow WTO Recommendations on Tourism Statistics. The major change in the current edition includes the addition of "Other" under "Arrivals by Purpose and Visit," to cover health and religious tourism. The data are based on reports received by WTO from member governments and tourist organizations.

CONTENTS
Sudan
Suriname
Swaziland
Sweden
Switzerland
Syrian Arab Republic
Taiwan
Thailand
Togo
Tonga
Trinidad and Tobago
Tunisia
Turkey
Turks and Caicos Islands
Tuvalu
Uganda
Former USSR
United Kingdom
United Republic of Tanzania
United States
United States Virgin Islands
Uruguay
Vanuatu
Venezuela
Yemen
Yugoslavia, Federal Republic of
Zaire
Zambia
Zimbabwe

World and Regional Totals (Blue Pages)

List of Tables
World Tourist Arrivals (1950-1993)
World Tourism Receipts (1950-1993)
Breakdown of Arrivals According to WTO Regional Commissions, 1988-1992
Breakdown of Receipts According to WTO Regional Commissions, 1988-1992
World Capacity (by Region), 1988-1992

YEARBOOK OF TOURISM STATISTICS

FACTS AT A GLANCE

Number of Pages: Volume One: 157; Volume Two: 445

Periodicity: Annual

Publisher: World Tourism Organization (WTO)

PURPOSE AND SCOPE

The purpose of the *Yearbook of Tourism Statistics* is to present the most important comparable international data for the analysis of global, regional, and national tourism statistics.

DATA ORGANIZATION

Volume I covers world aggregates, broken down by region and country, of the following main series: (1) international tourism arrivals at frontiers or in accommodation establishments; (2) arrivals by mode of transport; (3) accommodation capacity (number of rooms and beds); and (4) tourism receipts and expenditures. Volume II provides for 150 countries and territories data broken down by country of origin for total arrivals and overnight stays of international and inbound tourism.

METHODOLOGY

Based on WTO recommendations regarding collection and presentation of data. These recommendations promote comparability of data and compatibility of terms, concepts, definitions, and classifications used at the national and international levels. Not all data in the *Yearbook* are comparable in vintage or quality, and therefore they have only limited value.

CONTENTS

Volume I

A. Trends of Tourism Movements and Payments

1. Worldwide
Arrivals of tourists from abroad and receipts from international tourism, 1950-1993. World tourist arrivals and tourism receipts. Historical growth rates, 1950-1993. World selected series, 1988-1992. Arrivals of tourists from abroad by regions, 1980-1992. International tourism receipts by regions, 1980-1992. International tourism expenditure by regions, 1980-1992. International tourist arrivals; trends in regional market share, 1980-1993.

2. Selected Groupings
World Bank, 1980-1992. Developing countries, 1988-1992. Mediterranean countries, 1988-1992. OECD, 1988-1992. PATA, 1980-1992.

3. Country Rankings
World's top tourism destination, 1980-1992. World's top tourism earner, 1980-1992. World's top tourism spenders, 1980-1992. Top countries with highest receipts per tourist; with highest expenditure per trip abroad, 1985-1992. Ranking of countries by hotel capacity, 1985-1992.

B. Regional Summary

1. Africa
Arrivals of tourist from abroad and receipts from international tourism, 1950-1993. Tourist arrivals and tourism receipts in Africa; historical growth rates, 1950-1993.

2. Selected Series, 1988-1992
Africa. Eastern Africa. Middle Africa. Northern Africa. Southern Africa. Western Africa. Trends of tourist arrivals by country, 1988-1992. Trends of tourist arrivals by air, 1988-1992. Trends of tourism receipts by country, 1988-1992. Outbound travel by region of destination, 1988-1992. Trends of tourism expenditures by country, 1988-1992.

3. Americas
Arrivals of tourists from abroad and receipts from international tourism, 1950-1993. Tourist arrivals and tourism receipts in the Americas; historical growth rates, 1950-1993.

4. Selected Series, 1988-1992
Americas. Caribbean. Central America. Northern America. Southern America. LAIA. Trends of tourist arrivals by country, 1988-1992. Trends of tourist arrivals by air, 1988-1992. Trends of tourist receipts by country, 1988-1992. Outbound travel by region of destination, 1988-1992. Trends of tourism expenditure by country, 1988-1992.

5. East Asia/Pacific
Arrivals of tourists from abroad and receipts from international tourism, 1950-1993. Tourist arrivals

and tourism receipts in East Asia and the Pacific; historical growth rates, 1950-1993.

6. Selected Series, 1988-1992

East Asia/Pacific. Northeastern Asia. Southeastern Asia. Australasia. Melanesia. Micronesia. Polynesia. ASEAN. Trends of tourist arrivals by country, 1988-1992. Trends of tourist arrivals by air, 1988-1992. Trends of tourism receipts by country, 1988-1992. Outbound travel by region of destination, 1988-1992. Trends of tourism expenditure by country, 1988-1992.

7. Europe

Arrivals of tourists from abroad and receipts from international tourism, 1950-1993. Tourist arrivals and tourism receipts in Europe; historical growth rates, 1950-1993.

8. Selected Series, 1988-1992

Europe. Central/Eastern Europe. Northern Europe. Southern Europe. Western Europe. East Mediterranean Europe. European Community. EFTA. Trends of tourist arrivals by country, 1988-1992. Trends of tourist arrivals by air, 1988-1992. Trends of tourism receipts by country, 1988-1992. Outbound travel by region of destination, 1988-1992. Trends of tourism expenditure by country, 1988-1992.

9. Middle East

Arrivals of tourists from abroad and receipts from international tourism, 1950-1993. Tourist arrivals and tourism receipts in Middle East; historical growth rates, 1950-1993.

10. Selected Series, 1988-1992

Middle East. Trends of tourist arrivals by country, 1988-1992. Trends of tourist arrivals by air, 1988-1992. Trends of tourism receipts by country, 1988-1992. Outbound travel by region of destination, 1988-1992. Trends of tourism expenditure by country, 1988-1992.

11. South Asia

Arrivals of tourists from abroad and receipts from international tourism, 1950-1993. Tourist arrivals and tourism receipts in South Asia; historical growth rates, 1950-1993.

12. Selected Series, 1988-1992

South Asia. Trends of tourist arrivals by country, 1988-1992. Trends of tourist arrivals by air, 1988-1992. Trends of tourism receipts by country, 1988-1992. Outbound travel by region of destination, 1988-1992. Trends of tourism expenditure by country, 1988-1992.

C. Technical Notes

Volume II

A. Tourism from Abroad (by Country of Origin)

1. Arrivals at Frontiers of Tourists from Abroad, 1988-1992

2. Arrivals at Frontiers of Visitors from Abroad, 1988-1992
3. Arrivals of Tourists from Abroad in Hotels and Similar Establishments, 1988-1992
4. Arrivals of Tourists from Abroad in all Accommodation Establishments, 1988-1992
5. Nights of Tourists from Abroad in Hotels and Similar Establishments, 1988-1992
6. Nights of Tourists from Abroad in All Accommodation Etablishments, 1988-1992

TRADE

DIRECTION OF TRADE STATISTICS YEARBOOK

FACTS AT A GLANCE

Number of Pages: 427

Periodicity: Annual

Publisher: International Monetary Fund (IMF)

PURPOSE AND SCOPE

The *Direction of Trade Statistics* presents, for 161 countries (sovereign nations as well as non-sovereign territories), figures on the value of merchandise exports and imports by trading partners for the years 1986 through 1992 as well as regional and world aggregates showing major trade flows.

DATA ORGANIZATION

The countries are grouped into three categories: Industrialized Countries, Developing Countries, and Other Countries (former centralized planning economies). Export data are reported freight on board while import data are reported cost, insurance, and freight—uniformly assumed to be 10 percent of cost. All figures are reported in U.S. dollars. A number of analytical lines are included at the end of country tables based on the tabular data. One set of lines shows the percentage distribution of exports and imports from selected areas. The other set of lines shows the annual percentage change in total exports and imports and also in exports to and imports from selected areas.

METHODOLOGY

Data on exports and imports by trading partners reported to the International Monetary Fund (IMF) vary in frequency. Approximately 40 countries, including virtually all industrialized countries and about 20 developing countries report their data on a regular monthly basis. These 40 countries account for four-fifths of the value of recorded world exports and imports. Other countries report less current data either quarterly or annually. The availability of partner data makes it possible to estimate export and import figures for countries that do not report regularly to the IMF. Recourse to estimates and extrapolation is limited to a very small section of world trade, not more than two percent each of world exports and imports.

To provide guidance regarding the sources of the figures for the individual countries, certain symbols are used in the tables. These figures apply only to trade between two partner countries and not to world or regional totals. Such symbols indicate that data are received from partner records or by other methods of estimation as follows:

S - 6-11 months of reported data and 1-6 months of estimates

T - 1-5 months of reported data and 7-11 months of estimates

* Derived solely from partner records

Y - Other types of estimates or extrapolation sometimes using partner records, if available

... Data totally lacking

The summary tables for areas and the world are calculated in two ways. Part A shows the country and area distribution of the aggregate trade of the respective area or of the world. Part B presents the trade of the countries listed in the table with the area covered in that table.

Ideally, in the absence of problems of valuation, timing, and coverage, the value of exports in Part A would equal the value of imports in Part B and conversely the value of imports in Part A would equal the value of exports in Part B. However, the continuing mystery of international trade is that the total has never matched in all the years that records have been kept. The discrepancy has never been properly explained, but several factors are believed to contribute to it, including: (1) the difficulty of matching export flows recorded freight on board and import flows recorded cost, insurance, and freight; (2) time lags between the recording of an export by the exporting country and the recording of the same shipment as an import by the importing country; (3) shipments to third countries for clandestine re-export to another country; (4) underreporting of small items of merchandise; (5) the practice of bunching of import and export destinations under regions rather than countries; (6) poor reporting or the unavailability of data on weight and price; and (7) the existence of large-scale smuggling which may be recorded in one country but not in the other.

CONTENTS

Gambia, The
Germany
Eastern Germany
Ghana
Greece
Greenland
Grenada
Guadeloupe
Guatemala
Guiana, French
Guinea
Guinea-Bissau
Guyana
Haiti
Honduras
Hong Kong
Hungary
Iceland
India
Indonesia
Iran, Islamic Republic of
Iraq
Ireland
Israel
Italy
Jamaica
Japan
Jordan
Kenya
Korea
Kuwait
Lao, People's Democratic Republic of
Lebanon
Liberia
Libya
Macao
Madagascar
Malawi
Malaysia
Maldives
Mali
Malta
Martinique
Mauritania
Mauritius
Mexico
Morocco
Mozambique
Myanmar
Nepal
Netherlands
Netherlands, Antilles
New Caledonia
New Zealand
Nicaragua
Niger
Nigeria
North Korea
Norway
Oman
Pakistan

Panama
Papua New Guinea
Paraguay
Peru
Philippines
Poland
Portugal
Qatar
Reunion
Romania
Rwanda
St.Vincent and the Grenadines
Sao Tome and Principe
Saudi Arabia
Senegal
Seychelles
Sierra Leone
Singapore
Solomon Islands
Somalia
South Africa
Spain
Sri Lanka
Sudan
Suriname
Sweden
Switzerland
Syrian Arab Republic
Tanzania
Thailand
Togo
Tonga
Trinidad and Tobago
Tunisia
Turkey
Uganda
U.S.S.R. (former)
United Arab Emirates
United Kingdom
United States
Uruguay
Vanuatu
Venezuela
Viet Nam
Western Somoa
Yemen Arab Republic
Yemen, People's Democratic Republic of
Yugoslavia
Zaire
Zambia
Zimbabwe

EC-LATIN AMERICAN TRADE

FACTS AT A GLANCE

Number of Pages: 114

Periodicity: Irregular

Publisher: European Communities

PURPOSE AND SCOPE

EC -Latin American Trade is a compendium of data on the direction and composition of trade between the European Union (EU) and countries of the Western Hemisphere below the Rio Grande.

DATA ORGANIZATION

The data are organized in four parts: The first part is an overview that illustrates the importance of bilateral trade between the European Community and Latin America. Part II shows the structure and composition of the trade. Part III analyzes the trade by individual products and Part IV is a country-by-country break-down of the trade.

METHODOLOGY

The book has an annex which explains the method-ological bases, particularly the geographical and prod-uct classification, the source of data, and the way the indicators are devised.

CONTENTS

FOREIGN TRADE STATISTICS FOR AFRICA

FACTS AT A GLANCE

Number of Pages: 159

Periodicity: Annual

Publisher: United Nations

PURPOSE AND SCOPE

Foreign Trade Statistics for Africa provides comprehensive data on the foreign trade of African countries.

DATA ORGANIZATION

The data are organized in four regional sections dealing with North Africa, West Africa, Central Africa, and East and Southern Africa. For each country, the data provide breakdowns by countries and then by products and product categories.

METHODOLOGY

The data are drawn from the trade database maintained by the United Nations.

CONTENTS

Total African Trade by Countries

North Africa

West Africa

Central Africa

East and Southern Africa

FOREIGN TRADE STATISTICS OF ASIA AND THE PACIFIC

FACTS AT A GLANCE

Number of Pages: 520

Periodicity: Quadrennial

Publisher: United Nations (UN)

PURPOSE AND SCOPE

Foreign Trade Statistics of Asia and the Pacific presents foreign trade statistics of the countries and territories of the ESCAP region.

DATA ORGANIZATION

The data cover exports and imports of ESCAP countries broken down by commodities.

METHODOLOGY

The information is taken from magnetic tapes supplied by the UN Statistical Division.

CONTENTS

1. Total Imports and Exports by Countries of Provenance and Destination of SITC Rev. 2
2. Imports and Exports by Sections of SITC Rev. 2
3. Imports and Exports by Groups of SITC Rev. 2
4. Classification of Trade by Broad Economic Categories of SITC Rev. 2

INTERNATIONAL TRADE STATISTICS

FACTS AT A GLANCE

Number of Pages: 120

Periodicity: Annual

Publisher: General Agreement on Tariffs and Trade (GATT)

PURPOSE AND SCOPE

International Trade Statistics is the most comprehensive compilation of statistics on global trade as reported to GATT (the World Trade Organization—WTO).

DATA ORGANIZATION

International Trade Statistics presents data under three parts: Part I deals with world trade; Part II deals with merchandise trade by regions, and Part III deals with merchandise trade by products.

METHODOLOGY

The publication measures statistically, the flow of trade across national boundaries by product, trading partner, and region.

CONTENTS

I. World Trade
   Table I.1 World Exports of Merchandise and Commercial Services, 1992
   Chart I.1 Volume of World Merchandise Trade and Output, 1980-92
   Table I.2 World Merchandise Exports, Commodity Output, and Gross Domestic Product, 1980-92
   Table I.3 Composition of World Merchandise Exports by Region and Product, 1992
   Table I.4 Leading Exporters and Importers in World Merchandise Trade, 1992
   Table I.5 Leading Exporters and Importers in World Merchandise Trade (Excluding EC Intra-Trade), 1992
   Table I.6 Leading Exporters and Importers in World Trade in Commercial Services, 1992
   Table I.7 Merchandise Trade of Least Developed Countries, 1991

7. Clothing

Appendix Tables

INTERNATIONAL TRADE STATISTICS YEARBOOK

FACTS AT A GLANCE

Number of Pages: Volume One: 1,162; Volume Two: 804

Periodicity: Annual

Publisher: United Nations (UN)

PURPOSE AND SCOPE

The *International Trade Statistics Yearbook* provides complete information on the trade of individual countries in terms of trends in current value, volume and price, the importance of trading partners, and the significance of individual commodities imported or exported.

DATA ORGANIZATION

The *Yearbook* presents data for 159 countries or customs areas. Volume I contains detailed data for individual countries and a number of special tables. Table 1 shows 10 series, 5 for imports and 5 for exports: total merchandise trade, trade in gold, conversion factors, quantum index numbers, and unit value index numbers. Table 2 shows the percentage breakdown of imports by broad economic categories of end use and exports by industrial origin. The analysis for imports is based on the Classification by Broad Economic Categories and for exports on the Classification of Commodities by Industrial Origin. Table 3 shows the value in U.S. dollars of import and export trade analyzed by principal countries or areas of origin or destination. The analysis is made in accordance with the UN Standard Country or Area Codes for Statistical Use. A maximum of 50 trading partners are shown in order of magnitude with import and export values ranked separately. It is followed by a percentage breakdown of trade by regions and the percentage of trade accounted for by each of the first 10 trading partners. Tables 4 and 5 show the quantity and value in U.S. dollars of imports and exports analyzed by commodities, the value of which is equal to or greater than 0.3 percent of the total trade for the year. The commodities are shown in terms of SITC headings.

Volume I also contains special tables showing the contribution of the trade of each country to the trade of the region and of the world, the flow of trade between countries and regions, price fluctuations and goods loaded and unloaded in international transport. Volume II contains commodity tables showing total trade broken down by countries and regions. Commodity tables are presented in two parts, based on SITC levels. The values for both imports and exports are analyzed by regions and the 50 top trading partners.

METHODOLOGY

Regional and world totals are adjusted to include estimates when full data are not available or to eliminate incomparabilities. Monthly and quarterly data appear in the *Monthly Bulletin of Statistics.*

CONTENTS

Volume I

Abbreviations and Country Nomenclature
Explanation of Symbols
Magnetic Tapes and Diskettes
Introduction
Country Notes

Special Tables

A. Total Imports and Exports by Regions and Countries or Areas
B. World Exports by Commodity Classes and by Regions
C. Growth of World Exports by Commodity Classes and by Regions
D. Structure of World Exports by Commodity Classes and by Regions
E. Total Imports and Exports: Index Numbers by Countries or Areas
F. Total Exports and Imports: Index Numbers of Quantum, Unit Value, and Terms of Trade by Regions
G. Manufactured Goods Exports
H. Fuel Imports: Developed Economies
I. Some Indicators on Fuel Imports: Developed Economies
J. Export Price Index of Machinery and Transport Equipment for Selected Countries
K. Export Price Index Numbers of Primary Commodities and Non-ferrous Base Metals

Country Tables

Afghanistan
Algeria
Angola
Antigua and Barbuda
Argentina
Australia
Austria
Bahamas
Bahrain
Bangladesh
Barbados
Belgium-Luxembourg
Belize
Benin
Bermuda
Bolivia
Brazil
British Virgin Islands
Brunei Darussalam
Bulgaria
Burkina Faso
Burundi
Cameroon
Canada
Cape Verde
Cayman Islands
Central African Republic
Chile
China
Colombia
Comoros
Congo
Cook Islands
Costa Rica
Cote d'Ivoire
Croatia
Cuba
Cyprus
Former Czechoslovakia
Denmark
Djibouti
Dominica
Dominican Republic
Ecuador
Egypt
El Salvador
Equatorial Guinea
Ethiopia
Faeroe Islands
Fiji
Finland
France, including Monaco
French Guiana
French Polynesia
Gabon
Gambia
Germany
Ghana
Greece
Greenland
Grenada
Guadeloupe
Guatemala
Guyana
Haiti
Honduras
Hong Kong
Hungary
Iceland
India
Indonesia
Ireland
Israel
Italy
Jamaica
Japan
Jordan
Kenya
Kiribati
Korea, Republic of
Kuwait
Liberia
Libyan Arab Jamahiriya
Lithuania

Macau
Madagascar
Malawi
Malaysia
Mali
Malta
Martinique
Mauritania
Mauritius
Mexico
Morocco
Mozambique
Nepal
The Netherlands
Netherlands Antilles
New Caledonia
New Zealand
Nicaragua
Niger
Nigeria
Nieu
Norway, including Svalbard and Jan Mayen Islands
Oman
Pakistan
Panama
Papua New Guinea
Paraguay
Peru
Philippines
Poland
Portugal
Qatar
Reunion
Romania
Rwanda
Saint Kitts and Nevis
Saint Lucia
Saint Pierre and Miquelon
Saint Vincent and the Grenadines
Samoa
Saudi Arabia
Senegal Seychelles
Sierra Leone
Singapore
Solomon Islands
Somalia
Southern Africa, Customs Union of
Spain
Sri Lanka
Sudan
Suriname
Sweden
Switzerland, including Liechtenstein
Syrian Arab Republic
Thailand
Togo
Tonga
Trinidad and Tobago
Tunisia
Turkey
Tuvalu

Former Union of Soviet Socialist Republics
United Arab Emirates
United Kingdom
United Republic of Tanzania
United States
Uruguay
Vanautu
Venezuela
Yemen
Yogoslavia SFR
Zaire
Zambia
Zimbabwe

Volume II
Abbreviations, Country Nomenclature
Explanation of Symbols
Magnetic Tapes and Diskettes
Introduction
Commodity Tables:
    3-Digit SITC
    4- and 5- Digit SITC

TRANSPORT

ANNUAL BULLETIN OF TRANSPORT STATISTICS FOR EUROPE

FACTS AT A GLANCE

Number of Pages: 315

Periodicity: Annual

Publisher: United Nations (UN)

PURPOSE AND SCOPE

The purpose of the *Annual Bulletin of Transport Statistics for Europe* is to provide basic data on transport and related trends in European countries, Canada, and the United States.

DATA ORGANIZATION

The scope of the *Annual Bulletin* covers railroad and inland water sectors container transport, goods loaded and unloaded at seaports, transport by oil pipeline, and international goods transport by various modes of transport and commodity groups. The data refer to length of networks, number, capacity and power of vehicles, and internal and international traffic and transport. In the road sector, data are given on expenditure on roads. General information on the consumption of energy in transport is given in Table 5.

METHODOLOGY

Data are obtained from official and unofficial national publications supplemented by UN estimates.

CONTENTS

Index

Explanatory Notes

Tables

TRANSPORT ANNUAL STATISTICS

FACTS AT A GLANCE

Number of Pages: 247

Periodicity: Annual

Publisher: European Communities

SCOPE AND PURPOSE

Transport Annual Statistics contains the most important data on transport in the European Union and its member states for the period 1970 to 1989.

DATA ORGANIZATION

The *Yearbook* provides data on infrastructure, mobile equipment, distances covered by various modes of transport, such as rail, road, inland waterway, merchant shipping, and pipelines, and selected data for traffic accidents. Aviation is excluded with the exception of Tables 1 to 6.

METHODOLOGY

The Statistical Office of the European Communities (SOEC) collected the data from national statistical institutes, transport ministries in member states, and international organizations. The SOEC also publishes related transport data in *Basic Statistics* (international comparisons) and *Eurostat Review* (long-term series).

CONTENTS

1. General Tables
Basic data. Railways. Road. Inland waterways. Merchant shipping. Aviation. Infrastructure expenditures for three modes of transport.

2. Railways
Average length of lines by number of tracks and by type of traction. Average length of lines worked by type of traction and nature of traffic. Length of lines by current systems in use. Tractive stock by type of traction. Tractive power. Rolling stock for

passenger and goods transport. Rolling stock for passenger transport and number of seats. Rolling stock for goods transport by type of wagon. Tractive stock km. Hauled vehicles km Train km by type of traffic and mode of traction. Gross ton km worked by type of traffic and mode of traction. Passenger traffic. International passenger traffic. Goods traffic by type of traffic. International goods transport by traffic relations and NST/R chapters. Goods traffic by type of loading. Goods traffic by distance. Accompanied motor vehicles traffic. Fuel and energy consumption for tractive stock. Average staff strength. Railway casualties. Other networks.

3. Road

Length of road network category. Stock of vehicles by category. First registration of motor vehicles. Stock of goods vehicles and tractors by category and by type of transport. Stock of goods vehicles by category, type of transport, and load capacity. Goods traffic by type of traffic. National goods traffic by NST/R chapter (t). National goods traffic NST/R chapter (tkm). National goods traffic. International goods transport by traffic relations and NST/R chapters. Energy consumption of road transport. Energy—retail prices per 100 l. Accidents involving personal injury. Traffic casualties by their means of transport. Traffic casualties by age group and sex. Road traffic casualties per 10,000 inhabitants by age group and sex. Traffic casualties by means of transport and by age. Road traffic accidents with one or two implicated elements.

4. Inland Waterways

Length and density of traffic of some inland waterways. Length of navigable waterways by group. Goods-carrying vessels, tugs, and pushers by type (number). Goods-carrying vessels, tugs, and pushers by type (load-carrying capacity). Goods-carrying vessels by type and load-carrying capacity (number). Goods-carrying vessels by type and load-carrying capacity (t). Total goods-carrying vessels by type and by year of construction. Changes in the fleets by cause and by type of vessels. Number of enterprises for goods transport. Goods traffic by type of traffic (t). Goods traffic by type of traffic (tkm). International goods transport by traffic relations and NST/R chapters.

5. Merchant Shipping

All steam and motor ships. World fleet by type and flag. Merchant fleet. Merchant fleet by size group. Merchant fleet by age and country. Merchant fleet by type and age. Fishing vessels and factory trawlers by size and flag. Arrivals of ships. International traffic by flag. Relative part of flags in international traffic. Goods traffic. Petroleum products unloaded in international traffic.

TUNGSTEN STATISTICS

FACTS AT A GLANCE

Number of Pages: 71

Periodicity: Annual

Publisher: United Nations

PURPOSE AND SCOPE

Tungsten Statistics presents statistics relating to the production, consumption, trade, and prices of tungsten throughout the world.

DATA ORGANIZATION

The data are organized in six parts: (1) Prices; (2) Production; (3) Consumption; (4) Trade: Ores and Concentrates; (5) Trade: Tungsten Products; and (6) Stocks, which includes three charts.

METHODOLOGY

Tables have been compiled principally from answers to questionnaires, supplemented by data from national publications. Price series are from *Metal Bulletin, Metals Weeks,* and *Metal Powder Report.*

CONTENTS

Summary Table: Tungsten in Ores and Concentrates

Chart

I.   Price of Tungsten Concentrates, *Metal Bulletin*

II.   Price of Ferro-tungsten

III. Price of Amonium Paratungstate

Part One

Prices

1.1   Price of Tungsten Concentrates, *Metal Bulletin*

1.2   Price of Tungsten Products (Ferro-tungsten, Tungsten Powder) (Tungsten Carbide Powder)

1.3   Price of Tungsten Products: Amonium Paratungstate

Part Two

Production

2.1   Production of Tungsten in Ores and Concentrates

2.2   Production from Various Types of Mines and Number of Mines Operating

2.3   Cooperation of Other Metals from Mines Producing Various Types of Tungsten-bearing Ore

2.4   Mine Production Capacity

URBAN

PROSPECTS OF WORLD URBANIZATION

FACTS AT A GLANCE

Number of Pages: 204

Periodicity: Irregular

Publisher: United Nations

PURPOSE AND SCOPE

The *Prospects of World Urbanization* includes estimates
and projections of urban and rural populations for all
countries and areas of the world, urban agglomerations with a population of 2 million or more, and of
capital cities of countries with a population of 2 million or more.

DATA ORGANIZATION

For urban and rural populations the estimates cover a
75-year span from 1950 to 2025 and for urban
agglomerations the coverage is 50 years from 1950 to
2000. The report is organized in two chapters.
Chapter I deals with urban and rural population size
and growth while Chapter II relates to the size and
growth of urban agglomerations of 2 million or more.
Also included in the report are 10 annex tables.
Annex tables A1 through A8 provide for each country
or area the total urban and rural population size and
rates of growth, the percent of the national population living in urban areas, and the growth rate of the
urban component. Population trends of urban
agglomerations from 1950 to 2000 are given in Annex
table A-9. Additional summary statistics and indices
by countries on selected characteristics of the urban
and rural populations and urban agglomeration and
capital city populations are presented in Annex table
A-10.

METHODOLOGY

The major problem in urban data is the absence of
standardized criteria for defining cities. The threshold is only 200 persons in Denmark and Norway, but
20,000 in Mauritius and Nigeria and 30,000 in Japan.
Some countries adopt criteria other than population,
such as the number of dwellings, population density,
or type of economic activity. These definitions are
given in Annex table A-10.

There are similar discrepancies in the definition
of units variously known as cities, urban agglomerations, or metropolitan areas.

The method of projecting urban and rural populations is the urban-rural growth differences method.
The projections use the latest decennial census data
from which estimates are extrapolated.

The annex tables list all of the 206 countries covered in the report aggregated into 22 regions and 7
major areas.

CONTENTS

List of Tables

1. Percentage of Population Living in Urban Areas,
by Major Area and Region, 1970-2025
2. Total, Urban, and Rural Population, by Major
Area, 1970-2025
3. Average Annual Rate of Growth of Total, Urban,
and Rural Populations and Rate of Urbanization,
by Major Area or Region, 1970-2025
4. Countries with Percent Urban in 1985 of 80
Percent or More and 20 Percent or Less
5. Countries with Rate of Urbanization in 1980 of 3.0
Percent or More and 0.3 Percent or Less
6. Urban Agglomerations with Population of 2
Million or More in 1985 and their Average Annual
Rate of Population Growth, 1970-2000

STATISTICS OF WORLD LARGE CITIES

FACTS AT A GLANCE

Number of Pages: 156

Year of Publication: 1993

Periodicity: Irregular

Publisher: Statistics Division, Tokyo Metropolitan Government

PURPOSE AND SCOPE

Statistics of World Large Cities has been published since 1961.

DATA ORGANIZATION

This volume contains statistical information covering demographic, sociological, cultural, and other aspects of world large cities.

METHODOLOGY

The data are based on the data files collected and maintained by the Tokyo Metropolitan government. These files are derived from commercial reports of Japanese embassies and commercial organizations abroad.

CONTENTS

List of Data by City

Index of Cities

Land Area, Population, and Population Density by Nation, Capital, and Large City

Climate

Population by Sex

Population by Age

Vital Statistics

Deaths by Age

Deaths by Major Cause

Medical Facilities and Personnel

Establishments

Consumer Price Index

Education

Libraries and Museums

Electricity, Gas, and Waterworks

Post and Telecommunication

Transport

Water Carriage

Motor Vehicles

Number of Newly Constructed Dwellings

Roads and Parks

Police and Fire Service

Theaters and Cinemas

Appendix: Questionnaire of the Statistics of World Large Cities

WOMEN

COMPENDIUM OF STATISTICS AND INDICATORS ON THE SITUATION OF WOMEN

FACTS AT A GLANCE

Number of Pages: 592

Periodicity: Irregular

Publisher: United Nations (UN)

PURPOSE AND SCOPE

The purpose of the *Compendium of Statistics and Indicators on the Situation of Women* is to make available in a single source, a comprehensive selection of internationally comparable statistics and indicators on the situation of women. It also serves as a convenient reference guide to international sources of data for further research. The *Compendium* also provides a convenient summary of statistical concepts, definitions, and classifications used in data collections at national and international levels. The current edition is an expanded and updated version of the document, "Selected Statistics and Indicators on the Status of Women," prepared by the World Conference to Review and Appraise the Achievements of the United Nations Decade for Women: Equality, Development, and Peace held at Nairobi in 1985. The *Compendium* has been prepared on the basis of the UN Microcomputer Database on Women's Indicators and Statistics (WISTAT) completed in 1987 with the collaboration of the UN Population Fund, the UN Fund for Women in Development, the Centre for Social Development and Humanitarian Affairs, the International Research and Training Institute for the Advancement of Women (INSTRAW), the International Labour Organisation, the World Health Organization, the United Nations Educational, Scientific, and Cultural Organization, the Food and Agriculture Organization, and other groups. The work has been undertaken in pursuance of the World Plan of Action for the Implementation of the Objectives of the International Women's Year and the Programme of Action for the Second Half of the United Nations Decade for Women: Equality, Development, and Peace and the Nairobi Forward Looking Strategies for the Advancement of Women.

DATA ORGANIZATION

The *Compendium* brings together statistics and indicators for 178 countries and areas in 33 tables grouped into eight general subject fields:
Tables 1-3 Population
Tables 4-7 Households and Families, Marital Status, Fertility

Tables 8-15 Economic Participation and Population Not Economically Active
Tables 16-19 National Household Income and Expenditure
Tables 20-22 Education and Literacy
Tables 23-28 Health and Health Services, Disabled Persons
Tables 29-32 Public Affairs and Political Participation
Table 33 Criminal Justice

METHODOLOGY

The data in the *Compendium* are not designed to be authoritative. The volume does not include the detailed notes and qualifications that are found in the original sources. Serious researchers and policymakers are encouraged to consult these original sources.

CONTENTS

Preface

Explanatory Notes

Introduction

Improving Statistics and Indicators on the Situation of Women

Development of the United Nations Women's Indicators and Statistics Data Base for Microcomputers (WISTAT)

General Technical Notes

  A. Scope and Coverage of the Compendium

  B. Sources and Reliability of Data

  C. Urban and Rural Areas

I.   Population Composition, Distribution and Change: Tables 1-3

II.   Households and Families, Marital Status, Fertility: Tables 4-7

III.   Economic Participation and Population not Economically Active: Tables 8-15

IV.   National and Household Income and Expenditure: Tables 16-19

V.   Education and Literacy: Tables 20-22

VI.   Health and Health Services; Disabled Persons: Tables 23-27

VII.   Housing Conditions and Human Settlements: Table 28

VIII.   Public Affairs and Political Participation: Tables 29-32

IX.   Criminal Justice: Table 33

Notes

Statistical Sources

THE WORLD'S WOMEN: TRENDS AND STATISTICS

FACTS AT A GLANCE

Number of Pages: 120

Periodicity: Irregular

Publisher: United Nations

PURPOSE AND SCOPE

The idea behind producing *The World's Women: Trends and Statistics* is to provide the numbers and analysis needed to understand how conditions are changing or not changing for women—and to do it in a way that will reach women, the media, and women's advocates everywhere. In this approach the report is innovative and experimental for the United Nations. It provides concerned women and men with information they can use to inform people everywhere about how much women contribute to economic life, political life, and family life and to support appeals to persuade public and private decision-makers to change policies that are unfair to women.

The direction and the areas covered follow mandates already adopted in the United Nations, including the Convention on the Elimination of All Forms of Discrimination against Women (1979) and the Nairobi Forward-looking Strategies for the Advancement of Women (1985).

DATA ORGANIZATION

The World's Women: Trends and Statistics 1970-1990 is a new type of international statistical publication which follows the form of publications on "Social Trends and Statistics" developed at the national level in a few countries since the 1960s and 1970s. Sir Claus Moser, as consultant to the participating United Nations organizations, encouraged and assisted in planning this form of statistical publication. It is hoped that this format will be found particularly suited to the presentation of a wide diversity of social and human development indicators which, however important, do not lend themselves to presentation using a few aggregate series as do economic statistics and national accounts.

METHODOLOGY

The publication is also a statistical sourcebook. Country and area data were assembled on indicators that capture conditions of women and then grouped into regional averages. The regional averages were analyzed and interpreted for presentation in text and charts. A wide range of general and ad hoc statistics was assembled, but many gaps remain—gaps in coverage of important topics, in timeliness, in comparison with men, in comparisons over time, and in country coverage. The publication nevertheless provides a guide for accumulating and interpreting more information in coming years. It also provides the most complete presentation so far of how women fare in different parts of the world.

CONTENTS

Message from the Secretary General

Foreword

Preface

About the Chapters

Overview of *The World's Women*

1. Women, Families, and Households
The World's Women
Families
Households
Domestic Violence
Indicators
Table 1. Female Population and Age Groups
Table 2. Indicators on Families and Households

2. Public Life and Leadership
Top Positions
Political Participation
Community and Grass Roots Leadership
Women in the Public Sector
Women in Economic Decision Making
Peace
Indicators
Table 3. Indicators on Women in Public Life

3. Education and Taining
Advancing Literacy for Women
Primary and Secondary School Enrollments
University and College Enrollments
Fields of Advanced Study and Training
Women in Teaching
Indicators
Table 4. Indicators on Education and Training

4. Health and Child-bearing
Life Expectancy
Causes of Death
Women's Health
The Health of Girls
Child Bearing
AIDS and Other Threats to Women's Health
Indicators
Table 5. Indicators on Health and Child Bearing

5. Housing, Human Settlements, and the Environment
Human Settlements
Migration
Water, Sanitation, and Electricity
The Environment
Indicators
Table 6. Indicators on Housing, Human Settlements, and Environment

6. Women's Work and the Economy
Women's Working World

Women in the Labour Force
Women in Agriculture, Industry, and Services
The Informal Sector
Economic Crisis and the Impact of Stabilization and
Adjustment Policies on Women

Indicators
Table 7. Indicators on Time Use
Table 8. Indicators on Women's Economic Activity
Table 9. Indicators on the Economy and Women's
Work

I.   Nairobi Forward-looking Strategies for the
     Advancement of Women

II. Convention on the Elimination of All Forms of
     Discrimination against Women

III. Geographical Groups of Countries and Areas

Statistical Sources

YOUTH

STATISTICAL CHARTS AND INDICATORS ON YOUTH

FACTS AT A GLANCE

Number of Pages: 50

Periodicity: Annual

Publisher: United Nations (UN)

PURPOSE AND SCOPE

Statistical Charts and Indicators on Youth is a statistical
and analytical sourcebook that uses charts and graphs
to highlight main aspects of and trends in the social
and economic situation of youth from 1970 through
1990.

DATA ORGANIZATION

Each chapter contains 5 to 10 summary charts. Data
are presented in more detail at the end of each chapter. Charts and tables are accompanied by statements
on definition, sources, and interpretation.

METHODOLOGY

The tables provide regional and subregional averages.
Subregional averages are shown when regional averages conceal wide differences among countries. The
exceptions are when the countries are heterogeneous
even at the subregional level or when a subregion is
very small. In general, the countries and areas covered are the same as in the social statistics databases
of the UN Statistical Office.

CONTENTS

1. **The World's Youth Population**
   The world's youth: 519 million young men and
   493 young women in 1990. Indicators. Table 1 -
   population indicators on youth 1970-1990.

2. **Education and Training**
   World youth illiteracy: 62 million young men and
   107 million young women in 1990 in developing
   regions. Indicators. Table 2 - indicators on education and training.

3. **Economic Activity**
   World youth in the labor force: 509 million in
   developing regions and 103 million in developed
   regions in 1990. Indicators. Table 3 - indicators on
   economic activity.

4. **Health and Child-bearing**
   Health and child-bearing. Indicators. Table 4 -
   health and child-bearing.

5. **Households and Marital Status**
   Households and marital status. Indicators. Table 5
   - indicators on marital status and household head-
   ship.

Annex

Geographical Groupings of Countries and Areas

Statistical Sources

SECTION TWO:

ELECTRONIC DATABASES

The inclusion of an Electronic Database Section in this edition is an indication of things to come. Unlike literature and other creative arts, statistics are ideally suited for being presented in electronic formats. The ability to make quick changes in data, derive percentages and ratios, and visualize trends are only some of the advantages that the electronic format has over print. The most important is the abridgment of leadtime between collection, editing, and publication. Every electronic database gains a minimum of three years in currency when converted from its print form.

It has been estimated that in the past two decades electronic databases have grown by a factor of 122, and database entries have grown by a factor of 27. The number of producers continues to grow at a somewhat slower rate because individual producers create multiple databases. Similarly, the number of vendors also has grown at a slower rate because vendors bundle a number of services and some, such as DIALOG, offer hundreds of databases. While these trends indicate that the database industry is now solidly established, the real growth has been in the acceptance by users, measured in terms of the number of searches (which translates to connect time) and in terms of expenditures for searching.

Statistics—technically known as numeric databases—is only a small subset of the worldwide electronic database industry and global statistics is an even smaller subset. Nevertheless, the rising electronic tide has helped to lift nonprint statistics to a position where it can effectively compete with print. Virtually all the core print products in this field are being offered simultaneously in electronic form. Some products are offered in more than one platform, for example, online, CD-ROM, and diskette. Online represents 57 percent of the databases, CD-ROM—20 percent, diskette—10 percent, magnetic tape—7 percent, batch—5 percent, and handheld products—1 percent.

The growth of the database industry has been accompanied by an expansion of the production and marketing facilities. Producers of databases—sometimes called publishers—may also be hardcopy publishers, but many produce only electronic versions. Most offer their databases for lease or license to vendors who, in turn, offer search services to the marketplace on a fee basis. In the beginning, government databases (including those produced by the United Nations and related organizations) monopolized the production of electronic databases, but their market share has fallen significantly over the past decade. As a percentage of the total, official databases have decreased between 1977 and 1994 from 56 percent to 14 percent, while commercial databases have climbed during the same period from 22 percent to 76 percent. However, these percentages mask the fact that most commercial databases are built on official data.

Vendors—formerly called hosts in Europe—play a special role in the database industry. They provide value-added processing and offer search services. The three largest vendors of global statistical databases are The WEFA Group, Reuters Information Services, and DRI/McGraw-Hill.

This section is subdivided into five subsections: (1) Batch Access Products; (2) CD-ROMs; (3) Diskettes; (4) Magnetic Tapes; and (5) Online. Generally, each subsection contains entries that include the following information: title; publisher; address; phone number; fax number; type of database; content; subject; languages; coverage; time span; updating; vendor; system requirements; software; and price. The Online subsection contains additional information on online availability and alternate electronic formats.

GENERAL

ECONOMIST'S STATISTICS

Phone: (416) 964-0789
Fax: (416) 323-1961

James R. LymBurner & Sons, Ltd.
P.O. Box 289, Station A
Toronto, ON, Canada M5W 1B2

TYPE

Time series

CONTENT

Provides access to a full range of economic and financial data. Coverage includes currencies, collectibles, commodities, international interest rates, international Gross National Product statistics, real estate, and stock market indexes. Comprises the following data:

- Weekly Statistics—contains weekly and monthly time series on international interest rates and currency exchange rates; major stock market indexes and sub-indexes from London, New York, Toronto, Hong Kong, Singapore, Sydney, Paris, and Tokyo; commodity indexes from Reuters, Dow Jones, and *The Economist*; commodity prices for food and metals; prices for strategic metals; gold coin prices; and world shipping statistics. Includes future or forward prices for London, New York, and Chicago.

- Gross National Product Statistics—contains weekly, monthly, and quarterly time series of income and expenditure data for Canada, Germany, Japan, the United Kingdom, and the United States. Data are seasonally adjusted at annual rates.

SUBJECT

International economic and financial statistics

COVERAGE

International

TIME SPAN

Varies by series

UPDATING

As data become available

VENDOR

Search results are provided in hard copy or on diskette. Contact vendor for details

EDUCATION

SIRI DATA BANK

Phone: 02 2235582
Fax: 02 491875

United Nations Educational, Scientific, and Cultural Organization (UNESCO)
Officina Regional de Educacion para America Latina y el Caribe (OREALC)
Enrique Delpiano St. 2058
Providencia
Santiago, Chile

TYPE

Statistical

CONTENT

Contains statistical information on financial statements for educational systems on pre-primary, primary, and secondary school levels in 36 regions in Latin America and the Caribbean. Includes combined information for the entire region.

SUBJECT

Financial statistics for Latin American and Caribbean educational systems

LANGUAGES

English; Spanish

COVERAGE

Latin America and the Caribbean

TIME SPAN

1980 to date

UPDATING

Monthly

VENDOR

United Nations Educational, Scientific, and Cultural Organization (UNESCO), Officina Regional de Educacion para America Latina y el Caribe (OREALC)

PRICE

Contact vendor for details

INDUSTRY

INDEX NUMBERS OF INDUSTRIAL PRODUCTION

Phone: (212) 963-4120
Fax: (212) 963-4116

United Nations Statistical Division
2 United Nations Plaza, DC2-1620
New York, NY 10017

TYPE

Statistical

CONTENT

Provides indexes of country, regional, and world industrial production.

SUBJECT

Worldwide industrial production

TIME SPAN

1967 to 1991

VENDOR

United Nations Statistical Division

PRICE

Search results are provided on magnetic tape. Contact vendor for details

INDUSTRIAL STATISTICS

Phone: (212) 963-4120
Fax: (212) 963-4116

United Nations Statistical Division
2 United Nations Plaza, DC2-1620
New York, NY 10017

TYPE

Time series

CONTENT

Provides national output statistics for industries engaged in mining and quarrying, manufacturing, and the production and distribution of gas, electricity, and water. Comprises two sections: General Industrial Statistics and Commodity Production Statistics. Corresponds to Volume 1 and Volume 2 of the *Industrial Statistics Yearbook.*

SUBJECT

Mining; quarrying; manufacturing; and gas, electricity, and water industry statistics; questionnaires; tapes supplied by national sources; data furnished by the specialized agencies and similar bodies; national, international, and other publications; direct inquiry; censuses; and others

VENDOR

United Nations Statistical Division

PRICE

Depends on number of years needed. Search results are available on magnetic tape. Contact vendor for details

TRADE

EXTERNAL TRADE STATISTICS

Phone: (212) 963-4120
Fax: (212) 963-4116

United Nations Statistical Division
2 United Nations Plaza, DC2-1620
New York, NY 10017

TYPE

Statistical

CONTENT

Provides annual and some cumulative quarterly country, regional, and world statistics on external trade in commodities identified according to the Standard International Trade Classification. Detailed values in thousand U.S. dollars and quantity data in metric units for each trading partner exist to the extent provided by the reporting counties. Subsets of the data are made available upon request.

SUBJECT

Worldwide external trade

TIME SPAN

1962 to date

VENDOR

United Nations Statistical Division

PRICE

Search results are available on printouts, diskette, or on magnetic tape. Contact vendor for details

CORPORATIONS

WORLD VESTBASE™

Phone: (312) 266-0575
Fax: (616) 756-2288

World Vest-Base
1335 N. Dearborn Pkwy
Chicago, IL 60610

TYPE

Numeric

CONTENT

Provides comprehensive balance sheet and income statement data for 5,500 foreign industrial companies in 45 countries and 125 industry groups. For each company, provides name, balance sheet, per share values, stock price histories, annual percentage change, flow of fund statements, redefined values, price-related data with highs, lows, and averages, text note describing each company's activities along with tables from annual reports, economic data for each country, schedule of interim results on a semiannual or quarterly basis for each company, price history from 1980 (including share type for each company), performance estimates from broker-dealers (for most companies), current prices, and price ratios. Corresponds to the online World 'Vest-Base' database.

SUBJECT

Equity information on foreign industrial companies

COVERAGE

International, except the United States

TIME SPAN

1980 to date

UPDATING

Monthly

VENDOR

World Vest-Base

SYSTEM REQUIREMENT

Contact vendor for details

PRICE

Contact vendor for details

FINANCE

COMPUSTAT® PC PLUS GLOBAL VANTAGE

Phone: (303) 771-6510
(800) 525-8640
(303) 740-4687

Standard & Poor's Compustat
7400 S. Alton Court
Englewood, CO 80112

TYPE

Time series

CONTENT

Provides corporate financial data covering more than 2,500 U.S. companies and approximately 7,000 companies and financial services in 32 other countries. Covers companies that comprise the Morgan Stanley Capital International Index, as well as those used for local market indexes. Comprises the following three files:

- Financial File—contains more than 353 items obtained from shareholders' reports and company filings, including income statements, balance sheets, flow of funds statements, and supplementary income statement and balance sheet items. Data are stated in the currency used in the company's financial report.

- Issue File—contains monthly share prices, dividends, shares traded, high, low, and close prices from local exchanges, annual earnings per share, shares outstanding, and issued capital. Issue price histories reflect the currency of the exchange on which the stock is traded. Sources include U.S. Securities and Exchange Commission (SEC) 10K filings and filings with local stock exchanges.

- Currency File—provides currency data covering month-end rates, monthly averages, and 12-month moving averages for 57 currencies, and a currency translation matrix, which enables users to compare 39 currencies against the yen, Swiss franc, U.S. dollar, and British pound.

Enables the user to search by London Issuer Code for International Stock Exchanges, SEDOL code, and, for companies traded in North America, CUSIP and Trading Symbol codes. Corresponds to the GLOBAL Vantage online database.

SUBJECT

Financial and market information for companies in 32 countries; world currency markets

COVERAGE

International

TIME SPAN

1982 to date

UPDATING

Monthly

VENDOR

Standard & Poor's Compustat

SYSTEM REQUIREMENTS

IBM PC AT, PS/2, 80286- or 80396-based machines of higher; hard disk with 10MB free; 640K memory; MS-DOS 3.1 or higher; math coprocessor chip; color monitor recommended; CD-ROM drive

SOFTWARE

From Standard & Poor's Compustat

PRICE

Contact vendor for details

INTERNATIONAL FINANCIAL STATISTICS

Phone: (202) 623-6180
Fax: (202) 623-4661

International Monetary Fund (IMF)
Statistics Department
700 19th St., N.W.
Washington, DC 20431

TYPE

Time series

CONTENT

Contains more than 26,000 annual, quarterly, and monthly time series of economic and financial statistics on about 200 countries, supplemented by world and area aggregates for key time series. Annual series cover 1948 to date; quarterly and monthly series cover 1957 to date; some monthly series cover 1985 to date. Topics covered include exchange rates (e.g., averages and closings); international liquidity (e.g., reserves, foreign assets, and liabilities of deposit banks); money and banking (e.g., interest rates, domestic credit, and money); interest rates, prices, and production (e.g., wholesale and consumer prices, wages, industrial production, and crude petroleum production); government finance (e.g., revenues and expenditures); inter-

national transactions (e.g., value, volume, prices of exports and imports, and capital transactions); national accounts (e.g., private consumption, investment, and Gross Domestic Product); and population. Corresponds to the IMF publication *International Financial Statistics*, which provides additional information on sources of data, definitions, and other supplemental information, and to the online International Financial Statistics database.

SUBJECT

Financial and general economic time series

COVERAGE

International

TIME SPAN

Varies

UPDATING

Monthly

VENDOR

International Monetary Fund, Statistics Department

SYSTEM REQUIREMENTS

IBM PC or compatible; hard disk; MS-DOS 3.0 or higher; Microsoft CD-ROM Extensions; CD-ROM drive

PRICE

Contact vendor for details

WORLDSCOPE®

Phone: (203) 330-5261
Fax: (203) 330-5001

W/D Partners
1000 Lafayette Blvd.
Bridgeport, CT 06604

ALTERNATE DATABASE NAME

Disclosure/Worldscope

FORMER DATABASE NAME

Disclosure/Worldscope

TYPE

Directory; numeric

CONTENT

Contains financial data on more than 11,000 major corporations in 45 countries listed on leading stock exchanges around the world. Covers 25 industries, including aerospace, banking, chemicals, electronics, food and beverages, insurance, metal products manufacturing, and transportation. For U.S. companies, provides monthly data on more than 600 items; for non-U.S. companies, on more than 350 items. Includes fundamental data (e.g., financial statement, balance sheet), computed variables (e.g., current ratios), company-specific accounting standards, and descriptive information (e.g., name, address, names of executives). Sources include corporate annual and 10K reports, disclosure statements, newspapers, and wire services. Corresponds in part to *Worldscope Industrial Company Profiles* and *Worldscope Financial and Service Company Profiles* and the online Worldscope database.

SUBJECT

Fundamental, descriptive, and financial data for leading companies worldwide

COVERAGE

International

TIME SPAN

Most current 10 years

UPDATING

Varies by online service

UPDATING

Monthly

VENDOR

W/D Partners

SYSTEM REQUIREMENTS

IBM PC, PS/2, or compatible; hard disk with 2MB free; 640K memory; MS-DOS 3.1 or higher; Microsoft CD-ROM Extensions; CD-ROM drive

SOFTWARE

From W/D Partners

PRICE

Contact vendor for details

ENERGY

THE ETDE ENERGY DATABASE

Phone: 01 45248200
Fax: 01 45249988

International Energy Association (IEA)
Energy Technology Data Exchange (ETDE)
2, rue Andre Pascal
F-75775 Paris Cedex 16, France

TYPE

Bibliographic

CONTENT

Contains more than one million citations to the world's literature dealing with nuclear science and technology. Sources include journals, research reports, monographs, conference proceedings, theses, patents, and unpublished materials. Corresponds to the online International Nuclear Information System produced by the International Atomic Energy Agency; Energy Science and Technology database produced by the U.S. Department of Energy, Office of Scientific and Technical Information; and Coal Data Base produced by IEA Coal Research.

SUBJECT

Nuclear science and technology, including nuclear energy, coal, fossil and synthetic fuels, solar and other renewable energy, energy storage and conversion, and environmental sciences and related issues

COVERAGE

International

YEAR FIRST AVAILABLE

1993

TIME SPAN

1974 to date

UPDATING

Quarterly

VENDOR

SilverPlatter Information, Inc.

SYSTEM REQUIREMENTS

Contact vendor for details

SOFTWARE

PC SPIRS or WINSPIRS from SilverPlatter Information, Inc.

PRICE

Contact vendor for details

GENERAL

STATBANK™

Phone: (203) 966-1100
(800) 762-8182
Fax: (203) 966-6254

NewsBank, Inc.
58 Pine St.
New Canaan, CT 06840

TYPE

Statistical

CONTENT

Contains charts and tables of statistics on a worldwide basis. Covers a variety of categories relating to such subjects as agriculture, the fishing industry, mines and mine resources, transportation, crime and law enforcement, health, geography, education, labor, business and industry, income, communications, housing, state finances and taxation, demography, energy, social welfare, government and elections, and prices. Sources include more than 250 publications from U.S. federal government agencies, state government agencies, newspapers, business journals, and international sources.

SUBJECT

World statistics in all subject areas

COVERAGE

International

TIME SPAN

Current information

UPDATING

Quarterly

VENDOR

NewsBank, Inc.

SYSTEM REQUIREMENTS

Requires NewsBank Electronic Index Workstation; contact NewsBank, Inc. for details.

SOFTWARE

From NewsBank, Inc.

PRICE

Contact vendor for details

STATISTICAL ABSTRACTS FROM THE A MATTER OF FACT DATABASE

Phone: (313) 434-5530
(800) 678-2435
Fax: (313) 434-6409

Pierian Press, Inc.
P.O. Box 1808
Ann Arbor, MI 48106

TYPE

Bibliographic; statistical

CONTENT

Contains more than 50,000 citations, with abstracts and statistics, of textual materials on current political, social, economic, and environmental issues worldwide. Covers materials, with accompanying comparative statistical content, extracted from testimony presented at congressional hearings by witnesses considered to be experts in their field, the Congressional Record reflecting statements made by U.S. senators and representatives, and approximately 250 general-interest periodicals and selected newspapers. Items are indexed using the Library of Congress subject headings. Corresponds to *A Matter of Fact: Statements Containing Statistics on Current Social, Economic, and Political Issues* and the online A Matter of Fact database.

SUBJECT

Facts and research findings in social, economic, political, environmental, and other areas

COVERAGE

International

YEAR FIRST AVAILABLE

1993

TIME SPAN

1985 to date

UPDATING

Quarterly

VENDOR

SilverPlatter Information, Inc.

SYSTEM REQUIREMENTS

IBM PC, PS/2, or compatible; hard disk recommended; 640K memory; MS-DOS 2.1 or higher; monochrome or color monitor; Microsoft CD-ROM Extensions; CD-ROM drive; Apple Macintosh Plus, SE, or II series; hard disk recommended (two 800K floppy drives acceptable); 1mb memory (2MB recommended); System 6.0.2 or higher; AppleCD SC or compatible CD-ROM drive

SOFTWARE

PC SPIRS (for IBM) or MacSPIRS (for Macintosh) from SilverPlatter Information, Inc.

PRICE

Contact vendor for details

STATISTICAL MASTERFILE®

Phone: (301) 654-1550
(800) 638-8380
Fax: (301) 654-4033

Congressional Information Service, Inc. (CIS)
4520 East-West Hwy., Suite 800
Bethesda, MD 20814-3389

TYPE

Bibliographic

CONTENT

Contains statistical data published in the United States or by international intergovernmental organizations in the areas of population, business and financial activities, domestic and international trade, government programs, health, and other economic, demographic, social, and political issues. Comprises the following three files:

American Statistics Index—contains citations, with abstracts, to publications containing social, economic, demographic, and other statistical data collected and analyzed by the U.S. government since the mid-1960s. Covers statistical publications (or publications containing substantial statistical data) generated by executive, legislative, and judicial departments; research, administrative, and regulatory agencies; and special bodies created by the Congress or the president. Corresponds to *American Statistics Index* and to the online American Statistics Index database.

Index to International Statistics—contains citations, with abstracts, to statistical publications issued by 95 international intergovernmental organizations from 1983 to date. Sources include the United Nations and affiliated agencies, the European Community, the Organization of American States, and the Organization for Economic Cooperation and Development. Corresponds to the *Index to International Statistics.*

Statistical Reference Index—contains citations, with abstracts, to statistical publications released by non-U.S. government sources from 1981 to date. Sources include more than 1,000 associations, institutes, businesses, commercial publishers, state government agencies, and independent and university research centers. Corresponds to *Statistical Reference Index.*

Each database is searchable by CIS-assigned index terms or free text. Software enables the user to search all databases simultaneously.

SUBJECT

International station government and other publications containing the following types of data: population, business and financial activities, domestic and international trade, government programs, health, and other economic, demographic, social, and political trends

COVERAGE

International

TIME SPAN

Mid-1960s to date

UPDATING

Quarterly

VENDOR

Congressional Information Service, Inc.

SYSTEM REQUIREMENTS

IBM PC, PS/2, or compatible; hard disk with 2MB free; 640K memory; MS-DOS 3.1 or higher; monochrome or color monitor; Microsoft CD-ROM Extensions 2.0 or higher; CD-ROM drive

Software

Access from Quantum Access, Inc.

PRICE

Varies by index selected, ordering library budget, and subscription to printed indexes. Contact vendor for details

STATISTICAL YEARBOOK

Phone: (212) 963-4120
Fax: (212) 963-4116

United Nations Statistical Division
2 United Nations Plaza, DC2-1620
New York, NY 10017

CONTACT

Robert Johnston, Officer-in-Charge

TYPE

Statistical

CONTENT

Contains new database techniques developed by UNSTAT. Corresponds to the print version of the 38th issue of the *United Nations Statistical Yearbook.*

SUBJECT

Database techniques

YEAR FIRST AVAILABLE

1994

VENDOR

United Nations Statistical Division

SYSTEM REQUIREMENTS

IBM PC or compatible; CD-ROM drive

PRICE

Contact vendor for details

NORDIC COUNTRIES

STATISTICS ACROSS BORDERS: NORDIC STATISTICS ON CD-ROM

Phone: 3 9173917
Fax: 3 1184801

Danmarks Statistik
Sejrogade 11
DK-2100 Copenhagen 0, Denmark

TYPE

Numeric

CONTENT

Contains data on employment and foreign trade in Denmark. Includes annual data on company employment, turnover, accounts, household surveys, wages, and salaries. Includes monthly and quarterly foreign trade data classified by Harmonized Tariff Codes and Standard International Trade Classification codes. Also includes quarterly data on production. Corresponds to the online Erhvervsstatistisk Databank.

SUBJECT

Employment and foreign trade in Denmark

LANGUAGE

Danish

COVERAGE

Denmark

YEAR FIRST AVAILABLE

1993

TIME SPAN

1980 to date

UPDATING

Annual

VENDOR

Danmarks Statistik

SYSTEM REQUIREMENTS

Contact vendor for details

PRICE

Contact vendor for details

TRADE

WORLD TRADE ATLAS CD-ROM

Phone: (803) 765-1860

Global Trade Information Services Inc.
610 Hilton St., Suite 6
Columbia, SC 29205

TYPE

Statistical

CONTENT

Contains official U.S. government data on import, export, and balance-of-trade between the United States and more than 200 nations. Provides information on products, importing/exporting country, market share and percentage change, and quantity and average-unit price data among countries. Includes 2-, 4-, 6-, or 10-digit product Harmonized Codes information.

SUBJECT

U.S. imports and exports

COVERAGE

International

YEAR FIRST AVAILABLE

1994

TIME SPAN

Current three years

UPDATING

Monthly or quarterly

VENDOR

Global Trade Information Services Inc.

SYSTEM REQUIREMENTS

IBM PC or compatible; CD-ROM drive

PRICE

Contact vendor for details

WORLD TRADE DATABASE

Phone: (613) 951-9647
Fax: (613) 951-0117

Statistics Canada
International Trade Division
9 JT, Tunney's Pasture
Ottawa, ON, Canada K1A 0T6

ALTERNATE DATABASE NAME

Statistics Canada World Trade Database; La Base de
Donnees sur le Commerce Mondial

TYPE

Statistical

CONTENT

Contains 12 years of annual commodity and industry
flow statistics for the 160 member countries of the
United Nations, 600 commodities, and 300 industries.
Tracks commodity supply, and enables the user to
spot marketing potential, monitor import/export
activity, and calculate trends.

SUBJECT

Industry and commodity trade flow data

COVERAGE

International

YEAR FIRST AVAILABLE

1993

TIME SPAN

1980-1991

UPDATING

Not updated

VENDOR

OPTIM Corporation

SYSTEM REQUIREMENTS

IBM PC or compatible; hard disk with at least 1.5MB
free; floppy drive; MS-DOS 3.0 or higher; MS-DOA
CD-ROM Extensions 2.01 or higher; monochrome or
color monitor; CD-ROM drive

SOFTWARE

From Dataware Technologies, Inc.

PRICE

Contact vendor for details

Diskettes

AGRICULTURE

WORLD AGRICULTURE SUPPLY AND DISPOSITION (WASD)

Phone: (215) 667-6000
Fax: (215) 660-6477

The WEFA Group
401 City Line Ave., Suite 300
Bala Cynwyd, PA 19004-1780

TYPE

Time series

CONTENT

Contains more than 29,000 annual time series on the supply and disposition of crops, livestock, and meat commodities in more than 195 countries. Data include stocks; areas harvested, yield, and production; domestic use broken down by food and industrial use; imports, exports, and imports from the United States. Covers 52 commodities, including barley, beef and veal, cattle, coffee, corn, cottonseeds, oats, pigs, pork, poultry, poultry meat, soybeans, sugar, and wheat. Primary source of data is the U.S. Department of Agriculture, Foreign Agricultural Service.

SUBJECT

The worldwide supply and disposition of agricultural commodities, including coffee, cotton, eggs, dairy, grains (10 commodities), livestock (3 commodities), meat (12 commodities), oilseeds (23 commodities), tobacco, and sugar

COVERAGE

International

VENDOR

The WEFA Group

PRICE

Contact vendor for details

BUSINESS

INTERNATIONAL BUSINESS CLIMATE INDICATORS

Phone: (315) 472-1224
Fax: (315) 472-1235

IBC USA Licensing Inc.
Political Risk Services (PRS)
222 Teall Ave., Suite 200
P.O. Box 6482
Syracuse, NY 13217-6482

TYPE

Statistical

CONTENT

Contains tables extracted from Political Risk Services' print publication *Country Forecasts*. Provides rankings for 100 countries globally and regionally according to political, social, and economic variables. Covers data and forecasts on elections, political stability, market risk, work force, urban growth, unemployment, infant mortality, gross domestic product, inflation, capital investment, budget balance, debt service, current account, and currency change.

SUBJECT

European business climate indicators, including elections, regime stability, financial transfers, direct investments, export markets, inflation rates, capital investments, unemployment, currency fluctuation, population shifts, the workforce, and urban growth

COVERAGE

International

TIME SPAN

Current information

UPDATING

Semiannual

VENDOR

IBC USA Licensing Inc., Political Risk Services

SYSTEM REQUIREMENTS

IBM PC or compatible

PRICE

Contact vendor for details

CIVIL AVIATION

CIVIL AVIATION STATISTICS ON DISKETTE

Phone: (514) 286-6292
Fax: (514) 285-6744

International Civil Aviation Organization (ICAO)
Statistics Section
1000 Sherbrooke St., W.
Montreal, PQ, Canada H3A 2R2

TYPE

Statistical; directory

CONTENT

Contains statistical data on international commercial air carriers and airports. Covers data on air carrier traffic, traffic by flight stage, on-flight origin and destination, finance, and fleet and personnel. Also covers airport and route facility traffic and financial statistics. Corresponds to the *ICAO Digests of Statistics* series. Each file corresponds to one digest.

SUBJECT

International airport and air traffic

COVERAGE

International

TIME SPAN

1968 to date

UPDATING

Annual

VENDOR

International Civil Aviation Organization, Statistics Section

PRICE

Contact vendor for details

COMPUTERS

WORLD SEMICONDUCTOR TRADE STATISTICS

Phone: (408) 246-2711
Fax: (408) 246-2830
Semiconductor Industry Association (SIA)
4300 Stevens Creek Blvd., Suite 271
San Jose, CA 95129

TYPE

Statistical

SUBJECT

International semiconductor industry

COVERAGE

International

TIME SPAN

1976 to date

UPDATING

Monthly

VENDOR

Semiconductor Industry Association

PRICE

Contact vendor for details

DEBT

WORLD DEBT TABLES

Phone: (202) 477-1234
Fax: (202) 477-0661

The World Bank
International Economics Department
1818 H St., N.W.
Washington, DC 20433

TYPE

Time series

CONTENT

Contains more than 20,300 annual time series and some long-term forecasts on the external debt of approximately 138 developing countries and 6 regions worldwide. Data are published by the International Bank for Reconstruction and

Development (World Bank) in *World Debt Tables: External Finance for Developing Countries* and its supplements. Data, available by category of debt and by type of creditor, cover these major transactions for each creditor: commitments; disbursements; repayments of principal; payments of interest; debt outstanding; loan terms; and debt services projections. Corresponds to the online World Debt Tables database.

SUBJECT

External debt information, external finance, and capital flows

COVERAGE

International

TIME SPAN

1970 to date

UPDATING

Twice yearly

VENDOR

Haver Analytics

SYSTEM REQUIREMENTS

IBM PC or compatible; floppy drive; hard disk with 2.5MB free; 512K memory; MS-DOS 3.0 or higher; monochrome or color monitor

SOFTWARE

Data Link Express from Haver Analytics, Inc.

PRICE

Contact vendor for details

WORLD DEBT TABLES EXTRACTS (DX)

Phone: (202) 477-1234
Fax: (202) 477-0661

The World Bank
International Economics Department
1818 H St., N.W.
Washington, DC 20433

TYPE

Time series

CONTENT

Contains more than 20,300 annual time series and some long-term forecasts on the external debt of approximately 138 developing countries and 6 regions worldwide.

SUBJECT

External debt information, external finance, and capital flows

COVERAGE

International

UPDATING

Annual

VENDOR

The World Bank, International Economics Department

PRICE

Contact vendor for details

DEVELOPING COUNTRIES

OECD DAC EXTERNAL DEBT OF DEVELOPING COUNTRIES

Phone: 01 45249056
Fax: 01 45241650

Organization for Economic Cooperation and Development (OECD)

Development Assistance Committee (DAC)

2, rue Andre Pascal
F-75775 Paris Cedex 16, France

TYPE

Time series

CONTENT

Contains annual time series of historical and forecast data on the debt positions of 141 developing countries and territories. Provides total long- and medium-term outstanding external debt and debt service in U.S. dollars. Also provides selected indicators of economic performance for each country. Excludes short-term debt, military official debt, and International Monetary Fund credits. Corresponds to the online OECD DAC External Debt of Developing Countries database.

SUBJECT

Foreign debts of developing countries

COVERAGE

International

TIME SPAN

1975 to date

UPDATING

Annual

VENDOR

Organization for Economic Cooperation and Development, Development Assistance Committee

SYSTEM REQUIREMENTS

Contact the Development Assistance Committee for details

PRICE

Contact vendor for details

OECD DAC FINANCIAL FLOWS TO DEVELOPING COUNTRIES

Phone: 01 45249056
Fax: 01 45241650

Organization for Economic Cooperation and Development (OECD)

Development Assistance Committee (DAC)

2, rue Andre Pascal
F-75775 Paris Cedex 16, France

ALTERNATE DATABASE NAME

OECD Aid Flows to Developing Countries

TYPE

Time series

CONTENT

Contains annual time series of financial aid statistics for 216 developing countries. Includes recipient, donor, and amount and type of aid in U.S. dollars. Sources of data include reports from the Organization for Economic Development, Development Assistance Committees countries (Australia, Austria, Belgium, Denmark, Germany, Finland, France, Italy, Japan, The Netherlands, New Zealand, Norway, Sweden, Switzerland, United Kingdom, and the United States), the Commission of the European Communities, and reports from multilateral organizations. Corresponds to the online OECD DAC Financial Flows to Developing Countries database.

SUBJECT

Financial data pertaining to developing countries

COVERAGE

International

TIME SPAN

1968 to date

UPDATING

Annual

VENDOR

Organization for Economic Cooperation and Development, Development Assistance Committee

SYSTEM REQUIREMENTS

Contact vendor for details

PRICE

Contact vendor for details

DISABILITY

DISABILITY STATISTICS DATABASE (DISTAT)

Phone: (212) 963-4120
Fax: (212) 963-4116

United Nations Statistical Division
2 United Nations Plaza, DC2-1620
New York, NY 10017

CONTACT

Robert Johnston, Officer-in-Charge

TYPE

Statistical; numeric

CONTENT

Contains information on sources and availability of statistics on disability for 95 countries or areas, as well as detailed statistics on disabled persons from national censuses, surveys, and other data sources from 55 countries.

SUBJECT

Worldwide statistics on the handicapped

TIME SPAN

1960-1986

VENDOR

United Nations Statistical Division

PRICE

Contact vendor for details

ECONOMY

INTERNATIONAL COMPARISON PROGRAMME

Phone: (212) 963-4120
Fax: (212) 963-4116

United Nations Statistical Division
2 United Nations Plaza, DC2-1620
New York, NY 10017

CONTACT

Robert Johnston, Officer-in-Charge

CONTENT

Contains five Lotus 1-2-3 spreadsheet files. Provides the basic input, including 151 basic heading expenditures, purchasing power parities per U.S. dollar, and real values for the 60 participating countries in the United Nations Statistical Division phase IV comparison of 1980.

SUBJECT

Comparisons of expenditures and purchases among various countries

COVERAGE

International

YEAR FIRST AVAILABLE

1994

VENDOR

United Nations Statistical Division

PRICE

Contact vendor for details

INTLINE

Phone: (215) 667-6000
Fax: (215) 660-6477

The WEFA Group
401 City Line Ave., Suite 300
Bala Cynwyd, PA 19004-1780

TYPE

Time series

CONTENT

Contains approximately 7,000 daily, weekly, monthly, quarterly, and annual time series providing coverage of principal macroeconomic data for more than 40 countries worldwide, including Argentina, Australia, Austria, Belgium, Brazil, Canada, Chile, Colombia, Denmark, Finland, France, Germany, Greece, Hong Kong, India, Indonesia, Ireland, Italy, Japan, Korea, Malaysia, Mexico, The Netherlands, New Zealand, Norway, the Philippines, Singapore, South Africa, Spain, Sweden, Switzerland, Taiwan, Thailand, the United Kingdom and the United States. Corresponds to the online INTLINE database.

SUBJECT

International macroeconomic data for 40 countries, covering national accounts: government finance; cyclical indicators and business surveys; industrial production and producer price indexes; orders, stocks, and deliveries; wholesale and retail sales and consumer and wholesale prices; construction and housing starts; population; labor, wages, and unemployment rates; money and banking; interest bearing, charged, and interbank (LIBOR) rates; foreign exchange rates, forward rates, and Eurocurrency rates; foreign trade, exports, imports, and balance; balance of payments; and official reserves

COVERAGE

International

TIME SPAN

1901 to date

UPDATING

Daily

VENDOR

The WEFA Group (INTLINE)

PRICE

Contact vendor for details

NATIONAL ACCOUNTS STATISTICS

Phone: (212) 963-4120
Fax: (212) 963-4116

United Nations Statistical Division
2 United Nations Plaza, DC2-1620
New York, NY 10017

TYPE

Time series

CONTENT

Contains annual time series on the national income and product accounts of countries worldwide. Both market economies and centrally planned economies are included. Covers gross domestic product, gross capital formation, gross fixed capital formation, government consumption expenditures, private consumption expenditures; imports and exports, national income, savings, and net material products. Represents the transactions of corporate and quasi-corporate enterprises, financial and non-financial institutions, government, and households. Corresponds to data published by the United Nations in the *National Accounts Statistics: Main Aggregates and Detailed Tables* from 1970 to 1986, and in part to *National Accounts Statistics: Analysis of Main Aggregates.*

SUBJECT

National accounts data and material product balances

COVERAGE

International

TIME SPAN

1950 to 1990

UPDATING

Annual

VENDOR

United Nations Statistical Division

PRICE

Contact vendor for details

OECD ECONOMIC OUTLOOK

Phone: 331 49104265
Fax: 331 49104299

Organization for Economic Cooperation and Development (OECD)

Electronic Editions

2, rue Andre Pascal
F-75775 Paris Cedex 16, France

TYPE

Time series

CONTENT

Contains approximately 3,500 annual and semiannual time series of macroeconomic statistics and forecasts for OECD member countries, with information on OECD aggregates and non-OECD zones included. Covers national income, expenditures, household accounts, employment, production, interest rates, and balance of payments. Provides disaggregated data on national income, household accounts, interest rates, and balance of payments for seven major industrialized nations (Canada, Germany, France, Italy, Japan, United Kingdom, and the United States). Corresponds to the *OECD Economic Outlook* and to the online OECD Economic Outlook database.

SUBJECT

Macroeconomic financial data for member countries of the OECD and aggregates, including gross national product and its components; government, and households appropriation accounts; fiscal and monetary indicators; labor markets and supply indicators; wages, prices, and profitability; and international trade and payments

COVERAGE

International

TIME SPAN

Varies by series

UPDATING

Semiannual (June and December)

VENDOR

Organization for Economic Cooperation and Development, Electronic Editions

SYSTEM REQUIREMENTS

Contact the OECD for system requirements

PRICE

Contact vendor for details

OECD MAIN ECONOMIC INDICATORS

Phone: 331 49104265
Fax: 331 49104299

Organization for Economic Cooperation and Development (OECD)

Electronic Editions

2, rue Andre Pascal
F-75775 Paris Cedex 16, France

TYPE

Time series

CONTENT

Contains approximately 7,200 monthly, quarterly, and annual economic time series for the 25 OECD member countries and selected totals for North America, the European Community, OECD-Europe, and all OECD countries. Most series are available both seasonally adjusted and unadjusted. Software enables the user to retrieve data and analyze statistics. Corresponds to data in *Main Economic Indicators* and to the online OECD Main Economic Indicators database.

SUBJECT

Economic indicators for OECD member countries, including industrial productions, business surveys, deliveries, stocks and orders, constructions, domestic trade, labor, wages, prices, domestic and foreign finance, interest rates, foreign trade, and balance of payments

COVERAGE

International

TIME SPAN

1980 to date

UPDATING

Monthly

VENDOR

Organization for Economic Cooperation and Development, Electronic Editions

SYSTEM REQUIREMENTS

Contact the OECD for system requirements information

PRICE

Contact vendor for details

OECD QUARTERLY NATIONAL ACCOUNTS

Phone: 331 49104265
Fax: 331 49104299

Organization for Economic Cooperation and Development (OECD)

Electronic Editions

2, rue Andre Pascal
F-75775 Paris Cedex 16, France

TYPE

Time series

CONTENT

Contains aggregate data on the main national income accounts for 19 OECD member countries and the following four groups of countries: OECD Total, OECD-Europe, European Community, and the Major Seven. Includes gross national product; personal consumption expenditures; government consumption expenditures; gross capital formation; gross fixed capital formation; change in stocks, exports, and imports; operating surplus; savings income; indirect taxes and price deflators. Totals approximately 2,500 time series in both current and constant prices. Corresponds to data released in the *Quarterly National Accounts Bulletin* and in part to the online OECD Quarterly National Accounts database.

SUBJECT

National accounts for OECD member countries, including national income and production; personal and government consumption expenditures; fixed capital formation; imports and exports of goods and services, changes in stocks; and price deflators

COVERAGE

International

TIME SPAN

1970 to date

UPDATING

Quarterly

VENDOR

Organization for Economic Cooperation and Development, Electronic Editions

SYSTEM REQUIREMENTS

Contact the OECD for system requirements information

PRICE

Contact vendor for details

SHORT-TERM ECONOMIC INDICATORS: CENTRAL AND EASTERN EUROPEAN COUNTRIES

Phone: 331 49104265
Fax: 331 49104299

Organization for Economic Cooperation and Development (OECD)

Electronic Editions

2, rue Andre Pascal
F-75775 Paris Cedex 16, France

TYPE

Time series

CONTENT

Contains monthly and annual economic data on the following former Soviet Republics and Eastern Bloc countries: Russia, Bulgaria, the Czech Republic, the Slovak Republic, Estonia, Hungary, Latvia, Poland, Romania, Armenia, Azerbaijan, Belorussia, Kazakstan, Kirghizie, Lithuania, Moldavia, Tadzhikistan, Turkmenistan, and Uzbekistan. Covers industrial output, construction, prices, labor force, foreign trade, retail sales, and monetary and financial statistics.

Corresponds in part to the online OECD Economic Statistics of Central and Eastern Europe database.

SUBJECT

Economic data on Central and Eastern European countries

COVERAGE

Central and Eastern European countries

TIME SPAN

1980 to date

UPDATING

Quarterly

VENDOR

Organization for Economic Cooperation and Development, Electronic Editions

SYSTEM REQUIREMENTS

Contact the OECD for system requirements information

PRICE

Contact vendor for details

TES

Phone: 0352 430134567
Fax: 0352 436404

Commission of the European Communities (CEC)

Statistical Office of the European (Communities (EUROSTAT)

Information Office
Batiment Jean Monnet, B.P. 1907
Rue Alcide de Gasperi
L-2920 Luxembourg, Luxembourg

TYPE

Numeric; time series

CONTENT

Contains time series on the input-output tables for national accounts of the European Community. Covers factor prices and financial flows by sources (e.g., total domestic imports from the EC countries, imports from Third World countries). Includes from 50 to 100 tables for each country on intermediate consumption, final uses, and primary inputs. Data are obtained from statistical offices in the EC countries. Corresponds to data published in *National Accounts ESA Input-Output Tables* (1975) and *National Accounts ESA Input-Output Tables* (1980).

SUBJECT

National accounts statistics

LANGUAGE

English; French

COVERAGE

European Community countries

TIME SPAN

1959 to 1985

UPDATING

Every five years

VENDOR

Commission of the European Communities, Statistical Office of the European Communities, Information Office

SYSTEM REQUIREMENTS

IBM PC or compatible; 5 inch floppy drive; 360K memory; MS-DOS

PRICE

Contact vendor for details

ENERGY

ENERGY BALANCES OF OECD COUNTRIES

Phone: 331 49104265
Fax: 331 49104299

Organization for Economic Cooperation and Development (OECD)
Electronic Editions
2, rue Andre Pascal
F-75775 Paris Cedex 16 France

TYPE

Time series

CONTENT

Contains annual energy balance data on crude oil, coal, electricity, gas, heat, hydro energy, nuclear energy, and other solid fuels, as well as solar and wind energy of all OECD member countries. Corresponds to the online OECD Annual Energy Balance database.

SUBJECT

Energy balance statistics for OECD countries

COVERAGE

OECD member countries

TIME SPAN

1960 to date

UPDATING

Annual

VENDOR

Organization for Economic Cooperation and Development, Electronic Editions

SYSTEM REQUIREMENTS

Contact OECD for system requirements information

PRICE

Contact vendor for details

ENERGY STATISTICS

Phone: (212) 963-4120
Fax: (212) 963-4116

United Nations Statistical Division
2 United Nations Plaza, DC2-1620
New York, NY 10017

CONTACT

Robert Johnston, Officer-in-Charge

TYPE

Time series

CONTENT

Provides country statistics on production, imports, exports, stocks, and capacity of fuels, gases, and electricity. Data are supplied in either the basic reported units (i.e., measures of weight, volume, heat) or standardized to a common heat unit (coal equivalent or oil equivalent). Corresponds in part to the print publications *Energy Statistics Yearbook* and *Energy Balances and Electricity Profiles.*

SUBJECT

Energy statistics

TIME SPAN

1950 to 1991

VENDOR

United Nations Statistical Division

PRICE

Contact vendor for details

ENERGY STATISTICS OF OECD COUNTRIES

Phone: 331 49104265
Fax: 331 49104299

Organization for Economic Cooperation and Development (OECD)
Electronic Editions
2, rue Andre Pascal
F-75775 Paris Cedex 16 France

TYPE

Time series

CONTENT

Contains the basic energy statistics of the OECD member countries. Includes data on oil, gas, electricity, and solid fuels. Corresponds to the online OECD Basic Energy Statistics.

SUBJECT

Energy statistics for OECD countries

COVERAGE

OECD member countries

TIME SPAN

1960 to date

UPDATING

Annual

VENDOR

Organization for Economic Cooperation and Development, Electronic Editions

SYSTEM REQUIREMENTS

Contact OECD for system requirements information

PRICE

Contact vendor for details

FERTILIZER

WORLD FERTILIZER FORECAST

Phone: (215) 667-6000
Fax: (215) 660-6477

The WEFA Group
401 City Line Ave., Suite 300
Bala Cynwyd, PA 19004-1780

TYPE

Time series

CONTENT

Contains approximately 250 annual time series of historical and forecast data on nitrogen, potash, and phosphate fertilizers. Includes capacity, production, consumption, import, and export data for eight regions and the world.

SUBJECT

Nitrogen, potash, and phosphate fertilizers

COVERAGE

International

TIME SPAN

1963 to date

VENDOR

The WEFA Group

PRICE

Contact vendor for details

FINANCE

FINSTAT

Phone: 071-873 3000
Fax: 071-873 4610

FINSTAT, The Financial Times Statistical Service
Number One, Southwark Bridge
London SE1 9HL, England

CONTACT

Karen Bidmead

TYPE

Numeric

CONTENT

Contains price data on securities listed in the *Financial Times* (FT) newspaper. Covers U.K. and international equities, gilts, unit and investment trusts, insurance (life and pension) and offshore funds, dividends, FT-Actuaries Indices, and currency exchange rates. The datafeeds automatically update most major financial software applications for, among others, portfolio management, technical analysis, and sales support and presentations, as well as in-house systems.

SUBJECT

Financial Times Statistical data, including price and yield for traded securities and gilts on the London Stock Exchange; values for the various sectors that make up the FT-Actuaries Indices in addition to the FT 30 Share Index; and bid and offer prices, day's change and yields for authorized U.K. trusts, insurance funds (life and pension), and offshore funds

COVERAGE

United Kingdom and international

TIME SPAN

Current month

UPDATING

Monthly

VENDOR

FINSTAT, The Financial Times Statistical Service

SYSTEM REQUIREMENTS

Contact FINSTAT for details

PRICE

Contact vendor for details

FINSTAT - GLOBAL FINANCIAL DATABANK

Phone: (215) 667-6000
Fax: (215) 660-6477

The WEFA Group
401 City Line Ave., Suite 300
Bala Cynwyd, PA 19004-1780

TYPE

Time series

CONTENT

Contains approximately 1,400 time series of daily and end-of-month data on international exchange rates, Eurocurrency interest rates, London money rates, and gold prices. Also contains London and overseas stock indexes, including the Financial Times Actuaries and Financial Times Actuaries Fixed Interest indexes and some commodity prices. Data are supplied by FINSTAT, The Financial Times Statistical Service and maintained by the WEFA Group.

SUBJECT

Prices and indexes on equity, money, precious metal, and stock markets worldwide

COVERAGE

International

VENDOR

The WEFA Group

PRICE

Contact vendor for details

OECD FLOWS AND STOCKS OF FIXED CAPITAL

Phone: 331 49104265
Fax: 331 49104299

Organization for Economic Cooperation and Development (OECD)
Electronic Editions
2, rue Andre Pascal
F-75775 Paris Cedex 16, France

TYPE

Time series

CONTENT

Contains annual time series for 12 OECD member countries covering gross and net fixed capital stocks, gross fixed capital formation, and consumption of fixed capital, all at current and constant replacement cost. Data are further categorized by industry, product (e.g., construction and equipment), volumes, and local currencies. Corresponds to *OECD Flows and Stocks of Fixed Capital* and in part to the online OECD Flows and Stocks of Fixed Capital database.

SUBJECT

Fixed capital information for selected OECD member countries

LANGUAGE

English; French

COVERAGE

International

TIME SPAN

1964 to date

UPDATING

Every two years

VENDOR

Organization for Economic Cooperation and Development, Electronic Editions

SYSTEM REQUIREMENTS

Contact the OECD for system requirements information

PRICE

Contact vendor for details

GENERAL

ECONBASE: TIME SERIES AND FORECASTS

Phone: (215) 667-6000
Fax: (215) 660-6477

The WEFA Group
401 City Line Ave., Suite 300
Bala Cynwyd, PA 19004-1780

TYPE

Time series

CONTENT

Contains approximately 13,000 monthly, quarterly, and annual economic time series. Includes national, state, Metropolitan Statistical Area, and Consolidated Metropolitan Statistical Area data for the U.S., and national aggregate data for more than 30 other countries. Covers such areas as industry, demographics, employment, income and expenditures, prices, interest and exchange rates, finance, foreign transactions, and national accounts, and provides annual two-year forecasts for 1,100 major economic indicators. Sources of data include the Bureau of Economic Analysis, Bureau of Labor Statistics, Census Bureau, Federal Reserve Board, Organization for Economic Cooperation and Development, and national statistical agencies in other countries.

SUBJECT

Econometric data for agriculture; capital expenditures; construction and housing; consumer expenditures; cyclical indicators; employment, wages, and salaries; exchange rates; finance; government finance; industrial production; interest rates; labor force; manufacturers shipments, inventories, and orders; personal income; population; price indexes; retail sales; selected National Income Accounts; and transportation

COVERAGE

United States and international

TIME SPAN

1948 to date

UPDATING

Monthly

VENDOR

The WEFA Group

PRICE

Contact vendor for details

PC GLOBE

Phone: (415) 382-4400
(800) 521-6263

Broderbund Software, Inc.
500 Redwood Blvd.
Novato, CA 94948

TYPE

Image; directory; full text; numeric; audio

CONTENT

Contains map images and political, economic, demographic, cartographic, trade, and travel data on 177 countries. Includes maps of countries, continents, and the world with locations of major cities. Also includes information on population, age distribution, growth rate, literacy, urbanization, major industries, gross national product, commodities and agricultural products, balance of trade, imports and exports, languages, ethnic groups, religions, health statistics, political organizations and leaders, tourist attractions, visa requirements, amateur "Ham" radio, telex, and international dialing codes.

Software enables users to create map overlays; shift maps horizontally on the screen; select screen colors; compute statistics for pre-defined or user-defined country groupings (e.g., European Community, North Atlantic Treaty Organization, Organization of Petroleum Exporting Countries); convert currency using pre-defined or user-defined exchange rates; identify time zones; generate bar graphs; compute point-to-point distances using standard and metric systems; determine longitude and latitude coordinates; and export text files and map and flag image files.

Audio capabilities enable users to hear audio recordings of the national anthems from 175 countries. This feature was formerly maintained as a separate product under the name PC Nations.

SUBJECT

International cartographic, demographic, political, economic, and travel information

LANGUAGE

English; French; German; Spanish

COVERAGE

International

TIME SPAN

Current Information

UPDATING

Annual

VENDOR

Broderbund Software, Inc.

SYSTEM REQUIREMENTS

IBM PC, PS/2, or compatible; two floppy drives or hard disk; 640K memory; MS-DOS 2.0 or higher; CGA, EGA, VGA, or Hercules monochrome card and monitor; mouse (optional). A Hewlett-Packard LaserJet Series II, Hewlett Packard PaintJet, IBM Proprinter, IBM Color printer, or compatible printer required to print maps

SOFTWARE

From Broderbund Software, Inc.

PRICE

Contact vendor for details

INDUSTRY

INDUSTRIAL STATISTICS DATABASE

Phone: 0222 21131-3633
Fax: 0222 232156

United Nations Industrial Development Organization (UNIDO)

Industrial Statistics and Sectoral Surveys Branch

Vienna International Center
P.O. Box 300
A-1400 Vienna, Austria

CONTACT

John Bremer, Systems Analyst

E-MAIL

E.A.R.N. bitnet:UN1@UNIDO1. (bitnet);
UN1@IAEA1.IAEA.OR.AT (Internet)

ALTERNATE DATABASE NAME

UNIDO Industrial Statistics

TYPE

Numeric

CONTENT

Contains approximately 370,000 annual time series on industrial statistics worldwide. Data are available by three-digit United Nations International Standard Industrial Classification codes. Sources include more than 1,000 national publications (e.g., industrial censuses, annual surveys) collected and adjusted by UNIDO, and data provided by the United Nations Statistical Office, the World Bank, and other international organizations. Sources also include data obtained by UNIDO in specific countries. Corresponds in part to the *Handbook of Industrial Statistics.*

SUBJECT

Value added, gross output, wages and salaries, employment, and production indexes for 28 manufacturing industries in 152 countries

COVERAGE

International

TIME SPAN

1963 to 1991

UPDATING

Annual

VENDOR

United Nations Industrial Development Organization, Industrial Statistics and Sectoral Surveys Branch

SYSTEM REQUIREMENTS

IBM PC or compatible; floppy drive; 20MB hard disk; 640K memory; MS-DOS 2.1 or higher; monochrome or color monitor

SOFTWARE

From United Nations Industrial Development Organization

PRICE

Contact vendor for details

INTERNATIONAL INDUSTRIAL MARKETS

Phone: (215) 667-6000
Fax: (215) 660-6477

The WEFA Group
401 City Line Ave., Suite 300
Bala Cynwyd, PA 19004-1780

TYPE

Time series

CONTENT

Contains time series of industrial market data for the United States, the United Kingdom, Germany, Japan, France, Italy, Belgium, Austria, Korea, and Spain. Contains detailed forecast information on output, prices, trade consumption, investment, employment, and sales to major markets. Corresponds to the online International Industrial Markets database.

SUBJECT

Industry forecasts

COVERAGE

International

TIME SPAN

1960 to date

UPDATING

Quarterly

VENDOR

The WEFA Group

PRICE

Contact vendor for details

OECD INDICATORS OF INDUSTRIAL ACTIVITY

Phone: 331 49104265
Fax: 331 49104299

Organization for Economic Cooperation and Development (OECD)
Electronic Editions
2, rue Andre Pascal
F-75775 Paris Cedex 16, France

TYPE

Time series

CONTENT

Contains approximately 2,500 monthly, quarterly, and annual time series covering indexes of industrial production, producer prices, employment, new orders, and unfilled orders. Indicators are classified by industry groups according to the International Standard Industrial Classification. Corresponds to data released in the *Indicators of Industrial Activity* and in part to the online OECD Indicators of Industrial Activity database.

SUBJECT

International indicators of industrial activity, including production deliveries, prices, employment, new orders, and unfilled orders for each industrial grouping

COVERAGE

International

TIME SPAN

1985 to date

UPDATING

Quarterly

VENDOR

Organization for Economic Cooperation and Development, Electronic Editions

SYSTEM REQUIREMENTS
Contact the OECD for system requirements information

PRICE
Contact vendor for details

IRON AND STEEL

IRON AND STEEL

Phone: (215) 667-6000
Fax: (215) 660-6477

The WEFA Group
401 City Line Ave., Suite 300
Bala Cynwyd, PA 19004-1780

TYPE
Time series

CONTENT
Contains more than 2,000 weekly, monthly, quarterly, and annual historical time series on supply, demand, and trade for the U.S. and worldwide iron and steel industry. Includes prices by city for number one heavy melting steel scrap; data on pig iron, iron ore, and scrap iron; time series for steel industry employment; and crude steel production, consumption, imports, and exports for 75 countries. Sources include the American Iron and Steel Institute, the U.S. Bureau of Mines, and the International Iron and Steel Institute. Corresponds to the online Iron and Steel database.

SUBJECT
International steel and iron mill statistics, including shipments by product and grade (carbon, alloy, stainless), imports and exports by product, raw steel production by furnace type and region, and steel mill shipments by product by market

COVERAGE
United States and international

TIME SPAN
1972 to date

UPDATING
Weekly

VENDOR
The WEFA Group

PRICE
Contact vendor for details

LABOR

ECONOMICALLY ACTIVE POPULATION: ESTIMATES AND PROJECTIONS, 1950-2025

Phone: 227 996111
Fax: 227 988685
International Labour Office (ILO)
Bureau of Statistics
4, route des Morillons
CH-1211 Geneva 22, Switzerland

TYPE
Statistical

CONTENT
Contains approximately 30,000 items of historical and projected demographic data for all countries, territories, regions, and major geographical subdivisions of the world. Includes total population by sex and age group for 1950 to 2025, and data for the economically active population and economic activity rates in agriculture, industry, and services, by gender, for 1950 to 1980. Corresponds to the third edition of *Economically Active Population, Estimates and Projections: 1950-2025*, including Volume 1, *Asia*; Volume 2, *Africa*; Volume 3, *Latin America*; Volume 4, *Northern America, Europe, Oceania, USSR*; Volume 5, *World Summary*; and Volume 6, *Methodological Supplement*.

SUBJECT
Historical and projected demographic data for all areas of the world

COVERAGE
International

TIME SPAN
1950 to date

UPDATING
As needed

VENDOR
International Labour Office, Bureau of Statistics

SYSTEM REQUIREMENTS
IBM PC or compatible; floppy drive; MS-DOS 2.1 or higher

PRICE
Contact vendor for details

LABORSTAT

Phone: 227 996111
Fax: 227 988685
International Labour Office (ILO)
Bureau of Statistics
4, route des Morillons
CH-1211 Geneva 22, Switzerland

TYPE

Statistical

CONTENT

Contains approximately 110,000 statistical data items on all aspects of employment worldwide.

SUBJECT COVERAGE

Statistics on all aspects of employment, including consumer prices, hours of work, labor costs and statistics, occupational accidents, strikes, and unemployment

LANGUAGE

English; French; Spanish

GEOGRAPHIC COVERAGE

International

TIME SPAN

1945 to date

VENDOR

International Labour Office, Bureau of Statistics

PRICE

Contact vendor for details

OECD QUARTERLY LABOR FORCE STATISTICS

Phone: 331 49104265
Fax: 331 49104299

Organization for Economic Cooperation and Development (OECD)
Electronic Editions
2, rue Andre Pascal
F-75775 Paris Cedex 16, France

TYPE

Time series

CONTENT

Contains annual and quarterly data on the main components of the labor force, the breakdown of civilian employment by major economic sectors, and employment by gender and age group. Presented in three forms: absolute figures, indexes, and percentages.

Includes monthly, quarterly, and annual unemployment rates. Corresponds to data in *OECD Quarterly Labor Force Statistics* and to the online OECD Quarterly Labor Force Statistics database.

SUBJECT

International labor

COVERAGE

International (OECD Countries)

TIME SPAN

Current 10 years

UPDATING

Quarterly

VENDOR

Organization for Economic Cooperation and Development, Electronic Editions

SYSTEM REQUIREMENTS

Contact the OECD for system requirements information

PRICE

Contact vendor for details

LATIN AMERICA

LATIN AMERICA FORECAST

Phone: (215) 667-6000
Fax: (215) 660-6477

The WEFA Group
401 City Line Ave., Suite 300
Bala Cynwyd, PA 19004-1780

TYPE

Time series

CONTENT

Contains more than 1,500 time series of economic data and forecasts for nine countries in Latin America. Macroeconomics forecasts available for Argentina, Brazil, Chile, Colombia, Ecuador, Mexico, Peru, Uruguay, and Venezuela. Includes annual data and five-year forecasts. Covers inflation and exchange rates; balance of payments; imports, exports, and trade balances; major commodity exports and prices; financial indicators; industrial production; employment indicators; and national accounts. Corresponds to the online Latin America Forecast database.

SUBJECT

Macroeconomic forecasts for Argentina, Brazil, Chile, Colombia, Ecuador, Mexico, Peru, Uruguay, and Venezuela, including national income accounts (supply, demand, and factor income); balance of payments accounts; exports and imports by major categories; petroleum sector; financial and inflation indicators; and external debt and debt servicing

COVERAGE

Latin America

TIME SPAN

1970 to date

UPDATING

Quarterly

VENDOR

The WEFA Group

PRICE

Contact vendor for details

LEAD AND ZINC

INTERNATIONAL LEAD AND ZINC

Phone: (215) 667-6000
Fax: (215) 660-6477

The WEFA Group
401 City Line Ave., Suite 300
Bala Cynwyd, PA 19004-1780

TYPE

Time series

CONTENT

Contains approximately 1,400 monthly, quarterly, and annual time series on lead and zinc. Covers metal consumption, mine production, metal production, principal end uses, stocks, recovery of secondary lead and zinc, and trade with socialist countries. Data are obtained from the monthly publication *Lead and Zinc Statistics*, published by the International Lead and Zinc Study Group. Corresponds to the online International Lead and Zinc database.

SUBJECT

Worldwide lead and zinc statistics, covering metal consumption and production, mine production, principal end uses, stocks, recovery of secondary lead and zinc, and trade with socialist countries

COVERAGE

International

TIME SPAN

1955 to date

UPDATING

Monthly

VENDOR

The WEFA Group

PRICE

Contact vendor for details

MIDDLE EAST

MIDDLE EAST AND AFRICA FORECAST

Phone: (215) 667-6000
Fax: (215) 660-6477

The WEFA Group
401 City Line Ave., Suite 300
Bala Cynwyd, PA 19004-1780

TYPE

Time series

CONTENT

Contains approximately 1,600 annual time series of historical and forecast data on the economies of countries in the Middle East and Africa. Includes national income accounts; exports, imports, and petroleum trade balance; balance of payments accounts; financial and inflation indicators; and external debt. Countries covered are Algeria, Bahrain, Egypt, Ghana, Iran, Iraq, Ivory Coast, Kenya, Kuwait, Libya, Morocco, Nigeria, Oman, Qatar, Saudi Arabia, South Africa, Tunisia, United Arab Emirates, Zaire, Zimbabwe, Gabon, Turkey, and Cameroon.

SUBJECT

Economic data for the Middle East and Africa

COVERAGE

Middle Eastern and African countries

VENDOR

The WEFA Group

PRICE

Contact vendor for details

TRADE

EXTERNAL TRADE STATISTICS

Phone: (212) 963-4120
Fax: (212) 963-4116

United Nations Statistical Division
2 United Nations Plaza, DC2-1620
New York, NY 10017

CONTACT

Robert Johnston, Officer-in-Charge

TYPE

Statistical

CONTENT

Provides annual and some cumulative quarterly country, regional, and world statistics on external trade in commodities identified according to the Standard International Trade Classification. Detailed values in thousand U.S. dollars and quantity data in metric units for each trading partner exist to the extent provided by the reporting counties. Subsets of the data are made available upon request.

SUBJECT

Worldwide external trade

TIME SPAN

1962 to date

UPDATING

Annual; some quarterly data available

VENDOR

United Nations Statistical Division

PRICE

Contact vendor for details

UNITED NATIONS

UN-EARTH

Phone: 022 7988591
Fax: 022 7401269
United Nations
Advisory Committee for the Coordination of
Information Systems (ACCIS)
Palais des Nations
CH-1211 Geneva 10, Switzerland

TYPE

Full text; statistical

CONTENT

Contains selected contemporary information on the United Nations system, including objectives, membership, administrative offices, information services, databases of the organizations and agencies, human resources, development projects, and expenditures. Enables the user to view data by organization, country, region, politico-economic grouping, or globally. For each country, indicates membership of, and missions to the United Nations system, as well as United Nations system representation and information services and document collections in that country.

SUBJECT

United Nations

COVERAGE

International

TIME SPAN

Current information

VENDOR

United Nations, Advisory Committee for the Coordination of Information Systems

SYSTEM REQUIREMENTS

IBM PC or compatible; MS-DOS 3.0 or higher; 500K free RAM; hard disk with 12 MB free; VGA or EGA monitor recommended

PRICE

Contact vendor for information

AGRICULTURE

AGROSTAT

Phone: 06 57971

United Nations
Food and Agriculture Organization (FAO)
Statistics Division
Via delle Terme di Caracalla
I-00100 Rome, Italy

CONTACT

F. Pariboni, Statistician

TYPE

Time series

CONTENT

Covers statistical information from more than 200 countries and territories on approximately 800 agricultural commodities and 2,300 agriculture-related variables. Comprises the following four subfiles:

- FAO Production Yearbook—contains approximately 23,000 time series on crops, livestock numbers, products, and means of production.

- FAO Trade Yearbook—contains approximately 52,000 time series on the trade of agricultural commodities and agricultural requisites.

- FAO Yearbook of Forest Products and Trade—contains approximately 25,000 time series on forestry production and trade.

- FAO Fertilizer Yearbook—contains approximately 7,000 time series on production, trade, consumption, and prices paid by farmers. Corresponds to the *FAO Quarterly Bulletin of Statistics, FAO Production Yearbook, FAO Trade Yearbook, FAO Yearbook of Forest Products and Trade, FAO Fertilizer Yearbook*, and *Food Balance Sheets.*

SUBJECT

Worldwide food, agriculture, fishery, and forestry statistics, including data on human population, crops and livestock production, livestock numbers, agricultural machinery, pesticides, fertilizers, land use, irrigation, trade, fishery and forestry commodities, and related commodity production

COVERAGE

International

TIME SPAN

1981 to date

UPDATING

Quarterly

VENDOR

United Nations, Food and Agriculture Organization, Statistics Division

PRICE

Contact vendor for details

WORLD AGRICULTURE SUPPLY AND DISPOSITION (WASD)

Phone: (215) 667-6000
Fax: (215) 660-6477

The WEFA Group
401 City Line Ave., Suite 300
Bala Cynwyd, PA 19004-1780

TYPE

Time series

CONTENT

Contains more than 29,000 annual time series on the supply and disposition of crops, livestock, and meat commodities in more than 195 countries. Data include stocks; areas harvested, yield, production; domestic use broken down by food and industrial use; imports, exports and imports from the United States. Covers 52 commodities, including barley, beef and veal, cattle, coffee, corn, cottonseeds, oats, pigs, pork, poultry, poultry meat, soybeans, sugar, and wheat. Primary source of data is the U.S. Department of Agriculture, Foreign Agricultural Service.

SUBJECT

The worldwide supply and disposition of agricultural commodities, including coffee, cotton, eggs, dairy, grains (10 commodities), livestock (3 commodities), meat (12 commodities), oilseeds (23 commodities), tobacco, and sugar

COVERAGE

International

TIME SPAN

1960 to date

UPDATING

Quarterly

VENDOR

The WEFA Group

PRICE

Contact vendor for details

ASIA

ASIA FORECAST

Phone: (215) 667-6000
Fax: (215) 660-6477

The WEFA Group
401 City Line Ave., Suite 300
Bala Cynwyd, PA 19004-1780

TYPE

Time series

CONTENT

Contains detailed macroeconomic forecasts for Asian countries, covering national accounts, exports, imports, balance of payments, prices, debt, debt servicing, exchange rates, industrial production, labor, and population. Corresponds to the online Asia Forecast database.

SUBJECT

Macroeconomic forecasts for Australia, China, Hong Kong, India, Indonesia, Japan, Republic of Korea, Malaysia, Pakistan, the Philippines, Singapore, Taiwan, and Thailand

COVERAGE

Asian countries

TIME SPAN

1970 to date

UPDATING

Quarterly

VENDOR

The WEFA Group

PRICE

Contact vendor for details

BALANCE OF PAYMENTS

BALANCE OF PAYMENTS STATISTICS (BOPS)

Phone: (202) 623-6180
Fax: (202) 623-4661

International Monetary Fund (IMF)
Statistics Department
700 19th St., N.W.
Washington, DC 20431

ALTERNATE DATABASE NAME

IMF Balance of Payments

TYPE

Time series

CONTENT

Contains more than 63,000 quarterly and annual time series compiled by the IMF on the international economic transactions of 140 individual countries. Data are grouped by current account, long- and short-term capital, transfers, investments, and reserves. Corresponds to the IMF publication *Balance of Payments Statistics Yearbook* and to the Balance of Payments online database.

SUBJECT

Balance of payments components and aggregates

COVERAGE

International

TIME SPAN

1965 to date

UPDATING

Monthly

VENDOR

International Monetary Fund, Statistics Department

PRICE

Contact vendor for details

CIVIL AVIATION

CIVIL AVIATION STATISTICS ON TAPE

Phone: (514) 286-6292
Fax: (516) 285-6744

International Civil Aviation Organization (ICAO)
Statistics Section
1000 Sherbrooke St., W.
Montreal, PQ, Canada H3A 2R2

TYPE

Statistical; directory

CONTENT

Contains statistical data on international commercial air carriers and airports. Covers data on air carrier traffic, traffic by flight stage, on-flight origin and destination, finance, and fleet and personnel. Also covers airport and route facility traffic and financial statistics. Corresponds to the *ICAO Digests of Statistics* series. Each file corresponds to one digest.

SUBJECT

International airport and air traffic

COVERAGE

International

TIME SPAN

1968 to date

UPDATING

Annual

VENDOR

International Civil Aviation Organization, Statistics Section

PRICE

Contact vendor for details

DEBT

WORLD DEBT TABLES

Phone: (202) 477-1234
Fax: (202) 477-0661

The World Bank
International Economics Department
1818 H St., N.W.
Washington, DC 20433

TYPE

Time series

CONTENT

Contains more than 20,300 annual time series and some long-term forecasts on the external debt of approximately 138 developing countries and six regions worldwide. Data are published by the International Bank for Reconstruction and Development (World Bank) in *World Debt Tables: External Finance for Developing Countries* and its supplements. Data, available by category of debt and by type of creditor, cover these major transactions for each creditor: commitments; disbursements; repayments of principal; payments of interest; debt outstanding; loan terms; and debt services projections. Corresponds to the online World Debt Tables database.

SUBJECT

External debt information, external finance, and capital flows

COVERAGE

International

TIME SPAN

1970 to date

UPDATING

Annual

VENDOR

The World Bank, International Economics Department

PRICE

Contact vendor for details

ECONOMY

CRONOS

Phone: 0352 430134567
Fax: 0352 436404

Commission of the European Communities (CEC)
Statistical Office of the European Communities (EUROSTAT)
Information Office
Batiment Jean Monnet, B.P. 1907
Rue Alcide de Gasperi
L-2920 Luxembourg, Luxembourg

TYPE

Time series

CONTENT

Contains more than 900,000 time series of economic data on countries in the European Community (EC) and other countries worldwide. Data are obtained from the statistical offices of the EC countries. Corresponds to data available in various EUROSTAT publications and to the online CRONOS database. Comprises the following five files:

- General Statistics—contains 80,000 time series of short-term indicators and general economic information covering industry, agriculture, services, transportation, population, employment, trade, prices, finance, and balance of payments. Also contains 84,000 series on macroeconomic indicators for developing countries.

- National Accounts, Finance, Balance of Payments—contains 25,000 series (since 1960) on aggregate national account data; series on national account transactions related to goods and services; annual series (since 1970) on economic transactions between institutional sectors (companies, households); 200 annual series (since 1970) on the financial flows between institutional sectors; 32,000 series (since 1960) on the balance of payments, with geographic breakdowns, for EC countries, the U.S., and Japan; and 16,000 biannual series (since 1970) on budget expenditures for research and development.

- Industry and Services—contains 12,500 series from annual industrial surveys aggregated in accordance with the activities nomenclature of the European Community: 30,000 annual and quarterly series on production and foreign trade for industrial products; 23,500 series on annual energy balances and monthly statistics for production, stocks, and exchanges; and monthly series (since 1973) on production, supplies, stocks, and consumption in the steelmaking industries of the EC countries.

- Agriculture, Forestry, Fishing—contains 7,500 monthly series on the sale and purchase prices of agricultural commodities; monthly series (since 1970) on exports of agricultural products; 25,000 quarterly series on agricultural products, including number of livestock and milk, eggs, and meat production (since 1964), supply balances for animal products (since 1960) and for vegetable products (since 1973); 9,000 annual series of regional statistics for agricultural activity; and series (since 1970) on fishing statistics, including catches, quantities landed, and number and tonnage of boats.

- Foreign Trade—contains 185,000 quarterly and monthly series (since 1970) on international trade, by product and trading partner; quarterly series on imports of 250 basic products; and 127,000 annual series (since 1962) on foreign trade for African, Caribbean, and Pacific (ACP) countries.

SUBJECT COVERAGE

Economies of European Economic Community countries, associated overseas countries, and major third-world countries. Included are general statistics; foreign trade aggregates and trade with ACP and associated countries; developing countries; industrial survey and sectoral information; energy; agricultural products, prices, and accounts; balance of payments; financial accounts; national accounts; and research and development

LANGUAGE

English; French; German

GEOGRAPHIC COVERAGE

International

TIME SPAN

1960 to date

UPDATING

Periodically

VENDOR

Commission of the European Communities, Statistical Office of the European Communities, Information Office

PRICE

Contact vendor for details

ECONBASE: TIME SERIES AND FORECASTS

Phone: (215) 667-6000
Fax: (215) 660-6477
The WEFA Group
401 City Line Ave., Suite 300
Bala Cynwyd, PA 19004-1780

TYPE

Time series

CONTENT

Contains approximately 13,000 monthly, quarterly, and annual economic time series. Includes national, state, Metropolitan Statistical Area, and Consolidated Metropolitan Statistical Area data for the U.S., and national aggregate data for more than 30 other countries. Covers such areas as industry, demographics, employment, income and expenditures, prices, interest and exchange rates, finance, foreign transactions, and national accounts, and provides annual two-year forecasts for 1,100 major economic indicators. Sources of data include the Bureau of Economic Analysis, Bureau of Labor Statistics, Census Bureau, Federal Reserve Board, Organization for Economic Cooperation and Development, and national statistical agencies in other countries.

SUBJECT

Econometric data for agriculture; capital expenditures; construction and housing; consumer expenditures; cyclical indicators; employment, wages, and salaries; exchange rates; finance, government finance; industrial production; interest rates; labor force; manufacturers shipments, inventories, and orders; personal income; population; price indexes; retail sales; selected National Income Accounts; and transportation.

COVERAGE

United States and international

TIME SPAN

1948 to date

VENDOR

The WEFA Group

PRICE

Contact vendor for details

INTLINE

Phone: (215) 667-6000
Fax: (215) 660-6477
The WEFA Group
401 City Line Ave., Suite 300
Bala Cynwyd, PA 19004-1780

TYPE

Time series

CONTENT

Contains approximately 7,000 daily, weekly, monthly, quarterly, and annual time series providing coverage of principal macroeconomic data for more than 40 countries worldwide, including Argentina, Australia, Austria, Belgium, Brazil, Canada, Chile, Colombia, Denmark, Finland, France, Germany, Greece, Hong Kong, India, Indonesia, Ireland, Italy, Japan, Korea, Malaysia, Mexico, The Netherlands, New Zealand, Norway, the Philippines, Singapore, South Africa, Spain, Sweden, Switzerland, Taiwan, Thailand, the United Kingdom, and the United States. Corresponds to the online INTLINE database.

SUBJECT

International macroeconomic data for 40 countries, covering national accounts: government finance; cyclical indicators and business surveys; industrial production and producer price indexes; orders, stocks, and deliveries; wholesale and retail sales and consumer and wholesale prices; construction and housing starts; population; labor, wages, and unemployment rates; money and banking; interest bearing, charged, and interbank (LIBOR) rates; foreign exchange rates, forward rates, and Eurocurrency rates; foreign trade, exports, imports, and balance; balance of payments; and official reserves

COVERAGE

International

TIME SPAN

1901 to date

UPDATING

Daily

VENDOR

The WEFA Group (INTLINE)

PRICE

Contact vendor for details

NATIONAL ACCOUNTS STATISTICS

Phone: (212) 963-4120
Fax: (212) 963-4116

United Nations Statistical Division
2 United Nations Plaza, DC2-1620
New York, NY 10017

TYPE
Time series

CONTENT
Contains annual time series on the national income and product accounts of countries worldwide. Both market economies and centrally planned economies are included. Covers gross domestic product, gross capital formation, gross fixed capital formation, government consumption expenditures, private consumption expenditures, imports and exports, national income, savings, and net material products. Represents the transactions of corporate and quasi-corporate enterprises, financial and non-financial institutions, government, and households. Corresponds to data published by the United Nations in the *National Accounts Statistics: Main Aggregates and Detailed Tables* from 1970 to 1986, and in part to *National Accounts Statistics: Analysis of Main Aggregates.*

SUBJECT
National accounts data and material product balances

COVERAGE
International

TIME SPAN
1950 to 1990

UPDATING
Annual

VENDOR
United Nations Statistical Division

PRICE
Contact vendor for details

OECD INDICATORS OF ECONOMIC ACTIVITY

Phone: 331 49104265
Fax: 331 49104299

Organization for Economic Cooperation and Development (OECD)
Electronic Editions
2, rue Andre Pascal
F-75775 Paris Cedex 16, France

TYPE
Time series

CONTENT
Contains approximately 2,500 monthly, quarterly, and annual time series covering indexes of industrial production, producer prices, employment, new orders, and unfilled orders. Indicators are classified by industry groups according to the International Standard Industrial Classification. Corresponds to data released in the *Indicators of Industrial Activity* and in part to the online OECD Indicators of Industrial Activity database.

SUBJECT
International indicators of industrial activity, including production, deliveries, prices, employment, new orders, and unfilled orders for each industrial grouping

COVERAGE
International

TIME SPAN
1975 to date

UPDATING
Quarterly

VENDOR
Organization for Economic Cooperation and Development, Electronic Editions

PRICE
Contact vendor for details

OECD MAIN ECONOMIC INDICATORS

Phone: 331 49104265
Fax: 331 49104299

Organization for Economic Cooperation and Development (OECD)
Electronic Editions
2, rue Andre Pascal
F-75775 Paris Cedex 16, France

TYPE
Time series

CONTENT
Contains approximately 7,200 monthly, quarterly, and annual economic time series for the 25 OECD member countries and selected totals for North America, the European Community, OECD-Europe, and all OECD countries. Most series are available both sea-

sonally adjusted and unadjusted. Software enables users to retrieve data and analyze statistics. Corresponds to data in *Main Economic Indicators* and to the online OECD Main Economic Indicators database.

SUBJECT

Economic indicators for OECD member countries, including industrial production, business surveys, deliveries, stocks and orders, construction, domestic trade, labor, wages, prices, domestic and foreign finance, interest rates, foreign trade, and balance of payments

COVERAGE

International

TIME SPAN

1980 to date

UPDATING

Monthly

VENDOR

Organization for Economic Cooperation and Development, Electronic Editions

PRICE

Contact vendor for details

OECD QUARTERLY NATIONAL ACCOUNTS

Phone: 331 49104265
Fax: 331 49104299

Organization for Economic Cooperation and Development (OECD)
Electronic Editions
2, rue Andre Pascal
F-75775 Paris Cedex 16, France

TYPE

Time series

CONTENT

Contains aggregate data on the main national income accounts for 19 OECD member countries and the following four groups of countries: OECD Total, OECD-Europe, European Community, and the Major Seven. Includes gross national product; personal consumption expenditures; government consumption expenditures; gross capital formation; gross fixed capital formation; change in stocks, exports, and imports; operating surplus; savings income; indirect taxes; and price deflators. Totals approximately 2,500 time series in both current and constant prices. Corresponds to data released in the *Quarterly National Accounts Bulletin*

and in part to the online OECD Quarterly National Accounts database.

SUBJECT

National accounts for OECD member countries, including national income and production; personal and government consumption expenditures; fixed capital formation; imports and exports of goods and services; changes in stocks; and price deflators

COVERAGE

International

TIME SPAN

1955 to date

UPDATING

Quarterly

VENDOR

Organization for Economic Cooperation and Development, Electronic Editions

PRICE

Contact vendor for details

REGION-EUROSTAT

Phone: 0352 430134567
Fax: 0352 436404

Commission of the European Communities
Statistical Office of the European Communities (EUROSTAT)
Information Office
Batiment Jean Monnet, B.P. 1907
Rue Alcide de Gasperi
L-2920 Luxembourg, Luxembourg

TYPE

Statistical

CONTENT

Contains approximately 90,000 time series, primarily annual, of economic data on various regions, administrative units, and administrative unit subdivisions in countries of the European Community (EC). Covers demographics, unemployment, population, agriculture, industry, transportation, and finance.

SUBJECT

Regional statistics for the countries of the EC, including demography, economy, employment and labor force, industry, agriculture, community financial investment, and transport

LANGUAGE

English; French; German

COVERAGE

European Community countries

TIME SPAN

1975 to date

UPDATING

Varies by series

VENDOR

Commission of the European Communities, Statistical Office of the European Communities, Information Office

PRICE

Contact vendor for details

TES

Phone: 0352 430134567
Fax: 0352 436404

Commission of the European Communities
Statistical Office of the European Communities
(EUROSTAT)
Information Office
Batiment Jean Monnet, B.P. 1907
Rue Alcide de Gasperi
L-2920 Luxembourg, Luxembourg

TYPE

Numeric; time series

CONTENT

Contains time series on the input-output tables for national accounts of the European Community (EC). Covers factor prices and financial flows by sources (e.g., total domestic imports from the EC countries, imports from Third World countries). Includes from 50 to 100 tables for each country on intermediate consumption, final uses, and primary inputs. Data are obtained from statistical offices in the EC countries. Corresponds to data published in *National Accounts ESA Input-Output Tables* (1975) and *National Accounts ESA Input-Output Tables* (1980).

SUBJECT

National accounts statistics

LANGUAGE

English; French

COVERAGE

European Community countries

TIME SPAN

1959 to 1985

UPDATING

Every five years

VENDOR

Commission of the European Communities, Statistical Office of the European Communities, Information Office

PRICE

Contact vendor for details

ENERGY

ENERGY BALANCES OF OECD COUNTRIES

Phone: 331 49104265
Fax: 331 49104299

Organization for Economic Cooperation and Development (OECD)
Electronic Editions
2, rue Andre Pascal
F-75775 Paris Cedex 16 France

TYPE

Time series

CONTENT

Contains annual energy balance data on crude oil, coal, electricity, gas, heat, hydro energy, nuclear energy, and other solid fuels, as well as solar and wind energy of all OECD member countries. Corresponds to the online OECD Annual Energy Balance database.

SUBJECT

Energy balance statistics for OECD countries

COVERAGE

OECD member countries

TIME SPAN

1960 to date

UPDATING

Annual

VENDOR

Organization for Economic Cooperation and Development, Electronic Editions

PRICE

Contact vendor for details

ENERGY STATISTICS

Phone: (212) 963-4120
Fax: (212) 963-4116
United Nations Statistical Division
2 United Nations Plaza, DC2-1620
New York, NY 10017

CONTACT

Robert Johnston, Officer-in-Charge

TYPE

Time series

CONTENT

Provides country statistics on production, imports, exports, stocks, and capacity of fuels, gases, and electricity. Data are supplied in either the basic reported units (i.e., measures of weight, volume, heat) or standardized to a common heat unit (coal equivalent or oil equivalent). Corresponds in part to the print publications *Energy Statistics Yearbook* and *Energy Balances and Electricity Profiles*.

SUBJECT

Energy statistics

TIME SPAN

1950 to 1991

VENDOR

United Nations Statistical Division

PRICE

Contact vendor for details

ENERGY STATISTICS OF OECD COUNTRIES

Phone: 331 49104265
Fax: 331 49104299

Organization for Economic Cooperation and Development (OECD)
Electronic Editions
2, rue Andre Pascal
F-75775 Paris Cedex 16 France

TYPE

Time series

CONTENT

Contains the basic energy statistics of the OECD member countries. Includes data on oil, gas, electricity, and solid fuels. Corresponds to the online OECD Basic Energy Statistics.

SUBJECT

Energy statistics for OECD countries

COVERAGE

OECD member countries

TIME SPAN

1960 to date

UPDATING

Annual

VENDOR

Organization for Economic Cooperation and Development, Electronic Editions

PRICE

Contact vendor for details

FERTILIZER

WORLD FERTILIZER FORECAST

Phone: (215) 667-6000
Fax: (215) 660-6477
The WEFA Group
401 City Line Ave., Suite 300
Bala Cynwyd, PA 19004-1780

TYPE

Time series

CONTENT

Contains approximately 250 annual time series of historical and forecast data on nitrogen, potash, and phosphate fertilizers. Includes capacity, production, consumption, import, and export data for eight regions and the world.

SUBJECT

Nitrogen, potash, and phosphate fertilizers

COVERAGE

International

TIME SPAN

1963 to date

VENDOR

The WEFA Group

PRICE

Contact vendor for details

FINANCE

FINSTAT - GLOBAL FINANCIAL DATABANK

Phone: (215) 667-6000
Fax: (215) 660-6477

The WEFA Group
401 City Line Ave., Suite 300
Bala Cynwyd, PA 19004-1780

TYPE

Time series

CONTENT

Contains approximately 1,400 time series of daily and end-of-month data on international exchange rates, Eurocurrency interest rates, London money rates, and gold prices. Also contains London and overseas stock indexes, including the Financial Times Actuaries and Financial Times Actuaries Fixed Interest indexes and some commodity prices. Data are supplied by The Financial Times Statistical Service and maintained by the WEFA Group.

SUBJECT

Prices and indexes on equity, money, precious metal, and stock markets worldwide

COVERAGE

International

VENDOR

The WEFA Group

PRICE

Contact vendor for details

GLOBAL VANTAGE™

Phone: (303) 771-6510
(800) 525-8640
(303) 740-4687

Standard & Poor's Compustat
7400 S. Alton Court
Englewood, CO 80112

TYPE

Time series

CONTENT

Provides corporate financial data covering more than 2,500 U.S. companies and approximately 7,000 com-
panies and financial services in 32 other countries. Covers companies that comprise the Morgan Stanley Capital International Index, as well as those used for local market indexes. Comprises the following three files:

- Financial File—contains more than 353 items obtained from shareholders' reports and company filings, including income statements, balance sheets, flow of funds statements, and supplementary income statement and balance sheet items. Data are stated in the currency used in the company's financial report.

- Issue File—contains monthly share prices, dividends, shares traded, high, low, and close prices from local exchanges, annual earnings per share, shares outstanding, and issued capital. Issue price histories reflect the currency of the exchange on which the stock is traded. Sources include U.S. Securities and Exchange Commission 10K filings and filings with local stock exchanges.

- Currency File—provides currency data covering month-end rates, monthly averages, and 12-month moving averages for 57 currencies, and a currency translation matrix, which enables users to compare 39 currencies against the yen, Swiss franc, U.S. dollar, and British pound.

    Enables users to search by London Issuer Code for International Stock Exchanges, SEDOL code, and, for companies traded in North America, CUSIP and Trading Symbol codes. Corresponds to the GLOBAL Vantage online database.

SUBJECT

Financial and market information for companies in 32 countries; world currency markets

COVERAGE

International

TIME SPAN

1982 to date

UPDATING

Monthly

VENDOR

Standard & Poor's Compustat

PRICE

Contact vendor for details

INTERNATIONAL FINANCIAL STATISTICS

Phone: (202) 623-6180
Fax: (202) 623-4661

International Monetary Fund (IMF)
Statistics Department
700 19th St., N.W.
Washington, DC 20431

TYPE
Time series

CONTENT
Contains more than 26,000 annual, quarterly, and monthly time series of economic and financial statistics on about 200 countries, supplemented by world and area aggregates for key time series. Annual series cover 1948 to date; quarterly and monthly series cover 1957 to date; some monthly series cover 1985 to date. Topics covered include exchange rates (e.g., averages and closings); international liquidity (e.g., reserves, foreign assets, and liabilities of deposit banks); money and banking (e.g., interest rates, domestic credit, and money); interest rates, prices, and production (e.g., wholesale and consumer prices, wages, industrial production, and crude petroleum production); government finance (e.g., revenues and expenditures); international transactions (e.g., value, volume, prices of exports and imports, and capital transactions); national accounts (e.g., private consumption, investment, and Gross Domestic Product); and population. Corresponds to the IMF publication *International Financial Statistics*, which provides additional information on sources of data, definitions, and other supplemental information, and to the online International Financial Statistics database.

SUBJECT
Financial and general economic time series

COVERAGE
International

TIME SPAN
Varies

UPDATING
Monthly

VENDOR
International Monetary Fund Statistics Department

PRICE
Contact vendor for details

OECD FLOWS AND STOCKS OF FIXED CAPITAL

Phone: 331 49104265
Fax: 331 49104299

Organization for Economic Cooperation and Development (OECD)
Electronic Editions
2, rue Andre Pascal
F-75775 Paris Cedex 16, France

TYPE
Time series

CONTENT
Contains annual time series for 12 OECD member countries covering gross and net fixed capital stocks, gross fixed capital formation, and consumption of fixed capital, all at current and constant replacement cost. Data are further categorized by industry, product (e.g., construction and equipment), volumes, and local currencies. Corresponds to *OECD Flows and Stocks of Fixed Capital* and in part to the online OECD Flows and Stocks of Fixed Capital database.

SUBJECT
Fixed capital information for selected OECD member countries

LANGUAGE
English; French

COVERAGE
International

TIME SPAN
1955 to date

UPDATING
Every two years

VENDOR
Organization for Economic Cooperation and Development, Electronic Editions

PRICE
Contact vendor for details

GENERAL

A MATTER OF FACT (AMOF)

Phone: (313) 434-5530
(800) 678-2435
Fax: (313) 434-6409

Pierian Press, Inc.
P.O. Box 1808
Ann Arbor, MI 48106

TYPE

Bibliographic; statistical

CONTENT

Contains more than 50,000 citations, with abstracts and statistics, to textual materials on current political, social, economic, and environmental issues worldwide. Covers materials, with accompanying comparative statistical content, extracted from testimony presented at congressional hearings by witnesses considered to be experts in their field. Also covers the *Congressional Record* which reflects statements made by U.S. senators and representatives, and approximately 250 general-interest periodicals and selected newspaper items are indexed using the Library of Congress subject headings. Corresponds to *A Matter of Fact: Statements Containing Statistics on Current Social, Economic, and Political Issues* and the online A Matter of Fact database.

SUBJECT

Facts and research findings in social, economic, political, environmental, and other areas

COVERAGE

International

TIME SPAN

1985 to date

UPDATING

Semiannual

VENDOR

Pierian Press, Inc.

PRICE

Contact vendor for details

GOVERNMENT FINANCE

GOVERNMENT FINANCE STATISTICS YEARBOOK

Phone: (202) 623-6180
Fax: (202) 623-4661

International Monetary Fund (IMF)
Statistics Department
700 19th St., N.W.
Washington, DC 20431

TYPE

Time series

CONTENT

Contains approximately 35,000 time series on government finances in 132 countries. Includes data on various units of government, government accounts, government-owned enterprises and financial institutions, and government operations. Covers central government revenue, grants, expenditure, debt, financing, and lending. For some countries, includes tables of data for state and local government operations, as well as for consolidated general government. Corresponds to the *Government Finance Statistics Yearbook.*

SUBJECT

Government finance data

COVERAGE

International

TIME SPAN

1970 to date

UPDATING

Monthly

VENDOR

International Monetary Fund, Statistics Department

PRICE

Contact vendor for details

INDUSTRY

GENERAL INDUSTRIAL STATISTICS

Phone: (212) 963-4120
Fax: (212) 963-4116

United Nations Statistical Division
2 United Nations Plaza, DC2-1620
New York, NY 10017
Alternate Database Name: UNINDUST

TYPE

Time series

CONTENT

Contains approximately 17,500 annual time series for more than 100 countries on manufacturing, mining and quarrying, and public utilities. Covers labor force and employment, wages and salaries, investment, electricity consumption, output, and value added, along with industrial production indexes. Data are classified by four-digit International Standard Industrial Classification codes. Corresponds to the *Industrial Statistics Yearbook*.

SUBJECT

Mining, quarrying, and manufacturing; gas, electricity, and water industry statistics

COVERAGE

International

TIME SPAN

1953 to 1991

VENDOR

United Nations Statistical Division

PRICE

Contact vendor for details

INDEX NUMBERS OF INDUSTRIAL PRODUCTION

Phone: (212) 963-4120
Fax: (212) 963-4116

United Nations Statistical Division
2 United Nations Plaza, DC2-1620
New York, NY 10017

CONTACT

Robert Johnston, Officer-in-Charge

TYPE

Statistical

CONTENT

Provides indexes of country, regional, and world industrial production

SUBJECT

Worldwide industrial production

TIME SPAN

1967 to 1991

VENDOR

United Nations Statistical Division

PRICE

Contact vendor for details

INDUSTRIAL STATISTICS

Phone: (212) 963-4120
Fax: (212) 963-4116

United Nations Statistical Division
2 United Nations Plaza, DC2-1620
New York, NY 10017

CONTACT

Robert Johnston, Officer-in-Charge

TYPE

Time series

CONTENT

Provides national output statistics for industries engaged in mining and quarrying, manufacturing, and the production and distribution of gas, electricity, and water. Comprises two sections: General Industrial Statistics and Commodity Production Statistics. Corresponds to Volume 1 and Volume 2 of the *Industrial Statistics Yearbook*.

SUBJECT

Mining; quarrying; manufacturing; and gas, electricity, and water industry statistics; questionnaires; tapes supplied by national sources; data furnished by the specialized agencies and similar bodies; national, international, and other publications; direct inquiry; censuses; and others

VENDOR

United Nations Statistical Division

PRICE

Contact vendor for details

INDUSTRIAL STATISTICS DATABASE

Phone: 0222 21131-3633
Fax: 0222 232156

United Nations Industrial Development Organization (UNIDO)
Industrial Statistics and Sectoral Surveys Branch
Vienna International Center
P.O. Box 300
A-1400 Vienna, Austria

CONTACT

John Bremer, Systems Analyst

E-MAIL

E.A.R.N. bitnet:UN1@UNIDO1. (bitnet);
UN1@IAEA1.IAEA.OR.AT (Internet)

ALTERNATE DATABASE NAME

UNIDO Industrial Statistics

TYPE

Numeric

CONTENT

Contains approximately 370,000 annual time series on industrial statistics worldwide. Data are available by three-digit United Nations International Standard Industrial Classification codes. Sources include more than 1,000 national publications (e.g., industrial censuses, annual surveys) collected and adjusted by UNIDO, data provided by the United Nations Statistical Office, the World Bank, and other international organizations, and data obtained by UNIDO in specific countries. Corresponds in part to the *Handbook of Industrial Statistics.*

SUBJECT

Value added, gross output, wages and salaries, employment, and production indexes for 28 manufacturing industries in 152 countries

COVERAGE

International

TIME SPAN

1963 to 1990

UPDATING

Annual

VENDOR

United Nations Industrial Development Organization, Industrial Statistics and Sectoral Surveys Branch

PRICE

Contact vendor for details

INTERNATIONAL INDUSTRIAL MARKETS

Phone: (215) 667-6000
Fax: (215) 660-6477

The WEFA Group
401 City Line Ave., Suite 300
Bala Cynwyd, PA 19004-1780

TYPE

Time series

CONTENT

Contains time series of industrial market data for the United States, the United Kingdom, Germany, Japan, France, Italy, Belgium, Austria, Korea and Spain. Contains detailed forecast information on output, prices, trade consumption, investment, employment, and sales to major markets. Corresponds to the online International Industrial Markets database.

SUBJECT

Industry forecasts

COVERAGE

International

TIME SPAN

1960 to date

UPDATING

Quarterly

VENDOR

The WEFA Group

PRICE

Contact vendor for details

IRON AND STEEL

IRON AND STEEL

Phone: (215) 667-6000
Fax: (215) 660-6477

The WEFA Group
401 City Line Ave., Suite 300
Bala Cynwyd, PA 19004-1780

TYPE

Time series

CONTENT

Contains more than 2,000 weekly, monthly, quarterly, and annual historical time series on supply, demand, and trade for the U.S. and worldwide iron and steel industry. Includes prices by city for number one heavy melting steel scrap; data on pig iron, iron ore, and scrap iron; time series for steel industry employment; and crude steel production, consumption, imports, and exports for 75 countries. Sources include the American Iron and Steel Institute, the U.S. Bureau of Mines, and the International Iron and Steel Institute. Corresponds to the online Iron and Steel database.

SUBJECT

International steel and iron mill statistics, including shipments by product and grade (carbon, alloy, stainless), imports and exports by product, raw steel production by furnace type and region, and steel mill shipments by product by market

COVERAGE

United States and international

TIME SPAN

1970 to date

VENDOR

The WEFA Group

PRICE

Contact vendor for details

LABOR

ECONOMICALLY ACTIVE POPULATION: ESTIMATES AND PROJECTIONS, 1950-2025

Phone: 227 996111
Fax: 227 988685

International Labour Office (ILO)
Bureau of Statistics
4, route des Morillons
CH-1211 Geneva 22, Switzerland

TYPE

Statistical

CONTENT

Contains approximately 30,000 items of historical and projected demographic data for all countries, territories, regions, and major geographical subdivisions of the world. Includes total population by sex and age group for 1950 to 2025, and data for the economically active population and economic activity rates in agriculture, industry, and services, by gender, for 1950 to 1980. Corresponds to Volumes 1 through 6 of the third edition of *Economically Active Population, Estimates and Projections: 1950-2025*.

SUBJECT

Historical and projected demographic data for all areas of the world

COVERAGE

International

TIME SPAN

1950 to date

UPDATING

As needed

VENDOR

International Labour Office Bureau of Statistics

PRICE

Contact vendor for details

OECD ANNUAL LABOR FORCE STATISTICS

Phone: 331 49104265
Fax: 331 49104299

Organization for Economic Cooperation and Development (OECD)
Electronic Editions
2, rue Andre Pascal
F-75775 Paris Cedex 16, France

TYPE

Time series

CONTENT

Contains annual time series for 25 OECD member countries (Australia, Austria, Belgium, Canada, Denmark, Germany, Finland, France, Greece, Iceland, Ireland, Italy, Japan, Luxembourg, The Netherlands, New Zealand, Norway, Portugal, Spain, Sweden, Switzerland, Turkey, United Kingdom, United States, and Yugoslavia). Covers main labor force aggregates with breakdowns by major economic sector and detailed data for each country, including population by age and gender; major component of labor force; civilian employment by professional status and by major divisions of the International Standard Industrial Classification (ISIC) code; and manufacturing employment by ISIC. Corresponds to data published in the *OECD Labor Force Statistics Yearbook* and in part to the online OECD Annual Labor Force Statistics database.

SUBJECT

International labor force statistics

COVERAGE

International

TIME SPAN

Current 24 years

UPDATING

Annual

VENDOR

Organization for Economic Cooperation and Development, Electronic Editions

PRICE

Contact vendor for details

OECD QUARTERLY LABOR FORCE STATISTICS

Phone: 331 49104265
Fax: 331 49104299
Organization for Economic Cooperation and Development (OECD)
Electronic Editions
2, rue Andre Pascal
F-75775 Paris Cedex 16, France

TYPE

Time series

CONTENT

Contains annual and quarterly data on the main components of the labor force, the breakdown of civilian employment by major economic sectors, and employment by gender and age group. Presented in three forms: absolute figures, indexes, and percentages. Includes monthly, quarterly, and annual unemployment rates. Corresponds to data in the *OECD Quarterly Labor Force Statistics* and to the online OECD Quarterly Labor Force Statistics database.

SUBJECT

International labor

COVERAGE

International (OECD Countries)

TIME SPAN

Current 20 years

UPDATING

Quarterly

VENDOR

Organization for Economic Cooperation and Development, Electronic Editions

PRICE

Contact vendor for details

LATIN AMERICA

LATIN AMERICA FORECAST

Phone: (215) 667-6000
Fax: (215) 660-6477

The WEFA Group
401 City Line Ave., Suite 300
Bala Cynwyd, PA 19004-1780

TYPE

Time series

CONTENT

Contains more than 1,500 time series of economic data and forecasts for nine countries in Latin America. Macroeconomics forecasts available for Argentina, Brazil, Chile, Colombia, Ecuador, Mexico, Peru, Uruguay, and Venezuela. Includes annual data and five-year forecasts. Covers inflation and exchange rates; balance of payments; imports, exports, and trade balances; major commodity exports and prices; financial indicators; industrial production; employment indicators; and national accounts. Corresponds to the online Latin America Forecast database.

SUBJECT

Macroeconomic forecasts for Argentina, Brazil, Chile, Colombia, Ecuador, Mexico, Peru, Uruguay, and Venezuela, including national income accounts (supply, demand, and factor income); balance of payments accounts; exports and imports by major categories; petroleum sector; financial and inflation indicators; and external debt and debt servicing

COVERAGE

Latin America

TIME SPAN

1970 to date

UPDATING

Quarterly

VENDOR

The WEFA Group

PRICE

Contact vendor for details

LEAD AND ZINC

INTERNATIONAL LEAD AND ZINC

Phone: (215) 667-6000
Fax: (215) 660-6477

The WEFA Group
401 City Line Ave., Suite 300
Bala Cynwyd, PA 19004-1780

TYPE

Time series

CONTENT

Contains approximately 1,400 monthly, quarterly, and annual time series on lead and zinc. Covers metal consumption, mine production, metal production, principal end uses, stocks, recovery of secondary lead and zinc, and trade with Socialist countries. Data are obtained from the monthly publication *Lead and Zinc Statistics*, published by the International Lead and Zinc Study Group. Corresponds to the online International Lead and Zinc database.

SUBJECT

Worldwide lead and zinc statistics, covering metal consumption and production, mine production, principal end uses, stocks, recovery of secondary lead and zinc, and trade with socialist countries.

COVERAGE

International

TIME SPAN

1955 to date

UPDATING

Monthly

VENDOR

The WEFA Group

PRICE

Contact vendor for details

MIDDLE EAST

MIDDLE EAST AND AFRICA FORECAST

Phone: (215) 667-6000
Fax: (215) 660-6477

The WEFA Group
401 City Line Ave., Suite 300
Bala Cynwyd, PA 19004-1780

TYPE

Time series

CONTENT

Contains approximately 1,600 annual time series of historical and forecast data on the economies of countries in the Middle East and Africa. Includes national income accounts; exports, imports, and petroleum trade balance; balance of payments accounts; financial and inflation indicators; and external debt. Countries covered are Algeria, Bahrain, Egypt, Ghana, Iran, Iraq, Ivory Coast, Kenya, Kuwait, Libya, Morocco, Nigeria, Oman, Qatar, Saudi Arabia, South Africa, Tunisia, United Arab Emirates, Zaire, Zimbabwe, Gabon, Turkey, and Cameroon.

SUBJECT

Economic data for the Middle East and Africa

COVERAGE

Middle Eastern and African countries

VENDOR

The WEFA Group

PRICE

Contact vendor for details

POPULATION

DEMOGRAPHIC STATISTICS

Phone: (212) 963-4120
Fax: (212) 963-4116

United Nations Statistical Division
2 United Nations Plaza, DC2-1620
New York, NY 10017

CONTACT

Robert Johnston, Officer-in-Charge

FORMER DATABASE NAME

United Nations Demographics

TYPE

Statistical

CONTENT

Contains country, region, and world statistics covering all characteristics of populations. Includes vital natality, mortality, marriage, and divorce statistics, as well as migration data. Corresponds to the print publication *The Demographic Yearbook*.

SUBJECT

Worldwide demographic statistics

UPDATING

Annual

VENDOR

United Nations Statistical Division

PRICE

Contact vendor for details

RISK

COUNTRY REPORT SERVICES

Phone: (315) 472-1224
Fax: (315) 472-1235

IBC USA Licensing Inc.
Political Risk Services (PRS)
222 Teall Ave., Suite 200
P.O. Box 6482
Syracuse, NY 13217-6482

CONTACT

Mary Lou Walsh, Managing Director

TYPE

Full text

CONTENT

Contains the complete text of reports covering economic and political conditions for 100 countries worldwide. Basic data include name of capital, population, area, official languages, names and positions of leading government officials, government structure (e.g., administrative subdivisions, type of legislature, frequency of elections), currency exchange rate against the U.S. dollar, and currency exchange system (e.g., ties to currencies of trading partners). Sociodemographic data include population growth rates and urban-rural distribution, percentage of popula-

tion under age 15, labor force distribution by major industrial sector, and percentage of population in each major ethnic group. Also provides data on principal exports and imports, trading part and, for the previous five years, the following annual economic indicators: gross domestic product (GDP) in billions of U.S. dollars, per capita income, real growth rate, inflation rate, capital investment, unemployment rate, debt service ratio to exports, national accounts, imports and exports in billions of U.S. dollars, and percentage change in value of currency. Includes an Economic Performance Profile, which indicates each country's position by quartile relative to all 100 countries covered in the database. The profile is based on five-year averages for a variety of indicators.

Also provides 18-month and five-year forecasts for likely political scenarios, plus risk ratings in the areas of political turmoil, financial transfers, investments, and export markets. Probabilities are given in qualitative terms (e.g., same, more, much more) for risk factors (e.g., taxation discrimination on foreign businesses) under various political scenarios (e.g., a reformist military regime). Includes an assessment by at least three independent experts on the likelihood of specific political scenarios. Also provides brief commentary on the current political and economic situation, including a five-year forecast of GDP growth and the inflation rate. Also contains the complete text of *International Country Risk Guide*, providing country analyses, regional surveys, and economic and demographic data for 130 countries worldwide.

Corresponds to *Country and Executive Reports* produced by Political Risk Services and available individually or as part of the *World Service*, to *The European Community: Annual Five-Year Forecast for International Business*, to *Country Forecasts* (tables), and to the online Country Report Services database.

SUBJECT

Analysis of the political and economic conditions of countries worldwide, presenting three alternative scenarios and covering current and expected regime stability, political turmoil, international investment restrictions, trade restrictions, and economic policies

COVERAGE

International

TIME SPAN

Current information

UPDATING

Monthly

VENDOR

IBC USA Licensing Inc., Political Risk Services

PRICE

Contact vendor for details

SHIPPING

MARITIME TRANSPORT STATISTICS

Phone: (212) 963-4120
Fax: (212) 963-4116

United Nations Statistical Division
2 United Nations Plaza, DC2-1620
New York, NY 10017

CONTACT

Robert Johnston, Officer-in-Charge

TYPE

Statistical

CONTENT

Provides seaborne export data by exporting and destination coastal areas in quantity (in metric tons), shipping distance (in nautical miles), and their product (ton mileages). Covers all available one- through five-digit codes of the Commodity Classification for Maritime Transport Statistics.

SUBJECT

Maritime export data

TIME SPAN

1969

VENDOR

United Nations Statistical Division

PRICE

Contact vendor for details

TRADE

COMEXT

Phone: 0352 430134567
Fax: 0352 436404

Commission of the European Communities
Statistical Office of the European Communities
(EUROSTAT)
Information Office
Batiment Jean Monnet, B.P. 1907
Rue Alcide de Gasperi
L-2920 Luxembourg, Luxembourg

TYPE

Time series

CONTENT

Contains more than 4.5 million time series on trade between European Community Countries and their trading partners. Data are collected at the combined nomenclature product level. Trade data are available in monetary values, quantities (e.g., tons), and supplementary units (e.g., numbers, pairs, liters) for each product. Import values are based on cost, insurance, and freight and export values are based on free on board. Data are obtained from the statistical offices of EC countries. Corresponds to the online COMEXT database and in part to data published by EUROSTAT in analytical tables of foreign trade.

SUBJECT

External trade statistics for European Economic Community members

LANGUAGE

English; French

COVERAGE

European Community and all trading partners worldwide

TIME SPAN

1976 to date

UPDATING

Monthly

VENDOR

Commission of the European Communities, Statistical Office of the European Communities, Information Office

PRICE

Contact vendor for details

EXTERNAL TRADE STATISTICS

Phone: (212) 963-4120
Fax: (212) 963-4116

United Nations Statistical Division
2 United Nations Plaza, DC2-1620
New York, NY 10017

CONTACT

Robert Johnston, Officer-in-Charge

TYPE

Statistical

CONTENT

Provides annual and some cumulative quarterly country, regional, and world statistics on external trade in commodities identified according to the Standard International Trade Classification. Detailed values in thousand U.S. dollars and quantity data in metric units for each trading partner exist to the extent provided by the reporting counties. Subsets of the data are made available upon request.

SUBJECT

Worldwide external trade

TIME SPAN

1962 to date

UPDATING

Annual; some quarterly data available

VENDOR

United Nations Statistical Division

PRICE

Contact vendor for details

IMF DIRECTION OF TRADE

Phone: (202) 623-6180
Fax: (202) 623-4661

International Monetary Fund (IMF)
Statistics Department
700 19th St., N.W.
Washington, DC 20431

ALTERNATE DATABASE NAME:

IMF Direction of Trade

TYPE

Time series

CONTENT

Contains more than 60,000 monthly, quarterly, and annual time series of import and export statistics for about 160 countries and their trading partners. The annual series cover 1948 to date; quarterly series cover 1960 to date; monthly series cover 1965 to date. These country/partner data are supplemented by world and area aggregates. All exports are valued free on board and all imports are valued cost, insurance, and freight. All data are expressed in U.S. dollars. Corresponds to the IMF publication *Direction of Trade Statistics* and to the online IMF Direction of Trade database.

SUBJECT

Import and export trade statistics

COVERAGE

International

TIME SPAN

Varies

UPDATING

Monthly

VENDOR

International Monetary Fund, Statistics Department

PRICE

Contact vendor for details

OECD MONTHLY FOREIGN TRADE STATISTICS - SERIES A

Phone: 331 49104265
Fax: 331 49104299

Organization for Economic Cooperation and Development (OECD)
Electronic Editions
2, rue Andre Pascal
F-75775 Paris Cedex 16, France

TYPE

Time series

CONTENT

Contains approximately 14,000 monthly, quarterly, and annual time series on trade for OECD member countries, by origin and destination and by major commodity categories for the analysis of trade flows. These data cover 105 countries and regions with which the OECD countries are associated in trade. Data are organized by Standard Industrial Trade Classification (SITC) codes. Corresponds to the data published by OECD in *Statistics of Foreign Trade: Series A Monthly Bulletin* and in part to the online OECD Statistics of Foreign Trade: Series A database.

SUBJECT

Trade for OECD members

COVERAGE

International

TIME SPAN

1960 to date

UPDATING

Monthly

VENDOR

Organization for Economic Cooperation and Development, Electronic Editions

PRICE

Contact vendors for details

Online

AGRICULTURE

WORLD AGRICULTURE SUPPLY AND DISPOSITION (WASD)

Phone: (215) 667-6000
Fax: (215) 660-6477

The WEFA Group
401 City Line Ave., Suite 300
Bala Cynwyd, PA 19004-1780

TYPE

Time series

CONTENT

Contains more than 29,000 annual time series on the supply and disposition of crops, livestock, and meat commodities in more than 195 countries. Data include stocks; areas harvested, yield, and production; domestic use broken down by food and industrial use; total imports and exports; and selected imported commodities from the United States. Covers 52 commodities, including barley, beef and veal, cattle, coffee, corn, cottonseeds, oats, pigs, pork, poultry, poultry meat, soybeans, sugar, and wheat. Primary source of data is the U.S. Department of Agriculture, Foreign Agricultural Service.

SUBJECT

The worldwide supply and disposition of agricultural commodities, including coffee, cotton, eggs, dairy, grains (10 commodities), livestock (3 commodities), meat (12 commodities), oilseeds (23 commodities), tobacco, and sugar. Data provided covers stocks; areas harvested, yield, and production; domestic use (total, food, feed, and industrial uses); imports and exports; and imports of selected commodities from the United States.

COVERAGE

International

TIME SPAN

1960 to date

UPDATING

Quarterly

ONLINE AVAILABILITY

The WEFA Group (WASD)

ALTERNATE ELECTRONIC FORMATS

Diskette [World Agriculture Supply and Disposition (WASD)]; Magnetic Tape [World Agriculture Supply and Disposition (WASD)]

ASIA

ASIA FORECAST

Phone: (215) 667-6000
Fax: (215) 660-6477

The WEFA Group
401 City Line Ave., Suite 300
Bala Cynwyd, PA 19004-1780

FORMER DATABASE NAME

Far East Forecast Monthly Far East

TYPE

Time series

CONTENT

Contains detailed macroeconomic forecasts for Asian countries. Covers national accounts, exports, imports, balance of payments, prices, debt, debt servicing, exchange rates, industrial production, labor, and population.

SUBJECT

Macroeconomic forecasts for Australia, China, Hong Kong, India, Indonesia, Japan, Republic of Korea, Malaysia, Pakistan, the Philippines, Singapore, Taiwan, and Thailand

COVERAGE

Asian countries

TIME SPAN

1970 to date; five years (short-term forecasts); 10 years (long-term forecasts)

UPDATING

Quarterly (short-term forecasts); annual (long-term forecasts)

ONLINE AVAILABILITY

The WEFA Group (ASIA; FAREAST)

BALANCE OF PAYMENTS

BALANCE OF PAYMENTS STATISTICS (BOPS)

Phone: (202) 623-6180
Fax: (202) 623-4661

International Monetary Fund (IMF)
Statistics Department
700 19th St., N.W.
Washington, DC 20431

ALTERNATE DATABASE NAME

IMF Balance of Payments

TYPE

Time series

CONTENT

Contains more than 63,000 quarterly and annual time series compiled by the IMF on the international economic transactions of 140 individual countries. Data are grouped by current account, long- and short-term capital, transfers, investments, and reserves. Corresponds to the IMF publication *Balance of Payments Statistics Yearbook.*

SUBJECT

Balance of payments components and aggregates

COVERAGE

International

TIME SPAN

1965 to date (annual data); 1970 to date (quarterly data)

UPDATING

Monthly

ONLINE AVAILABILITY

The WEFA Group

ALTERNATE ELECTRONIC FORMAT

Magnetic Tape (Balance of Payments)

BUSINESS

EIU: BUSINESS INTERNATIONAL

Phone: (212) 460-0600

The Economist Intelligence Unit
215 Park Ave. S.
New York, NY 10003

TYPE

Full text

CONTENT

Provides full-text business information on 57 countries in Europe, Asia, and Latin America. Includes political and economic trends, market analyses and corporate strategies. Corresponds to *Business Asia, Business Eastern Europe, Business Europe, Business International, Business Latin America, Country Profiles, Country Reports, Forecasting Services, Investing, Licensing & Trading Conditions Abroad, Doing Business with Eastern Europe, Eastern Europe Industrial Monitors, Business International Money Report, Financing Foreign Operations,* and *Worldwide Financial Regulations.*

SUBJECT

International business

COVERAGE

Europe, Asia, and Latin America

TIME SPAN

1989 to date

UPDATING

Weekly

ONLINE AVAILABILITY

DIALOG Information Services, Inc.

IFAX INTERFAX (IFAX)

INTERFAX Deutschland
Stephanstr. 1
D-60313 Frankfurt, Germany

ALTERNATE DATABASE NAME

Interfax CIS-States News Agency

TYPE

Full text; numeric

CONTENT

Contains the following reports *Business Weekly, Business Reports, Business Law Reports,* and *Statistical Reports,* issued by the statistical offices of the CIS states.

SUBJECT

German and English reports authorized by the statistical offices of the CIS-States

LANGUAGE

German; English

COVERAGE

CIS-States

YEAR FIRST AVAILABLE

1994

TIME SPAN

March 1994 to date

UPDATING

Weekly

ONLINE AVAILABILITY

GENIOS Wirtschaftsdatenbanken (IFAX: DM4.50/connect minute; DM4.00//full record online)

INTERNATIONAL BUSINESS CLIMATE INDICATORS

Phone: (315) 472-1224
Fax: (315) 472-1235

IBC USA Licensing Inc.
Political Risk Services (PRS)
222 Teall Ave., Suite 200
P.O. Box 6482
Syracuse, NY 13217-6482

TYPE

Statistical

CONTENT

Contains tables extracted from Political Risk Services print publication *Country Forecasts.* Provides rankings for 100 countries globally and regionally according to political, social, and economic variables. Covers data and forecasts on elections, political stability, market risk, work force, urban growth, unemployment, infant mortality, gross domestic product, inflation, capital investment, budget balance, debt service, current account, and currency change.

SUBJECT

European business climate indicators, including elections, regime stability, financial transfers, direct investments, export markets, inflation rates, capital investments, unemployment, currency fluctuation, population shifts, the workforce, and urban growth.

COVERAGE

International

TIME SPAN

Current information

UPDATING

Semiannual

ONLINE AVAILABILITY

NewsNet, Inc. (contact vendor for details)
Also Online as Part of: Country Report Services

ALTERNATE ELECTRONIC FORMATS

Diskette (International Business Climate Indicators)

WORLD VEST-BASE™

Phone: (312) 266-0575
Fax: (616) 756-2288

World Vest-Base
1335 N. Dearborn Pkwy
Chicago, IL 60610

TYPE

Numeric

CONTENT

Provides comprehensive balance sheet and income statement data for 5,500 foreign industrial companies in 45 countries and 125 industry groups. For each company, provides name, balance sheet, per share values, stock price histories, annual percentage change, flow of fund statements, redefined values, price-related data with highs, lows, and averages, text notes describing each company's activities along with tables from annual reports, economic data for each country, schedule of interim results on a semiannual or quarterly basis for each company, price history from 1980 (including share type for each company), performance estimates from broker-dealers (for most companies), current prices, and price ratios.

SUBJECT

Equity information on foreign industrial companies

COVERAGE

International, except the United States

YEAR FIRST AVAILABLE

1987

TIME SPAN

1984 to date (historical coverage); 1980 to date (additional coverage)

UPDATING

Daily

ONLINE AVAILABILITY

Telekurs AG (available by subscription)

ALTERNATE ELECTRONIC FORMATS

CD-ROM (World Vest-Base™); Magnetic Tape (World Vest-Base™)

WORLDSCOPE

Phone: (203) 330-5261
Fax: (203) 330-5001

W/D Partners
1000 Lafayette Blvd.
Bridgeport, CT 06604

ALTERNATE DATABASE NAME

Disclosure/Worldscope

TYPE

Directory; numeric

CONTENT

Contains financial data on more than 11,000 major corporations in 45 countries listed on leading stock exchanges around the world. Covers 25 industries, including aerospace, banking, chemicals, electronics, food and beverages, insurance, metal products manu-facturing, and transportation. For U.S. companies, provides monthly data on more than 600 items; for non-U.S. companies, on more than 350 items. Includes fundamental data (e.g., financial statement, balance sheet), computed variables (e.g., current ratios), company-specific accounting standards, and descriptive information (e.g., name, address, names of executives). Sources include corporate, annual, and 10K reports, disclosure statements, newspapers, and wire services. Corresponds in part to *Worldscope Industrial Company Profiles* and *Worldscope Financial and Service Company Profiles*.

SUBJECT

Fundamental, descriptive, and stock for leading com-panies worldwide

COVERAGE

International

TIME SPAN

Varies by online service

UPDATING

Varies by online service

ONLINE AVAILABILITY

Dow Jones News/Retrieval (contact vendor for details); Bridge Information Systems, Inc; FactSet Data Systems, Inc; LEXIS (WLDSCP); Randall-Helms International, Inc.

Also Online as Part of: M.A.I.D (Market Analysis and Information Database)

ALTERNATE ELECTRONIC FORMATS

CD-ROM (Worldscope®); Diskette (Worldscope®); Magnetic Tape (Worldscope®)

COAL

COAL STATISTICS MONTHLY

Phone: 0932 761444
Fax: 0932 781425

FT Business Enterprises Ltd.
Number One
Southwark Bridge
London SE1 9HL, England

TYPE

Full text; statistical

CONTENT

Contains the complete text of *Coal Statistics Monthly*, a newsletter providing statistics and analyses of coal pro-duction, imports, exports, prices, and consumption worldwide.

SUBJECT

Coal production and trade worldwide

COVERAGE

International

TIME SPAN

1987 to date

UPDATING

Semimonthly

ONLINE AVAILABILITY

Available Online as Part of: Financial Times Business Reports: Energy (described in a separate entry)

COMPUTERS

WORLD SEMICONDUCTOR TRADE STATISTICS (WSTS)

Phone: (408) 246-2711
Fax: (408) 246-2830

Semiconductor Industry Association (SIA)
4300 Stevens Creek Blvd., Suite 271
San Jose, CA 95129

TYPE
Statistical

CONTENT
Provides information on orders and shipments of worldwide semiconductor manufacturers in the world market. Contains detailed data for major product families and key product lines, shipment and order data reported by companies worldwide, and aggregate data estimated for nonreporting organizations. Includes monthly and yearly summaries and sales forecasts.

SUBJECT
International semiconductor industry

COVERAGE
International

TIME SPAN
1976 to date

UPDATING
Monthly

ONLINE AVAILABILITY
Dataquest, Inc.

DEBT

OECD DAC EXTERNAL DEBT OF DEVELOPING COUNTRIES

Phone: 01 45249056
Fax: 01 45241650

Organization for Economic Cooperation and Development (OECD)
Development Assistance Committee
2, rue Andre Pascal
F-75775 Paris Cedex 16, France

TYPE
Time series

CONTENT
Contains annual time series of historical and forecast data on the debt positions of 141 developing countries and territories. Provides total long- and medium-term outstanding external debt and debt service in U.S. dollars. Also provides selected indicators of economic performance for each country. Excludes short-term debt, military official debt, and International Monetary Fund credits.

SUBJECT
Foreign debts of developing countries

COVERAGE
International

TIME SPAN
1975 to date

UPDATING
Annual

ONLINE AVAILABILITY
Reuters Information Services (Canada) Ltd. (OECDEXD; OECD External Debt of Developing Countries)

ALTERNATE ELECTRONIC FORMATS
Diskette (OECD DAC External Debt of Developing Countries)

WORLD DEBT TABLES

Phone: (202) 477-1234
Fax: (202) 477-0661

The World Bank
International Economics Department
1818 H St., N.W.
Washington, DC 20433

TYPE
Time series

CONTENT
Contains more than 20,300 annual time series on the external debt of approximately 138 developing countries and 6 regions worldwide. Data are published by the International Bank for Reconstruction and Development (World Bank) in *World Debt Tables: External Finance for Developing Countries* and its supplements. Data, available by category of debt and by type of creditor, cover these major transactions for each creditor: commitments; disbursements; repayments of

principal; payments of interest; debt outstanding; loan terms; and debt services projections.

SUBJECT

External debt information, external finance, and capital flows

COVERAGE

International

TIME SPAN

1970 to date, with some 10-year forecasts

UPDATING

Annual, with minor updates twice a year

ONLINE AVAILABILITY

GSI-ECO; The WEFA Group; GE Information Services (GEIS)

ALTERNATE ELECTRONIC FORMATS

Diskette [World Debt Tables; World Debt Tables Data Extracts (DX)]; Magnetic Tape (World Debt Tables)

DEVELOPING COUNTRIES

OECD DAC FINANCIAL FLOWS TO DEVELOPING COUNTRIES

Phone: 01 45249056
Fax: 01 45241650

Organization for Economic Cooperation and Development (OECD)
Development Assistance Committee
2, rue Andre Pascal
F-75775 Paris Cedex 16, France

ALTERNATE DATABASE NAME

OECD Aid Flows to Developing Countries

TYPE

Time series

CONTENT

Contains annual time series of financial aid statistics for 216 developing countries. Includes recipient, donor, and amount and type of aid in U.S. dollars. Sources of data include reports from the Organization for Economic Development, Development Assistance Committees countries (Australia, Austria, Belgium, Denmark, Germany, Finland, France, Italy, Japan, The Netherlands, New Zealand, Norway, Sweden, Switzerland, United Kingdom, and the United States), the Commission of the European Communities, and reports from multilateral organizations.

SUBJECT

Financial data pertaining to developing countries

COVERAGE

International

TIME SPAN

1968 to date

UPDATING

Annual

ONLINE AVAILABILITY

Reuters Information Services (Canada) Ltd. (OECD-DAC)

ALTERNATE ELECTRONIC FORMATS

Diskette (OECD DAC Financial Flows to Developing Countries)

ECONOMY

BANQUE DE DONNÉES MACROECONOMIQUE (BDM)

Phone: 01 45400614
France Institut National de la Statistique et

des Etudes Economiques (INSEE)
18, blvd. Adolphe Pinard
F-75675 Paris Cedex 14, France

TYPE

Time series

CONTENT

Contains more than 300,000 time series of macroeconomic data on France and on countries of the European Community (EC) and the Organization for Economic Cooperation and Development (OECD). Data on France include general statistics (e.g., demography, employment, revenues, consumption), production and price indexes, national accounts, and financial statistics (e.g., public finance, money and credit, balance of payments, foreign commerce) originating from government sources and the central French bank. Data on other countries are derived from reports of the statistical services of the EC countries, the Statistical Institutes of the EC, the OECD, the International Monetary Fund, and Citibase.

SUBJECT

Economic and related data for France and selected national and international sectors

LANGUAGE

French

COVERAGE

Economic and related data for France and selected national and international sectors

TIME SPAN

1945 to date

UPDATING

Periodically, as new data become available

ONLINE AVAILABILITY

GSI-ECO

ALTERNATE ELECTRONIC FORMATS

Batch Access [Banque de Donnees Macroeconomique (BDM)].

CHELEM

Phone: 01 48426414
Fax: 01 48425912

Center d'Etudes Prospectives et d'Informations Internationales (CEPII)
9, rue Georges Pitard
F-75015 Paris, France

ALTERNATE DATABASE NAME

Comptes Harmonises sur les Echanges et l'Economie Mondiale/ Harmonized Trade and World Economy Accounts

TYPE

Time series

CONTENT

Contains information on international trade, world economics, foreign economies, economic models, international finance systems, and related topics.

Comprises the following five data files:

- International Trade—covers 71 product categories in 32 import and export areas for the years 1967 to date.

- Balance of Payments—covers 32 geographic areas and 112 accounts.

- Gross National Products—provides value and volumes in dollars for 166 countries since 1960.

- National Accounts—provides value and volume in dollars for 32 geographic areas since 1960.

- World Demand—covers 55 categories of manufactured products since 1970.

SUBJECT

World trade and economics, including international trade economic models and international economies and finance systems

LANGUAGE

English; French

COVERAGE

International

TIME SPAN

Varies by type of data, with earliest dating from 1960

UPDATING

Annual

ONLINE AVAILABILITY

GSI-ECO (CHELEM International Trade File)

ALTERNATE ELECTRONIC FORMATS

CD-ROM (CHELEM)

COMPARATIVE ECONOMIC TRENDS

Phone: (617) 345-2526

Technical Data
22 Pittsburgh St.
Boston, MA 02210

TYPE

Numeric

CONTENT

Contains all relevant macroeconomic indicators, tracking and reporting government statistics on gross national product, consumer and wholesale prices, unemployment, reserves, imports and exports, percent of import cover, trade balance, current account, business conditions, and monetary aggregates.

SUBJECT

Macroeconomic indicators, including gross national product, consumer and wholesale prices, unemployment, reserves, and imports and exports

COVERAGE

International

TIME SPAN

Current information

UPDATING

Continuous

ONLINE AVAILABILITY

Telerate Systems Inc.

COUNTRY ECONOMIC PROFILES (CEP)

Phone (416) 365-5361
(800) 387-1588
Fax: (416) 364-0646

Reuters Information Services (Canada) Ltd.
Data Services Division
Exchange Tower, Suite 2000, P.O. Box 418
2 First Canadian Place
Toronto, ON, Canada M5X 1E3

TYPE

Time series

CONTENT

Contains quarterly and annual economic data for 193 countries including developed, developing, and centrally planned economies. Coverage includes: demographics; employment; national accounts (i.e., gross domestic product measured in terms of consumption, creation, and distribution of goods and services); production (e.g., major exports, allocation of industrial capacity); money, finance, and prices; external sector (e.g., balance of trade); aid flows (the amount of aid given out or taken in); energy (e.g., Organization of Petroleum Exporting Countries trade balance, oil, or natural gas production and consumption government (e.g., revenues, expenditures); and currency exchange rates against the U.S. dollar. Also contains average annual growth rates in each category for the last five years and for the last two years or last two comparable quarters. Sources include the International Monetary Fund, Organization for Economic Cooperation and Development, United Nations, World Bank, and such national agencies, as the Australian Bureau of Statistics, Statistics Canada, and U.K. Central Statistical Office.

SUBJECT

National economies and economic policies of 193 countries

COVERAGE

International

TIME SPAN

Current five years

UPDATING

Monthly

ONLINE AVAILABILITY

Reuters Information Services (Canada) Ltd.

COUNTRY REPORTS AND FORECAST OF KEY INDICATORS

Phone: (201) 575-8333
Fax: (201) 575-8474

Multinational Computer Models, Inc. (MCM)
333 Fairfield Rd.
Fairfield, NJ 07004

TYPE

Time series

CONTENT

Contains monthly historical and forecast data on more than 50 key economic indicators for 75 countries as well as annual and five-year forecasts for 75 currencies.

SUBJECT

International economic indicators and currencies

COVERAGE

International

TIME SPAN

Most recent five years, historical data; one-year quarterly forecasts, forecast data

UPDATING

Monthly or quarterly, depending on type of data
Online Availability: Multinational Computer Models, Inc.

COUNTRY STATISTICS AND ANALYSIS

Phone: (617) 345-2526

Technical Data
22 Pittsburgh St.
Boston, MA 02210

FORMER DATABASE NAME

Country Analysis and Comparisons

TYPE

Numeric

CONTENT

Contains appraisals of the economic and political conditions of key countries, including the United States, Canada, Japan, the United Kingdom, Germany, Switzerland, France, Italy, The Netherlands, and Belgium.

SUBJECT

Economic and political indicators

COVERAGE

International

ONLINE AVAILABILITY

Telerate Systems, Inc.

CRONOS

Phone: 0352 430134567
Fax: 0352 436404

Commission of the European Communities
Statistical Office of the European Communities
(EUROSTAT)
Information Office
Batiment Jean Monnet, B.P. 1907
Rue Alcide de Gasperi
L-2920 Luxembourg, Luxembourg

TYPE

Time series

CONTENT

Contains more than 900,000 time series of economic data on countries in the European Community (EC) and other countries worldwide. Corresponds to data available in various EUROSTAT publications.

- General Statistics—contains 80,000 time series of short-term indicators and general economic information covering industry, agriculture, services, transportation, population, employment, trade, prices, finance, and balance of payments. Also contains 84,000 series (since 1970) on macroeconomic indicators for developing countries.

- National Accounts, Finance, Balance of Payments—contains 25,000 series (since 1960) on aggregate national account data; series on national account transactions related to goods and services; annual series (since 1970) on economic transactions between institutional sectors (companies, households); 2,000 annual series (since 1970) on the financial flows between institutional sectors; 32,000 series (since 1960) on the balance of payments, with geographic breakdowns, for EC countries, the U.S., and Japan; and 16,000 biannual series (since 1970) on budget expenditures for research and development.

- Industry and Services—contains 12,500 series from annual industrial surveys aggregated in accordance with the activities nomenclature of the European Community; 30,000 annual and quarterly series on production and foreign trade for industrial products; 23,500 series on annual energy balances and monthly statistics for production, stocks, and exchanges; and monthly series (since 1973) on production, supplies, stocks, and consumption in the steelmaking industries of the EC countries.

- Agriculture, Forestry, Fishing—contains 7,500 monthly series on the sale and purchase prices of agricultural commodities; monthly series (since 1970) on exports of agricultural products; 25,000 quarterly series on agricultural products, including number of livestock and milk, eggs, and meat production (since 1964), supply balances for animal products (since 1960), and for vegetable products (since 1973); 9,000 annual series of regional statistics for agricultural activity; and series (since 1970) on fishing statistics, including catches, quantities landed, and number and tonnage of boats.

- Foreign Trade—contains 185,000 quarterly and monthly series (since 1970) on international trade, by product and trading partner; quarterly series on imports of 250 basic products; and 127,000 annual series (since 1962) on foreign trade for ACP (African, Caribbean, and Pacific) countries.

SUBJECT

Economies of European Economic Community countries, associated overseas countries, and major third-world countries. Included are general statistics; foreign trade aggregates and trade with African, Caribbean, Pacific, and associated countries; developing countries; industrial survey and sectoral information; energy; agricultural products, prices, and accounts; balance of payments; financial accounts; national accounts; and research and development

LANGUAGE

English; French; German

COVERAGE

International

TIME SPAN

1950 to date

UPDATING

Daily (for short-term indicators); monthly (or longer, depending on the statistical field covered)

ONLINE AVAILABILITY

GSI-ECO (EUROSTAT CRONOS); Datacentralen A/S (DKK 15/connect minute, DKK 15 per time series accessed); The WEFA Group; Statistical Office of the European Communities (EUROSTAT) (Accessible to internal and privileged users)

ALTERNATE ELECTRONIC FORMATS

Diskette; Magnetic Tape (CRONOS)

CURRENT ECONOMIC INDICATORS (CEI)

Phone: 331 49104265
Fax: 331 49104299

Organization for Economic Cooperation and
Development (OECD)
Electronic Editions
2, rue Andre Pascal
F-75775 Paris Cedex 16, France

TYPE

Time series

CONTENT

Contains monthly and quarterly time series of economic indicators for the G-7 economic grouping of
nations (Canada, France, Germany, Italy, Japan,
United Kingdom, and the United States). Covers total
imports, total exports, consumer price index, money
supply, and rate of unemployment.

SUBJECT

Economic indicators for G-7 member nations

COVERAGE

Canada, France, Germany, Italy, Japan, United
Kingdom, the United States

TIME SPAN

1989 to date

UPDATING

United States and Canada, daily; all others, weekly

ONLINE AVAILABILITY

Reuters Information Services (Canada) Ltd.

DRI/TBS WORLD FORECAST

Phone: (617) 863-5100
DRI/McGraw-Hill

Data Products Division
24 Hartwell Ave.
Lexington, MA 02173

CONTACT

Client Services

TYPE

Time series

CONTENT

Contains more than 7,000 historical and forecast economic time series for 46 countries and five world
regions. For each country, provides approximately
100 indicators adjusted to accommodate cross-country
comparisons. Covers balance of payments and trade,
central government revenues and expenditures, external assets, debt and debt service, industrial output,
interest rates, currency exchange rates, money supply
and prices, national income accounts, population,
labor force, employment, and wages and incomes.
Also provides regional aggregate data for key indicators. Regional forecasts are available.

SUBJECT

Economic, financial, and social forecasts for 46 countries, covering approximately 100 concepts, including
national income accounts; balance of payments and
merchandise trade; central government revenues,
spending, and balances; external assets, debt, and
debt service; industrial output and productivity; interest and exchange rates; money supply and prices;
population, labor force, and employment; and wages
and incomes

COVERAGE

International

TIME SPAN

Earliest series from 1950s, with 10- to 15-year forecasts

UPDATING

Varies by country

ONLINE AVAILABILITY

DRI/McGraw-Hill (@INTL/MODELBANK)

GLOBAL REPORT

Phone: (212) 898-7425
(800) 842-8405
Fax: (212) 742-8769

Citicorp
77 Water St., 2nd Floor
New York, NY 10043
Alternate Database Name: Citibank Global Report

TYPE

Full text; numeric

CONTENT

Contains information on worldwide business and
finance. Comprises the following six files:

• Foreign Exchange—contains real-time spot and
  cross rates for 100 currencies, spot and forward
  rates for all major currencies, historical rates for
  26 countries, and a summary of central bank activity. Includes weekly recommendations, technical
  forecasts from FOREXIA and MMS International,
  and the International Finance Alert from

Financial Times Business Information, which provides daily hedging recommendations. Provides information on exchange regulations and the tax implications of alternative buying and selling strategies. Also includes market commentary and analyses.

- Country Reports—contains news on 100 countries and information on conditions affecting business in the following 15 countries: Australia, Brazil, Canada, France, Germany, Great Britain, Hong Kong, Italy, Japan, Mexico, the Netherlands, Spain, Sweden, Switzerland, and the United States. Covers the position of each country's currency on world markets, economic indicators, business practices and regulations, and current political and economic news. Currency information, provided by Business International, includes the annual average exchange rates against the U.S. dollar for the past five years, five-year forecasts, and five-year monthly closings and averages; a consensus forecast from financial staff of major international companies of high, low, and mean forward rates for the next 3-, 6-, and 121-month periods; and an analysis of current factors affecting the position of the currency in world markets. Also provides information on domestic financing, credit conditions, economic indicators, current investment yields, trade restrictions, key tax provisions, tax treaties, comparative tax rates, and new or proposed changes to tax laws.

- Money Markets—contains real-time rates for money market instruments in major world markets. Covers Eurocurrency and Eurodollar deposits, certificates of deposit, U.S. Treasury bills, mortgage-backed securities, issuer-placed commercial paper, U.S. federal agency discount notes, short-term financing rates, and money market futures. Also provides U.S. interest rate data, including Federal Reserve weekly rates and the prime rate, and news and commentary on international money market activity. Sources include Financial Times Business Information, Knight-Ridder Financial Information, and MMS International.

- Bonds—contains rates and prices for major fixed income markets. Includes corporate, municipal, treasury, and mortgage-backed bonds, Eurobonds, and interest rate futures.

- Companies—contains news, company profiles, and financial information on 10,000 companies, including 800 foreign firms, traded on the New York, American, Over-the-Counter, and regional exchanges, as well as current securities quotes on publicly traded companies from major exchanges worldwide. Also contains profiles of 20,000 leading companies in Italy and the United Kingdom. Data on securities include last sale price, bid, ask, open, high, low, volume, and stock and bond descriptions, including latest Standard & Poor's ratings. Also provides background and earnings information, including location, directors, earnings, financing, sales, operating statistics, litigation, new offerings, new products, mergers, acquisitions, and leveraged buyouts. Information sources also include Comtex, Databank SpA, II Sole 24 Ore, and Extel.

- Industries—contains news of 30 broad industry groups (e.g., leisure and recreation) and 60 specific market segments (e.g., sports equipment). Covers company news, including mergers, acquisitions, and sales; new product announcements; and litigation affecting the industry. Sources include Comtex, Extel, Standard & Poor's, and Knight-Ridder.

- News—contains business news and stories, as well as weather reports, from wire services around the world. Sources include Comtex, Extel, and Knight-Ridder, and its *Knight-Ridder Financial News* publication.

SUBJECT

International news covering world events, countries, U.S. and European companies, industries, foreign exchange and money markets, equities, bonds, commodities, and other business affairs

COVERAGE

International

TIME SPAN

Varies by file, with earliest data from 1982 and currency rate forecasts through 1994

UPDATING

Continuously, throughout the day

ONLINE AVAILABILITY

FAME Information Services, Inc.; Info Globe Online; CompuServe Information Service (contact vendors for details)

GLOBO LANDERBERICHTE (GLOB)

Phone: 0711 7821790
Fax: 0711 7822025

Deutscher Sparkassenverlag GmbH
Am Wallgraben 115
D-70565 Stuttgart 80, Germany

ALTERNATE DATABASE NAME

Country Report Tables International

TYPE

Numeric

CONTENT

Offers country reports consisting of more than 500 tables covering economic information on 76 countries.

SUBJECT

Gross national product, economic growth, exports, imports, inflation, depreciation, currency, and gold reserves

LANGUAGE

German

COVERAGE

International

YEAR FIRST AVAILABLE

1993

TIME SPAN

Current information

UPDATING

Monthly—each country report is updated semiannually

ONLINE AVAILABILITY

GENIOS Wirtschaftsdatenbanken (GLOB: DM4.50/connect minute; DM5.00//full record online)

INTERNATIONAL COMPARISONS

Phone: (212) 986-9300
Fax: (212) 986-5857

Haver Analytics
60 E. 42nd St., Suite 620
New York, NY 10165

TYPE

Time series

CONTENT

Contains 36 economic time series for 14 nations adjusted for comparability with U.S. statistics. Data are obtained from unpublished U.S. Bureau of Labor Statistics documents.

SUBJECT

Worldwide economic indicators, including labor force employment, and unemployment; gross domestic product converted to common units using Purchasing Price Parity rather than market exchange rates and manufacturing productivity

COVERAGE

International

TIME SPAN

Varies by series, with earliest data from 1959

UPDATING

Monthly

ONLINE AVAILABILITY

GE Information Services (GEIS) (A Haver Analytics File)

INTERNATIONAL MACROECONOMIC DATABASE

Phone: (201) 575-8333
Fax: (201) 575-8474

Multinational Computer Models, Inc. (MCM)
333 Fairfield Rd.
Fairfield, NJ 07004

FORMER DATABASE NAME

Globe Star

TYPE

Time series

CONTENT

Contains approximately 45,000 time series of monthly, quarterly, and annual data on more than 50 key economic variables for 125 countries. Covers exchange rates, international liquidity, money and banking, international trade, prices, production, government finance, and interest rates. Corresponds in part to International Financial Statistics (described in a separate entry).

SUBJECT

International Financing

COVERAGE

International

TIME SPAN

1948 to date

UPDATING

Daily

ONLINE AVAILABILITY

Multinational Computer Models, Inc. (MCM)

INTLINE

Phone: (215) 667-6000
Fax: (215) 660-6477

The WEFA Group
401 City Line Ave., Suite 300
Bala Cynwyd, PA 19004-1780

FORMER DATABASE NAME

International Online Database

TYPE

Time series

CONTENT

Contains approximately 7,000 daily, weekly, monthly, quarterly, and annual time series providing coverage of principal macroeconomic data for more than 40 countries worldwide, including Argentina, Australia, Austria, Belgium, Brazil, Canada, Chile, Colombia, Denmark, Finland, France, Germany, Greece, Hong Kong, India, Indonesia, Ireland, Italy, Japan, Korea, Malaysia, Mexico, The Netherlands, New Zealand, Norway, the Philippines, Singapore, South Africa, Spain, Sweden, Switzerland, Taiwan, Thailand, the United Kingdom, and the United States.

SUBJECT

International macroeconomic data for 40 countries, covering national accounts: government finance; cyclical indicators and business surveys; industrial production and producer price indexes; orders, stocks, and deliveries; wholesale and retail sales and consumer and wholesale prices; construction and housing starts; population; labor, wages, and unemployment rates; money and banking; interest bearing, charged, and interbank (LIBOR) rates; foreign exchange rates, forward rates, and Eurocurrency rates; foreign trade, exports, imports, and balance; balance of payments; and official reserves.

COVERAGE

International

TIME SPAN

1901 to date

UPDATING

Daily

ONLINE AVAILABILITY

The WEFA Group (INTLINE)

ALTERNATE ELECTRONIC FORMATS

Diskette (INTLINE); Magnetic Tape (INTLINE)

ITIS

Phone: 02 2801777
Fax: 02 2303453

CERVED International S.A.
85-87, blvd Clovis
B-1040 Bruxelles, Belgium

ALTERNATE DATABASE NAME

Files on Foreign Countries

TYPE

Statistical; directory

CONTENT

Contains information on the political and economic structures of more than 100 countries and the commercial prospects for Italian entrepreneurs in these countries. Includes a general picture of the economy, commercial prospects and main imports, statistical data on the economic situation, shipping documents, and addresses.

SUBJECT

Business and political structures for countries worldwide

LANGUAGE

Italian; Italy's country profile text is available in both Italian and English

COVERAGE

International

UPDATING

Continuous

ONLINE AVAILABILITY

CERVED International, S.A. (contact vendor for details)

OECD ANNUAL NATIONAL ACCOUNTS

Phone: 331 49104265
Fax: 331 49104299

Organization for Economic Cooperation and Development (OECD)
Electronic Editions
2, rue Andre Pascal
F-75775 Paris Cedex 16, France

TYPE

Time series

CONTENT

Contains approximately 22,000 quarterly and annual time series of national accounts data for 25 member countries, 44 industries classified by the International Standard Industrial Classification code, and 4 aggregate totals. Covers main national income account aggregates; government and private expenditures in current and constant prices; imports and exports of goods and services; indirect taxes, savings; gross domestic product by kind of economic activity; employment by kind of activity; gross fixed capital formation; employment, including self-employed, employees, and total man hours by employees; and industrial cost components, including employee compensation, capital consumption, operating surplus, indirect taxes, subsidies, and value-added price and volume indexes. Corresponds to data in *National Accounts of OECD Countries*.

SUBJECT

National income accounts for OECD member countries, including distribution of national income; employment by activity; gross capital formation, financing, and composition; household income, outlays, and consumption; private consumption expenditure by type and purpose; production, income and outlay, and capital accumulation accounts by sector; and volume indices and price deflators

COVERAGE

International

TIME SPAN

1960 to date, with some series from 1950 to date

UPDATING

Semiannual; Reuters and The WEFA Group, annual

ONLINE AVAILABILITY

DRI/McGraw-Hill (@OECDNIA)

Reuters Information Services (Canada) Ltd. (OECDANA1 Main Aggregates File, OECDANA2 Detailed Tables File); The WEFA Group (ANIA); Wirtschafts- und Sozialwissenschaftliches Rechenzentrum (WSR)

OECD ECONOMIC OUTLOOK

Phone: 331 49104265
Fax: 331 49104299

Organization for Economic Cooperation and Development (OECD)
Electronic Editions
2, rue Andre Pascal
F-75775 Paris Cedex 16, France

TYPE

Time series

CONTENT

Contains approximately 3,500 annual and semiannual time series of macroeconomic statistics and forecasts for OECD member countries, with information on OECD aggregates and non-OECD zones included. Covers national income, expenditures, household accounts, employment, production, interest rates, and balance of payments. Provides disaggregated data on national income, household accounts, interest rates, and balance of payments for seven major industrialized nations (Canada, Germany, France, Italy, Japan, United Kingdom, and the United States). Forecasts correspond to data published in the *OECD Economic Outlook*.

SUBJECT

Macroeconomic financial data for member countries of the OECD and aggregates, including gross national product and its components; government and households appropriation accounts; fiscal and monetary indicators; labor markets and supply indicators; wages, prices, and profitability; and international trade and payments

COVERAGE

International

TIME SPAN

Varies by series, with earliest data from 1960

UPDATING

Semi-annual (June and December)

ONLINE AVAILABILITY

Reuters Information Services (Canada) Ltd. (OECDEOL)

ALTERNATE ELECTRONIC FORMATS

Diskette (OECD Economic Outlook); Magnetic Tape

OECD ECONOMIC STATISTICS - CENTRAL AND EASTERN EUROPE

Phone: 331 49104265
Fax: 331 49104299

Organization for Economic Cooperation and Development (OECD)
Electronic Editions
2, rue Andre Pascal
F-75775 Paris Cedex 16, France

TYPE

Time series

CONTENT

Contains monthly and annual economic data on the following former Soviet Republics and Eastern Bloc countries: Russia, Bulgaria, the Czech Republic, the Slovak Republik, Estonia, Hungary, Latvia, Poland, Romania, Armenia, Azerbaijan, Belorussia, Kazakstan, Kirghizie, Lithuania, Moldavia, Tadzhikistan, Turkmenistan, and Uzbekistan. Covers industrial output, construction, prices, labor force, foreign trade, retail sales, and monetary and financial statistics.

SUBJECT

Economic data on Central and Eastern European countries

COVERAGE

Central and Eastern European countries

TIME SPAN

1980 to date

UPDATING

Monthly

ONLINE AVAILABILITY

Wirtschafts- und Sozialwissenschaftliches Rechenzentrum (WSR)

ALTERNATE ELECTRONIC FORMATS

Diskette (Short-Term Economic Indicators: Central and Eastern European Countries)

OECD MAIN ECONOMIC INDICATORS

Phone: 331 49104265
Fax: 331 49104299

Organization for Economic Cooperation and Development (OECD)
Electronic Editions
2, rue Andre Pascal
F-75775 Paris Cedex 16, France

TYPE

Time series

CONTENT

Contains approximately 7,200 monthly and quarterly economic time series for OECD member countries and selected totals for North America, the European Community, OECD-Europe, and all OECD countries. Most series are available both seasonally adjusted and unadjusted. Corresponds to data in Main Economic Indicators.

NOTE: On DRI, data from OECD Indicators of Industrial Activity (described in a separate entry) and

OECD Labor Force Statistics (described in a separate entry) are also included.

SUBJECT

Economic indicators for OECD member countries, including industrial production, business surveys, deliveries, stocks and orders, construction, domestic trade, labor, wages, prices, domestic and foreign finance, interest rates, foreign trade, and balance of payments

COVERAGE

International

TIME SPAN

1960 to date

UPDATING

Monthly

ONLINE AVAILABILITY

DRI/McGraw-Hill (OECDMEI); GSI-ECO (PIE); Reuters Information Services (Canada) Ltd. (OECD-MEI); The WEFA Group (PIE); FAME Information Services, Inc; Wirtschafts -und Sozialwissenschaftliches Rechenzentrum (WSR)

ALTERNATE ELECTRONIC FORMATS

Diskette (OECD Main Economic Indicators);
Magnetic Tape (OECD Main Economic Indicators)

OECD QUARTERLY NATIONAL ACCOUNTS

Phone: 331 49104265
Fax: 331 49104299

Organization for Economic Cooperation and Development (OECD)
Electronic Editions
2, rue Andre Pascal
F-75775 Paris Cedex 16, France

TYPE

Time series

CONTENT

Contains aggregate data on the main national income accounts for 19 OECD member countries and the following four groups of countries: OECD Total, OECD-Europe, European Community (EC), and the Major Seven. Includes gross national product; personal consumption expenditures; government consumption expenditures; gross capital formation; gross fixed capital formation; change in stocks, exports, and imports; operating surplus; savings income; indirect taxes and price deflators. Totals approximately 2,500 time series in both current and constant prices. Corresponds to data released in the *Quarterly National Accounts Bulletin*.

SUBJECT

National accounts for OECD member countries, including national income and production; personal and government consumption expenditures; fixed capital formation; imports and exports of goods and services; changes in stocks; and price deflators

COVERAGE

International

TIME SPAN

1960 to date, with some series from 1955 to date

UPDATING

Quarterly

ONLINE AVAILABILITY

Reuters Information Services (Canada) Ltd. (OEC-DONA); The WEFA Group (QNA); Wirtschafts- und Sozialwissenschaftliches Rechenzentrum (WSR)

ENERGY

INTERNATIONAL ENERGY ANNUAL

Phone: (416) 364-5361
(800) 387-1588
Fax: (416) 364-0646

Reuters Information Services (Canada) Ltd.
Data Services Division
Exchange Tower, Suite 2000, P.O. Box 418
2 First Canadian Place
Toronto, ON, Canada M5X 1E3

TYPE

Numeric

CONTENT

Provides annual time series of energy-related data compiled for more than 190 countries and regions. Corresponds to U.S. Department of Energy, Energy Information Administration's *International Energy Annual*. Comprises the following 11 files:

- IEAPROD—covers world energy production of coal, crude oil, dry and liquid natural gas, hydro-electric power, and nuclear electric power, expressed both in natural units and British Thermal Units.

- IEAPSD—covers world supply and disposition of crude oil and refined petroleum products.

- IEAICEO—covers imports, exports, output, and apparent consumption of refined petroleum products.

- IEASTK—covers Organization for Economic Cooperation and Development petroleum stocks.

- IEARC—covers world refinery capacity.

- IEACSP—covers world crude oil selling prices.

- IEAPPP—covers world prices for petroleum products.

- IEANGPSD—covers world natural gas production, supply, and disposition.

- IEAFLOW—covers international flow of crude oil, natural gas, and coal.

- IEACOAL—covers world coal production, supply, and disposition.

- IEARES—covers world crude oil and natural gas reserves and estimates recoverable coal reserves.

SUBJECT

Energy, including reserves, refining capacity, production, supply, dispositions, stocks, prices, product flow, and imports and exports for such energy commodities as coal, crude oil, dry and liquid natural gas, hydroelectric power, nuclear energy, and refined petroleum products

COVERAGE

International

TIME SPAN

Varies by file, with most data from 1973

UPDATING

Annual

ONLINE AVAILABILITY

Reuters Information Services (Canada) Ltd.

OECD ANNUAL ENERGY BALANCE

Phone: 331 49104265
Fax: 331 49104299

Organization for Economic Cooperation and Development (OECD)
Electronic Editions
2, rue Andre Pascal
F-75775 Paris Cedex 16, France

TYPE

Time series

CONTENT

Contains annual energy balance data on crude oil, coal, electricity, gas, heat, hydro energy, nuclear energy, and other solid fuels, as well as solar and wind energy of all OECD member countries.

SUBJECT

Energy balance statistics for OECD countries

COVERAGE

OECD member countries

TIME SPAN

1960 to date

UPDATING

Annual

ONLINE AVAILABILITY

Wirtschafts- und Sozialwissenschaftliches Rechenzentrum (WSR)

ALTERNATE ELECTRONIC FORMATS

Diskette (Energy Balances of OECD Countries); Magnetic Tape (Energy Balances of OECD Countries)

OECD BASIC ENERGY STATISTICS

Phone: 331 49104265
Fax: 331 49104299

Organization for Economic Cooperation and Development (OECD)
Electronic Editions
2, rue Andre Pascal
F-75775 Paris Cedex 16, France

TYPE

Time series

CONTENT

Contains the basic energy statistics of the OECD member countries. Includes data on oil, gas, electricity, and solid fuels.

SUBJECT

Energy statistics for OECD countries

COVERAGE

OECD member countries

TIME SPAN

1960 to date

UPDATING

Annual

ONLINE AVAILABILITY

Wirtschafts- und Sozialwissenschaftliches Rechenzentrum (WSR)

ALTERNATE ELECTRONIC FORMATS

Diskette (Energy Statistics of OECD Countries); Magnetic Tape (Energy Statistics of OECD Countries)

FINANCE

FINSTAT - GLOBAL FINANCIAL DATABANK

Phone: (215) 667-6000
Fax: (215) 660-6477

The WEFA Group
401 City Line Ave., Suite 300
Bala Cynwyd, PA 19004-1780

FORMER DATABASE NAME

Financial Times Currency and Share Index Databank

TYPE

Time series

CONTENT

Contains approximately 1,400 time series of daily and end-of-month data on international exchange rates, Eurocurrency interest rates, London money rates, and gold prices. Also contains London and overseas stock indexes, including the Financial Times Actuaries and Financial Times Actuaries Fixed Interest indexes and some commodity prices. Data are supplied by FINSTAT, The Financial Times Statistical Service and maintained by the WEFA Group.

SUBJECT

Prices and indexes on equity, money, precious metal, and stock markets worldwide

COVERAGE

International

TIME SPAN

1976 to date (monthly data); 1979 to date (daily data)

UPDATING

Daily

ONLINE AVAILABILITY

The WEFA Group

ALTERNATE ELECTRONIC FORMATS

Diskette (FINSTAT - Global Financial Databank); Magnetic Tape (FINSTAT - Global Financial Databank)

THE FOREX WATCH

Phone: (617) 345-2526

Technical Data
22 Pittsburgh St.
Boston, MA 02210

TYPE

Full text

CONTENT

Covers world financial and economic developments. Contains current reports and current and historical data on international currency exchange markets, economic and political news, and economic indicators. Comprises the following 10 files:

- U.S. Money Market Report—contains a current analysis of the short-term dollar market, including forces affecting interest rates, general market outlook, and the futures market in relation to cash in the U.S. Includes comparative tables, including opening domestic certificates of deposit rates, opening Treasury bill rates, and spread between domestic and Euro certificates of deposit.

- Individual Country Reports—contains reports on political and economic conditions for each of 10 industrial countries (Belgium, Canada, Germany, France, Italy, Japan, The Netherlands, Switzerland, United Kingdom, and the United States). News Alerts contains daily summaries of economic and political news. Statistical Profile contains tables of key economic indicators for each country showing the percent changes from the previous month and year and average annual change for the past two years. Includes consumer prices, wholesale prices, industrial production, unemployment, and trade data. Risk Assessment covers, for each country, businesses' confidence in the investment climate and profitability; assessment of political risk, covering each government's ideological position, strengths, weaknesses, and prospects for current administrations remaining in power; and economic outlook, analyzing key economic indicators.

- Comparative Economic Indicators—contains tables comparing individual economic indicators for all countries covered. Includes consumer prices, wholesale prices, industrial production, unemployment, reserves, imports, exports, trade balance, and current account. Each table shows percent changes from previous month and year, and annual average change for the past two years.

- Asia/Pacific Regional Reports—contains reports on trends in individual Asian and Pacific Rim countries.

- American Regional Reports—contains reports on trends in individual Latin American countries.

- Mediterranean Regional Reports—contains reports on trends in individual Mediterranean countries.

- Nordic Regional Reports—contains reports on trends in individual Scandinavian countries.

- Calendar of Market Affecting News—a weekly calendar of events affecting the market. Covers speeches by heads of major monetary institutions and releases of national economic statistics.

- Update Status of the Various Reports—contains date or time of last update for most reports and statistics.

- Historical Data Base—contains monthly or quarterly data on economic indicators for 10 countries (Belgium, Canada, Germany, France, Italy, Japan, the Netherlands, Switzerland, United Kingdom, and the United States). Data are stated in the units originally reported. Also includes New York daily opening spot rates for 10 foreign currencies, Euro-deposit rates, and 1-, 3-, 6-, and 12-month forward rates.

SUBJECT

World financial and economic developments

COVERAGE

International

TIME SPAN

Historical Database, 1976 to date; all others, current information

UPDATING

Daily

ONLINE AVAILABILITY

Telerate Systems Inc.

IIF COUNTRY DATABASE

Phone: (202) 856-3600

Institute of International Finance (IIF)
2000 Pennsylvania Ave., N.W., Suite 8500
Washington, DC 20006

TYPE

Time series, full text

CONTENT

Contains economic data for approximately 50 developing countries, with primary emphasis on the economic conditions and debt positions of borrowing nations. Includes annual time series of historical, current estimated, and forecast data covering central government budget information, balance of payments, long-term and total debt, and key economic indicators. Also contains commentaries on economic publications released by each country (e.g., statistical reports, restructuring reports, special analyses).

SUBJECT

Economies and debt positions of major debtor nations

COVERAGE

International

TIME SPAN

1978 to date

UPDATING

Periodically, as new data become available

ONLINE AVAILABILITY

GE Information Services (GEIS) (IIFDB, a Haver Analytics file. Available to IIF members only); Reuters Information Services (Canada) Ltd. (Institute of International Finance Country Evaluation System: Available to IIF members only)

INTERNATIONAL FINANCIAL STATISTICS

Phone: (202) 623-6180
Fax: (202) 623-4661

International Monetary Fund
Statistics Department
700 19th St., N.W.
Washington, D.C. 20431

TYPE

Time series

CONTENT

Contains more than 26,000 annual, quarterly, and monthly time series of economic and financial statistics on approximately 200 countries, supplemented by world and area aggregates for key time series. Topics covered include exchange rates (e.g., averages and closings); international liquidity (e.g., reserves, foreign assets, and liabilities of deposit banks); money and banking (e.g., interest rates, domestic credit, and money); interest rates, prices, and production (e.g., wholesale and consumer prices, wages, industrial production, and crude petroleum production); government finance (e.g., revenues and expenditures); international transactions (e.g., value, volume, prices of exports and imports, and capital transactions); national accounts (e.g., private consumption, investment, and gross domestic product); and population. Corresponds to the IMF publication *International Financial Statistics* (which provides additional information on sources of data, definitions, and other supple-

mental information) and the related computer tape subscription.

SUBJECT

Financial and general economic time series

COVERAGE

International

TIME SPAN

Annual series, 1948 to date; quarterly and monthly series, 1957 to date

UPDATING

Varies by online service, from monthly to every two months

ONLINE AVAILABILITY

FAME Information Services, Inc; DRI/McGraw-Hill (IMF); GE Information Services (GEIS); GSI-ECO; Reuters Information Services (Canada) Ltd.(IFS); The WEFA Group; Alternate Electronic

ALTERNATE ELECTRONIC FORMATS

CD-ROM (International Financial Statistics); Magnetic Tape (International Financial Statistics)

OECD FLOWS AND STOCKS OF FIXED CAPITAL

Phone: 331 49104265
Fax: 331 49104299

Organization for Economic Cooperation and Development (OECD)
Electronic Editions
2, rue Andre Pascal
F-75775 Paris Cedex 16, France

TYPE

Time series

CONTENT

Contains annual time series for 12 OECD member countries covering gross and net fixed capital stocks, gross fixed capital formation, and consumption of fixed capital, all at current and constant replacement cost. Data are further categorized by industry, product (e.g., construction and equipment), volumes, and local currencies. Data are presented "as is" and not standardized by the OECD, so not all series are available for all countries.

SUBJECT

Fixed capital information for selected OECD member countries

LANGUAGE

English; French

COVERAGE

International

TIME SPAN

1955 to date

UPDATING

Every two years

ONLINE AVAILABILITY

Reuters Information Services (Canada) Ltd. (OECD-CAP)

ALTERNATE ELECTRONIC FORMATS

Diskette (OECD Flows and Stocks of Fixed Capital); Magnetic Tape (OECD Flows and Stocks of Fixed Capital)

REUTER MONITOR CAPITAL MARKETS SERVICE

Phone: 071-250 0122
0800 010701
Fax: 071-696 8761

Reuters Ltd.
85 Fleet St.
London EC4P 4AJ, England

TYPE

Full text, numeric

CONTENT

Provides 13 services containing prices and commentary of interest to international capital markets. Includes subsets from approximately 60 files of financial, securities, commodities, energy, and general news information.

- Money/Financial Futures—International Money Service covers foreign exchange rates, money rates, bank note rates, and market commentary. Domestic Money Service covers U.S. government securities, bankers acceptances, certificates of deposit, commercial paper, discount notes, federal funds, domestic bonds, IBF rates, Canadian domestic money market, and market commentary.

- Grain/Livestock—contains grains and oilseeds market quotations, livestock market quotations, stock market indexes, and split page news files. Optionally includes grains and oilseeds news headlines, livestock news, National Provisioner, and business and market news and indexes.

- Metals—contains metal market quotations, stock market indexes, and news headlines. Includes con-

tributed coins and precious metals prices (North America), contributed coins and precious metals prices (International), and news headlines. Optionally includes business and market news and indexes, and metals news.

- Softs—contains coffee, cocoa, sugar, and orange juice market quotations, stock market indexes, and news headlines. Optionally includes coffee, cocoa, sugar, and cotton news headlines and business and market news and indexes.

- Energy—contains energy service, Energy Traders Service, The Reuter Pipeline, stock market indexes, and news headlines. Optionally includes U.S. industry and stock markets news, Petroleum Argues Report, Instant Oil Market analyses from Petroleum Analysis, Inc., and Petro Flash, and business and market news and indexes.

- Securities—contains Toronto Exchange quotations, options quotations, NASDAQ quotations, stock market indexes, news headlines, New York Stock Exchange (NYSE) consolidated quotations, and American Stock Exchange (AMEX) and regional consolidated quotations. Optionally includes Equity Market Analysis from MMS International, covering factors affecting the U.S. equity market, U.S. industry news and stock markets news, Canadian industry news, Newcomb securities, and business and market news and indexes.

- Optional News—contains U.S. industry and stock markets news, grains and oilseeds news, livestock news, coffee, cocoa, sugar, and cotton news, Canadian industry news, business and market news and indexes, metals news, money news and market quotations, energy news, and Reuters' money market statistics.

- Optional Domestic Data—contains financial and currency futures quotations, grains and oilseeds market quotations, livestock market quotations, coffee, cocoa, sugar, and orange juice market quotations, wood market quotations, metals market quotations, and AMEX gold coin exchange.

- Optional International Data—contains energy service, arbitrage of cocoa, copper, silver, sugar, and coffee, London metals quotations, and London-Paris soft commodities quotations.

- Optional Securities Quotations—contains Toronto Exchange quotations, options quotations, Montreal Exchange quotations, NASDAQ quotations, NYSE consolidated quotations, AMEX and regional consolidated quotations.

- Tickers—contains NYSE composite, AMEX composite, Chicago Board of Trade, Chicago Mercantile Exchange, coffee-cocoa-sugar, international monetary market-IOM, New York Commodity Exchange, London Commodities Exchange, Winnipeg Commodity Exchange, combined Canadian stock exchanges, NYSE 15-

minute-delayed composite, and AMEX 15-minute-delayed composite.

- Contributed Information—contains data on bids and offers furnished by companies trading in markets that have no central exchange. Covers international foreign exchange, domestic foreign exchange, U.S. government securities, domestic coins, international coins, non-ferrous and strategic metals, and Mocatta commodity options.

SUBJECT

International Capital Markets

COVERAGE

International

TIME SPAN

Current

UPDATING

Continuous

ONLINE AVAILABILITY

Reuters Ltd.

REUTER PRICELINK

Phone: 071-250 0122
0800 010701
Fax: 071-696 8781

Reuters Ltd.
85 Fleet St.
London EC4P 4AJ, England

TYPE

Numeric

CONTENT

Provides financial pricing and volume data from markets worldwide. Covers equities, market indicators, futures, mutual funds/unit trusts, options, bonds, Eurobonds, foreign exchange rates, and money market rates.

SUBJECT

Financial markets worldwide

ONLINE AVAILABILITY

Reuters Ltd.

REUTER SNAPSHOT

Phone: 071-250 0122
0800 010701
Fax: 071-696 8781

Reuters Ltd.
85 Fleet St.
London EC4P 4AJ, England

TYPE

Numeric

CONTENT

Contains quotes for more than 160,000 financial instruments traded on more than 100 exchanges worldwide. Covers equities, bonds, mutual and money market funds, futures, options, and index funds. Includes bid, ask, high, low, open, last trade, previous day's close, volume, and open interest rates. Also provides spot rates for 33 currencies and forward rates for 26 currencies, gold and silver prices, and more than 450 exchange and non-exchange market indexes, including the Dow Jones Average, Morgan Stanley Capital International, Value Line Averages, and Moody's. Quotes are available after a delay that varies by exchange.

SUBJECT

Financial prices covering equities, commodities, financial futures, options, indices, bonds, foreign exchange, and money market rates, and mutual funds.

COVERAGE

International

TIME SPAN

Current

UPDATING

Continuous

ONLINE AVAILABILITY

Reuters Ltd.

GENERAL

A MATTER OF FACT

Phone: (313) 434-5530
(800) 678-2435
Fax: (313) 434-6409

Pierian Press, Inc.
P.O. Box 1808
Ann Arbor, MI 48106

TYPE

Bibliographic; statistical

CONTENT

Contains more than 50,000 citations, with abstracts and statistics, to textual materials on current political, social, economic and environmental issues worldwide. Covers materials, with accompanying comparative statistical content, extracted from testimony presented at Congressional hearings by witnesses considered to be experts in their field, the *Congressional Record* reflecting statements made by U.S. senators and representatives, and approximately 250 general-interest periodicals and selected newspapers. Items are indexed using the Library of Congress (LC) subject headings. Corresponds to *A Matter of Fact: Statements Containing Statistics on Current Social, Economic and Political Issues.*

SUBJECT

Facts and research findings in social, economic, political, environmental, and other areas

COVERAGE

International

TIME SPAN

1985 to date

UPDATING

Semiannual

ONLINE AVAILABILITY

OCLC EPIC; OCLC First Search Catalog

ALTERNATE ELECTRONIC FORMATS

CD-ROM (Statistical Abstracts from the A Matter of Fact Database); Magnetic Tape (A Matter of Fact)

THE ECONOMIST

Phone: 0932 761444
Fax: 0932 781425

FT Business Enterprises Ltd.
Number One
Southwark Bridge
London SE1 9HL, England

TYPE

Full text

CONTENT

Contains the complete text of *The Economist*, a periodical providing worldwide coverage of politics, economics, business, finance, science, and technology. Emphasis is on developments in the United Kingdom, the United States, and continental Europe. Does not

include letters to the editor or reviews prior to June 1984.

SUBJECT

United Kingdom and international business and economic news

COVERAGE

United Kingdom, with some international, United States, and European coverage

TIME SPAN

1975 to date, NEXIS; December 26, 1981 to date, FT PROFILE

UPDATING

Weekly

ONLINE AVAILABILITY

NEXIS; FT PROFILE

Also Online as Part of: Reuter TEXTLINE (September 1980 to date) and LEXIS Country Information Service

ALTERNATE ELECTRONIC FORMATS

CD-ROM (*The Economist* on CD-ROM)

ECONOMIST INTELLIGENCE UNIT INTERNATIONAL STATISTICS

Phone: 071-493 6711
Fax: 071-499 9767

The Economist Intelligence Unit Ltd.
40 Duke St.
London W1A 1DW, England

FORMER DATABASE NAME

Country Credit Risk Service

TYPE

Time series; Full text

CONTENT

Contains more than 200 time series of macroeconomic data on non-Organization for Economic Cooperation and Development (OECD) countries. Includes monthly data for 66 developing countries and annual time series for seven Eastern-bloc countries. Covers national accounts (e.g., gross domestic product), population, trade, and national debt. Provides assessments of the credit worthiness of country economies by comprising data on political risk factors, economic and financial status, and short-term foreign exchange risk. Corresponds in part to *Country*

Credit Risk Service Handbook and *Economic Data Reference Guide.*

SUBJECT

Credit risk assessment of 66 developing countries

COVERAGE

International

TIME SPAN

1978 to date

UPDATING

Monthly

ONLINE AVAILABILITY

Reuters Information Services (Canada) Ltd.

ALTERNATE ELECTRONIC FORMATS

Diskette

LEXIS® COUNTRY INFORMATION SERVICE

Phone: (513) 865-6800
(800) 227-4908
Fax: (513) 865-6909

Mead Data Central, Inc.
9443 Springboro Pike
P.O. Box 933
Dayton, OH 45401-0933

TYPE

Full text

CONTENT

Contains international business and country assessment information. Comprises the following four files:

- Current News Alert (ALERT)—contains current international business, political and economic news items selected by Comtext Scientific Corporation from newswires worldwide. Updated every three hours.

- Country Analysis Reports Library (REPORT)—contains profiles of 64 countries, covering politics, economics, international trade, industrial development, business conditions, and corporate finances. Examples include *Australia Country Reports, Poland Country Reports,* and *Spain Country Reports.* Updated periodically, as new data become available.

- European News Library (EUROPE)—contains news, financial data, analysis, and legal/regulatory information. In addition to in-depth coverage of European topics, it offers particular value in its coverage of the European Community and 1992.

- International News (INTNEW)—contains the complete text of articles on international relations and foreign affairs from more than 40 periodicals.

SUBJECT

Economic and political analysis of the following countries/regions: Algeria, Argentina, Asia/Pacific, Australia, Austria, Belgium, Brazil, Canada, Chile, China, Columbia, Denmark, Ecuador, Egypt, Europe, Finland, France, East Germany, West Germany, Greece, Hong Kong, India, Indonesia, Ireland, Israel, Italy, Japan, Kuwait, South Korea, Libya, Malaysia, Mexico, Middle East/Africa, The Netherlands, New Zealand, Nigeria, North/South America, Norway, Pakistan, Panama, Peru, Philippines, Portugal, Saudi Arabia, Singapore, South Africa, Soviet Union, Spain, Sweden, Switzerland, Taiwan, Thailand, Turkey, United Arab Emirates. United Kingdom, the United States, Venezuela, and Yugoslavia; worldwide business and financial news

COVERAGE

International

TIME SPAN

Varies by source

UPDATING

Varies by file

ONLINE AVAILABILITY

LEXIS (ALERT, REPORT, EUROPE, INTNEW)

PREDICASTS FORECASTS

Phone: (415) 378-5000
(800) 321-5388
Fax: (415) 358-4759

Information Access Company
352 Lakeside Dr.
Foster City, CA 94404

FORMERLY PRODUCED BY

Predicasts

FORMER DATABASE NAME

PTS U.S. Forecasts and PTS International Forecasts

TYPE

Full text; numeric

CONTENT

Contains citations and data from published forecasts in trade journals, business and financial publications, key newspapers, government reports, and special studies. Coverage ranges from thousands of detailed products to entire economies, including forecasts, products, industries, demographics, and national income. Records generally contain historical base period data for one year, a short-term forecast, and a long-term forecast. There are currently more than one million records online. The files correspond to *Predicasts Forecasts* and *Worldcasts.*

NOTE: The U.S. and international forecasts are included in a single database through Data-Star. They are in separate databases through DIALOG Information Services, Inc.

SUBJECT

Economic forecasts

COVERAGE

United States and international

TIME SPAN

DIALOG, July 1971 to date; Data-Star, 1978 to date

UPDATING

Monthly

ONLINE AVAILABILITY

Data-Star (PTFC); DIALOG Information Services, Inc. (contact vendor for details); NEXIS (UFRCST, IFRCST: Transaction pricing, per-search pricing, and connect hour charging options available; contact vendor for details)

REUTER ECONLINE

Phone: (202) 898-8300

Reuters Information Services Inc.
1333 H St., N.W., Ste. 410
Washington, DC 20005

TYPE

Time series

CONTENT

Contains historical and forecast economic and financial time series for more than 200 countries. Includes international comparative statistics as well as detailed country-specific data for Australia, Canada, Germany, the United Kingdom, and the United States, covering population, labor force activity, industrial production, prices, national accounts, government finance, national debt, foreign trade, balance of payments, money supply, and currency exchange and interest rates. Also includes trade data for more than 3,000 commodities, and currency exchange and money market rates in various international markets. International sources include The Economist Intelligence Unit, International Monetary Fund, Organization for Economic Cooperation and Development, United Nations, Vienna Institute of

Comparative Economic Studies, and the World Bank. National sources include the Australian Bureau of Statistics, Citicorp Database Services, Deutsche Bundesbank, Statistics Canada, U.K. Central Statistical Office, U.S. Department of Labor, and the U.S. Federal Reserve Bank.

SUBJECT

Current and historical economic data worldwide

COVERAGE

International

TIME SPAN

1960 to date, with historical data back to 1913

UPDATING

Continuous

ONLINE AVAILABILITY

Reuters Ltd.

REUTER COUNTRY REPORTS

Phone: 071-250 0122
0800 010701
Fax: 071-696 8781

Reuters Ltd.
85 Fleet St.
London EC4P 4AJ, England

TYPE

Full text, numeric

CONTENT

Contains news and analyses of economic and political conditions worldwide. Includes the complete text of items from Reuters global newswire service covering 190 countries and territories. Also contains detailed reports on 100 countries, covering demographics, politics, membership in international organizations, geography and climate, banking and finance, local stock exchange activity, industry, agriculture, raw materials, armed forces, labor unions, communications, social welfare, and local customs. Reports also include biographies of leading political and business leaders, economic indicators (e.g., trade balance, net external debt), names and titles of leading government officials and summaries of recent key news events.

SUBJECT

Country profiles, including demographics, local customs, public holidays, geography and climate, power structure, politics, banking and finance, international financial data, national economic and financial data, companies and stock exchanges, industry, energy, raw materials, agriculture, transportation, communications and the media, armed forces, unions, social security and welfare, membership in international organizations, government officials, and news

COVERAGE

International

TIME SPAN

Current 90 days

UPDATING

Continuous

ONLINE AVAILABILITY

Reuters Ltd.

WORLD INFORMATION SERVICES

Phone: (415) 622-1446
(800) 645-6667
Fax: (415) 622-0909

Bank of America
World Information Services
Dept. 3015
P.O. Box 37000
San Francisco, CA 94137

TYPE

Full text; numeric

CONTENT

Provides a full range of global economic information covering 80 countries worldwide. Contains the following three report services:

- Country Outlooks—provides in-depth analysis of the business, financial, and economic environment expected for the coming two years for 30 countries.

- Country Data Forecasts—for 80 countries, provides major economic, financial, and demographic data, including 23 key economic indicators covering six years, an estimate for the current year, and five years of forecasts.

- Country Risk Monitor—contains business risk evaluations for 80 countries, including such criteria as income per capita, governmental fiscal responsibility, involvement in international trade, strength of trade performance, foreign indebtedness, and capacity to pay foreign debt.

SUBJECT

Economic and business risk assessment for 80 countries

COVERAGE

International

TIME SPAN

Current information

UPDATING

Semiannual

ONLINE AVAILABILITY

NEXIS (contact vendor for details)
Also Online as Part of: Quest Economics Database

WORLD FORECAST DATABASE

Phone: (215) 667-6000
Fax: (215) 660-6477

The WEFA Group
401 City Line Ave., Suite 300
Bala Cynwyd, PA 19004-1780

TYPE

Time series

CONTENT

Contains 7,000 annual time series of historical and forecast economic data for 23 Organization for Economic Cooperation and Development (OECD) countries and South Africa. Also includes 500 quarterly time series of historical and forecast economic data for Canada, Germany, France, Japan, the United Kingdom, and the United States. Includes expenditures on gross domestic product by use in nominal and real terms; foreign trade, including value and volume of imports and exports; balance of payments on current and capital accounts in local currency and U.S. dollars; and wages and employment. Also contains aggregate data for developing countries, oil-producing countries, centrally planned economies, developed nations, and world total. Sources include the International Monetary Fund, OECD, United Nations, and national source data.

SUBJECT

Economic data for 23 Organization for Economic Cooperation and Development and South Africa

COVERAGE

International, with emphasis on OECD countries

TIME SPAN

Annual data, 1960 to date, with six-year forecasts; quarterly data, 1970 to date, with 24-quarter short-term forecasts and 20-year long-term forecasts

UPDATING

Quarterly for quarterly forecast; biannual for long-term forecast

ONLINE AVAILABILITY

The WEFA Group

GERMANY

FAKT

Phone: 89 5600251
Fax: 89 5801996
Infratest Burke AG

Bereich Information und Dokumentation
Landsbergerstr. 338
D-80687 Munich 21, Germany

ALTERNATE DATABASE NAME

Economy and Market Tables and Reviews

TYPE

Statistical; Full text

CONTENT

Contains current statistical information relating to business, the economy, public affairs, social welfare, health care, media, technology, society, energy, and the environment in Germany and worldwide as reported in the German general and business press. Provides market data, market overviews, trends, market research, and economic indicators and forecasts. Records contain tabular data, usually with an informative abstract. Sources include some 150 newspapers, journals, and magazines as well as published Infratest Burke market research reports.

SUBJECT

German business, economy, public affairs, social welfare, health care, media technology, society, energy, and the environment

LANGUAGE

German; English titles, descriptors, subject classification, and country names

COVERAGE

Germany and Europe, with some international coverage

TIME SPAN

1989 to date

UPDATING

Monthly

ONLINE AVAILABILITY

Data-Star (FAKT); FIZ Technik; GENIOS Wirtschaftsdatenbanken (FAKT, Markt- und Wirtschaftsinformationen: DM 4.50/connect minute, DM 8.00/full record online); Gesellschaft fur Betriebswirtschaftliche Information mbH (GBI) (FAKT)

GOVERNMENT FINANCE

OECD REVENUE STATISTICS

Phone: 331 49104265
Fax: 331 49104299

Organization for Economic Cooperation and Development (OECD)
Electronic Editions
2, rue Andre Pascal
F-75775 Paris Cedex 16, France

TYPE

Time series

CONTENT

Contains annual time series of tax revenue statistics for OECD member countries. Provides breakdowns by government sector (e.g., supranational, central, state, local) and class of tax (e.g., import, export, consumption). Includes data on social security and payroll taxes paid by governments.

SUBJECT

Government tax revenues for member countries of OECD

COVERAGE

International

TIME SPAN

General government revenues, 1965 to date; revenues by government sector, 1973 to date

UPDATING

Annual

ONLINE AVAILABILITY

IBM Information Network Services-Europe (dropped); Nomura Securities Co., Ltd; DRI/McGraw-Hill;. GSI-ECO; Reuters Information Services (Canada) Ltd; The WEFA Group

INDUSTRY

INTERNATIONAL INDUSTRIAL MARKETS

Phone: (215) 667-6000
Fax: (215) 660-6477
The WEFA Group
401 City Line Ave., Suite 300
Bala Cynwyd, PA 19004-1780

TYPE

Time series

CONTENT

Contains time series of industrial market data for the United States, the United Kingdom, Germany, Japan, France, Italy, Belgium, Austria, Korea, and Spain. Contains detailed forecast information on output, prices, trade consumption, investment, employment, and sales to major markets.

SUBJECT

Industry forecasts

COVERAGE

International

TIME SPAN

1960 to date, with five-year forecasts

UPDATING

Quarterly

ONLINE AVAILABILITY

The WEFA Group

ALTERNATE ELECTRONIC FORMATS

Diskette (International Industrial Markets); Magnetic Tape (International Industrial Markets)

OECD INDICATORS OF INDUSTRIAL ACTIVITY

Phone: 331 49104265
Fax: 331 49104299

Organization for Economic Cooperation and Development (OECD)
Electronic Editions
2, rue Andre Pascal
F-75775 Paris Cedex 16, France

TYPE

Time series

CONTENT

Contains approximately 6,300 quarterly time series covering indexes of industrial production, deliveries, production prices, employment, new orders, and unfilled orders. Indicators are classified by industry groups according to the International Standard Industrial Classification. Corresponds to data released in the Indicators of Industrial Activity.

NOTE: On The WEFA Group, monthly and annual series are also available.

SUBJECT

International indicators of industrial activity, including production deliveries, prices, employment, new orders, and unfilled orders for each industrial grouping

COVERAGE

International

TIME SPAN

1975 to date

UPDATING

Quarterly

ONLINE AVAILABILITY

DRI/McGraw-Hill; GSI-ECO (IAI: OECD Industrial Activity Indicators); Reuters Information Services (Canada) Ltd. (OECDIIA); The WEFA Group (IAI)

Also Online as Part of: OECD Main Economic Indicators

ALTERNATE ELECTRONIC FORMATS

Diskette (OECD Indicators of Industrial Activity); Magnetic Tape (OECD Indicators of Economic Activity)

IRON AND STEEL

IRON AND STEEL

Phone: (215) 667-6000
Fax: (215) 660-6477

The WEFA Group
401 City Line Ave., Suite 300
Bala Cynwyd, PA 19004-1780
Former Database Name: World Steel; U.S. Steel

TYPE

Time series

CONTENT

Contains more than 2,000 weekly, monthly, quarterly, and annual historical time series on supply, demand, and trade for the U.S. and worldwide iron and steel industry. Includes prices by city for number one heavy melting steel scrap; data on pig iron, iron ore, and scrap iron; time series for steel industry employment; and crude steel production, consumption, imports, and exports for 75 countries. Sources include the American Iron and Steel Institute, the U.S. Bureau of Mines, and the International Iron and Steel Institute.

SUBJECT

International steel and iron mill statistics, including shipments by product, by grade (carbon, alloy, stainless), imports and exports by product, raw steel production by furnace type and region, and steel mill shipments by product by market

COVERAGE

United States and international

TIME SPAN

1972 to date, with additional data from as early as 1960

UPDATING

Weekly

ONLINE AVAILABILITY

The WEFA Group

ALTERNATE ELECTRONIC FORMATS

Diskette (Iron and Steel); Magnetic Tape (Iron and Steel)

LABOR

OECD ANNUAL LABOR FORCE STATISTICS

Phone: 331 49104265
Fax: 331 49104299

Organization for Economic Cooperation and Development (OECD)
Electronic Editions
2, rue Andre Pascal
F-75775 Paris Cedex 16, France

TYPE

Time series

CONTENT

Contains annual time series for 25 OECD member countries (Australia, Austria, Belgium, Canada, Denmark, Germany, Finland, France, Greece, Iceland, Ireland, Italy, Japan, Luxembourg, the Netherlands, New Zealand, Norway, Portugal, Spain, Sweden, Switzerland, Turkey, United Kingdom, the United States, and Yugoslavia). Covers main labor force aggregates with breakdowns by major economic sector and detailed data for each country, including population by age and gender; major component of labor force; civilian employment by professional status and by major divisions of the International Standard Industrial Classification (ISIC) code; and manufacturing employment by ISIC. Corresponds to data published in *OECD Labor Force Statistics Yearbook*.

Also includes quarterly (with some monthly) time series on the main components of the labor force for 14 OECD member countries (Australia, Austria, Canada, Germany, Finland, France, Italy, Japan, Norway, Spain, Sweden, Switzerland, the United Kingdom, and the United States). Includes breakdown of civilian employment by major economic sectors and unemployment by gender and age group. Corresponds to data in *Quarterly Labor Force Statistics*.

NOTE: On Reuters Information Services (Canada) Ltd., data are available in two separate databases: the Organization for Economic Cooperation and Development Annual Labour Force Statistics and Quarterly Labour Force Statistics.

SUBJECT

International labor force statistics

COVERAGE

International

TIME SPAN

1963 to date

UPDATING

Annual

ONLINE AVAILABILITY

Reuters Information Services (Canada) Ltd. (OEC-DALF); Wirtschafts- und Sozialwissenschaftliches Rechenzentrum (WSR)

Also Online as Part of: OECD Main Economic Indicators

ALTERNATE ELECTRONIC FORMATS

Magnetic Tape (OECD Annual Labor Force Statistics)

OECD QUARTERLY LABOR FORCE STATISTICS

Phone: 331 49104265
Fax: 331 49104299

Organization for Economic Cooperation and Development (OECD)
Electronic Editions
2, rue Andre Pascal
F-75775 Paris Cedex 16, France

TYPE

Time series

CONTENT

Contains annual and quarterly data on the main components of the labor force, the breakdown of civilian employment by major economic sectors, and employment by gender and age group. Presented in three forms: absolute figures, indexes, and percentages. Corresponds to data in *OECD Quarterly Labor Force Statistics*.

SUBJECT COVERAGE

International labor

COVERAGE

International (OECD countries)

TIME SPAN

1965 to date

UPDATING

Quarterly

ONLINE AVAILABILITY

Reuters Information Services (Canada) Ltd. (OECDQLF)

Also Online as Part of: OECD Main Economic Indicators

ALTERNATE ELECTRONIC FORMATS

Diskette (OECD Quarterly Labor Force Statistics); Magnetic Tape (OECD Quarterly Labor Force Statistics)

LATIN AMERICA

DRI LATIN AMERICAN FORECAST

Phone: (617) 863-5100
DRI/McGraw-Hill
Data Products Division
24 Hartwell Ave.
Lexington, MA 02173

TYPE

Time series

CONTENT

Contains annual historical and forecast time series for eight Latin America economies. Includes more than 100 series for Brazil, Mexico, and Venezuela; more than 50 series for Argentina, Chile, Colombia, Ecuador, and Peru; and 20 series for all countries combined. Covers gross domestic product (GDP) by type of expenditure, inflation, foreign debt positions, money supply, exchange rates, trade and balance of payments, industrial production, income, and population. Forecasts are linked to DRI projections for other world economies. Data are derived from DRI Developing Countries Data Bank, DRI External Debt Data Base, DRI Latin American Models, and IMF International Financial Statistics Data Bank.

SUBJECT

Latin American economy and finance, including GDP by type of expenditure; inflation rates; income; population; trade and balance of payments accounts; industrial production; foreign debt positions; money supply; and exchange rates

COVERAGE

Latin America

TIME SPAN

Earliest series from 1970s, with 10-year forecasts

UPDATING

Quarterly

ONLINE AVAILABILITY

DRI/McGraw-Hill (@LATAM/MODELBANK)

LEAD AND ZINC

INTERNATIONAL LEAD AND ZINC

Phone: (215) 667-6000
Fax: (215) 660-6477

The WEFA Group
401 City Line Ave., Suite 300
Bala Cynwyd, PA 19004-1780

TYPE
Time series

CONTENT
Contains approximately 1,400 monthly, quarterly, and annual time series on lead and zinc. Covers metal consumption, mine production, metal production, principal end uses, stocks, recovery of secondary lead and zinc, and trade with Socialist countries. Data are obtained from the monthly publication *Lead and Zinc Statistics*, published by the International Lead and Zinc Study Group.

SUBJECT
Worldwide lead and zinc statistics, covering metal consumption and production, mine production, principal end uses, stocks, recovery of secondary lead and zinc, and trade with socialist countries

COVERAGE
International

TIME SPAN
1955 to date

UPDATING
Monthly

ONLINE AVAILABILITY
The WEFA Group (BMETAL)

ALTERNATE ELECTRONIC FORMATS
Diskette (International Lead and Zinc); Magnetic Tape (International Lead and Zinc)

MIDDLE EAST

DRI MIDDLE EAST AND AFRICA FORECAST

Phone: (617) 863-5100

DRI/McGraw-Hill
Data Products Division
24 Hartwell Ave.
Lexington, MA 02173

CONTACT
Client Services

TYPE
Time series

CONTENT
Contains more than 500 annual historical and forecast time series for 10 Middle Eastern and African economies. Covers gross domestic product (GDP) by type of expenditure; inflation rates; income; population; trade and balance of payments accounts; oil production; foreign debt positions; money supply; and exchange rates.

SUBJECT
Middle East and Africa economy and finance

COVERAGE
Middle Eastern and African countries

TIME SPAN
Earliest series from 1950, with 10- to 15-year forecasts

UPDATING
Quarterly

ONLINE AVAILABILITY
DRI/McGraw-Hill

MIDDLE EAST AND AFRICA FORECAST

Phone: (215) 667-6000
Fax: (215) 660-6477

The WEFA Group
401 City Line Ave., Suite 300
Bala Cynwyd, PA 19004-1780

TYPE
Time series

CONTENT

Contains approximately 1,600 annual time series of historical and forecast data on the economies of countries in the Middle East and Africa. Includes national income accounts; exports, imports, and petroleum trade balance; balance of payments accounts; financial and inflation indicators; and external debt. Countries covered are Algeria, Bahrain, Egypt, Ghana, Iran, Iraq, Ivory Coast, Kenya, Kuwait, Libya, Morocco, Nigeria, Oman, Qatar, Saudi Arabia, South Africa, Tunisia, United Arab Emirates, Zaire, Zimbabwe, Gabon, Turkey, and Cameroon.

SUBJECT

Middle Eastern and African countries

COVERAGE

Middle Eastern and African countries

TIME SPAN

Most data from the 1970s, with some earlier data from 1965; five-year forecasts

UPDATING

Quarterly for South Africa, Tunisia, and Turkey; annual for all other countries

ONLINE AVAILABILITY

The WEFA Group

ALTERNATE ELECTRONIC FORMATS

Diskette (Middle East and Africa Forecast); Magnetic Tape (Middle East and Africa Forecast)

PETROLEUM

APIBIZ

Phone: (212) 366-4040
Fax: (212) 366-4298

American Petroleum Institute (API)
Central Abstracting & Information Services
275 Seventh Ave., 9th Floor
New York, NY 10001-6708

ALTERNATE DATABASE NAME

API Energy Business News Index

FORMER DATABASE NAME

P/E News

TYPE

Bibliographic

CONTENT

Contains more than 645,000 citations to the petroleum and energy business news literature. Covers news of plans and actions of government agencies, corporations, and other organizations; economic factors, such as supply, demand, taxation, and labor matters; and environmental issues. Sources include *Middle East Economic Survey, The Oil Daily, The Petroleum Economist, Petroleum Intelligence Weekly, Platt's Oilgram News, Oil and Gas Journal, National Petroleum News, Asian Oil and Gas, Comparative Appraisal Report, Lubricants World, The Lundberg Letter, International Petroleum Finance, Petroleum Outlook, U.S. Oil Week, Bulletin de l'Industrie Petroliere, Petroleum Market Intelligence, Oil Prices Information Service, World Gas Intelligence,* and *World Oil*.

Also contains citations to statistical information on capital and exploration outlays, comparative product costs, salaries for petroleum engineers, refineries under construction, crude reserves, and tanker freight rates. Corresponds to the *Guide to Petroleum Statistical Information*.

SUBJECT

Political, social, economic, government, corporation, and personal news related to all aspects of the petroleum and energy industries ranging from exploration and drilling contracts to marketing of products

COVERAGE

International

TIME SPAN

1975 to date

UPDATING

650 records a week

ONLINE AVAILABILITY

Data-Star (contact vendor for details); DIALOG Information Services, Inc. (contact vendor for details); ORBIT•QUESTEL (contact vendor for details)

DRI/TBS WORLD OIL FORECAST

Phone: (617) 863-5100
DRI/McGraw-Hill

Data Products Division
24 Hartwell Ave.
Lexington, MA 02173

CONTACT

Client Services

TYPE

Time series

CONTENT

Contains approximately 250 quarterly and annual forecasts of production, stocks, consumption, and prices of crude oil worldwide. Covers seven major industrial countries (Canada, Germany, France, Italy, Japan, the United Kingdom, and the United States), Organization of Petroleum Exporting Countries (OPEC), Mexico, other less-developed countries, communist countries, and non-communist countries. Forecasts reflect worldwide growth, currency exchange rates, crude inventories, and OPEC and non-OPEC supply policies in specific countries.

SUBJECT

Worldwide crude oil production, supply stocks, consumption, and prices

COVERAGE

International

TIME SPAN

15- to 20-year forecasts, with historical series from 1975

UPDATING

Quarterly

ONLINE AVAILABILITY

DRI/McGraw-Hill

IEA QUARTERLY OIL STATISTICS

Phone: 01 45249887

Organization for Economic Cooperation and Development (OECD)
International Energy Agency (IEA)
2, rue Andre Pascal
F-75775 Paris Cedex 16, France

TYPE

Time series

CONTENT

Contains time series data covering oil supply and demand in the OECD countries. Figures are given in thousands of metric tons except natural gas, which is in millions of cubic meters. Covers balances of production, trade, refinery intake and output, final consumption, and stock levels and changes for crude oil, natural gas liquids, feed stocks, and nine product groups; imports and exports by origin and destination for liquefied petroleum gases, naphtha, and the main

product groups; natural gas supply and consumption; and deliveries to international civil aviation by product group. Data are derived from OECD-member countries, national statistical agencies, and international organizations.

SUBJECT

Oil supply and demand

COVERAGE

International

TIME SPAN

1974 to 1982

UPDATING

Not updated

ONLINE AVAILABILITY

Reuters Information Services (Canada) Ltd. (QOS)

INTERNATIONAL PETROLEUM ANNUAL

Phone: (202) 586-8800

U.S. Energy Information Administration
1000 Independence Ave., S.W.
Washington, DC 20585

CONTACT

National Energy Information Center

TYPE

Time series

CONTENT

Contains approximately 2,100 annual time series from Table 6 of the Department of Energy's International Petroleum Annual covering international supply and demand for crude oil and petroleum products for more than 100 countries and geographic regions. Statistics include domestic production, imports, exports, stocks, refineries, refinery outputs, and domestic demand.

SUBJECT

Crude petroleum and refined petroleum products, including production, exports, imports, stocks, refinery output, and domestic demand for more than 100 countries

COVERAGE

International

TIME SPAN

1960 to 1978

UPDATING

Not updated

ONLINE AVAILABILITY

Reuters Information Services (Canada) Ltd. There is no subscription fee for this database

Also Online as Part of: Petroleum Supply Monthly

OECD OIL AND GAS STATISTICS

Phone: 331 49104265
Fax: 331 49104299

Organization for Economic Cooperation and Development (OECD)
Electronic Editions
2, rue Andre Pascal
F-75775 Paris Cedex 16, France

TYPE

Time series

CONTENT

Contains monthly, quarterly, and annual oil and gas statistics of the OECD member countries. Includes statistics on production and import and export data of each member country.

SUBJECT

Oil and gas statistics

COVERAGE

OECD member countries

TIME SPAN

1970 to date

UPDATING

Monthly

ONLINE AVAILABILITY

Wirtschafts- und Sozialwissenschaftliches Rechenzentrum (WSR)

REUTER PIPELINE

Phone: (202) 898-8300

Reuters Information Services Inc.
1333 H St., N.W., Ste. 410
Washington, DC 20005

TYPE

Full text; numeric

CONTENT

Contains information on European and U.S. petroleum markets for gasoline, gas oil, naphtha, and kerosene. Includes spot market prices and notification of confirmed sales for Arab Light, Brent, Durbai, and West Texas Intermediate crudes and crudes from Libya, Egypt, and Indonesia. Includes netback calculations for topping and cracking refineries in the U.S. Gulf Coast, Singapore, northwest Europe, and the Mediterranean.

SUBJECT

European and U.S. petroleum markets

COVERAGE

International

TIME SPAN

Current two months

UPDATING

Daily, usually by 4:00pm Central Time (close of trading in Houston, Texas)

ONLINE AVAILABILITY

Reuters Ltd.; Reuters Information Services (Canada) Ltd.

REUTER SPOTLINE

Phone: 071-250 0122
0800 010701
Fax: 071-696 8781

Reuters Ltd.
85 Fleet St.
London EC4P 4AJ, England

TYPE

Time series; full text

CONTENT

Contains current and historical time series on spot and futures prices for crude oil, natural gas, petroleum products, and petrochemicals. Covers spot prices for major crudes, refined petroleum products, and petrochemicals worldwide, and spot prices for natural gas in various U.S. regional markets; netback values for 20 world crudes and for refined petroleum products for European, Asian, and U.S. markets; and futures prices from the New York Mercantile Exchange and the International Petroleum Exchange for crude oil and refined petroleum products. Also includes market analyses and commentary. Sources include the ICIS-LOR group, Petroleum Argues, Reuters, and others.

SUBJECT

Energy markets

COVERAGE

International

TIME SPAN

Varies by series, with earliest data from 1973

UPDATING

Continuous

ONLINE AVAILABILITY

Reuters Ltd.

REUTER SUPPLYLINE

Phone: 071-250 0122
0800 010701
Fax: 071-696 8781

Reuters Ltd.
85 Fleet St.
London EC4P 4AJ, England

TYPE

Numeric

CONTENT

Contains current and historical volumetric time series on oil and gas exploration, production, inventories, and imports and exports worldwide. Covers land and marine seismic crews and rigs; international production of primary energy products and crude oil; Organization of Petroleum Exporting Countries production estimates; and U.S. refinery output; international imports and exports of crude oil, gas, and coal; U.S. imports and exports of crude oil and refined petroleum products; and Japanese imports of crude oil and refined petroleum products; and petroleum stock for Organization for Economic Cooperation and Development countries and the United States. Also includes data on refinery operations and transportation, sales, and consumption of energy products in the U.S. and worldwide. Sources include the American Petroleum Institute, Baker Hughes, Chemical Market Associates, Inc., DeWitt and Company, ICIS-LOR Group, Japanese Ministry of Trade and Industry, Society of Exploration Geophysicists, the U.S. Department of Energy, and others.

SUBJECT

Energy industry statistics, including oil drilling exploration, production, imports and exports, and crude oil supplies and products

COVERAGE

International

TIME SPAN

Varies by series, with earliest data from 1971

UPDATING

Varies by series

ONLINE AVAILABILITY

Reuters Ltd.

WORLD PETROCHEMICAL INDUSTRY SURVEY

Phone: 02 4801979
Fax: 02 48008107

Parpinelli TECNON srl
Via Egadi 7
I-20144 Milan, Italy

FORMER DATABASE NAME

European Petrochemical Industry Computerized System (EPICS)

TYPE

Time series; full text

CONTENT

Contains time series, analyses, and forecasts covering the worldwide energy, petroleum, and petrochemical industries. Covers developments and trends, and includes information on producers. Typical data elements include plant location, capacity, production, raw materials requirements, total imports and exports, and consumption.

SUBJECT

The worldwide energy, petroleum, petrochemical industry, covering such products as ethylene, propylene, butadiene, benzene, toluene, petrochemical intermediates, olefins, plastics, resins, feed stocks, rubbers, and fibers

COVERAGE

International

TIME SPAN

1978 to 2005

UPDATING

Annual

ONLINE AVAILABILITY

Parpinelli TECNON srl

ALTERNATE ELECTRONIC FORMATS

Diskette (World Petrochemical Industry Survey)

POPULATION

UN DEMOGRAPHICS

Phone: (212) 754-3217

United Nations
Department of International Economic
  and Social Affairs
Population Division, Estimates and
  Projection Section
New York, NY 10017

TYPE

Time series

CONTENT

Contains approximately 9,200 time series in five-year intervals of historical and forecast demographic data for 165 countries and regional aggregates. Includes ratios of total population by age groups; birth, death, growth, reproduction, and fertility rates; life expectancies; and urban and working-age populations. Data may be retrieved by country and international region. Sources of data include *World Population Prospects as Assessed in 1984* and *Demographic Indicators of Countries*.

SUBJECT

Worldwide historical and forecast demographic data

COVERAGE

International

TIME SPAN

1950 to date; projections to 2025

UPDATING

Annual

ONLINE AVAILABILITY

GE Information Services (GEIS) (UNPOP: United Nations Population Statistics); The WEFA Group (UNPOP)

RISK

INTERNATIONAL COUNTRY RISK GUIDE

Phone: (315) 472-1224
Fax: (315) 472-1236

IBC USA Licensing Inc.
Political Risk Services (PRS)
222 Teall Ave., Suite 200
P.O. Box 6482
Syracuse, NY 13217-6482

TYPE

Full text

CONTENT

Contains the complete text of *International Country Risk Guide*, a monthly publication providing analyses of economic, financial, and political risks that may affect business opportunities in more than 130 countries. Each in-depth analysis provides both current information and forecasts.

Coverage is provided in five separate files arranged by region: The Americas, Europe, Middle East and North Africa, Sub-Saharan Africa, and Asia and the Pacific.

SUBJECT

Political and economic analysis of countries worldwide

COVERAGE

International

YEAR FIRST AVAILABLE

1991

TIME SPAN

1991 to date

UPDATING

Monthly

ONLINE AVAILABILITY

NewsNet, Inc. IT11-IT14, IT16: (contact vendor for details)

Also Online as Part of: Newsletter Database

WORLD RISK ANALYSIS PACKAGE (WRAP)

Phone: (212) 838-0141

S.J. Rundt & Associates
130 E. 63rd St.
New York, NY 10021

TYPE
Full text; numeric

CONTENT
Contains complete text of risk-analysis business reports for 61 countries throughout the world, covering S.J. Rundt's assessments of a country's socio-political, domestic-economic, and external accounts prospects. Includes a socio-political prognosis (e.g., prospects for stability, official attitude toward foreign investment, labor market trends, role of government in the economy); domestic market forecast (e.g., economic growth prospects, market potential, outlook for inflation and credit conditions, monetary and fiscal policies); and external account projections (e.g., current-account balance of payments, exchange reserves and foreign debt, trade restrictions and collection reliability, exchange controls and currency outlook). Also provides a generic risk rating for each country. Statistical tables accompanying the text present current and historical data derived from local government releases, private surveys, and such organizations as the International Monetary Fund and the World Bank.

SUBJECT
Worldwide economic, financial, political, and social conditions relating to international business

COVERAGE
International

TIME SPAN
Current Information

UPDATING
Periodically, as new data become available; each country updated at least once a year

ONLINE AVAILABILITY
Reuters Information Services (Canada) Ltd. (SJRUNDT: Available by subscription)

ALTERNATE ELECTRONIC FORMATS
Diskette

TRADE

DIRECTION OF TRADE STATISTICS (DOTS)

Phone: (202) 623-6180
Fax: (202) 623-4661

International Monetary Fund (IMF)
Statistics Department
700 19th St., N.W.
Washington, DC 20431

ALTERNATE DATABASE NAME
IMF Direction of Trade

TYPE
Time series

CONTENT
Contains more than 60,000 monthly, quarterly, and annual time series of import and export statistics for 160 countries and their trading partners. These country/partner data are supplemented by world and area aggregates. All exports are valued on FOB (free on board) and all imports are valued on CIF (cost, insurance, and freight). All data are expressed in U.S. dollars. Corresponds to the IMF publication *Direction of Trade Statistics* and the related IMF computer tape subscription.

SUBJECT
Import and export trade statistics

COVERAGE
International

TIME SPAN
1948 to date (annual data); 1960 to date (quarterly data); 1965 to date (monthly data)

UPDATING
Monthly

ONLINE AVAILABILITY
DRI/McGraw-Hill (IMFDOT); Reuters Information Services (Canada) Ltd. (DOT); The WEFA Group

ALTERNATE ELECTRONIC FORMATS
Magnetic Tape (IMF Direction of Trade)

DRI/TBS WORLD SEA TRADE FORECAST

Phone: (617) 863-5100

DRI/McGraw-Hill
Data Products Division
24 Hartwell Ave.
Lexington, MA 02173

CONTACT

Client Services

TYPE

Time series

CONTENT

Contains more than three million historical and forecast time series on worldwide waterborne trade. Covers 205 major trading routes (e.g., U.S. Southern Pacific Coast to Japan), 40 commodity categories, and 18 vessel types, and provides data by metric tonnage, 20-foot equivalent units (TEUs), and value.

SUBJECT

Cargo movements over major trade routes worldwide

COVERAGE

International

TIME SPAN

Annual series, 1981 to date; quarterly series, 1985 to date; five-year forecasts

UPDATING

Quarterly

ONLINE AVAILABILITY

DRI/McGraw-Hill

DRI/TBS WORLD TRADE FORECAST

Phone: (617) 863-5100

DRI/McGraw-Hill
Data Products Division
24 Hartwell Ave.
Lexington, MA 02173

CONTACT

Client Services

FORMER DATABASE NAME

DRI World Trade Forecast

TYPE

Time series

CONTENT

Contains approximately 82,000 annual historical and forecast time series on import and export volumes, and prices in current U.S. dollars. Covers trade for 43 commodity types between 19 member countries of the Organization for Economic Cooperation and Development (OECD) and 25 regions of the world. Data are derived from the DRI ITIS Detailed Monthly Trade Monitor database, DRI ITIS Trade Series C, and DRI World Trade Model.

SUBJECT

Foreign trade forecasts for OECD countries that import and export more than 40 commodities within 25 regions worldwide

COVERAGE

International

TIME SPAN

Earliest series from 1978, with five-year forecasts

UPDATING

Quarterly

ONLINE AVAILABILITY

DRI/McGraw-Hill

OECD OVERALL TRADE BY COUNTRY

Phone: 331 49104265
Fax: 331 49104299

Organization for Economic Cooperation and Development (OECD)
Electronic Editions
2, rue Andre Pascal
F-75775 Paris Cedex 16, France

TYPE

Statistical

CONTENT

Contains monthly historical bilateral trade data between OECD member countries and other countries throughout the world. Includes other significant foreign trade data as well.

SUBJECT

OECD trade data, including seasonally adjusted import and export figures for individual OECD countries; volume, price, and average value indexes for OECD countries by main commodity categories;

monthly trade by single-digit SITC sections for some OECD countries; and foreign trade of OECD member countries by partner countries

COVERAGE

International (OECD Countries)

TIME SPAN

1960 to date

UPDATING

Monthly

ONLINE AVAILABILITY

Reuters Information Services (Canada) Ltd. (OECD-TRA): Foreign Trade Statistics

OECD STATISTICS OF FOREIGN TRADE: SERIES A (OECDTRA)

Phone: 331 49104265
Fax: 331 49104299

Organization for Economic Cooperation and Development (OECD)
Electronic Editions
2, rue Andre Pascal
F-75775 Paris Cedex 16, France

TYPE

Time series

CONTENT

Contains approximately 31,000 monthly, quarterly, and annual time series on trade for OECD member countries, by origin and destination and by major commodity categories for the analysis of trade flows. These data cover 105 countries and regions with which the OECD countries are associated in trade. Data are organized by Standard Industrial Trade Classification (SITC) codes. Corresponds to the data published by OECD in *Statistics of Foreign Trade: Series A Monthly Bulletin.*

SUBJECT

Trade for OECD members

COVERAGE

International

TIME SPAN

1960 to date

UPDATING

Monthly

ONLINE AVAILABILITY

Reuters Information Services (Canada) Ltd; Wirtschafts- und Sozialwissenschaftliches Rechenzentrum (WSR)

ALTERNATE ELECTRONIC FORMATS

Diskette; Magnetic Tape (OECD Monthly Foreign Trade Statistics - Series A)

SICE: FOREIGN TRADE INFORMATION SYSTEM

Phone: (202) 458-3725
Fax: (202) 458-3907

Organization of American States (OAS)
General Secretariat
1889 F St., N.W.
Washington, DC 20006-4413

ALTERNATE DATABASE NAME

Sistema de Informacion al Comercio Exterior (SICE)

TYPE

Full text; directory; numeric; statistical

CONTENT

Provides information on the U.S. import and export markets as well as some coverage of the markets of Organization of American States member countries. Coverage is expected to include European Community countries and Japan.

Comprises the following 11 subfiles:

- U.S. Harmonized Tariff Schedule, Annotated - 1992—provides the official Harmonized Tariff Schedule classification number, article description, units of measurement, and applicable rates of duty.

- U.S. Imports for Consumption Statistics—covers U.S. imports for consumption statistics by product; each table contains tariff schedule commodity classification number, article description, units of measurement, country of origin, imported quantity, dollar value, CIF (cost, insurance, and freight) value, duty value, actual duties paid, duty percentage rate, and aggregate amount for each column.

- U.S. Exports - Statistics—covers U.S. export statistics by product.

- U.S. Directory of Importers—contains information on U.S. companies engaged in importing goods; provides company name and address, contact person, bank utilized by importer for transactions, broker or agent, usual ports of entry, Harmonized Tariff Schedule commodity classification number and description of imported articles, country of origin, and registered trade names used by company.

- U.S. Directory of Exporters—contains information on U.S. companies engaged in exporting goods; provides company name and address, contact person, bank utilized by exporter for transactions, broker or agent, usual ports of exit, statistical classification number (Schedule B) and description of exported articles, country of destination, and registered trade names used by company.

- U.S. Import/Export Maritime Bills of Lading—each bill of lading provides country of origin or destination of the merchandise, name of exporter/shipper, arrival date, shipping line, port of origin and of discharge, commodity description, units of measurement, weight in metric tons, and name of U.S. consignee/importer.

- U.S. Markets Primary Wholesale Selling Prices—provides wholesale prices on the following commodities traded on U.S. markets and/or exchanges: cotton, grain, dairy products, livestock, poultry, fruits, vegetables, nuts, ornamentals and honey, tobacco, fresh and frozen fish and shellfish, spices, some frozen and canned foods and juices, and crop production forecasts; prices are updated daily.

- U.S. Code of Federal Regulations (CFR)—provides the complete text of those CFR titles that directly or indirectly affect international trade in the United States; revised annually.

- U.S. Federal Register—contains the complete text of the regulations and legal notices issued by U.S. government agencies; updated each working day.

- Business Opportunities of Supply and Demand—enables the user to learn of or place advertising for supplies and demands of products and services.

- Mexico - Directory of Exporters/Importers—provides the following information: company name and address, contact person, bank utilized for transactions, broker or agent, classification number at the four-digit level and description of products, country of destination or origin, number of employees, and year when company initiated its trading activities.

Online consultation and electronic mail capabilities are also available.

SUBJECT

U.S. import and export markets

LANGUAGE

English; Spanish

COVERAGE

International

TIME SPAN

1983 to date

UPDATING

Varies by file

ONLINE AVAILABILITY

Organization of American States, General Secretariat (contact vendor for details.)

UN WORLD TRADE STATISTICS

Phone: 1 515190
Fax: 1 5134258

Wirtschafts- und Sozialwissenschaftliches
Rechenzentrum (WSR)
Wollzeile 1-3
POB 622
A-1010 Vienna, Austria

TYPE

Numeric

CONTENT

Contains world trade flow data on Standard Industrial Trade Classifications (SITC) 3 digit commodity groups for some 100 reporting countries and their trade partners worldwide. Import and export data can be obtained on a value and quantity basis. The data are collected by the United Nations.

SUBJECT

World trade data

COVERAGE

International

TIME SPAN

1989 to date

UPDATING

Semiannual

ONLINE AVAILABILITY

Wirtschafts- und Sozialwissenschaftliches
Rechenzentrum (WSR)

UNITED NATIONAL COMMODITY TRADE STATISTICS

Phone: (416) 364-5361
(800) 387-1588
Fax: (416) 364-0646

Reuters Information Services (Canada) Ltd. Data
Services Division
Exchange Tower, Suite 2000, P.O. Box 418
2 First Canadian Place
Toronto, ON, Canada M5X 1E3

TYPE

Time series

CONTENT

Contains value and quantity statistics of international
commodity trade in 3,000 commodities for 31
selected reporting countries. Includes details on trade
with 270 other countries and country groupings
defined according to the Standard International
Trade Classification (SITC) Revision Two. Quantity
data is available only for commodities at the four- and
five-digit level of classification. (The SITC is a hierar-
chical, five-digit classification system in which each
digit describes successive levels of detail.) Data are
provided by the United Nations Statistical Division
and used with the permission of the United Nations.

COVERAGE

International commodity trade statistics

COVERAGE

International

TIME SPAN

1976 to date

UPDATING

As needed

ONLINE AVAILABILITY

Reuters Information Services (Canada) Ltd. (SITC)

WORLD TRADE STATISTICS DATABASE (TRADSTAT)

Phone: 071-930-5503
Fax: 071-930-2581

Data-Star
Haymarket House
1 Oxenden St.
London SW1Y 4EE, England

TYPE

Numeric

CONTENT

Contains approximately 50 million annual and
monthly time series on imports and exports of more
than 65,000 commodities and products between 16
major trading countries and all of their trading partners. For each commodity or product, provides
reporting country, value of shipment, weights, alternative volume unit, trading countries, price, month, and
cumulative year-to-date figures. Trend analyses,
deduced trading reports, and monthly currency
exchange rates are also available. Also includes
annual data for selected other countries. Data are
obtained from national statistical and customs offices.

SUBJECT

Import and export trade statistics for a variety of
products traded worldwide

COVERAGE

International

TIME SPAN

1981 to date

UPDATING

Daily, as new data become available

ONLINE AVAILABILITY

Data-Star

APPENDIX A:

DIRECTORY OF PUBLISHERS

This Appendix includes contact information for publishers represented in the *Global Data Locator* as well as other authoritative publishing organizations around the world. Arranged alphabetically by publisher, it is intended to be used by readers seeking further references to organizations that compile and publish international data.

Asian Productivity Organization: 4-14 Akasaka, 8-chome Minato-ku, Tokyo 107

Association of European Airlines: 350 Avenue, Louise Bte 4, 1050 Brussels

Association of Southeast Asian Nations: 70A Keboyoran Baru, P. O. Box 2072, Jakarta 12110

Basil Blackwell: 108 Cowley Road, Oxford OX4 1JF, United Kingdom

British Geological Survey: Keyworth, Nottingham NG12 5GG, United Kingdom

British Paper and Board Industry Federation: Papermakers House, Rivenhall Road, Westlea, Swindon, SN5 7BE United Kingdom

British Petroleum Company: Britannic House, 1 Finsbury Circus, London EC2M 7BA

Caribbean Community Secretariat: P. O. Box 10827, Bank of Guyana Building, Third Floor, Avenue of the Republic, Georgetown, Guyana

Chamber of Shipping: 30-32 St. Mary Axe, London EC3A 8ET

Chemical Industries Association: King's Building, Smiths Square, London SW1P 3JJ

Civil Aviation Authority: Greville House, 37 Grafton Road, Cheltenham, Gloucestershire GL50 2BN United Kingdom

Commonwealth Secretariat: Marlborough House, Pall Mall, London SW1Y 5HX

Confederation of British Industry: Centre Point, 103 New Oxford Street, London WC1A 1 DU

Council of Europe: Strasbourg, France

Croom Helm: 11 New Fetter Lane, London EC4P 4EE

Drewry Shipping Consultants: 11 Heron Quay, London E14 4JF

E. A. Gibson Shipbrokers: P. O. Box 278, Audrey House, 16-20 Ely Place, London EC1P 1HP

E. D. & F. Man Cocoa Limited: Sugar Quay, Lower Thames Street, London EC3R 6DU

Elsevier Advanced Technology: Mayfield House, 256 Banbury Road, Oxford OX2 7DH United Kingdom

Euromonitor: 87-88 Turnmill Street, London EC1M 5 QU

European Aluminum Association: Avenue de Broqueville, 12 B-1150 Brussels

Eurostat: Batiment Jean Monnet: L 2920 Luxembourg

European Conference of Ministers of Transport: 19 rue de Franqueville, F-75775 Paris Cedex 16

European Free Trade Association: 9-11 rue de Varembe, CH-1211 Geneva 20

European Paper Institute: 42 rue Galile, 75116 Paris

European Patent Office: Erhardstrasse 27 D-800 Munich 2

Fearnleys: P. O. Box 1158, Sentrum 0107 Oslo 1

F. O. Licht: P. O. Box 1220, D-2418 Ratzeburg, Germany

Food and Agriculture Organization: Via Delle Terme Di Caracella 00100 Rome

General Agreement on Tariffs and Trade: Centre William Rappard, rue de Lausanne 154, CH 1211, Geneva 21

Horwath International: 415 Madison Avenue, New York, NY 10017

Institute of Petroleum: 61 New Cavendish Street, London W1M 8AR

Institute of Shipping Economics and Logistics: Universitatsallee GW1 Block A, D-2800 Bremen 33 Germany

Inter-American Development Bank: 13000 New York Avenue, Washington, DC 20577

International Agency for Research on Cancer: 150 Cours Albert Thomas, F-69372 Lyon Cedex 08 France

International Air Transport Association: 3rd Floor, Sceptre House, 75-81 Staines Road, Hounslow, TW3 3HW, United Kingdom

International Association of Horticultural Producers: Bezuidenhoutseweg 153, Postbus 93099, NL-2509 AB's-Gravenhage, Netherlands

International Bauxite Association: 36 Trafalgar Road, P. O. Box 551, Kingston 5 Jamaica

International Civil Aviation Organization: 1000 Sherbrooke Street, West Montreal, PQ H3A 2RZ

International Cocoa Council Organization: 22 Berners Street, London W1P 3DB

International Commission for the Conservation of Atlantic Tunas: Calle Principe de Vergara, 17-7 28001 Madrid

International Cotton Advisory Committee: 1901 Pennsylvania Avenue, N.W., Suite 201, Washington, DC 20006

International Dairy Federation: 41 Square Vergote, B-1040 Brussels

International Energy Agency: IEA 2 rue Andre Pascal, F-75775 Paris Cedex 16

International Fertilizer Industry Association: 28 rue Marbeuf, 75008 Paris

International Institute of Synthetic Rubber Producers: 2077 South Gessner Road, Suite 133 Houston TX 77063

International Iron and Steel Institute: rue Colonel Bourg, 120-B 11140 Brussels

International Labour Organisation: 4 Route de Murillons, CH-1211 Geneva 22

International Lead and Zinc Study Group: Metro House, 58 St. James Street, London SW1A 1LD

International Monetary Fund: 700 19th Street, N.W., Washington. DC 20431

International North Pacific Fisheries Commission: 6640 Northwest Marine Drive, Vancouver V6T 1X2

International Pacific Halibut Commission: P. O. Box 5009 University Station, Seattle, WA 98145

International Rice Research Institute: P. O. Box 933, 1099 Manila

International Road Federation: CH-1202, 63 rue de Lausanne, Geneva

International Road Transport Union: Centre International, BP 44, 3 rue de Varembe, CH-1211 Geneva 20

International Rubber Study Group: York House, Empire Way, Wembley HA9 0PA United Kingdom

International Sugar Organization: 1 Canada Square, Canary Wharf, London E14 5AA

International Tea Committee: Sir John Lyon House, 5 High Timber Street, London, EC4V 3NH

International Telecommunication Union: Place de Nations, CH-1211 Geneva 20

International Textile Manufacturers Federation: Am Schanzengraben 29, Postfach 8039 Zurich

International Tropical Timber Organization: SF/Pacifico-Yokohama, H-1 Minato-Mirai, Nishi-ku, Yokohama 220 Japan

International Union of Railways: 16 rue Jean-Rey, 75015 Paris

International Whaling Commission: The Red House, Station Road, Histon, Cambridge CB4 4NP United Kingdom

International Wheat Council: Haymarket House, 28 Haymarket, London SW1Y 4SS

International Wool Secretariat: Development Centre, Valley Drive, Ilkley, West Yorkshire, LS29 8PB United Kingdom

Inter-Parliamentary Union: Place du petit saconnex, CP 438, CH-1211 Geneva 19

Iron and Steel Statistics Bureau: Canterbury House, 2 Sydenham Road, Croyden CR9 2LZ United Kingdom

Ista Mielk: 2100 Hamburg 90 Langenberg 25 Germany

Jaakko Poyry: Third Floor, Century House, Station Way, Cheam, Surrey SM3 8SW United Kingdom

Johnson Matthey: Blounts Court, Sonning Common, Reading RG 4 9NH United Kingdom

Lloyds Register of Shipping: 71 Fenchurch Street, London EC3M 4BS

Macmillan Press, Houndmills: Basingstoke, Hampshire RG21 2XS United Kingdom

Meat and Livestock Commission: P. O. Box 44 Winterhill House, Snowdon Drive, Milton Keynes MK6 1AX United Kingdom

Metal Bulletin Books: Park House, Park Terrace, Worcester Park, Surrey KT4 7HY United Kingdom

Milk Marketing Board: Portsmouth Road, Thames Ditton, Surrey KT7 OEL United Kingdom

Mining Journal: 60 Worship Street, London EC2A 2HD

Ministry of Housing, Physical Planning, and the Environment: P. O. Box 20951, 2500 EZ The Hague

Nordic Statistical Secretariat: Sejogade 11, DK-2100 Copenhagen 0

North Atlantic Treaty Organization: B-1110 Brussels

North West Atlantic Fisheries Organization: P. O. Box 638 Dartmouth BZY 3Y9 Canada

Organization for Economic Cooperation and Development: 2 rue Andre Pascal, F-75775 Paris, Cedex 16

Organization of Petroleum Exporting Countries: Obere Donaustrasse 93, A-1020 Vienna 11

Pannell Kerr Forster: 262 North Belt East, Suite 300, Houston, TX 77060

Pulp and Paper International: 123a Chaussee de Charleroi, B-1060 Brussels

Satra Footwear Technology Centre: Satra House, Rockingham Road, Kettering, Northamptonshire, NN16 9JH United Kingdom

Society of Motor Manufacturers and Traders: Forbes House, Halkin Street, London SW1X 7DS

South Pacific Commission: Anse Vata, BPD5 Noumea Cedex, New Caledonia

United Nations: New York, NY 10017

United Nations Economic and Social Commission for Asia and the Pacific: Rajadamern Avenue, Bangkok 10200

United Nations Economic Commission for Africa: P.O. Box 3001, Addis Ababa

United Nations Economic Commission for Europe: Palai de Nations, CH-1211 Geneva 10

United Nations Centre for Human Settlements: Habitat, P.O. Box 30030, Nairobi

United Nations Environment Programme: P.O. Box 30552, Nairobi

United Nations Conference on Trade and Development: Palais de Nations, CH-1211 Geneva 10

United Nations Educational, Scientific, and Cultural Organization: 7 Place de Fontenoy, F-75700 Paris

United Nations Industrial Development Organization: Vienna International Centre, P.O. Box 300, A-1400 Vienna

World Bank: 1818 H Street, N.W., Washington, DC 20433

World Bureau of Metal Statistics: 27 High Street, Ware, Hertfordshire SG12 9BQ

World Food Programme: 426 Via Cristofor Colombo, 1-00145 Rome

World Health Organization: CH-1211, Geneva 27

World Intellectual Property Organization: Case Postale 2300, 41AV Giuseppe Motta, CH-1211 Geneva 2

World Tourism Organization: Calle Capitan Haya 42, Madrid 28020

Wye College, University of London: Wye, Ashford, Kent TN25 5AH United Kingdom

APPENDIX B:

THE INTERNATIONAL STATISTICAL SYSTEM AND THE INTERNATIONAL STATISTICAL SERIES

THE INTERNATIONAL STATISTICAL SYSTEM

The international statistical system is a very diversified group of organizations engaged in the collection, processing, presentation, and analysis of global or regional statistics with a topical or multitopical focus. It draws on the national statistical systems which serve as catchment areas funneling data into the global system. The system does not have a central governing body but it is guided by the needs of the global system as perceived by the principal international organizations.

The principal responsibility falls on the United Nations Statistical Division (UNSTAT) which sets the standards, coordinates methodologies and definitions, monitors data collections, produces print and electronic publications, and provides technical assistance to organizations active in the field. Because the collection agencies have their own agendas, missions, and priorities, UNSTAT serves as an advisory and watchdog agency.

The main body for the coordination of the international system is the Working Group on International Statistical Programmes and Coordination of the United Nations Statistical Commission, one of the specialized commissions of the UN Economic and Social Council. In addition, the Subcommittee on Statistical Activities of the Administrative Committee on Coordination is composed of the representatives of the statistical services of international agencies.

Fundamental Principles of Official Statistics

During the 27th session of the UN Statistical Commission in 1993, the following fundamental principles of official international statistics were endorsed.

1. Official statistics provide an indispensable element in the information system of a democratic society, serving the government, the economy, and the public with data about the economic, demographic, social, and environmental situation. To this end, official statistics that meet the test of practical utility are to be compiled and made available on an impartial basis by official statistical agencies to honor citizens' entitlement to public information.

2. To retain trust in official statistics, the statistical agencies need to decide according to strictly professional considerations, including scientific principles and professional ethics, on the methods and procedures for the collection, processing, storage, and presentation of statistical data.

3. To facilitate the correct interpretation of the data, the statistical agencies are to present information according to scientific standards on the sources, methods, and procedures of the statistics.

4. The statistical agencies are entitled to comment on the erroneous interpretation and misuse of statistics.

5. Data for statistical purposes may be drawn from all types of sources, be they statistical surveys or administrative records. Statistical agencies are to choose the source with regard to quality, timeliness, costs, and burden on respondents.

6. Individual data collected by statistical agencies for statistical compilation, whether they refer to natural or legal persons, are to be strictly confidential and used exclusively for statistical purposes.

7. The laws, regulations, and measures under which statistical systems operate are to be made public.

8. Coordination among statistical agencies within countries is essential to achieve consistency and efficiency in the statistical system.

9. The use by statistical agencies in each country of international concepts, classifications, and methods promotes the consistency and efficiency of the statistical system.

10. Bilateral and multilateral cooperation in statistics contributes to the improvement of systems of official statistics in all countries.

UN Economic and Social Information System

The heart of UN statistical activities is the UNSTAT, but the driving force is the UN Economic and Social

Information System established by the UN Department for Economic and Social Information and Policy Analysis in cooperation with the regional commissions. UNSTAT serves as the secretariat to the subcommittee on Statistical Activities of the Administrative Committee on Coordination which includes the United Nations and all of its specialized agencies. The Regional Commissions also play a major role in UN statistical activities. UNSTAT has given special attention to strengthening international statistical cooperation. The Inter-Secretariat Working Group on National Accounts is the task force on national accounts for the development of the conceptual framework of the new System of National Accounts.

Regional Work

In Africa, under the aegis of the Economic Commission for Africa, a Coordinating Committee on African Statistical Development and four subcommittees (on the organization and management of the national statistical systems, training, data processing, and research methods and standards) were established in 1992 to help realize the goals set out in the strategy for the implementation of the Addis Ababa Plan of Action for Statistical Development in Africa.

In Europe, the Economic Commission for Europe, the Statistical Office of the European Communities (now, the European Union), and OECD have integrated their statistical work programs through the Conference of European Statisticians. Similar cooperation exists in the Western Hemisphere between the Organization of American States and the Economic Commission for Latin America and the Caribbean. In Asia, the Committee on Statistics was reestablished and the ESCAP Working Group of Statistical Experts first met in 1993. Finally, a statistical committee has been established by the Economic and Social Commission for Western Asia.

Other UN Agencies

1. The United Nations Centre for Human Settlements (HABITAT) is the principal agency concerned with urban statistics. In cooperation with the Network on Urban Research in the European Community (NUREC), the International Statistical Institute (ISI), and the International Union of Local Authorities, HABITAT is carrying out a project—Large Cities Statistics. Urban data from all cities of the world with more than 100,000 inhabitants will be collected in the CitiBase, a database developed in HABITAT's City Data Programme (CDP) and published in ISI's *International Statistics of Large Towns*. The data collected are also part of the second edition of the *Compendium of Human Settlements Statistics* and the computerized Human Settlements Statistical Database. The data will also form the Statistical Annex to the *Second Global Report on Human Settlements*.

2. International Civil Aviation Organization (ICAO)

3. The International Labour Organisation (ILO) has an extensive statistical program that sets standards for labor statistics and assists governments in producing useful, reliable, and comparable labor statistics. It sponsors the International Conference of Labor Statisticians who try to devise internationally acceptable definitions of terms and concepts in labor statistics.

4. Food and Agriculture Organization (FAO). The FAO Constitution specifies the collection, analysis, interpretation, and dissemination of data relating to nutrition, food, and agriculture as one of the primary functions of the organization. FAO's statistical system comprises data on 800 agricultural commodities and 250 fishery and forestry products in 30 countries. The three primary components of the FAO statistical division are the World Agricultural Information Centre (WAICENT), FAOSTAT—the FAO statistical database, and AGROSTAT, a global database on production, trade, and consumption of crops, livestock, and livestock products in the form of food balance sheets.

5. International Monetary Fund (IMF). The IMF Statistical Department maintains a comprehensive database that forms the basis of the Fund's central role in the international monetary system. The Statistical Department collects data, provides technical assistance to monetary authorities around the world, and develops statistical methodologies in such areas as balance of payments. Its database of macroeconomic statistics called the Economic Information System, contains more than three million monthly time series of internationally comparable historical data. IMF's technical assistance efforts in statistics has expanded considerably since the collapse of the Soviet Union. It conducts training activities in Washington, DC or in one of the recipient countries, and also maintains Resident Statistical Advisors in some countries. In the area of statistical methodologies, the Fund has actively participated in the revision process of the UN's System of National Accounts, particularly on such subjects as the attribution of output of financial intermediaries. The IMF Statistical Department participates in a wide range of international statistical commissions and working groups, notably the Task Force on Financial Statistics and the Balance of Payments Statistics Committee.

6. World Bank. Although the World Bank is primarily a data user and not producer, it has a number of statistical activities and publications that enhance international statistical efforts. It has a decentralized statistical system with each department maintaining a statistics department. The central database draws from all of these units. This database, in turn forms the nucleus of the

publication department which produces such widely read statistical annuals as the *World Development Report, World Bank Atlas, World Tables, World Debt Tables,* and *Social Indicators of Development.*

7. International Telecommunication Union (ITU). The ITU's Telecommunication Development Bureau maintains a statistical database of internationally comparable telecommunication statistics going back to 1960 and covering 200 countries and territories.

8. The Universal Postal Union (UPU) maintains a statistical database on items of interest to postal administrations, such as mail volume, number of post offices, etc.

9. Organization for Economic Cooperation and Development (OECD). The OECD is the largest source of statistics on the industrial economies of the world and produces a wide range of publications both by itself and in collaboration with EUROSTAT. Among its more important contributions to international statistics are the *International Direct Investment Statistics Yearbook* and the *Geographical Distribution of Financial Flows to Developing Countries.*

10. EUROSTAT is the Statistical Office of the Office for Official Publications of the European Communities. It produces two categories of documents—one for specialists and the other for the public. The former is presented in great detail using standardized formats and using scientific methodology. The latter are selected and annotated for certain audiences interested only in narrow topics. The vast majority of EUROSTAT's work is in direct support of the European Union's work, particularly in agriculture, industry, social affairs, and policy. EUROSTAT is also at the forefront of the efforts to protect statistical confidentiality.

11. The International Statistical Institute (ISI) was established in 1885 and is one of the oldest international scientific organizations. The Institute, whose permanent office is in Voorburg, near The Hague, is an autonomous society which seeks to develop and improve statistical methods and their application through international cooperation. The ISI is composed of 1,700 indidivuals, many of whom are among the world's leading statisticians. The membership is drawn from over 120 countries. In addition, ISI has affiliated societies with 3,300 members. ISI has consultative status with the UN Economic and Social Council and with UNESCO. Among the goals of ISI are the promotion of international cooperation among statisticians, integration of statistical work with other forms of developmental activity, advancement of statistical theory and research, and improvement of international comparability of statistical data.

There are five ISI sections: (1) Bernoulli Society for Mathematical Statistics and Probability; (2) International Association of Survey Statisticians; (3) International Association for Statistical Computing; (4) International Association for Official Statistics; and (5) International Association for Statistical Education. In addition, ISI has 10 international and regional affiliates and 33 national affiliates as follows:

International and Regional: Biometric Society, Econometric Society, Inter-American Statistical Institute, International Association for Research in Income and Wealth, International Institute for the Scientific Study of Population, Institute of Mathematical Statistics, American Society for Quality Control, International Actuarial Association, European Organization for Quality Control, and the Institute for Management Sciences.

National: Statistical Society of Argentina, Statistical Society of Australia, Austrian Statistical Society, Brazilian Statistical Association, Association des Statisticiens du Cameroun, Statistical Society of Canada, National Statistical Society of China, Danish Society for Theoretical Statistics, Ethiopian Statistical Association, Finnish Statistical Society, Association pour la Statistique et ses Utilisations, Societe de Statistique de Paris, Societe de Statistique de France, German Statistical Society, Union of German Municipal Statisticians, Greek Statistical Institute, Hungarian Statistical Association, Indian Society of Agricultural Statistics, Indian Statistical Institute, Israel Statistical Association, Italian Society for Economics, Demography and Statistics, Italian Statistical Society, Japan Statistical Society, Korean Statistical Association, Netherlands Society for Statistics and

Operations Research, New Zealand Statistical Association, Norwegian Statistical Society, Sociedade Portuguesa de Estatistica e Investigacao Operacional, Sociedad de Estadistica e Investigacion Operativa, Swedish Statistical Association, Societe Swiss de Statistique et d'Economie Politique, Royal Statistical Society of the United Kingdom, and the American Statistical Association.

12. The International Association for Official Statistics (IAOS) is an affiliate of the International Statistical Institute. It is the most actively involved in the study of national official statistics programs. One unit of IAOS is the Standing Committee on Regional and Urban Statistics (SCORUS).

THE INTERNATIONAL STATISTICAL SERIES

Listed below are some of the most popular titles from each of the publishers in the International Statistical Series.

United Nations Statistical System

Statistical Yearbook

World Statistics in Brief

Demographic Yearbook

Compendium of Social Statistics

Population and Vital Statistics Report

Yearbook of National Accounts

Yearbook of International Trade Statistics

Commodity Trade Statistics

World Trade Annual

World Energy Supplies

Yearbook of Industrial Statistics

Yearbook of Construction Statistics

Compendium of Housing Statistics

Monthly Bulletin of Statistics

Population and Vital Statistics Report

Monthly Commodity Price Bulletin

United Nations Economic Commission for Europe

Statistical Indicators of Short-Term Economic Changes in ECE Countries

Annual Bulletin of Coal Statistics for Europe

Annual Bulletin of General Energy Statistics for Europe

Quarterly Bulletin of Coal Statistics for Europe

Annual Bulletin of Electric Energy Statistics for Europe

Semi-Annual Bulletin of Electric Energy Statistics for Europe

Annual Bulletin of Gas Statistics for Europe

Quarterly Bulletin of Steel Statistics for Europe

Annual Bulletin of Steel Statistics for Europe

Statistics of World Trade in Steel

Bulletin of Statistics on World Trade in Engineering Products

Annual Bulletin of Housing and Building Statistics for Europe

Annual Bulletin of Transport Statistics for Europe

Statistics of Road Traffic Accidents in Europe

Annual Bulletin of Trade in Chemical Products

Annual Review of the Chemical Industry

Standardized Input/Output Tables of ECE Countries

United Nations Economic and Social Commission for Asia and the Pacific

Statistical Yearbook for Asia and the Pacific

Quarterly Bulletin of Statistics for Asia and the Pacific

Statistical Indicators for Asia and the Pacific

Foreign Trade Statistics for Asia and the Pacific

Electric Power in Asia and the Pacific

Handbook on Cereal and Fertilizer Statistics for Asia and the Pacific

United Nations Economic Commission for Latin America

Statistical Yearbook for Latin America

United Nations Economic Commission for Africa

African Statistical Yearbook

Foreign Trade Statistics for Africa Series A, B, and C

Statistical Information Bulletin for Africa

United Nations Economic Commission for Western Asia

Statistical Abstract of the Arab World

United Nations Conference of Trade and Development

Handbook of International Trade and Development Statistics

Monthly Commodity Price Bulletin

Tungsten Statistics

International Narcotics Control Board

Statistics on Narcotic Drugs/Maximum Levels of Opium Stocks

Estimated World Requirements of Narcotic Drugs and Estimates of World Production of Opium

International Labour Organisation

Yearbook of Labour Statistics

Bulletin of Labour Statistics

Household Income and Expenditure Statistics

Cost of Social Security

Labour Force Estimates and Projections, 1950-2025

Food and Agriculture Organization

Production Yearbook

Trade Yearbook

Annual Fertilizer Review

Monthly Bulletin of Statistics

Three-Year Average Food Balance Sheets

Economic Accounts for Agriculture
Review of Food Consumption Surveys
Report on the 1960 World Census of Agriculture
Yearbook of Forest Products
World Forest Products Statistics: A Ten-Year
Summary
World Forest Inventory
World Pulp and Paper Capacity Survey
World Survey of Production Capacity for Plywood,
Particleboard, and Fiberwood
Yearbook of Fishery Statistics
Food Aid Quarterly Bulletin
Food Outlook Quarterly

United Nations Educational, Scientific, and Cultural Organization

UNESCO Statistical Yearbook

Education Statistics

Summary Statistical Review of Education in the World

International Civil Aviation Organization

Civil Aviation Statistics of the World

Digest of Statistics:

  Airline Traffic

  Traffic by Flight Stage

  Financial Data

  Flight and Personnel Data

  Non-Scheduled Air Transport

  Civil Aircraft on Register

  Airport Traffic

World Health Organization

World Health Statistics Annual

World Health Statistics Quarterly

World Epidemiological Record

Cancer Incidence on Five Continents

World Bank

World Bank Atlas

World Tables

World Development Report and Indicators

Trends in Developing Countries

World Economic and Social Indicators

Commodity Trade and Price Trends

World Debt Tables

International Monetary Fund

International Financial Statistics

Direction of Trade

Balance of Payments Yearbook

Government Finance Statistics Yearbook

Universal Postal Union

Statistique des Services Postaux

International Telecommunication Union

Yearbook of Common Carrier Telecommunication
Statistics

Radiocommunication Statistics

Table of International Telex Relations and Traffic

Statistical Table of Coast Stations

Statistical Table of Ship Stations

World Intellectual Property Organization

Industrial Property Statistics

Food and Agriculture Organization/Economic Commission for Europe

Timber Bulletin for Europe

Review of Agricultural Situation in Europe

Recent Developments of Agricultural Trade in Europe

Prices of Agricultural Products and Selected Inputs

Outputs, Expenses, and Income of Agriculture

Organization for Economic Cooperation and Development

Main Economic Indicators

Historical Statistics

Historical Statistics - Supplement

Industrial Production - Quarterly Supplement

Industrial Production - Historical Statistics

National Accounts of OECD Countries

Quarterly National Accounts Bulletin

Quarterly National Accounts Bulletin - Historical
Statistics

Statistics of Foreign Trade:

  Series A Monthly Bulletin

  Series B Trade by Commodities - Country Summaries

  Series C Trade by Commodities - Market Summaries

OECD Financial Statistics

Revenue Statistics of OECD Member Countries

Labor Force Statistics

Energy Statistics

Energy Balances of OECD Countries

Oil Statistics - Supply and Disposal

Quarterly Oil Statistics

Short-Term Economic Indicators for Manufacturing Industries

National Accounts in Developing Countries of Asia

National Accounts of Less Developed Countries

Geographical Distribution of Financial Flows to Developing Countries

Interest Rates

Maritime Transport

Education Statistics Yearbook

Electricity Supply Industry

Engineering Industries in OECD Member Countries: Basic Statistics

OECD Economic Surveys

OECD Economic Outlook

Expenditure and Trends in OECD Countries

Food Consumption Statistics

Statistics of Area, Production, and Yield of Crop Products in OECD Member Countries

Meat Balances of OECD Member Countries

Tourism Policy and International Tourism in OECD Member Countries

Patterns of Resources Devoted to Research and Experimental Development in OECD

Organization of American States

Statistical Bulletin of OAS

Office for Official Publications of the European Communities

Brief Statistics of the Community

National Acounts - ESA: Aggregates

Balance of Payments - Global Data

Yearbook of Agricultural Statistics

Yearbook of Foreign Trade of the Maghreb and Mashrek Countries

Bulletin of Central Statistics

National Acounts - ESA: Detailed Tables

Balance of Payments - Geographical Breakdown

Tax Statistics

Accounts and Statistics of General Government

Public Expenditure on Research and Development

Population and Employment

Social Accounts - Accounts of Social Protection

Social Indicators

Statistics of Education

Agricultural and Forestry Accounts

Land Utilization and Production

Production of Vegetables and Fruit

Prices of Fruit, Vegetables, and Potatoes

Forestry Statistics

Supply Balance Sheets in Agricultural Production

Fishery Statistics I

Fishery Statistics II

EC Index Producer Prices

EC Index Means of Production

Yearbook of Iron and Steel

Raw Material Balance Sheets

Annual Investment Survey

Yearbook of Energy Statistics

Overall Energy Balance Sheets

Electrical Energy Statistics

Coal Statistics

Gas Statistics

Petroleum Statistics

Statistics on Operation of Nuclear Power Stations

Foreign Trade - ECSC Products

Statistics of Third Countries with Some State Trading

Yearbook of Foreign Trade with the ACP

Yearbook of Transport and Communication Tourism

Regional Accounts - Aggregates

Regional Statistics - Community's Financial Participation in Investments

Regional Statistics - Agriculture

Regional Statistics - Industry

Regional Statistics - Population

Rapid Statistics on the ACP

Labor Costs - Hours of Work

Crop Production

Monthly Statistics of Meat

Sugar

Monthly Statistics of Milk

Monthly Statistics of Eggs

Prices of Vegetable Products

Prices of Animal Products

Prices of Means of Production

EC Index of Producer Prices of Agricultural Products

EC Index of the Prices of the Means of Production

Fishery Statistics

Industrial Conjecture Indicators

Quarterly Bulletin of Industrial Production

Quarterly Bulletin of Iron and Steel

Monthly Bulletin of Foreign Trade

Trade Flows

Monthly Bulletin: Coal

Monthly Bulletin: Oil and Natural Gas

Monthly Bulletin: Electrical Energy

Monthly Tables of Transport

World Tourism Organization

World Travel Statistics

Regional Breakdown of World Travel Statistics

Statistics on International Tourism Receipts

European Free Trade Association

EFTA Trade

Annual Review of Agriculture Trade

International Cotton Advisory Committee

Cotton - World Statistics

Cotton: Monthly Review of World Situation

International Lead and Zinc Study Group

Lead and Zinc Statistics

International Rubber Study Group

Rubber Statistical Bulletin

International Rubber Digest

World Rubber Statistics Handbook

International Sugar Organization

Sugar Yearbook

Statistical Bulletin

International Tea Committee

Annual Bulletin of Statistics

Monthly Statistical Summary

International Tin Council

Monthly Statistical Bulletin

Tin Statistics

Tin Prices

International Wheat Council

World Wheat Statistics

Review of World Wheat Situation

Organization of Petroleum Exporting Countries

Annual Statistical Bulletin

APPENDIX C:

LIST OF PUBLICATIONS BY PUBLISHER

Below you will find a listing of the titles in the *Global Data Locator* arranged by publisher.

AT&T

The World's Telephones

African Development Bank

Compendium of Statistics

Selected Statistics of Regional Member Countries

American Automobile Manufacturers Association

World Motor Vehicle Data

Asian and Pacific Coconut Community

Coconut Statistical Yearbook

Asian Development Bank

Key Indicators of Developing Asian and Pacific Countries

British Petroleum Company

BP Review of World Gas

BP Statistical Review of World Energy

Central Intelligence Agency

Handbook of International Economic Statistics

Economist Intelligence Unit

Country Forecasts

Country Reports

The Country Risk Service

Energy Information Administration

International Energy Annual

International Energy Outlook

European Communities

ACP Basic Statistics

Agriculture: Statistical Yearbook

Basic Statistics of the Community

Earnings in Agriculture

EC-Latin American Trade

Employment and Unemployment: Aggregates

Forestry Statistics

Labour Force Sample Survey

Research and Development: Annual Statistics

Social Indicators for the European Community

Transport Annual Statistics

Food and Agriculture Organization

FAO Fishery Statistics Yearbook: Catches and Landings

FAO Fishery Statistics: Commodities

FAO Production Yearbook

FAO Trade Yearbook

Fertilizer Yearbook

The State of Food and Agriculture

World Crop and Livestock Statistics

Yearbook of Forest Products

Gale Research

Gale Country and World Rankings Reporter

Statistical Abstract of the World

General Agreement on Tariffs and Trade (World Trade Organization)

International Trade Statistics

INTERPOL

International Criminal Statistics

Institute of Contemporary Jewry

World Jewish Population: Trends and Policies

International Air Transport Association

World Air Transport Statistics

International Cocoa Organization

Quarterly Bulletin of Cocoa Statistics

The World Cocoa Market

International Commission for the Conservation of Atlantic Tuna

Statistical Bulletin (Tuna)

International Cotton Advisory Committee

Cotton: World Statistics

World Cotton Trade

World Textile Demand

International Iron and Steel Institute

Steel Statistical Yearbook

World Steel in Figures

International Labour Organisation

Yearbook of Labour Statistics

International Lead and Zinc Study Group

Lead and Zinc Statistics

International Monetary Fund

Balance of Payments Statistics Yearbook

Direction of Trade Statistics Yearbook

Government Finance Statistics Yearbook

International Financial Statistics Yearbook

International Road Federation

World Road Statistics

International Rubber Study Group

Key Rubber Indicators

Rubber Statistical Bulletin

World Rubber Statistics Handbook

International Tea Committee

Annual Bulletin of Statistics

International Telecommunication Union

ITU Statistical Yearbook

World Telecommunication Development Report

International Textile Manufacturers Federation

International Cotton Industry Statistics

International Textile Machinery Shipment Statistics

International Union of Railways

International Railway Statistics

Lloyds Register of Shipping

World Fleet Statistics

M.E. Sharpe

The Illustrated Book of World Rankings

NTC Publications

World Drink Trends: International Beverage, Alcohol Consumption, and Production Trends

National Center for Health Statistics

National Health Data Reference Guide

Nordic Statistical Secretariat

Nordic Research Library Statistics

Yearbook of Nordic Statistics

Organization for Economic Cooperation and Development

Coal Information

Development Cooperation

Employment Outlook

Energy Balances of OECD Countries

Energy Policies of OECD Countries

Energy Statistics of OECD Countries

Environmental Indicators

External Debt Statistics

Geographical Distribution of Financial Flows to Developing Countries

Historical Statistics

Industrial Structure Statistics

The Iron and Steel Industry

Labour Force Statistics

Maritime Transport

National Accounts

Oil and Gas Information

OECD Environmental Data

The Pulp and Paper Industry

Revenue Statistics of OECD Member Countries

Review of Fisheries in OECD Member Countries

The State of the Environment

The Steel Market in 1992 and the Outlook for 1993

Organization of Petroleum Exporting Countries

Annual Statistical Bulletin

Facts and Figures

Oxford University Press

National Health Systems of the World

World Resources

Routledge

INSTAT: International Statistics Sources

Siemens

International Telecom Statistics

Stockton Press

International Historical Statistics: Europe

International Historical Statistics: The Americas

Tokyo Metropolitan Government, Statistics Division

Statistics of World Large Cities

U.S. Arms Control and Disarmament Agency

World Military Expenditures and Arms Transfers

U.S. Bureau of the Census

World Population Profile

U.S. Bureau of Mines

Minerals Yearbook

U.S. Department of Agriculture

Patterns and Trends in World Agricultural Land Use

Union Bank of Switzerland

Prices and Earnings Around the Globe

United Nations

African Statistical Yearbook

Annual Bulletin of Coal Statistics for Europe

Annual Bulletin of Electric Energy Statistics for Europe

Annual Bulletin of Gas Statistics for Europe

Annual Bulletin of General Energy Statistics for Europe

Annual Bulletin of Housing and Building Statistics for Europe

Annual Bulletin of Steel Statistics for Europe

Annual Bulletin of Transport Statistics for Europe

Asia-Pacific in Figures

Child Mortality in Developing Countries

Commodity Yearbook

Compendium of Social Statistics and Indicators

Compendium of Statistics and Indicators on the Situation of Women

Demographic Yearbook

Disability Statistics Compendium

Electric Power in Asia and the Pacific

Energy Balances and Electricity Profiles

Energy Statistics Yearbook

Foreign Trade Statistics for Africa

Foreign Trade Statistics of Asia and the Pacific

Human Development Report

Human Settlements: Basic Statistics

International Trade Statistics Yearbook

The Least Developed Countries: A Statistical Profile

Narcotic Drugs: Estimated World Requirements

National Accounts Statistics: Main Aggregates and Details

Prospects of World Urbanization

Psychotropic Substances

Report on the World Social Situation

The Sex and Age Distribution of the World Population

The State of World Population

Statistical Abstract of the Region of the Economic and Social Commission for Western Asia

Statistical Charts and Indicators on Youth

Statistical Indicators for Asia and the Pacific

Statistical Yearbook for Asia and the Pacific

Statistical Yearbook for Latin America and the Caribbean

Statistics of Road Traffic Accidents in Europe

Statistics on World Trade in Engineering Products

Statistics of World Trade in Steel

Tungsten Statistics

United Nations Statistical Yearbook

World Industrial Robot Statistics

World Industry Development Indicators

World Population Prospects

World Statistics in Brief: United Nations Statistical Pocketbook

The World's Women: Trends and Statistics

United Nations Educational, Scientific, and Cultural Organization

Compendium of Statistics on Illiteracy

UNESCO Statistical Yearbook

Universal Postal Union

Postal Statistics

Vatican Secretariat Central Statistics Office

Statistical Yearbook of the Church

World Bank

Commodity Trade and Price Trends

Social Indicators of Development

World Bank Atlas

World Debt Tables

World Development Report

World Tables

World Economic Forum

National Competitiveness Report

World Health Organization

Maternal Mortality: A Global Factbook

World Health Statistics Annual

World Tourism Organization

Compendium of Tourism Statistics

Yearbook of Tourism Statistics

INDEX

The Bernan Press
U.S. DataBook Series™

 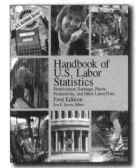 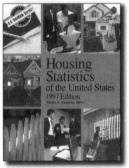

The **Bernan Press U.S. DataBook Series**™ is designed to provide essential, yet hard-to-find government statistics in a printed format. Our team of well-known editors has held high-ranking positions in the Department of Commerce, the Bureau of the Census, the Bureau of Labor Statistics, and other federal and national organizations.

Business Statistics of the United States: 1996 Edition *
Courtenay M. Slater, Editor

Based on the popular Business Statistics, (formerly published by the Bureau of Economic Analysis), this essential reference work presents annual and time series data on business trends through 1995. You'll find current information on: construction and housing; mining, oil, and gas; manufacturing; transportation, communications, and utilities; retail and wholesale trade; services; and government.

It also features a full statistical picture of the overall U.S. economy, including data on: gross domestic product; consumer income and spending; industrial production; money and financial markets; and more. Contains numerous charts and tables illustrating economic trends.

January 1997, Pbk, 424pp,
ISBN 0-89059-063-X, $59.00,
Standing Order No. 077.05375

Handbook of U.S. Labor Statistics: Employment, Earnings, Prices, Productivity, and Other Labor Data: First Edition
Eva E. Jacobs, Editor

Based on the Handbook of Labor Statistics, (formerly published by the Bureau of Labor Statistics), this comprehensive research tool presents historical data on labor market trends through 1995. Topics include: population, labor force, and employment status; consumer prices; producer prices; export and import prices; consumer expenditures; and productivity.

A special feature in this edition is the recently released Bureau of Labor Statistics projections of employment by industry and occupation for 1994-2005.

March 1997, Pbk, 316pp,
ISBN 0-89059-062-1, $59.00,
Standing Order No. 077.43472

Housing Statistics of the United States: First Edition
Patrick A. Simmons, Editor

This completely new reference work is the first ever comprehensive source for current and historical information on households, housing, and housing finance. Data includes: household characteristics; prices, rents, and affordability; housing production and investment; home mortgage lending; housing stock characteristics; and federal housing programs. An ideal source for data that can be used for producing or benchmarking market reports, trend analysis, and research.

Forthcoming Summer 1997,
Pbk, approx. 300pp,
ISBN 0-89059-065-6, $59.00,
Standing Order No. 077.43481
***

***Advanced Information

To order, contact Customer Relations at (800) 274-4447 or mail/fax the order form on the back page of this book.

Bernan Associates Order Form

4611-F Assembly Drive ■ Lanham, MD 20706 USA

If using a purchase order, please attach this form

Quantity	ISBN	Title	Begin Standing Order?		Price
	—	Standing Order Catalog	—		Free
	—	Internet Connection Newsletter (Sample)	—		Free
	0-89059-071-0	1997 County and City Extra	Yes ☐	No ☐	$109.00
	0-89059-063-X	Business Statistics of the U.S., '96 Edition	Yes ☐	No ☐	$59.00
	0-89059-062-1	Handbook of U.S. Labor Statistics, First Edition	Yes ☐	No ☐	$59.00
	0-89059-065-6	Housing Statistics of the U.S., First Edition	Yes ☐	No ☐	$59.00

Subtotal	
Postage & Handling*	
Tax**	
Total	

*Add Postage and Handling as follows:
U.S. 5%, minimum $4.00
Canada and Mexico 8%, minimum $5.00
Outside North America 20%, minimum $12.00
**MD and NY add applicable sales tax;
  Canada add GST

Rush Service
A Rush Service fee of $15.00 will be applied toward all rush orders.

Methods of Payment

Deposit Account
Requires a minimum initial deposit of $100.00 and an ongoing balance of $50.00. Upon receipt of the check or money order, an account will be established and a special account number will be assigned. The cost of ordered publications will be deducted from the funds on deposit.

Invoice Statement Account
Send in the order on an authorized purchase order, an invoice will be included with the shipment of publications. An account number will be assigned after the first purchase. All future orders can be charged against this account number with an authorized purchase order.

Prepayment
Prepay all orders with a check or money order in U.S. dollars, drawn from a U.S. bank, payable to Bernan Associates.

Prices are subject to change

Terms: Net 30 days

Return Policy
Customers may review any Bernan Press publication for 30 days. If not completely satisfied, you may return it to Bernan Press for a full refund or credit to your account.

MAKE RE-ORDERING EASY WITH STANDING ORDERS!

Place your publications on *Standing Order* and you are guaranteed automatic delivery of each new edition as it is published!

☐ **Check here to put the Bernan Press U.S. DataBook Series™ on *Group Standing Order*.**
You'll automatically receive all forthcoming titles in the U.S. DataBook Series as they are published.
Group Standing Order No. 077.00.111

☐ Check or Money Order enclosed
☐ Bill Me P.O.#_____ Date_____
☐ MC ☐ Visa Exp. Date _____
Card # _____
Signature _____

YES!
I'd like to open a Deposit Account.
Enclosed is a check for _____
  (minimum $100)
Account # _____
Tax Exempt # _____

Bill To
Name _____
Organization _____
Address _____
_____
Phone_____ Fax _____

Ship To
Name _____
Organization _____
Address _____
_____
Phone_____ Fax _____

Call Toll Free 1•800•274•4447   Fax Toll Free 1•800•865•3450   ✉mail: order@bernan.com